Practical Rails Social Networking Sites

Alan Bradburne

Apress®

Practical Rails Social Networking Sites

Copyright © 2007 by Alan Bradburne

ISBN-13 (pbk): 978-1-59059-841-2

ISBN-10 (pbk): 1-59059-841-5

Printed and bound in the United States of America 9 8 7 6 5 4 3 2 1

Lead Editors: Matthew Moodie, Chris Mills
Technical Reviewer: Paul Bentley
Editorial Board: Steve Anglin, Ewan Buckingham, Gary Cornell, Jonathan Gennick, Jason Gilmore, Jonathan Hassell, Chris Mills, Matthew Moodie, Jeffrey Pepper, Ben Renow-Clarke, Dominic Shakeshaft, Matt Wade, Tom Welsh
Project Manager: Kylie Johnston
Copy Edit Manager: Nicole Flores
Copy Editor: Heather Lang
Assistant Production Director: Kari Brooks-Copony
Production Editor: Kelly Winquist
Compositor: Susan Glinert
Proofreader: Elizabeth Berry
Indexer: Becky Hornyak
Artist: April Milne
Cover Designer: Kurt Krames
Manufacturing Director: Tom Debolski

Distributed to the book trade worldwide by Springer-Verlag New York, Inc., 233 Spring Street, 6th Floor, New York, NY 10013. Phone 1-800-SPRINGER, fax 201-348-4505, e-mail orders-ny@springer-sbm.com, or visit http://www.springeronline.com.

For information on translations, please contact Apress directly at 2855 Telegraph Avenue, Suite 600, Berkeley, CA 94705. Phone 510-549-5930, fax 510-549-5939, e-mail info@apress.com, or visit http://www.apress.com.

The source code for this book is available to readers at http://www.apress.com in the Source Code/Download section.

For Mayumi

Contents at a Glance

About the Author xvii

About the Technical Reviewer xix

Acknowledgments xxi

Introduction xxiii

■CHAPTER 1   Ruby, Ruby on Rails, and the RailsCoders Project 1

■CHAPTER 2   Developing a Content Management System 21

■CHAPTER 3   Adding Users and Groups 47

■CHAPTER 4   Building a News Blog with RSS Feeds and an API 83

■CHAPTER 5   Building a Discussion Forum 117

■CHAPTER 6   Building a Blogging Engine with Web Services Support 153

■CHAPTER 7   Building a Photo Gallery 191

■CHAPTER 8   Sending E-mail and Building a Newsletter Mailing List 217

■CHAPTER 9   Adding Friends with XFN Details 247

■CHAPTER 10   Adding Tags to the Photo Gallery 277

■CHAPTER 11   Creating Mashups and Integrating with Web 2.0 301

■CHAPTER 12   Adding User-Created Themes to the Blogging Engine 329

■CHAPTER 13   Adding a Mobile Interface 351

■CHAPTER 14   Deploying, Optimizing, and Scaling the Application 379

■INDEX 397

Contents

About the Author xvii

About the Technical Reviewer xix

Acknowledgments xxi

Introduction xxiii

■CHAPTER 1   Ruby, Ruby on Rails, and the RailsCoders Project 1

The RailsCoders Project 1

Ruby and Ruby on Rails 2

    A Brief History of Ruby 3

    What Is Ruby on Rails?. 4

Software Required to Build RailsCoders 7

Upgrading Rails 8

Installing Ruby, Rails, and MySQL 8

    Installing on Windows 9

    Mac OS X. 11

    Linux. 12

Creating the Skeleton of the Rails Application 14

    Watching the Rails Logfiles 16

Setting up the Database 17

    Creating the Database 18

    Configuring Rails to Use the Database. 18

    Testing the Database 19

Summary 20

■CHAPTER 2   Developing a Content Management System 21

Specifying the Feature Requirements 21

Rails, Routing, and REST 21

    Traditional Rails Routes 22

    RESTful Rails Routes 22

Creating a Site Layout 23

Designing the Pages and Page Editor 26

    The Page Model 26

    The Page Controller 27

Creating the Page Model 28
 Migrations 28
 Creating the Model 29
 Creating the Controller 33
 Setting Up a Default Page 41
 Adding a Link from the Sidebar Menu 41
Testing 42
 Creating the Testing Database 42
 Developing Unit Tests for the Page Model 42
Extending the Content Management System 44
Summary 45

■CHAPTER 3 Adding Users and Groups 47

Specifying the Feature Requirements 47
 Defining the User Model 47
 The Role Model and Join Table 48
 The Controllers 49
 Sessions and Cookies 50
Creating the User Model 51
The Session-Handling Library 53
Creating the Controllers 55
 The Users Controller 55
 The Account Controller 57
Creating the User Account Views 58
 The New User View 58
 The Login View 61
 The Show User View 62
Adding Administration Views 63
 Listing All Users in the Index View 64
 Editing a User with edit.rhtml 66
Testing 67
 Unit Testing 67
 Functional Testing 68
Adding Roles 72
 Creating the Role Model and Join Table 72
 Checking a User's Roles 74
 Administering Roles 76
Testing the Roles Functionality 79
Extending the User Management System 81
Summary 81

CHAPTER 4   Building a News Blog with RSS Feeds and an API 83

Specifying the Feature Requirements 83
  Textile Markup 83
  The Article Model 84
  Defining the Category Model............................ 85
  The Editor Role 85
  The Articles Controller 86
  The Categories Controller 86
Installing the RedCloth Gem 86
Creating the Article and Category Models 87
  Writing the Database Migrations......................... 87
  Defining the Relationships Among Models 88
  Defining the Validations 89
  Automatically Nullifying category_id on Deletion 89
  Automatically Updating the published_at Field............... 89
  Adding the Editor Role 90
Creating the Articles Controller and Views 91
  Mapping the REST Resources........................... 91
  The Articles Controller 92
  The Article Views 98
Using the Articles Feature 101
  Testing the XML API 101
  Adding HTTP Authentication for the API.................... 103
  Testing the API Authentication 104
Creating the Categories' Controller and Views 105
  The Categories Controller 105
  The Category Views 108
  Adding a Link from the Sidebar Menu 109
Manually Testing the News Blog System 110
Testing the News Blog 110
  Functional Tests 112
  Integration Tests..................................... 114
Further Development of the News System 115
Summary 116

■CHAPTER 5   **Building a Discussion Forum** 117

Specifying the Discussion Forum Requirements 117
    Defining the Forum Model................................. 118
    Defining the Topic Model................................. 118
    Defining the Post Model.................................. 119
    The Moderator Role 119
    The Forum, Topic, and Post Controllers..................... 119
Building the Forum 120
    Building the Forum, Topic, and Post Models................. 120
    Checking a User's Roles for Moderator Rights 126
    Adding the Nested Resource Route Mappings 126
    Modifying the Layout Template and Style Sheet.............. 126
    The Forums Controller and Views.......................... 127
    The Topics Controller and Views.......................... 131
    The Posts Controller and Views........................... 136
    Adding a Link to the Sidebar Menu 141
    Testing the Topics and Posts 141
    Restricting Actions to Moderators......................... 142
Testing the Forum 143
    Creating Test Fixtures 143
    Creating the Functional Tests 144
Further Development of the Discussion Forum 150
Summary 151

■CHAPTER 6   **Building a Blogging Engine
with Web Services Support** 153

Specifying the Blog Engine Requirements 153
    The Entry Model 153
    The Comment Model 154
    The User Model.. 154
    The Entries Controller................................... 155
    The Comments Controller 155
    The Blogs Controller.................................... 155
    Blogging APIs 155
Building the Blogging System 156
    Generating the Blogging Scaffolding Code 156
    Writing the Migrations 158
    The Models' Relationships and Validations 160
    Creating the Resource Mapping 161
    The Blog Name Helper Method 161

Adding the Blog Title to the Edit User Profile Page 162

The Controllers and Views 163

Testing the Entries Controller 171

Creating and Testing the Comments Controller 173

Adding the Latest Blog Entries to User Profiles 177

The Blogs Controller 178

Creating an XML-RPC Blogging Interface 180

Action Web Service 181

Generating the Web Service Code 181

Defining the API Method Calls 182

Writing the Blogging API Method Code 184

Testing the Web Services 186

Testing Using a Desktop Blogging Client 186

Automated Testing of the Blogging API 188

Further Development of the Blogging System 189

Summary 189

■CHAPTER 7   **Building a Photo Gallery** 191

Working with Uploaded Files 191

The attachment_fu Plug-in 192

The Photo Gallery Requirements 194

Defining the Photo Model 195

The Photos Controllers 195

Installing ImageMagick, RMagick,
and attachment_fu 195

Installing on Windows 196

Installing on OS X 196

Installing on Linux 196

Installing the attachment_fu Plug-in 196

Building the Photo Gallery 197

Generating the Scaffolding Code 197

Writing the Migration 198

Creating the Photo Model and Its Relationships 199

Mapping the Photos Resource 200

The Photos and User Photos Controllers 200

The Photo Views 203

Manually Testing the Gallery 208

Writing the Test Cases 210
Creating the Photo Fixtures 210
Unit Testing 210
Functional Tests 212
Further Development of the Photo Gallery 215
Summary 215

■CHAPTER 8   **Sending E-mail and Building
a Newsletter Mailing List** 217

Using ActionMailer 217
Configuring ActionMailer 217
Specifying the E-mail Feature Requirements 218
E-mail Notifications of New Comments 219
E-mail Newsletters 219
Building the New Comment Notifier 220
Creating the Mailer 220
Manually Testing E-mail Creation 223
Calling the Mailer from the Comments Controller 226
Testing the Mailer from Within the Application 227
Automating the Mailer Tests 228
Building the Newsletter Feature 230
Installing ar_mailer 230
Creating the Skeleton Resource 232
Mapping the Newsletter Resource 233
The Newsletter Model 234
Writing the Newsletter Controller and Views 234
Creating the Newsletter Mailer 241
Add the Newsletters to the Sidebar 241
Testing the Newsletter Mailer 242
Further Development of the E-mail System 244
Summary 244

■CHAPTER 9   **Adding Friends with XFN Details** 247

Microformats and XFN 247
The Friends Feature Requirements 249
The Friends Resource 249
Showing Users' Latest Activities 251

Building the Friends Resource 251

    Creating the Database Migrations 251

    Building the Friends Resource 254

    Updating the User's Latest Activity......................... 257

    The Friends Controller and Views.......................... 258

    Adding Friends Links to the Sidebar Menu 267

Styling the Friends List 269

Testing 272

Further Development of the Friendship Feature 274

Summary 275

■CHAPTER 10   **Adding Tags to the Photo Gallery** 277

The Gallery Tagging Requirements 277

Tagging with Rails 278

The acts_as_taggable_on_steroids Plug-in 279

Building the Photo Tagging Feature 282

    Installing the acts_as_taggable_on_steroids Plug-in 282

    Creating the Database Tables.............................. 283

    Updating the Models...................................... 284

    Creating the Controllers 285

    Adding the Resource Mappings 285

    Writing the Controllers and Views.......................... 286

    Adding Tags to a Photo 290

    Linking to the Tag Browser 295

Manually Testing 296

Further Development of the Tagging System 298

Summary 299

■CHAPTER 11   **Creating Mashups and Integrating with Web 2.0** 301

Integrating the Google Maps API 301

    The Mapping Feature Requirements 302

    Building the Mapping Feature.............................. 303

Integrating the Flickr API 316

    The Flickr Feature Requirements 317

    Building the Flickr Integration Feature....................... 317

Further Development Using Mashups 326

Summary 327

■CHAPTER 12 **Adding User-Created Themes**
to the Blogging Engine 329

The Blog Template Requirements 329
Liquid Templates 330
    The Liquid API... 331
    Liquid Markup... 331
Installing Liquid 332
Building the Blog Templates Feature 333
    Creating the Liquid Drops 333
    Creating the Liquid Filters 336
    The Usertemplate Model 337
    The Usertemplates Controller 338
    The Usertemplate Views 340
    Rendering Liquid Templates 342
Manual Testing 343
Testing the Usertemplates Controller 346
Further Development of the User Templates 348
Summary 349

■CHAPTER 13 **Adding a Mobile Interface** 351

The Mobile Web 351
The RailsCoders Mobile Site Requirements 352
    The Layout... 353
    User Profiles 354
    Accounts 354
    Pages 354
    News Articles 354
    Forums.. 354
    Blogs 354
    Photo Gallery... 355
Developing Mobile RailsCoders 355
    Structure of the Mobile Application 355
    Creating the Mobile Layout and Style Sheet 356
    The Resource Mappings 357
    The Mobile Controllers and Views......................... 360
Manual Testing 375
Testing the Mobile Site 375
Further Development of the Mobile Site 377
Summary 377

■**CHAPTER 14** **Deploying, Optimizing, and Scaling the Application** 379

Deploying RailsCoders 379
Development Mode vs. Production Mode 379
Session Storage 380
Choosing a Host 381
Choosing a Web Server 382
Automating Deployment with Capistrano and Deprec 383
Optimizing and Scaling RailsCoders 392
Watching the Log Files................................... 392
Caching 393
Benchmarking.. 395
Summary 396

■**INDEX** 397

About the Author

ALAN BRADBURNE is an independent Rails developer providing consulting services and developing applications for companies, both large and small. Alan has over ten years' experience in the Web and mobile industries, and has worked for Motorola, Nextel, and Sun Microsystems. In 2002, he created Phlog.net, one of the world's first dedicated mobile photo blogging communities. He then went on to work with 20six, helping to develop their blogging community software.

Since 2005, he has been working with Rails full time, developing applications for web start-ups and enterprise clients. He has spoken at a number of events on Rails development and has presented on agile development techniques and Rails coding.

He lives in Reading, England, with his wife, Mayumi. In his spare time, he enjoys learning Japanese, playing the occasional game of Go, and traveling as often as possible. You can find him online at http://alanbradburne.com.

About the Technical Reviewer

PAUL BENTLEY has been writing software professionally for over a decade. He has experience in many areas of computing, from embedded devices to 3-D graphics. He is especially proficient in the telephony world and is experienced with both traditional computer telephony and SIP-based solutions. He is currently working with Rails, developing web applications for corporations that want stable solutions to a variety of problems.

As an avid Go player, he tries to play every day—though he admits he still has a lot to learn before he can even be considered an amateur. He lives with his girlfriend and daughter in Harrogate, UK. If you feel like challenging Paul to a game of Go, he can be tracked down via `paulbentley.net`.

Acknowledgments

This book could not have been written without the help, guidance, and support of many people from Apress, the Ruby and Rails communities, friends, and family.

First of all, thanks to Peter Cooper for planting the seed of the idea to write this book and putting me in touch with Apress.

I would like to thank Keir Thomas for his encouragement and guidance during the early stages of the book. His advice and support were invaluable in my initial planning and writing.

Thanks to Kylie Johnston for being a wonderful project manager. She has been there every step of the way supporting me and keeping things moving.

Huge thanks go to Paul Bentley, Matt Moodie, and Chris Mills for doing such a fine job reviewing the book and providing constructive feedback.

I would also like to thank Heather Lang for her great work in copy editing the book and everybody else at Apress involved in the creation of this book.

Many thanks to the Rails community as a whole for making this such an exciting, interesting, and generally pleasant industry to work in. Special thanks go to Yukihiro Matsumoto and David Heinemeier Hansson for creating Ruby and Rails respectively.

Finally, I would like to thank my family and friends for their support during the writing of this book. Thanks go to my parents and Mayumi's parents for their encouragement and for putting up with my writing over Christmas and New Year. Special thanks must go to my wife, Mayumi, for her constant support and endless patience.

Introduction

Social networking sites have become increasingly popular and important for users of the Internet. Many people keep in touch with friends with sites such as Facebook and MySpace, and other sites such as LinkedIn allow people to connect and discuss topics in a business context.

Ruby on Rails has dramatically lowered the barriers to developing complex, maintainable, and scaleable web applications. This makes it a great tool to allow developers to easily build social sites that are tailored for the unique needs of a specific community.

I wrote this book to show you how to make use of Ruby on Rails and some of the available plug-ins and tools to build a unique site for your own community.

Who This Book Is For

Practical Rails Social Networking Sites is for developers who want to learn how to build a real-world web application using Ruby on Rails. This book is aimed at developers who have already worked through some Rails tutorials and have developed an application and now wish to build their skills and develop a social networking site using Rails.

How This Book Is Structured

Throughout the book, I will build a real-world social networking site called RailsCoders. In each chapter, I will address a different feature of the site, specifying the requirements of the feature and writing the code for it. You can use all of the code in the book to easily build your own social networking site or adapt the code for each feature to meet your own requirements.

This book is designed to be a practical guide to developing a site, rather than a reference book or a tutorial to Rails; I will point out useful resources for further information throughout this book.

I encourage you to get involved in the RailsCoders site itself at `http://railscoders.net`. You can use the forums to discuss topics from this book or create a blog to discuss your own Rails development experiences.

Downloading the Code

You can download a zip file containing the source code from the book from both the Apress web site at http://apress.com and the RailsCoders site at http://railscoders.net.

Contacting the Author

You can reach Alan Bradburne by e-mail at abradburne@gmail.com or follow his blog at http://alanbradburne.com.

CHAPTER 1

■ ■ ■

Ruby, Ruby on Rails, and the RailsCoders Project

Practical Rails Social Networking Sites is for developers who wish to build real-world community and social networking web sites using Ruby on Rails. In this book, we will develop a real-world community web site called RailsCoders, which you can find on the web at http://railscoders.net; the site is built on the same code that is developed in this book.

By learning how this community site was built, you can easily use the same code to run your own online community site or adapt and develop the code to suit your own site's requirements.

In this chapter, I will start by discussing the high-level requirements for the RailsCoders project. Next, I will give you some background on Ruby and Ruby on Rails and discuss some of the features of Ruby and Rails that make using them to develop web applications very quick and easy. I will provide instructions on how to install Ruby, Rails, and MySQL on your system and create the database required for the project. After that, I'll show you how to create the skeleton code for the application and make sure that Rails can connect to the database correctly.

You may already have installed Ruby and Rails on your machine and worked through some tutorials, or you may be familiar with developing a project in Rails. If so, you may wish to fast-forward through the installation section of this chapter, but you should ensure that you have the correct versions of the software installed and check that you are using a similar setup.

The RailsCoders Project

The RailsCoders site is aimed at both new and experienced developers working with Rails. Along with providing a general Rails developer community, it will also host a news and discussion forum for this book itself.

The two main features of the site will be a news blog containing articles on Rails and news about this book and a discussion forum to enable users to help each other and discuss issues with developing Rails web applications. To help build a community rather than just a collection of forum posts, the aim is to allow users to develop their profiles on the site by letting them to create blog posts and upload photos and allowing them to integrate profiles from other online communities, such as Flickr.

1

From this goal, we can produce a high-level list of features required for the site:

- *A system to allow users to create user accounts and add profiles about themselves*: This requires them to log in with a username and a password.

- *A simple way for you to maintain the information pages on the site*: These pages are likely to remain static most of the time. However, when they do need updating, you don't want to have to go in and edit HTML pages. Therefore, a simple content management system is required.

- *A news blog*: This will allow an editor of the site to create news articles and publish them.

- *A discussion forum system*: A forum moderator should be able to create a number of forums in which users can create new topics. Each topic can have any number of posts.

- *A blogging engine*: This will allow users of the site to create their own blogs about their projects and Rails development experiences. It should allow users to post blog entries using desktop blogging clients as well as the web.

- *A photo gallery for each user of the site*: This allows users to upload their photos to their profiles and should support showing thumbnails of each photo.

- *An e-mail newsletter*: The newsletter can be sent to all users of the site that opt in to receiving e-mails from the site.

- *Browser options*: The site should be able to be viewed from both a desktop web browser and from a mobile web browser on a cell phone.

Since many users will already have accounts on other online communities, the site should be able to integrate with these communities too. The RailsCoders project contained in this book will allow users to display their latest photos from their accounts on Flickr as well as providing RSS feeds of the users' blogs, enabling other community sites to access the users' data on RailsCoders.

Since RailsCoders will hopefully become popular, we need to make sure that it can scale to deal with a large number of simultaneous users. It also needs to be stable and secure.

Ruby and Ruby on Rails

I am sure you are eager to start developing the site (I know I am), but before we do, it is worth spending a bit of time getting to know what Ruby and Ruby on Rails are and how they relate to each other.

Ruby on Rails has drastically changed the way a lot of web development teams and individuals develop web applications, allowing a small team to rapidly develop stable, scalable, maintainable applications very quickly and easily. Rails provides results that are quick without being dirty, meaning that application development can be done very rapidly and interactively yet also be stable and well built.

Understanding where this dynamic duo of language and framework came from will help you get the most out of them and understand what makes them so productive and fun to work with.

A Brief History of Ruby

Ruby and Ruby on Rails are often mentioned in the same breath, and it is easy to think that they are one and the same. Looking at Rails code doesn't help much either, as it is difficult to see where Ruby ends and Ruby on Rails begins.

Ruby is simply a programming language much like Perl, PHP, or Java. However, there are a number of things that separate Ruby from other languages. First of all, Ruby was designed as an object-oriented language, rather than having object-oriented features added as an after-thought like Perl or PHP. Unlike Java or C#, Ruby is completely object oriented, meaning that everything in Ruby is an object—there are no primitives.

Also, Ruby is a dynamic language, which basically means that programs written in Ruby can change their structure as they are run. Ruby is dynamically typed: variables are not restricted to a particular type (such as an integer or a string); they can change their types during the execution of the application. This may not be unusual if you are coming from another dynamic language such as Perl or Python, but it may be a little unusual if you are coming from a C++ or Java background.

Ruby was conceived and developed by Yukihiro "Matz" Matsumoto and first released to the public in 1995. It quickly gained a lot of support in its native Japan, soon beating Python in popularity. However, it remained relatively unknown in the West. In 2000, it started to be noticed by developers who found its unique design and efficiency appealing, but it was not until the first release of Ruby on Rails in 2004 that it started attracting large amounts of attention (more on this in the next section).

The one thing that really sets Ruby apart from any other language that you are likely to have used is the philosophy behind its development. Matsumoto designed Ruby with the primary goal of making programmers happy. It does this by reducing the amount of menial work that you have to do as a programmer so that you can concentrate on the creative part of solving problems. All of the design decisions behind the language have this goal in mind.

Ruby has gained a lot of respect and recognition for being intuitive and, most of all, fun. Because of the design of the language and the fact that it allows you to quickly express your ideas in code, a lot of developers find that they have more fun writing in Ruby.

■**Note** Ruby's home on the web, `http://ruby-lang.org`, is a great place to learn more about it. You can find the online collection of Ruby documentation at `http://ruby-doc.org`.

OTHER USES OF RUBY

Ruby is used not only for developing web applications but also for system administration tasks and tool development. The standard libraries and increasingly extensive third-party libraries allow you to quickly develop scripts, tools, and applications. As you spend more time developing in Ruby, you may like to try developing other types of tools and applications with it. There are Ruby frameworks for developing desktop applications too.

For Mac OS X, a framework called RubyCocoa allows you to write desktop applications using the Apple Cocoa framework. You can find more out more information at `http://rubycocoa.sourceforge.net`.

WxRuby is a framework that allows you to create desktop applications for Windows, Linux, or OS X using the WxWidget GUI library. Visit `http://wxruby.rubyforge.org` for more information.

There is even a game development framework called Shattered Ruby that allows you to develop 3-D games. Find out more at `http://shatteredruby.com`.

What Is Ruby on Rails?

Ruby on Rails is simply a set of libraries and tools written in Ruby to allow rapid development of web applications. This package of tools is known as a framework.

This framework was not originally conceived as a stand-alone product; it was written as part of a real-world application and extracted from that. This is one of the reasons that Rails has proved to be so practical in the real world. David Heinemeier Hansson, the brain behind Ruby on Rails, started developing the web-based project management tool Basecamp for 37signals. 37signals can be found at `http://37signals.com`, and you can try out Basecamp at `http://basecamphq.com`.

Hansson had become frustrated with PHP and Java and had recently discovered the joy of programming in Ruby. He convinced the founder of 37signals, Jason Fried, to take a chance and let him develop the application in Ruby, and in the three months that it took to develop the first version of Basecamp, Ruby on Rails was born. After Basecamp was released, Hansson extracted the framework from the application and released it as open source.

Rails follows the design philosophy of Ruby, in that it focuses on making your life as a web developer easy and happy. Rails has a couple of main design principles that help achieve these goals: don't repeat yourself (DRY) and convention over configuration.

DRY is self-explanatory. If you have defined something once, you should not have to define it elsewhere. For instance, once you have defined the column names in a database schema, you should not have to repeat them elsewhere in your code. This reduces the amount of work and prevents inconsistencies in your code.

Hansson and 37signals made the decision to release the framework as open source, mainly because they believe that opening the framework up to other users to use and contribute to will help it rapidly grow and improve.

■**Note** When you install Rails, you are installing the actual Ruby source code to Rails. It is there on your hard drive to examine, reference, learn from, and even add to and improve. Do not be afraid to look through the code, as you can learn a lot from it. You can also browse the source code, along with checking the bug tracker, online at `http://dev.rubyonrails.org`.

Rails is simply a collection of Ruby packages, most importantly, ActiveRecord and ActionPack. They are supported by other utility components, such as `ActionMailer`, `ActionWebService`, and `ActiveSupport`.

Models, Views, and Controllers

The Ruby on Rails framework implements the model-view-controller (MVC) architecture. MVC is a set of design patterns that allows you to separate the data model, the user interface, and the control logic of your application. Separating your code into these three layers, as follows, allows you to work on one layer without affecting any other code:

- The *model* is the application-specific code that operates on your data. Any actions on the raw data stored by your application go through this layer. If you change or add any meaning to the data stored, it should be done in this code.

- The *view* is the presentation layer, where your page layouts and forms go. It controls how the result of your application is presented to the user.

- The *controller* contains the control logic of your application. The code that controls the flow of your program and what should happen when a user performs an action lives here.

The advantage of using an MVC architecture is that your code is cleanly separated into logical sections that are easy to develop, understand, maintain, and control.

■**Tip** If you wish to learn more about design patterns, you can find an overview on Wikipedia at `http://en.wikipedia.org/wiki/Design_pattern_(computer_science)` or see the book *Design Patterns: Elements of Reusable Object Oriented Software* by Erich Gamma, Richard Helm, Ralph Johnson, and John Vlissides (Addison Wesley, 1995).

Because Rails make such architectural decisions for you, you can spend that extra time working on your application and less time worrying about the information flows within your system.

Exactly how you write code that fits into this architecture and what happens when you request a page will be explained in later chapters as we develop the application.

Models: ActiveRecord

ActiveRecord is what is known as an Object/Relationship Mapping (ORM) library. An ORM library maps the data stored in a database to a class in your application. This allows you to access your data without having to worry about the SQL queries or even exactly how the data is accessed. The rows in each database table become instances of an object. Although this sounds complex, in practice, it makes working with a database incredibly simple and easy.

In a Rails application, all of the interaction with the database is performed through ActiveRecord, so learning how to get the most from it is important. Throughout this book, I will show you different ways of working with it and how to get the most from it.

Views and Controllers: ActionPack

ActionPack is simply a collection of libraries and tools to help you build web applications. These provide the "view" and "controller" of the MVC stack.

The view part of ActionPack is used to create the web pages themselves. Since virtually all of the pages in our site will be dynamic (i.e., not static HTML files), ActionPack provides a lot of helper functions to allow us to insert the dynamic data into a page.

The controller part of ActionPack is the glue that holds your application together. The controllers contain the code that responds to user requests through the web browser.

Metaprogramming

One of the reasons that it is sometimes difficult to tell Ruby and Ruby on Rails apart is that Rails uses a technique called metaprogramming to create what is known as a domain-specific language (DSL). A DSL is a programming language that is designed to solve problems in a specific domain. In this case, web applications are the domain, and Rails is a language that helps you describe your problem within this domain.

The ORM ActiveRecord (as described in the "Models: ActionRecord" section) provides a DSL for accessing your data, which means that we can use commands like `find_user_by_username('alan')` instead of having to go through lengthy sections of code that connect to a database, perform a SQL query, and then process the results. As you start writing applications using ActiveRecord finder methods, you will find it increasingly difficult to go back to writing SQL by hand.

Ruby makes it easy to create DSLs. As your Ruby skills improve, you should find yourself starting to think about how you can develop your application to best use the concept of DSLs. This will lead you to extend the feature set of Rails to enable it to work better within your application domain.

Built-in Testing

When developing web applications, testing the application often gets left to the end of the project or not given the amount of time or respect that it deserves. Often, the reason for this is that developing tests for the application may be difficult or time consuming.

The Rails framework comes complete with integrated automated testing tools. These tools make it incredibly simple to write unit, functional, and integration tests. Because writing the tests is so simple, you will find it makes sense to write the tests at the same time that you develop your code.

TEST-DRIVEN DEVELOPMENT

Some development teams use a development practice known as test-driven development (TDD). This involves writing your tests before you write your code. You then write your code to pass the tests. The test plans that you write are incredibly important and should be the result of use cases and user stories.

If you are interested in trying out TDD, there is a lot of documentation on the web about how to get started. The best place to start is the TDD page on the Rails wiki `http://wiki.rubyonrails.org/rails/pages/HowToDoTestDrivenDevelopmentInRails`.

Software Required to Build RailsCoders

To develop a web application using Ruby on Rails, you need to install a few things installed on your computer.

In this book, I am going to be using Ruby on Rails version 1.2 and MySQL 5.0. If you already have these installed and configured on your system, ensure that you have the latest version of Rails installed by following the instructions in the "Upgrading Rails" section; then skip ahead to the section called "Creating the Skeleton of a Rails Application."

If you do not have Rails already installed, follow the instructions in this section for your operating system.

Ruby uses a packaging system called RubyGems for distributing tools, applications, and extensions. Gems make it easy to install extra Rails plug-ins (small tools that extend the Rails functionality) and other Ruby tools. In fact, the Rails developers recommend that Rails itself is installed as a gem. Gems also make it easy to stay up to date with the updating command. You can find more information at `http://www.rubygems.org`.

By their very nature, community web sites require some kind of database to store the site's data (such as pages, users, and forum posts). Rails can work with most open source and commercial databases, but this book will use MySQL 5.0. If you are more familiar with another database, you may prefer to use that. If you use another database, you should refer to the Rails wiki at `http://wiki.rubyonrails.org` for instructions on how to configure Rails for your choice of database server.

You will also need a text editor. You probably already have a favorite, so stick with that. However, if you are using Windows, you may want to take a look at RadRails, a Rails integrated development environment (IDE). On the Mac, TextMate by MacroMates is a favorite with the Rails community and is used by most of the core Rails development team.

■**Tip** If you are using Windows and want to stick with the default text editor installed on your machine, make sure that you use Wordpad rather than Notepad. However, I highly recommend that you use a more developer-friendly editor.

IDE OR TEXT EDITOR?

If you are coming from a development environment such as Visual Studio or Eclipse, you may be a little worried about the thought of going back to just a text editor. But language-aware text editors designed especially for programmers, such as TextMate, have most of the features that you are likely to need.

TextMate is an advanced and flexible programmer's editor for Mac OS X by MacroMates. You can download a trial version from `http://macromates.com`.

RadRails is an IDE based on Eclipse and is rapidly becoming a favorite in the Windows Rails community. It is also available for Mac. You can download it from `http://radrails.com`.

Upgrading Rails

New releases of Rails are reasonably common. When a new version is released, updating your system to the latest version is very simple. Just open the command window for your Rails environment, and type the following line:

```
$ gem update rails --include-dependencies
```

Note If you are using OS X or Linux, you will have to prefix this command with `sudo` to perform the action as the root user. You will be prompted to enter your password.

This updates the version of Rails installed on your system but does not update any scripts or JavaScript libraries within your individual applications. To update these, run the `rails railscoders` command again in the directory above your application root directory. The script will ask you if it should overwrite files that already exist. You should select "yes" only to the files in the `script` and `public` directories, and select "no" to everything else.

Installing Ruby, Rails, and MySQL

As both Ruby and Rails are open source software and have diverse developer communities, they have been developed to run on almost any operating system in active use today. The applications you develop in Ruby can normally be run on any platform with no or very few modifications (as long as you take a few precautions, particularly when performing system or file system calls).

Many developers choose to develop their Rails applications on one platform then deploy on another. Linux or FreeBSD are the most popular choices for running a production server because of their stability and the fact that they are open source, and therefore free of charge.

Installing on Windows

There are a number of ways to install Rails onto your PC but the quickest and easiest way to get up and running is to use Instant Rails. This consists of a package of Ruby, Rails, Apache, MySQL, and some gems put together by Curt Hibbs.

Instant Rails is self-contained and can happily coexist with other installations of MySQL or Apache on your PC, so don't worry if you already have them installed.

To install Instant Rails, follow these steps:

1. Go to `http://instantrails.rubyforge.org`, and click the Download link.

2. From the list of downloads, right-click the latest version, and save it to your hard drive.

3. Copy the contents of the zip file to a new folder on your computer, such as `C:\InstantRails`. You must make sure that there are no spaces in the folder path, so a folder on your desktop or in your My Documents folder will not work.

4. Open the folder, and run the Instant Rails application.

5. Instant Rails will detect that it is in a new location and ask if it may regenerate your configuration files. Click OK.

6. An Instant Rails window similar to the one shown in Figure 1-1 will open and automatically start MySQL and Apache.

■**Caution** Windows may ask you if you want to unblock your web server port (port 80). Since we are just setting up a development system rather than a live server, you should tell Windows to keep blocking this port. Unblocking ports on your machine may be a security risk.

Figure 1-1. *The Instant Rails status window*

That's it! You should spend some time exploring the Instant Rails web site at `http://instantrails.rubyforge.org` to learn more about configuring Instant Rails.

To work with the Rails command-line utilities and to create and work with a new application, you need to open a console window for Instant Rails. To do this, click on the I button in the Instant Rails window, and select Rails Applications ➤ Open Ruby Console Window, as shown in Figure 1-2.

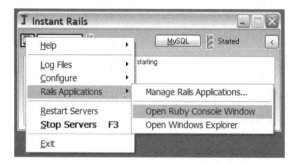

Figure 1-2. *Opening the Ruby console window in Instant Rails*

This will open a Windows command window, as shown in Figure 1-3, and change your working directory to the rails_apps directory within the Instant Rails path. All of the commands that you will enter in this book need to be typed into a command window opened through Instant Rails; otherwise, the path will not be set correctly.

```
C:\WINDOWS\system32\cmd.exe

C:\INSTAN~1>CD C:\InstantRails

C:\InstantRails>PATH C:\InstantRails\ruby\bin;C:\InstantRails\mysql\bin;C:\WINDO
WS\system32;C:\WINDOWS;C:\WINDOWS\System32\Wbem;C:\INSTAN~1\ruby\bin;C:\INSTAN~1
\Apache;C:\INSTAN~1\PHP

C:\InstantRails>cd rails_apps

C:\InstantRails\rails_apps>dir
 Volume in drive C has no label.
 Volume Serial Number is 0000-5844

 Directory of C:\InstantRails\rails_apps

10/09/2006  18:38    <DIR>          .
10/09/2006  18:38    <DIR>          ..
19/04/2006  07:00    <DIR>          cookbook
19/04/2006  07:00    <DIR>          typo-2.6.0
               0 File(s)              0 bytes
               4 Dir(s)  10,814,619,648 bytes free

C:\InstantRails\rails_apps>
```

Figure 1-3. *The Ruby console in Instant Rails*

After you have created a new application (which we will cover later in the chapter), you can start and stop your application from the Instant Rails application manager. To open this window, click on the I button, and select Rails Applications ➤ Manage Rails Applications. This window will be similar to the one shown in Figure 1-4.

From here you can choose which application is active. This is very useful if you are developing multiple Rails projects.

Figure 1-4. *The Instant Rails application manager*

Mac OS X

The quickest and easiest way to get Ruby on Rails up and running on your Mac is using a tool called Locomotive by Ryan Raaum. Locomotive is a package of Ruby, Rails, and a collection of tools and libraries together with a front end for administering your applications.

To install Locomotive, simply do the following:

1. Head over to `http://locomotive.raaum.org`, and click Download Now. Select a Source-Forge mirror to download from.

2. Open the downloaded `.dmg` file, and drag the `Locomotive 2` folder to your `Applications` directory.

3. Run the Locomotive application.

Locomotive does not come with MySQL as one of the preinstalled packages. If you do not already have MySQL on your system, install MySQL:

1. Go to `http://dev.mysql.com`, and click Downloads.

2. Select MySQL Community Server, and scroll down to the "Mac OS X downloads" section. Making sure that you choose the correct version for your Mac (i.e., PowerPC or x86/Intel), select the Standard package to download. Ensure that you download the `.dmg` file rather than a `.tar` file.

3. Open the downloaded `.dmg` file and run the `mysql-standard pkg` file. Follow the on-screen instructions to install MySQL.

4. Run `MySQL.prefPane` to install the System Preferences panel. This will allow you to start and stop the MySQL server from your Mac System Preferences panel. Start the server now.

Finally, you need to add the MySQL path to Locomotive, so that you can access the MySQL command-line tools easily. To do this, open the Locomotive preferences window from the menu bar. Click the Terminal icon, and add /usr/local/mysql/bin to the Additional Path(s) field, as shown in Figure 1-5.

Figure 1-5. *Adding MySQL to the Locomotive path*

You can easily create new Rails applications by simply selecting the menu option Applications ➤ Create New.

This will create a new Rails application in your home directory and automatically add a project in the Locomotive main window. If you select this application, you can then work on this application using the tools in the Applications menu. If you select Applications ➤ Open Terminal, Locomotive will open a terminal window that is set up with the correct paths to work with your selected application. When entering commands provided in this book, make sure that you do so in a terminal window opened from within Locomotive; otherwise, the correct paths will not be set.

You can also start and stop an application using the Run and Stop buttons in the main Locomotive window.

Linux

As with most things related to Linux, there are a multitude of ways to install Ruby and Rails, mostly depending on your choice of distribution. I will explain how to install for Ubuntu 6. Ubuntu is a very user-friendly Linux distribution that is available for free in both desktop and server versions. You can download it at http://ubuntu.com.

If you wish to install on a different Linux distribution, take a look at the installation pages on the official Rails wiki http://wiki.rubyonrails.org/rails/pages/HowtosInstallation. There are instructions for all main Linux distributions and most of the main flavors of Unix.

To install with Ubuntu, first log in and open a terminal window. Then follow these instructions:

1. Edit your `/etc/apt/sources.list` file, and ensure that the following lines are uncommented. This allows you access to the `universe` packages. Unless you are logged in as root, you will need to open this file using `sudo`, for example, `sudo vi /etc/apt/sources.list`.

   ```
   deb http://us.archive.ubuntu.com/ubuntu dapper universe
   deb-src http://us.archive.ubuntu.com/ubuntu dapper universe
   ```

2. Make sure your system is up to date by entering the following command:

   ```
   $ sudo apt-get update
   ```

   Enter your password if you are prompted to do so.

3. Install Ruby, some Ruby development libraries, and `irb` (interactive ruby):

   ```
   $ sudo apt-get install ruby ruby1.8 ruby1.8-dev irb
   ```

   Then install some extra Ruby libraries:

   ```
   $ sudo apt-get install rdoc libzlib-ruby libopenssl-ruby
   ```

4. Install MySQL and the MySQL Ruby bindings with the following command:

   ```
   $ sudo apt-get install mysql-server libmysql-ruby
   ```

5. Download and Install RubyGems by entering the following commands:

   ```
   $ wget http://rubyforge.org/frs/download.php/11289/rubygems-0.9.0.tgz
   $ tar xfvz rubygems-0.9.0.tgz
   $ cd rubygems-0.9.0
   $ sudo ruby setup.rb
   ```

   You can now delete the RubyGems `.tar` file and directory.

6. You should now run the gem automatic updater, just to check that the installer itself is up to date. You can do this by entering the following command:

   ```
   $ sudo gem update --system.
   ```

7. Now install Rails itself with the following command:

   ```
   $ sudo gem install rails --include-dependencies
   ```

8. Finally, install the Mongrel application server with the following command:

   ```
   $ sudo gem install mongrel
   ```

That's it! You now have Ruby and Ruby on Rails installed.

> ### SOURCE CONTROL MANAGEMENT
>
> I will not be discussing source control management (SCM) techniques in this book, but I strongly recommend that you consider using an SCM such as CVS (Concurrent Versions System) or Subversion (SVN). Developing using a versioning system is simply good practice and can save you a lot of stress and work if something goes wrong and you lose or break some code.
>
> You will find that most Rails and Ruby projects including Rails itself are developed using Subversion. You can find out more information about Subversion at `http://subversion.tigris.org`.

Creating the Skeleton of the Rails Application

Now that you have Ruby and Rails installed, it is finally time to start writing our Rails application. As I have mentioned, Rails has a lot of features to make writing a web application easier. To create a new application, we use the `rails` command to generate the skeleton code for a new Rails application. Open your Rails console window, and enter the command:

```
$ rails railscoders --database=mysql
```

■**Tip** If you are using Locomotive on OS X, it is preferable to use the menu option Applications ➤ Create New rather then using the command line. This will automatically add the newly created application to the Locomotive project window. After the application has been created, open a new terminal window for this application using the Application ➤ Open Terminal command.

The `--database=mysql` switch will automatically configure our application to use MySQL. If you are using a different database server, you can specify it using this command.

Running the command will create a directory for your application called `railscoders` and inside it, create a skeleton application. The command will output a listing of all the directories and files that it has created similar to the following:

```
create
create   app/controllers
create   app/helpers
create   app/models
create   app/views/layouts
...
create   log/production.log
create   log/development.log
create   log/test.log
```

This output might seem confusing, but you don't have to worry about most of these files for now. Change to the application directory that you've just created, and take a look around:

```
$ cd railscoders
$ ls -p
```

README	components/	doc/	public/	tmp/
Rakefile	config/	lib/	script/	vendor/
app/	db/	log/	test/	

Note On a Windows computer, use `dir` instead of `ls`; this is the only Windows-specific command.

The important directories for now are the app directory, which contains the code for all the models, views, and controllers, and the `script` directory, which contains a set of tools to help us build and run the application.

One of these tools is `server`, which starts an application server for the Rails application we are developing. Depending on the configuration of your machine, it may run WEBrick, lighttpd, or Mongrel. Try running this script now:

```
$ script/server
```

Note If you are running Instant Rails on Windows, you should use the Instant Rails application manager window, as described previously. Select the check box for the `railscoders` application, and click the Start with Mongrel button. If you are running Locomotive, click the Run button.

This will output information similar to the following:

```
=> Booting Mongrel (use 'script/server webrick' to force WEBrick)
=> Rails application starting on http://0.0.0.0:3000
=> Call with -d to detach
=> Ctrl-C to shutdown server
** Starting Mongrel listening at 0.0.0.0:3000
** Starting Rails with development environment...
** Rails loaded.
** Loading any Rails specific GemPlugins
** Signals ready.  TERM => stop.  USR2 => restart.  INT => stop (no restart).
** Rails signals registered.  HUP => reload (without restart).  It might not ➥
work well.
** Mongrel available at 0.0.0.0:3000
** Use CTRL-C to stop.
```

■Note If you are running Locomotive and start your application with the Run button, you will not see this
output.

This command starts an application server running your new Rails application. By default,
the server is listening on port 3000.

To test that the server is running, open a web browser, and go to `http://localhost:3000`.
You will be presented with the Rails welcome page, similar to the one shown in Figure 1-6.

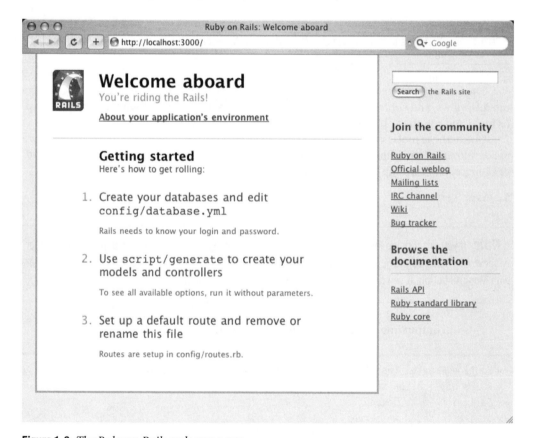

Figure 1-6. *The Ruby on Rails welcome page*

Ruby and Rails are now up and running correctly.

Watching the Rails Logfiles

While developing a Rails application, it is a good idea to keep an eye on the log file that is generated by Rails as it processes the requests to the server. The log files can be found in the `log`
directory of your Rails project.

These log files display the incoming request (along with any parameters that are sent), any SQL queries that are performed by the application, and the result of the request, for example, a page render or a redirection. You can also add messages to the log file from your controller files for debugging purposes using the `logger` object.

If you take a look in this directory now, you will see that there are number of log files. Depending on the configuration of your computer, there may be files generated by the application server (such as Mongrel) or web server (such as lighttpd). However, you will always find the three main log files: `development.log`, `test.log`, and `production.log`. Since we are running the server in development mode at this point in time, all requests will be logged to the `development.log` file.

On Linux and OS X, you can use the following command to keep a continuous display of the log file:

```
$ tail -f log/development.log
```

There is not a built-in tail command on Windows, but you can download a free tool from Bare Metal Software at `http://www.baremetalsoft.com/baretail`.

THE RAILS DEVELOPER COMMUNITY

Now that you are running Rails, it is worth spending a few minutes becoming familiar with the Rails community and how to keep updated with the latest news. The Ruby and Rails communities are incredibly friendly, so do not be worried about asking questions.

The official Rails blog is at `http://weblog.rubyonrails.com`. The Rails core development team maintains this blog, so the news is straight from the source.

There are number of Google Groups set up, including a Rails security list, which will alert you if there are any important security alerts:

- *rubyonrails-talk* is a discussion on general Ruby on Rails topics located at `http://groups.google.com/group/rubyonrails-talk`.

- *rubyonrails-spinoffs* is a discussion about the JavaScript libraries script.aculo.us and Prototype used within a Rails environment and can be found at `http://groups.google.com/group/rubyonrails-spinoffs`.

- *rubyonrails-security* provides important security announcements at `http://groups.google.com/group/rubyonrails-security`.

- rubyonrails-core is a discussion list for Ruby on Rails core development and is located at `http://groups.google.com/group/rubyonrails-core`.

Setting up the Database

Now that Rails is up and running, you should set up your database software and make sure that Rails can communicate properly with it. You should also create a new database for your project and configure Rails to use this development database.

Creating the Database

Rails applications actually expect three separate databases: one for development, one for testing, and another for production. Of course, it's highly unlikely that you will run the production version on your development and testing machine (in fact, I highly recommended that you do not!), so you do not have to worry about setting up everything right away. For now, you just need a development database.

I will use the MySQL command-line tools. If you are happier using a graphical tool or web interface, there are many open source and commercial tools available. However, having a good understanding of MySQL's command line will be a big advantage when you are trying to optimize and scale your database.

Open a command-line prompt, and enter the following command:

```
mysqladmin -u root create railscoders_development
```

This will create a new database accessible by the MySQL root user. Since we are just using a local development database that isn't publicly accessible, logging in as the root user is fine.

Note While accessing the database for development and testing as the root database user is OK, in a production environment, I highly recommend making the database more secure and using a different user name and password. I will talk about best practices for configuring your production environment in Chapter 14.

Configuring Rails to Use the Database

Now that you have a database, you need to configure your Rails application to connect to it. Thankfully, that is a simple task. When you created the `railscoders` application, you will remember that it created a whole variety of directories and files. The database configuration is stored in the `database.yml` file in the `config` directory. Open the file in a text editor, and take a look. The section that we are currently interested in is the section for development. It should look like this:

```
development:
  adapter: mysql
  database: railscoders_development
  username: root
  password:
  host: localhost
```

The style of markup should be pretty self-explanatory. It is written in YAML Ain't Markup Language (YAML), a non-verbose, lightweight text format for storing structured data that has been adopted by Rails for use in its configuration files. You can find more information on YAML at http://www.yaml.org.

■**Tip** You can also make use of YAML to store your own data for use in your application; for example, you could store your error or information messages in a YAML file, allowing easy editing without having to touch your code.

You will notice that it is already configured to use MySQL (since you specified the database system when you created the application with the `rails railscoders --database=mysql` command earlier in this chapter). You will also notice that the database name is already filled in with the correct name, in this case `railscoders_development`. This is another example of Rails preferring convention over configuration—it simply uses the application name together with development, test, or production. This saves us time and means that all Rails applications use the same naming convention. Of course, you could call your database anything, but you would have to edit this database configuration.

Since you are using the root user to connect to the database along with a blank password, no changes need to be made. Of course, if you are using a different database server or have set up a different user, you will have to change these settings.

■**Note** Rails only reads the `database.yml` configuration file when you first start up an instance of your application. So if you make any changes, you will have to restart your server by pressing Ctrl+C and running `script/server` again if you are running from the command line, clicking the Stop Server button if you are using Instant Rails, or clicking the Restart button if you are using Locomotive.

Testing the Database

You should just do a quick test to make sure that everything is set up and that Rails can connect to the database correctly. The simplest way to do that is to perform a migration; a migration is simply a way of altering your database structure through Rails.

I will talk more about migrations and how to write them in Chapter 2, but for the purposes of testing your database connection, you will just run the migrate command without any database changes. This will connect to your database, find that there are no changes to be made, and disconnect. If there are problems with the Rails application connecting to your database, they will be reported here.

To run an empty migration, enter the following command:

```
$ rake db:migrate
```

```
(in /Users/alan/Projects/rails/railscoders).
```

If no errors are reported, your database connection was successful. If an error is reported, check that your database server is running, check that the `railscoders_development` database is accessible, and check the configuration of your `database.yml` file.

This simply verifies our configuration to ensure that everything is set up correctly. We will start creating the database structure in Chapter 2 as well. Rails allows us to create the database schema incrementally as we develop the application, so each chapter will create the database schema necessary for that chapter.

Summary

In this chapter, I talked about the project to be developed throughout this book and gave a high-level specification for the project. I also discussed where Ruby on Rails came from and described the basic components of the framework. I showed you how to install and configure Ruby, Ruby on Rails, and MySQL on your computer and how to check to make sure everything is working correctly. I also described creating the skeleton code for the project using the `rails` command.

In the next chapter, I will show you how to build a simple content management system for the RailsCoders site that allows the site maintainer to create and maintain a number of pages that can be accessed by visitors to the site.

CHAPTER 2

■■■

Developing a Content Management System

In this chapter, we will start building the RailsCoders site by creating a content management system, which allows us to easily create, edit, and display pages through a web interface. Creating the content management system will provide the beginnings of the RailsCoders site and demonstrate how easily you can create a functional application in Rails.

To build the content management system, we will create and implement a Rails resource called Pages, together with a model for the resource and a collection unit tests. We will also build a layout for the site and create a style sheet that we will build on throughout the project.

Let's get this project under way.

Specifying the Feature Requirements

Before we start coding, we should decide on the requirements of the feature we're creating. Almost any interactive web site will require a number of information pages that are more or less static. They provide information about the site's contents, as well as maybe FAQ or help pages. These pages need to be created and maintained by an administrator but do not change very often. The RailsCoders site definitely needs some information pages.

For the RailsCoders site, we require a series of pages giving information about the site and what features it provides for our users. These pages need to be presented in the same style as the rest of the site, so creating new pages should be very simple.

These pages should be easily maintainable through a web interface, since we do not want to have to go through the process of using FTP to upload a file every time we make a small change.

This feature, therefore, will consist of a single resource called Page, which will store all of the details of a page that can be managed and presented by the site.

Rails, Routing, and REST

As you will recall from the discussion of MVC architecture in Chapter 1, our application is split into three distinct parts: the models, the views, and the controllers.

The controllers are the user's interface into the application. Whenever a user requests a page, clicks a button, or submits a form, the request is made to a URL, which is then routed to a method in a controller. Each controller consists of a number of methods, known as actions.

Each action performs a specific task and either returns a view to the user or redirects the browser to another action. The user never accesses a model directly, only through a controller. These actions allow the user to do things like show, create, or destroy pages.

The way that Rails knows to which method and controller to pass the request is specified in the file `config/routes.rb`.

Traditional Rails Routes

The `config/routes.rb` file allows you to configure how a URL should be parsed. If you look in this file now, you will see two route mappings at the bottom of the file:

```
map.connect ':controller/:action/:id.:format'
map.connect ':controller/:action/:id'
```

These are the default Rails mappings, and they allow you to call a particular controller and action method, together with an object ID through a URL.

For instance, if you wanted to call an action called `show` of a controller called page with an object ID of 4, the URL would be `page/show/4`.

If you wanted to request the `index` action of a controller, you could use `page/index` or simply `page/`.

RESTful Rails Routes

While traditional Rails routes allow mappings to be easily set up between URLs and controllers, using them also means that you have no standard way of accessing an object. One person might choose to use an action called `show` to display an object, whereas another might use `display`. However, Rails 1.2 supports a different way of specifying mappings between URLs and controllers based on the concept of Representational State Transfer (REST).

REST describes a set of architectural principles for building a system such as the Web. By REST principles, the Web is considered to simply be a collection of resources, and a web page is a representation of a specific resource. By utilizing the HTTP protocol, we can perform actions on these resources, such as getting, setting, or deleting objects. We could also provide other representations of resources, such as in XML.

To make building REST resources easy, you can state that a controller provides access to a resource in the Rails routes file. Doing this automatically sets up a number of mappings. You then simply need to provide the code to implement the standard REST methods that Rails expects.

Rails uses the HTTP request methods GET, POST, PUT, and DELETE together with the URL, meaning that the same URL can have different responses depending on which HTTP method is used.

The Rails action methods, URLs, and HTTP methods for a pages resource are shown in Table 2-1.

If you wish to provide other actions besides the standard actions described, you can specify extra actions for a collection or for a member of the resource in the routes file. I will demonstrate this later in the book.

Also, Rails allows you to respond to requests for XML responses of these actions, which we will look at later in this book.

Table 2-1. *Rails REST Mappings*

Rails Action	URL	HTTP Method	Description
index	/pages	GET	Return a collection of resources
show	/pages/1	GET	Return one specific resource
new	/pages/new	GET	Return a form for creating a new resource
create	/pages	POST	Create a new resource
edit	/pages/1;edit	GET	Return form for editing a resource
update	/pages/1	PUT	Update a resource
destroy	/pages/1	DELETE	Delete a resource

Creating a Site Layout

Before we build the content management feature, our application requires a layout. Layouts are used by Rails to break down the page content into nonchanging layout parts and dynamic parts. The parts of the page that never change are things like the XHTML header, a page header, or a menu bar.

Since the RailsCoders site will contain many different sections, we want to include a sidebar menu that lists all of the parts of the site. This will be on-screen for all pages of the site, so it can be part of our layout. A sketch of our page layout is shown in Figure 2-1.

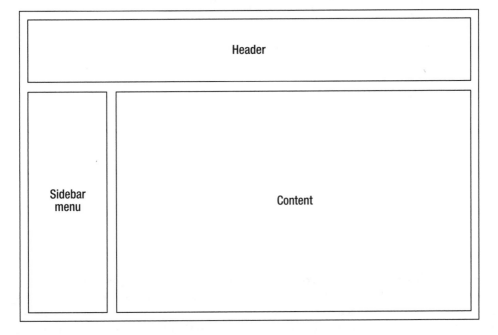

Figure 2-1. *The RailsCoders page layout*

Layout files are Rails template files written in ERb. ERb is a simple templating system for Ruby that allows Ruby code to be embedded within a text file. In this case, that text file is an XHTML file. All layout and template files in Rails have the suffix .rhtml.

By default, Rails looks for layout files in the app/views/layouts/ directory. If a layout exists that has the same name as the controller being requested, it will use that. This allows for each controller to have individual layouts without any extra coding.

If that file does not exist, it will look for a layout called application.rhtml. This easily allows for an entire site to use the same template.

Create the layout file app/views/layouts/application.rhtml now. Enter the code shown in Listing 2-1 into this file.

Listing 2-1. *The Application Layout File*

```
<!DOCTYPE html PUBLIC "-//W3C//DTD XHTML 1.0 Transitional//EN"
  "http://www.w3.org/TR/xhtml1/DTD/xhtml1-transitional.dtd">
<html xmlns="http://www.w3.org/1999/xhtml">
  <head>
    <title>RailsCoders</title>
    <%= stylesheet_link_tag 'main' %>
    <%= javascript_include_tag :defaults %>
    <%= yield :head %>
  </head>
  <body>
    <div id="container">
      <div id="header">
        <%= image_tag 'logo.png', :alt => "RailsCoders" %>
      </div>
      <div id="sidemenu">
        <%= render :partial => 'layouts/menu' %>
      </div>
      <div id="content">
        <% if flash[:notice] -%>
          <div id="notice"><%= flash[:notice] %></div>
        <% end -%>
        <% if flash[:error] -%>
          <div id="error"><%= flash[:error] %></div>
        <% end -%>
        <%= yield %>
      </div>
    </div>
  </body>
</html>
```

As you will have noticed, this looks like a standard XHTML file, except with Ruby code embedded within the <%= %> and <% %> tags. The important thing to note here is that <%= %> tags output the result of the executed code, whereas <% %> has no output. So you can see that the if and end statements do not output anything to the rendered HTML, whereas image_tag and render are output to the page.

The yield tags are used to insert the output of the relevant view.

The code stylesheet_link_tag 'main' will create a link to a CSS file called stylesheets/main.css. Since this CSS file is static, we should create it in the directory public/.

Create the file public/stylesheets/main.css, and add the CSS in Listing 2-2.

Listing 2-2. *Stylesheet for the RailsCoders Site*

```
body {
  margin: 0;
  padding: 0;
  background: #fff;
  font-family: Arial, Helvetica, sans-serif;
}

#header {
  background: #fff url(/images/h-grad.png) repeat-x;
  height: 60px;
  margin-top: 10px;
  text-align: left;
  padding-top: 1px;
}

#container {
  width: 760px;
  min-width: 760px;
  margin: 0 auto;
  padding: 0px;
}

#sidemenu {
  font-size: 80%;
  float: left;
  width: 100px;
  padding: 0;
}

#sidemenu ul {
  list-style: none;
  margin-left: 0px;
  padding: 0;
}

a { color: #b00; }
a:hover { background-color: #b00; color: #eee; }

#content { float: right; width: 650px; }
```

```
th { background-color: #933; color: #fff; }
tr.odd { background-color: #fcc; }
tr.even { background-color: #ecc; }
```

This provides some basic styling for the site, which we will add to as our site develops. You will notice that the layout and style sheet refer to two images: logo.png and h-grad.png. You can download both of these files from the Apress web site.

If you look back at the application.rhtml layout file, you will notice the following statement at line 16: render :partial => 'menu'. This instructs Rails to insert another template at this point, specifically a partial. A partial is another ERb file that is a snippet of code that we want to insert into another template. I have chosen to break out the sidebar menu into a partial file to allow us to easily maintain the menu over time and separate the menu from the content structure. Partials' names have an underscore (_) for a prefix.

Now, create the partial file app/views/layouts/_menu.rhtml. Since the site is currently empty, there's not a lot to add apart from a link to the index page. As we build new features, we will add them to this menu. Add the code shown in Listing 2-3.

Listing 2-3. *The Sidebar Menu Partial File*

```
<ul>
  <li><%= link_to 'Home', '/' %></li>
</ul>
```

We can now move on to building the content management feature.

Designing the Pages and Page Editor

To store the page data, the application needs a database structure to store the data, a model definition that allows the code to access and modify that data, and a user interface to actually allow the user to work on the content. So how does this convert into Rails code?

The Page Model

What should the Page model consist of? First of all, since each record is unique and needs to be referenced by a unique identifier, it needs a primary key. In this case, the MySQL auto-incrementing integer field is fine. By default, Rails expects all primary key fields to be called id.

A page needs a title, so a title field would make sense. Since we want to limit titles to a sensible length, we are going to use a MySQL string type, rather than an unlimited-length text type. This will limit the title field to 255 characters, which should be more than enough.

Of course, a page needs to have real content, so we need a body field. Since pages could be very large, we are going to use a text field type. This allows an unlimited-length string to be stored. However, it makes sense to put a sensible limit on the length of the page, though this will be done in the Rails model code, rather than the database definition. A maximum page length of 10,000 characters will be fine.

For the URL, the application could just use the primary key id to identify the page to show. However, that would not be very friendly to the user and does not provide very good search engine optimization. Therefore, I want the page to be accessible by a permalink—a few words that describe the page and can be part of the URL. The permalink should be reasonably short, so a string type will be fine. It will be automatically generated by the model from the title field.

To make the title into a URL-friendly string, we will remove any characters that are not alphanumeric, and spaces will be renamed to underscores.

It would be very useful to keep a record of when each page was created and when it was last updated, and luckily Rails thoughtfully provides an automatic way of doing this. If we add created_at and updated_at fields to our table, they are automatically detected and updated by ActiveRecord when pages are created or updated.

Table 2-2 summarizes our database structure.

Table 2-2. *The Page Model Database Structure*

Field Name	Field Type	Description
id	integer	The primary key
title	string	The title of the page
permalink	string	A URL-friendly version of the title
body	text	The body of the page
created_at	datetime	The date and time that the page was created
updated_at	datetime	The date and time that the page was last updated

The Page Controller

To access the Page model, all requests are handled by the pages controller file. This controller file lives, along with all other controller files, in the directory app/controllers/. When creating a new model or controller for a Rails application, the best practice is to use a Rails generator. Generators create all necessary files for a new model or controller.

Since we will be using Rails controllers to act as REST resources, Rails expects a number of default actions to be defined and maps these to default URLs as discussed earlier.

Therefore, we need to implement the actions index, show, new, create, edit, update, and destroy.

How should the page model be accessed by the user? Because we are going to use the built-in Rails REST support, we need to use the following default action method names:

- First of all, the application needs a way to display the page on the screen for a visitor to the site, so a show method is needed. This will take the id as a parameter.

- For the administration of the site, a number of methods are needed for listing, editing, saving, creating, and deleting pages.

  - To list the pages, the index method will be used.

  - For creating a new page, there will be two methods: new and create. The new method will show a page for entering the page details, and create will save this data.

  - To edit a page, there will be two methods: edit and update. The edit page will show the existing data, and the update method will validate and save that data.

  - A method called destroy will delete a page.

Creating the Page Model

Before you write the model code, you are going to need to define your database schema that will be used to store the pages. Rails makes defining your database incredibly easy using a feature called migrations.

Migrations

Migrations are simply a way of describing the changes in your database to allow it to migrate from one version to another, which includes setting up your initial database schema.

Rails migrations are interesting in that they are written in Ruby, rather than in SQL like a traditional database schema. This has some advantages:

- It allows you to add conditional statements or create records as part of the migration. In fact, you can access your full Rails application from a migration script, which allows you to perform complex tasks.

- You can work independently of the type of database that is running. This means that if you wish, you can develop on one type of database server, test with another, and deploy on yet another.

A common use of migrations is to use MySQL for developing on a local machine, since it is very simple to set up and use. Testing may be performed with a very fast, in-memory database such as SQLite. Then in production, you might choose to use another database such as PostgreSQL, depending on your server configuration.

IN-MEMORY TESTING WITH SQLITE

SQLite is a small, embedded database engine that provides the majority of the standard SQL features but in a very small, self-contained library. Ruby support for SQLite is provided by a gem called `sqlite-ruby`, and you can easily configure ActiveRecord to use SQLite as your database engine.

Using SQLite as a database engine to run your tests is a great way of speeding up your test cycle, but it is a little difficult to set up. Chris Roos first pioneered the procedure, which you can read on his blog at

`http://blog.seagul.co.uk/articles/2006/02/08`

Geoffrey Grosenbach then created a plug-in to make this procedure incredibly simple. You can find this plug-in at

`http://nubyonrails.com/articles/2006/06/01`

Using SQLite for testing allows your tests to run 30 to 50 percent faster then with MySQL or PostgreSQL. You can find more information about SQLite at `http://sqlite.org`, and the SQLite-Ruby interface documentation can be found at `http://sqlite-ruby.rubyforge.org`.

You can create a new migration script at any time using the `script/generate migration` command, but a new migration script is automatically created every time that you use the generate script to create a new model, so I'm going to use automatically generated migration this time.

Creating the Model

As you saw in the previous chapter, when we created a new application using the `rails` command, several directories were created. Rails provides a number of utility commands within the generated `script` directory to help you build your application. The generate script automatically generates the necessary files for a new model, controller, or migration.

To create the Page model, open a command window for the application, and enter the following command:

```
$ ruby script/generate model Page
```

This will produce output similar to the following:

```
exists  app/models/
exists  test/unit/
exists  test/fixtures/
create  app/models/page.rb
create  test/unit/page_test.rb
create  test/fixtures/pages.yml
create  db/migrate
create  db/migrate/001_create_pages.rb
```

As you can see, a number of files have been created for you. Open the generated migration file `db/migrate/001_create_pages.rb` in your text editor. Each time you perform a migration, the version number of the database is increased and stored in a database table called `schema_info`. The version number is reflected by the number prefix of the migration file and automatically incremented by the migration generator.

This file is the first migration file, describing how to migrate your database (in this case, an empty one) to the desired state. This migration is described using the ActiveRecord DSL. This allows you to add, alter, or remove tables and columns.

Inside the migration file, you will notice that there are two methods in the `CreatePages` class: `self.up` and `self.down`. These methods are for migrating up and down, respectively. This means that if you are at version 5 of your database, you can migrate back to version 4. The migration script simply follows the `down` method for the migration script number 4.

ACTIVERECORD MIGRATIONS

Within migrations, you can create, drop, or rename tables; create, edit, or remove columns within a table; and add or remove indexes.

The following database transformations are available:

- `create_table(table_name, options)`

- `drop_table(table_name)`

- `rename_table(old_name, new_name)`

- `add_column(table_name, column_name, column_type, options)`

- `rename_column(table_name, old_column_name, new_column_name)`

- `change_column(table_name, column_name, column_type, options)`

- `remove_column(table_name, column_name)`

- `add_index(table_name, column_name, index_type, index_name)`

- `remove_index(table_name, index_name)`

The full API reference can be found at `http://api.rubyonrails.com/classes/ActiveRecord/Migration.html`.

To add the actions to get the database schema to version 1, edit the skeleton `self.up` method as shown in Listing 2-4.

Listing 2-4. *The Migration for the Pages Model*

```
class CreatePages < ActiveRecord::Migration
  def self.up
    create_table :pages do |t|
      t.column :title, :string
      t.column :permalink, :string
      t.column :body, :text
      t.column :created_at, :datetime
      t.column :updated_at, :datetime
    end
  end

  def self.down
    drop_table :pages
  end
end
```

You might have noticed that the primary key id is not defined in this migration. ActiveRecord automatically adds the id column unless you tell it not to. If you have a table that explicitly requires there not to be an id column, you need to add the statement :id => false as part of the create_table command.

When this migration is run, it will create a new empty table called pages. However, it would be useful if there were at least an index page in the database, rather than leaving it empty. This will give us a page to get started with.

To create a page as part of the migration, add the following code before the end of the self.up method:

```
Page.create(:title => "RailsCoders Home",
            :permalink => "welcome-page",
            :body => "Welcome to RailsCoders")
```

This will create a new page record in the database. To actually run the migration and create the table, go back to the command line and run the following command:

```
$ rake db:migrate
```

This will output the result of the migration, similar to the following:

```
== CreatePages: migrating ========================================================
-- create_table(:pages)
   -> 0.0173s
== CreatePages: migrated (0.0173s) ===============================================
```

RAKE

rake is a Ruby build tool that allows you to define a set of tasks to be performed in order to build or make your application before running. However, within Rails, it is possible to do much more than just build an application—you can develop rake tasks to manage your databases, deploy your code to your servers, or perform tests.

Since rake scripts are written in Ruby, they can take advantage of the Rails framework, and developing tasks specific to your problem is simple.

You can see a list of all the rake scripts that are available to Rails by using the following command:

```
$ rake -T
```

If you write any new rake tasks for your application, simply create a rake file (a Ruby file with the file suffix .rake) in the directory lib/tasks/; then, you can run them from your command line with rake <task>.

You can learn more about rake and how to write tasks at http://rake.rubyforge.org/.

You should take a look at the railscoders_development database, either using the MySQL command line or a GUI front-end tool. You will see that the pages table has been created as well as the default page record.

■**Note** If you wish to downgrade to a specific version of the database, specify the desired version number as part of the migrate command: add `VERSION=<version number>` to the `rake db:migrate` command.

Mapping the Resource

We now need to declare the page model as a REST resource. This is done in the `config/routes.rb` file. The routes file allows you to define how URLs relate to your controllers and actions. You will see that there is already a catch-all route defined at the end of the file:

```
map.connect ':controller/:action/:id'
```

To define a REST resource, add the following line before the catch-all route:

```
map.resources :pages
```

This will map the URL /pages/. . . to your pages controller but predefines a collection of actions that are expected. You need to make sure that the correct action names are used.

Adding Validations

The database table to store the page data in is now created, but a model can (and should) do more than just store and retrieve data.

The first thing you should do is add some validations to the model. This simply allows you to define what each field can (and can't) contain. Because all data that is stored in the database has to pass through your model, you have complete control over what is allowed to be stored or rejected. This allows you to check the validity of all data before it gets into your database. You can specify if these validation checks should be performed every time an object is saved or just when it is created.

If the controller attempts to save invalid data, that data will get caught by your validation checks; any relevant errors will be added to the object; and the object will not get saved and will return `false` to the controller. You can then act on the returned value by displaying the error messages and asking the user to change the input data.

To add validations to your model, edit the `app/models/page.rb` file. At the moment, it is simply a class definition inheriting from the `ActiveRecord::Base` class. You can add a simple validation as follows:

```
class Page < ActiveRecord::Base
  validates_presence_of :title, :body
end
```

`validates_presence_of` is simply a Rails validation method that does pretty much what is says—it checks to make sure that each of the fields are present, that is, not empty or null.

This validation is a good start, but it only checks that a user enters something in each field, rather than checking if what they have entered is suitable.

Another useful check would be to ensure that the fields are a sensible length (especially since the title field is stored in a string database type where the length is limited to 255 characters). Do this by adding some more validations:

```
validates_length_of :title, :within => 3..255
validates_length_of :body, :maximum => 10000
```

The validates_length_of method checks for—yes, you guessed it—the length of the specified fields. I have specified a maximum length for the body field and a range for the title field. You can also specify a minimum or exact length using the parameters :minimum and :is.

As well as allowing validations, you can also automatically perform processing on the object at various stages of its life cycle; for instance, you could automatically encrypt a password before it is saved in the database, or you could update another object when a record is deleted. These hooks into the object life cycle are called callbacks. There are 20 different callbacks.

In this case, I want to autogenerate a permalink from the contents of the title field, replacing the regular text with a URL-friendly version. I want to do this before the object is created, so I will use the before_create callback.

There are a number of ways of writing a callback, but the simplest way is to write a method matching the callback that you require. So in the page.rb model file, add the following callback code inside the class definition:

```
def before_create
  @attributes['permalink'] =
    title.downcase.gsub(/\s+/, '_').gsub(/[^a-zA-Z0-9_]+/, '')
end
```

The regular expression code isn't pretty, but it will generate clean, URL-friendly permalinks by substituting an underscore for spaces and removing any nonalphanumeric characters.

Now, whenever a new page object is created, a permalink is generated and subsequently saved with the other object attributes.

Creating the Controller

We will also use the Rails generate script to create the controller file. The generate controller command takes the controller name as a parameter, along with any actions that you wish to define for this controller. We need to specify that we want a controller called "pages" and then list the action names necessary to work with the REST resource, as we discussed earlier. If you need to add extra methods later, you can just add a new method in the controller and add a view file.

Enter the following generate command:

```
$ ruby script/generate controller Pages index show new create edit update destroy
```

This will output details about created files as follows:

```
exists  app/controllers/
exists  app/helpers/
create  app/views/pages
exists  test/functional/
create  app/controllers/pages_controller.rb
create  test/functional/pages_controller_test.rb
create  app/helpers/pages_helper.rb
create  app/views/pages/index.rhtml
create  app/views/pages/show.rhtml
create  app/views/pages/new.rhtml
create  app/views/pages/create.rhtml
create  app/views/pages/edit.rhtml
create  app/views/pages/update.rhtml
create  app/views/pages/destroy.rhtml
```

Open the controller file app/controllers/pages_controller.rb. You will see that there are empty method definitions for the action methods specified in the generate command.

Listing the Available Pages Using index

To start with, it would be useful to see a list of the pages. This will be shown by the index method.

This action will use ActiveRecord's find method to retrieve the pages. If you look in the API documentation, you will see that the find method is very flexible and allows you to specify exactly what you want to search for and how you want to find it; it's similar to the SQL SELECT command, except much friendlier. In this instance, you want to find all pages, so edit the index method in the pages_controller.rb file as shown:

```
def index
  @pages = Page.find(:all)
end
```

This defines what will happen when the index page for the page controller is called. The command simply finds all of the page objects and stores them in the @pages variable. The @ symbol specifies an instance variable that will be accessible from the view.

The view for this action is stored in app/views/pages/index.rhtml. RHTML files are simply HTML that includes embedded Ruby code.

Open the index.rhtml file, delete the placeholder HTML, and add the code shown in Listing 2-5.

Listing 2-5. *The Pages Index View*

```
<h2>All Pages</h2>
<ul>
  <% @pages.each do |page| %>
    <li><%= page.permalink %> : <%= page.title %></li>
  <% end %>
</ul>
```

You will notice that is just regular HTML, but with some Ruby embedded in the <% %> and <%= %> tags.

Now is a good time to try running this code to see what happens when you access this method. Recall from Chapter 1 that, to run the Rails development server, you start the Rails server using either the command script/server from a command prompt or a GUI, such as InstantRails or Locomotive. When the server has started, open a web browser, and go to http://localhost:3000/pages. You will see a page listing the one page in your database, the welcome-page page, as shown in Figure 2-2.

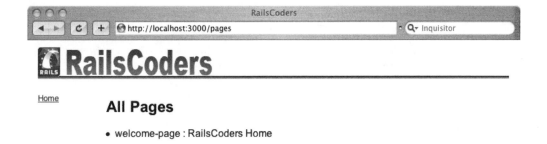

Figure 2-2. *The pages index view*

However, we now want to be able to see the full page, so that should be the next action to write. But first, we can add links to allow the pages listed in the page list to be shown.

Rails provides a helper method to write HTML links; helper methods are simply methods that are designed to make writing views easier. To change the view to include a link to the show action for each page, edit the index.rhtml file as shown in Listing 2-6.

Listing 2-6. *The Updated Index View*

```
<ul>
  <% @pages.each do |page| %>
    <li>
      <%= link_to page.permalink, page_path(page) %> : <%= page.title %>
    </li>
  <% end %>
</ul>
```

The link_to method here is a helper method. A lot of helper methods are built into Rails, including helpers to create links, create forms, display dates, and accomplish other common tasks that are required when writing HTML views.

You can also write your own helper methods. If you add a helper to one of the helper files in app/helpers that corresponds to a controller file, the helper method will only be available in views for that controller. If you add a helper method to the `app/helpers/application_helper.rb` file, it will be available to all views. Our application will make use of both Rails built-in helpers and custom helper methods.

Displaying a Page Using the show Action

Go back to the `pages_controller.rb` file where an empty `show` action is already defined. Add the following bold line to it:

```
def show
  @page = Page.find(params[:id])
end
```

The instance variable `@page` is now available to the view in `show.rhtml`. Open the `app/views/pages/show.rhtml` file, and replace the placeholder text with the code in Listing 2-7.

Listing 2-7. *The Page Show View*

```
<h2><%= @page.title %></h2>
<p><%= @page.body %></p>
```

As you might expect, this displays the page and the header.

Now, in your browser, go to `http://localhost:3000/pages`. As you saw before, this lists the pages in the database. If you click the `welcome-page` link, it will take you to `http://localhost:3000/pages/welcome-page`, which displays the welcome message.

Creating Links and Permalinks

Currently, the link that the `link_to` method creates in the index view is to `/pages/1`. Because the pages controller is defined as a REST resource, this is accessible by the shortcut `page_path(page)`. Notice here that we are not specifically asking for the `id` of the `page` object, we just supply the `page` object as a parameter. Each ActiveRecord object inherits the method `to_param`, which by default returns just the `id` of the object.

Since we want to include the page's permalink in the URL of the `page` item, we can override the `to_param` method of the page model, making it return the permalink together with the ID. We will still use the ID to find the page, but the URL and the `id` parameter subsequently passed to the controller will contain the permalink. All we have to do is use the Ruby method `to_i` to convert the `id` parameter to an integer. This will take the first group of integers from the parameter string. We can then use this as the `id` to retrieve the page object.

First, we will first override the page model's `to_param` method. Open the model file, `app/models/page.rb`, and add the following method within the `Page` class:

```
def to_param
  "#{id}-#{permalink}"
end
```

We now need to change the `show` action method of the page's controller to convert this parameter to an integer before attempting to find the `page` object. Open the page's controller file, `app/controllers/pages_controller.rb`, and change the `show` action method as follows:

SQL) will automatically do this conversion for you. However,
ood idea to add this to your controllers. You could also over-
http://www.notsostupid.com/blog/2006/07/07/

dex view, http://localhost:3000/pages, you will see
welcome-page. Try visiting this link to make sure that

te

eeds to have a page in which to enter the page infor-
aves the data. These actions will be called new and

e definition of the new action as follows:

Page model and stores it in the variable @page. This
simply created in memory.
tml file as shown in Listing 2-8.

```
html => { :method => :post } do |f| -%>
e, :size => 60 %></p>
<p>body:<br /><%= f.text_area :body, :rows => 20, :cols => 60 %></p>
<%= submit_tag 'Save' %> or <%= link_to 'cancel', pages_url %>
<% end -%>
```

There are a number of interesting methods introduced here. First of all, the
error_messages_for helper method is an easy way of showing all the errors (if there are any)
that arise from validating an object.

The form_for helper method is a way of creating an HTML form for a specific model object.
The URL to post the form to is specified simply as pages_url. The real URL is then derived from
the resource mapping that you defined in the routes.rb file earlier on.

The text_field and text_area methods create a text input field and a text input area, respectively, and the submit_tag creates a submit button for the form.

If a user fills in the form and clicks the Save button, the form will be submitted as an HTML POST to the page model resource URL. Because the page model is mapped as a REST resource, the resource URL (in this case http://localhost:3000/pages) responds not just to the URL itself, but also to the HTTP calling method—be it GET, POST, PUT, or DELETE. So if the /pages URL is accessed with HTTP GET, the pages_controller index method will be performed. However, through the magic of Rails routing of REST resources, if the same URL is accessed with HTTP POST (as in the case of submitting this form), the create method will be performed. This greatly simplifies the URL structure and makes the methods of accessing your objects very consistent, not just within your application but also as a REST web service.

So to actually save this page data, write the following create method in pages_controller.rb:

```
def create
  @page = Page.new(params[:page])
  @page.save!
  flash[:notice] = 'Page saved'
  redirect_to :action => 'index'
rescue ActiveRecord::RecordInvalid
  render :action => 'new'
end
```

This method creates and attempts to save an instance of the Page model, except this time it is instantiated with the parameters from the form. These are automatically available through the params variable. If the save fails and raises a RecordInvalid exception, it is caught by the rescue clause. The new page is rendered again, but the validation errors will be shown by the error_messages_for :page statement in the view.

When an attempt is made to save this object (which actually tries to create the database record), validation is performed, along with any callbacks. If the validations and saving are successful, true is returned.

A success notice is then stored in the flash, a temporary storage for values for the current session. By default, when something is stored in the flash, it is available for the next page request and cleared on the next successful request. This makes it ideal for passing error or status messages from page to page. If you look back at the layout template app/views/layouts/application.rhtml that we created at the beginning of this chapter, you will see that this template will display any flash messages if they are present.

The method then redirects the browser to the index method, which lists the available pages.

It would also be useful to add a link to the "Create new page" action on the page list view. Edit app/views/pages/index.rhtml, and add the following line below the h2 tag:

```
<p><%= link_to 'Create new page', new_page_url %></p>
```

Now you can test adding a new page. Go to http://localhost:3000/pages in your browser. Click the "add new page" link. This should now display the Create New Page form. To try it out, create a new test page, giving it a title and a body, and save the page. Your page will be created, and you will be returned to the list of pages—now including your new page. You will see that the permalink field has been created for you. Click the permalink of your new page to see it displayed.

Editing Pages Using edit and update

The code and views for editing pages are very similar to those for creating new pages. However, instead of creating an instance of a new empty model, you need to get an existing page from the database. To do this, edit the pages_controller.rb:

```
def edit
  @page = Page.find(params[:id].to_i)
end
```

In the same way as in the show method, we should make sure that the id parameter is converted to an integer before we try to search for the object.

The corresponding view is essentially identical to the view for the view action, since it displays the same fields. However, notice that the URL that the page is submitted to now specifies the ID of the page being edited and the :method has changed from :post to :put. This means Rails interprets HTTP POST methods as creating a new record and HTTP PUT methods as modifying an existing record.

Edit the file app/views/pages/edit.rhtml as shown in Listing 2-9.

Listing 2-9. *The Edit Page View*

```
<h2>Edit Page</h2>

<%= error_messages_for :page %>

<% form_for :page, :url => page_url(@page), :html => {:method=>:put} do |f| -%>
  <p>Title:<br /><%= f.text_field :title, :size => 60 %></p>
  <p>Body:<br /><%= f.text_area :body, :rows => 20, :cols => 60 %></p>
  <%= submit_tag 'Save' %> or <%= link_to 'cancel', pages_url %>
<% end -%>
```

When this form is submitted, it is handled by the update method in pages_controller.rb. Edit this method as follows:

```
def update
  @page = Page.find(params[:id].to_i)
  @page.attributes = params[:page]
  @page.save!
  flash[:notice] = "Page updated"
  redirect_to :action => 'index'
rescue
  render :action => 'edit'
end
```

This performs a similar action to the create method, except this time, instead of creating a new page based on the form parameters, you are retrieving the page from the database and attempting to update the attributes of this object. This will also be validated and callbacks that are defined will be run.

Now, you just need to add a link to the edit form from the page list by updating the `index.rhtml` file as shown in Listing 2-10.

Listing 2-10. *The Updated Page Index View*

```
<% @pages.each do |page| -%>
  <li>
    <%= link_to page.permalink, page_path(page) %>
      [<%= link_to 'edit', edit_page_path(page) %>]
      : <%= page.title %>
  </li>
<% end -%>
```

This adds a link to the edit page. Give it a try. You can now edit any page just by clicking on the edit link.

Deleting a Page Using destroy

The `destroy` method simply finds a given record and destroys it, adding a flash notice if the deletion was successful or an error message if it was not.

```
def destroy
  @page = Page.find(params[:id].to_i)
  if @page.destroy
    flash[:notice] = "Page deleted"
  else
    flash[:error] = "There was a problem deleting the page"
  end
  redirect_to :action => 'index'
end
```

To avert deletions by accidental mouse clicks, when you create the delete link in the index view, you can specify a pop-up confirmation box. Edit the `index.rhtml` view file again, adding a link to the destroy method as follows:

```
<li><%= link_to page.permalink, page_path(page) %>
  [ <%= link_to 'edit', edit_page_url(page) %>
  | <%= link_to 'delete', page_url(page), :method => :delete,
        :confirm => 'Are you sure you wish to delete this page?' %> ]
  : <%= page.title %>
</li>
```

The link to the `destroy` method is simply a normal page URL except with an HTTP DELETE method. This is specified by the `:method=>:delete` parameter. The `:confirm` parameter specifies the pop-up alert box.

Go ahead and try deleting a page now. Don't delete the welcome page!

Setting Up a Default Page

You will notice that if you just go to the index page of your application (i.e., `http://localhost:3000/`), you are still presented with the default Rails "Welcome aboard" page. This is because it is a static HTML page stored in the public folder of your application.

When you request a page through the browser, Rails first checks the public directory to see if any static files are there that match the request. If so, it will send that file rather than routing the request through your Rails application.

This feature is incredibly useful, as it allows the web server to very quickly serve static files that your application relies on, such as JavaScript files or images, without having to process the request in Ruby. Rails also makes use of this feature for caching pages.

To change your application so that your users will be presented with your own index page rather than the Rails default page, you need to set up a default route for an empty request and remove (or rename) the static `index.html` file.

Edit `config/routes.rb`, and add the default route as the first map statement:

```
map.index '/', :controller => 'pages',
                :action => 'show',
                :id => '1-welcome-page'
```

The `map.index` statement connects the root URL, `'/'`, to a particular action with a specific parameter. This particular named route is called `index`, and as you saw earlier, you can use a shortcut to reference this mapping. If you wanted to redirect a user back to the index page after performing an action, you would simply use this line:

```
redirect_to index_url
```

which is much easier to read than the equivalent command:

```
redirect_to '', :controller => 'pages', :action => 'show', :id => '1-welcome-page'
```

Another advantage is that you can change the mapping at any time just by editing the `routes.rb` file, rather than trying to find every instance of the index page in your code.

Finally, delete (or rename) the static index file `public/index.html`; otherwise, this will always be the default page loaded for your site!

Adding a Link from the Sidebar Menu

To make it easy to access the pages controller, we should add a link to the `index` action from the sidebar menu.

Open the partial view file, `app/views/layouts/_menu.rhtml`, and add a link to the page's index action. You should also change the URL for the home link to the `index_url` mapping that we just defined.

Edit the file to match the code shown in Listing 2-11.

Listing 2-11. *The Updated Menu View File*

```
<ul>
  <li><%= link_to 'Home', index_url %></li>
  <li><%= link_to 'Edit Pages', pages_path %></li>
</ul>
```

Now, reload the page, and test out the links and actions to ensure that the site is working as expected.

Testing

You may have noticed that when you first created the application with the `rails` command, a collection of directories and files was created under the `test` directory in the Rails application.

If you take a look at the `test` directory now, you'll see there are directories for fixtures, functional tests, integration tests, mocks, and unit tests. I will describe all of these in time, but for testing the page model, we will make use of the unit tests.

Creating the Testing Database

Before you start testing, you need to create another database. In Chapter 1, you created a database called `railscoders_development`. Now, you need another database, this time called `railscoders_test`. The advantage of running our tests with a separate database is that our development and production databases stay clean and free of any test data.

You can do this by opening a command prompt and entering the following line:

```
$ mysqladmin -u root create railscoders_test
```

Now that you have a test database, you need to create the necessary tables to make it the same as your development database. To do this, enter the following command:

```
$ rake db:test:prepare
```

You now should have a fresh database that has the same structure as your development database. You can now start writing some tests.

Developing Unit Tests for the Page Model

Open the `test/unit/page_test.rb` file. You will see that there is already a test defined—`test_truth`. You need to now replace this with your own tests.

So, what do you need to test for? You defined a number of validations on the page model, and these should be tested. If you look back at the page model, the first validation performed is that the two fields `title` and `body` are present. This should be the first test.

Unit tests in Rails are written as assertions; an assertion is a method that states what you expect to be true. For example, you might expect something to fail validation or you might expect an object to be saved correctly. By covering both positive and negative tests, you can be sure that the model is working correctly.

To check that the object is invalid if any of the attributes are missing, you can write the test as follows:

```
def test_invalid_if_any_field_empty
  page = Page.new
  assert !page.valid?
  assert page.errors.invalid?(:title)
  assert page.errors.invalid?(:body)
end
```

As you can see, this will create a new page object and check a number of assertions. If any of these assertions fail, this test will fail. The first assertion checks that the Page model is invalid by asserting a not valid test. The next two assertions check that each of the fields is invalid.

Next, we should check that a valid page can be saved. You could write the test by specifying all of the fields in the test code, but if you had a lot of tests, this could get quite repetitive and awkward. To make life easier, you can specify test data as fixtures; a fixture is a set of data that is used to create an object for testing. Unsurprisingly, these are stored in the test/fixtures directory. If you go there now, you will see that there is already a file called pages.yml that has a couple of placeholders for your fixture data. Fixtures are stored in YAML, the same as the database configuration file that you looked at in Chapter 1.

Since you want to test both valid and invalid data for the page model and check that the automatic permalink generation works, you should specify a number of fixtures as shown in Listing 2-12, replacing the placeholders that have been automatically generated in the file.

Listing 2-12. *The Page Test Fixtures File*

```
valid_page:
  id: 1
  title: Welcome Page
  permalink: welcome-page
  body: Welcome to RailsCoders
invalid_page_short_title:
  id: 2
  title: a
  permalink: a
  body: The title is shorter than 3 character
valid_with_auto_permalink:
  id: 3
  title: Another Page, but without a permalink
  body: No permalink is given so it should be automatically generated
```

Now, you need to write the tests that make use of these fixtures. Go back to your page_test.rb file. To test if you can save a valid page object, write a test_valid_fields stest as follows:

```
def test_valid_fields
  page = pages(:valid_page)
  assert page.valid?
end
```

You can access each of the fixtures that you defined using pages(:fixure_name). In this case, you retrieve the valid_page fixture and check that the page is valid. Now, try running your tests again:

```
$ ruby test/unit/page_test.rb
```

The results of the tests will be shown as follows:

```
Loaded suite test/unit/page_test
Started
..
Finished in 0.064965 seconds.

2 tests, 4 assertions, 0 failures, 0 errors
```

Each of the periods in the output represents a pass. If a test fails, this will show an F, and an E represents an error. You will be notified which test failed along with the line number where it failed.

You can now add more cases to test for too-short titles and to test the automatic permalink generator:

```
def test_invalid_short_title
  page = pages(:invalid_page_short_title)
    assert !page.valid?
end

def test_auto_permalink
  page = pages(:valid_with_auto_permalink)
  assert page.valid?
end
```

Again, run the tests, and make sure that they all pass. You should now have confidence in your object model, and if you make any changes, make sure you add the relevant tests. By keeping your tests up to date, you can add to and alter models without having to worry about having broken something. I will explore more ways of testing your code later.

Extending the Content Management System

The content management system that we have developed could be extended in many ways such as adding a JavaScript WYSIWYG editor, such as FCKeditor (www.fckeditor.net) or TinyMCE (http://tinymce.moxiecode.com), to the page-creation and editing pages. These will make creating a complex page much easier than having to write your own HTML markup.

You may also wish to improve the layout of the index view, for instance, you might put the list of pages into a table.

Summary

In this chapter, you saw how quickly and easily you can build a simple content management system that will allow content for the RailsCoders site to be written and maintained through a simple web interface.

To store the page content, we used ActiveRecord migrations to write a database schema. Next, we built a model for the page data, complete with validations. We utilized callbacks to autogenerate a search-engine-friendly permalink based on the title of the page and adapted the model to automatically show these permalinks on all links to the pages.

We also created a test database and wrote unit tests for the page model, ensuring that the validations and callbacks work as expected.

And we did all of this with only a handful of lines of code!

Now that the RailsCoders site has a welcome page, we can start to build on these foundations and add more features.

In the next chapter, we will add users and user roles to the system, which will allow us to add permissions to different actions. By adding permissions, we can create administrator users who are capable of editing the site, whereas regular visitors can only view it.

CHAPTER 3

■■■

Adding Users and Groups

In this chapter, we will add user accounts and a role-based group system. This will allow your users to create accounts and log in to the site and allow you to maintain control by adding an administrator role to regulate who can administer the site.

We will create a web interface to allow the administrator to manage the permissions of each user, including disabling accounts.

The code for the user authentication system in this chapter has been adapted from a Rails plug-in called `restful_authentication` written by Rick Olson. If you wish to find out more about this plug-in, go to `http://agilewebdevelopment.com/plugins/restful_authentication`.

Specifying the Feature Requirements

To start, you will add a user account system to the site, along with an interface to allow users to sign up, log in, and log out. You will also add an administration interface to allow the site administrators to add and remove permissions for user accounts and to disable or reset user accounts.

This will require two models and three database tables. First, we need a user model to hold the user data itself; it will store information such as the user's login details, e-mail address, and so on.

We also need a model called "Role." Our site requires users to have different permissions so that we can have editors, moderators, and administrators along with regular users of the site. This Role model will store what the role is called.

To link these models together and assign roles to users, we will create a join table called `roles_users`. A join table is a special type of table that simply allows Rails to link two other models together.

Defining the User Model

The User model will hold the account information. Here, we will define the information that will be stored about the users and how a user's input can be validated on sign-up. As you saw in Chapter 2, the User model will, by default, use a database table called `users`.

Before we specify the required fields, we need to consider how we will store sensitive information, in particular the user's password.

The user needs to log in to the site with a password, so we will require a `password` field. The simplest way to store this would be as clear text, but this raises a number of security issues. Many people use the same password across a number of sites, so having them accessible and stored as plain text just isn't fair to your users and generally not a good idea.

A better way of storing the passwords is using a one-way hashing algorithm. A hash is like a digital fingerprint of data. This data could be a file, or it might just be a string.

As it happens, the commonly used hashing algorithm SHA-256 is part of the standard Ruby libraries. By storing the hashed value of the user's password in the database, you can check that the user has entered the correct password by calculating the hash of the entered password and comparing that to the hashed value stored in the database.

The hashes created by the SHA-256 hashing algorithm are 64 characters long, so the database field to store the SHA-256 hash needs to be a string field capable of storing 64 characters.

Since users will enter their own passwords when signing up, we want to have the users confirm their passwords by repeating them in a confirmation text field to catch any typos. This will not actually be stored in the database—we will simply compare the password and password_confirmation fields when the user creation form is submitted to ensure that the user intends the entered password and didn't make a mistake.

The required database fields for this users table are shown in Table 3-1.

Table 3-1. *The Database Fields Required for the User Model*

Field Name	Field Type	Description
id	integer	This will be used as the primary key.
username	string	A unique name that the user will use as a nickname on the site. This should have a minimum length of 3 characters and a maximum of 64 characters.
email	string	Since we want the option of sending e-mails to the user from the site, this will hold their e-mail addresses, with a maximum length of 128 characters.
password	string	This will store the SHA-256 hash of the entered password.
enabled	boolean	If a user wants to remove his or her account, it needs to be disabled. A Boolean enabled field will allow a user's account to be enabled or disabled. By default, it should be set to true.
profile	text	Users will have the option of entering extra information, up to a maximum of 1,000 characters, about themselves.
created_at	datetime	The date and time that the user was created.
updated_at	datetime	The date and time that the user was last updated.

We want to be able to view users' profiles by specifying their usernames as well as by the primary keys, so we should make sure that the an index on the username field is created by the database.

The Role Model and Join Table

In order for us to assign different permissions to different users, we will create a Role model to store the different roles of users on the site. This will not store what the role is capable of, just the name of the role. We will define the actual capabilities or restrictions in the code. The required fields of the roles database table are shown in Table 3-2.

Table 3-2. *The Database Fields Required for the Role Model*

Field Name	Field Type	Description
id	integer	The primary key
name	string	The name of the role

We will then link the User and Role models together using a join table. A join table simply stores the IDs of two separate models and links them together. In your model code, you need to specify a many-to-many relationship by stating that each model has and belongs to many of the other model. For example, in this case, the User model has and belongs to many Roles, and the Role model has and belongs to many Users. The required fields are shown in Table 3-3.

Table 3-3. *The Database Fields Required for the Roles_Users Join Table*

Field Name	Field Type	Description
user_id	integer	The ID of the user
role_id	integer	The ID of the role

The Controllers

Implementing this technology will require three controllers: a users controller, an account controller, and a roles controller.

The users controller will provide the RESTful resource for the User model. This will provide the methods to display and edit the user account.

The account controller will provide the supporting web actions that allow the user to sign up, log in, and log out.

The roles controller will provide a RESTful resource for assigning and revoking roles from a specific user.

The reason for separating the tasks among three controllers is to keep the REST actions cleanly separated from the web-only methods, allowing much easier use of the site through a REST API.

The Account Controller

The account controller needs the following methods to allow a person to join the site, log in, and log out:

- The signup method will allow users to enter their details to become new members of the site.

- The login method will check the e-mail addresses and passwords of the users to allow them to log in to the site.

- So users can log out of the site, a logout method will be provided.

The Users Controller

The users controller will provide the usual REST methods for accessing the User model. Of course, you will want to limit use of some of these methods to only administrators. However, that functionality will be added later in this chapter.

- All the normal REST actions are provided: index, show, new, create, edit, update, and destroy. However, since I don't want to actually delete a user account, the destroy action will simply disable the user's account by setting the enabled field to false.

- In order for users to see other users' profiles in a pretty URL of /user/<username>, a show_by_username method will be provided to display the profiles of users referenced by their usernames.

- To allow an administrator to re-enable a user's account, an enable action will be provided.

The Roles Controller

The roles controller will be a nested resource under the users controller. This means that the controller will only be accessible when it is prefixed by a valid user in the URL. For example, /users/4/roles will show all of the roles assigned to user 4. The URL /users/6/roles/1 with the HTTP method of PUT (meaning that we want to update the object) would assign role ID 1 to user ID 6.

Through this controller we want to be able to perform three actions:

- List the roles that are assigned to a specified user. This will be performed by the index action.

- Add a role to a user's assigned roles list. This will be performed by the update action. Both the user ID and the role ID need to be specified.

- Remove a role from a user's assigned roles list. This will be performed by the destroy action.

Sessions and Cookies

Any web application that allows multiple people to log in and see views unique to them needs a way of tracking a user and knowing the identity of that user. Rails applications are stateless, meaning that each request made to the web application is independent and that the server does not have any knowledge of the previous actions of the user.

So, to keep track of the user's actions, you need to use sessions. A session is simply a unique ID assigned to each user that allows our application to track which user is requesting the page. This session ID is stored on the user's machine as a browser cookie. The cookie is sent along with every request to the web application, which can then be used by the application to work out which user submitted the request.

Rails session handling is very flexible and allows you to decide how you want to store session data: in files, a database, or an in-memory cache, such as memcached. Throughout this book, I will use the default file-based session store. I will discuss the benefits of a database or memcached session store and how you implement a database session store in Chapter 14.

We will also add a Ruby module for all of the session-handling code. Ruby modules are simply a way of grouping together reusable code. In Rails, modules live in the lib directory.

Creating the User Model

The first step is to use the generate script to create a new model. As you saw in the previous chapter, this will create the skeleton files that we need, along with a new migration script for adding the database migration details.

Open a terminal window, and enter the following command:

```
$ ruby script/generate model User
```

The relevant model files are created for you. First of all, edit the database migration script db/migrate/002_create_users.rb, and add the details of the users database table, as shown in Listing 3-1.

Listing 3-1. *The User Table Migration File*

```
class CreatesUsers < ActiveRecord::Migration
  def self.up
    create_table :users do |t|
      t.column :username, :string, :limit => 64, :null => false
      t.column :email, :string, :limit => 128, :null => false
      t.column :hashed_password, :string, :limit => 64
      t.column :enabled, :boolean, :default => true, :null => false
      t.column :profile, :text
      t.column :created_at, :datetime
      t.column :updated_at, :datetime
      t.column :last_login_at, :datetime
    end
    add_index :users, :username
  end

  def self.down
    drop_table :users
  end
end
```

Since it is a requirement to be able to search the users based on their usernames, we have added an index for the username column to speed up the database searching.

You can now run the migration:

```
$ rake db:migrate
```

This will create the new table:

```
== CreateUsers: migrating ========================================================
-- create_table(:users)
   -> 0.7473s
-- add_index(:users, :username)
   -> 0.2982s
== CreateUsers: migrated (1.0542s) ===============================================
```

Edit the model file, user.rb. As before, we need to define the validations for the model, matching the specification from the beginning of the chapter. Edit the file as shown in Listing 3-2.

Listing 3-2. *The User Model File*

```ruby
require 'digest/sha2'
class User < ActiveRecord::Base
  attr_protected :hashed_password, :enabled
  attr_accessor :password

  validates_presence_of :username
  validates_presence_of :email
  validates_presence_of :password, :if => :password_required?
  validates_presence_of :password_confirmation, :if => :password_required?

  validates_confirmation_of :password, :if => :password_required?

  validates_uniqueness_of :username, :case_sensitive => false
  validates_uniqueness_of :email, :case_sensitive => false

  validates_length_of :username, :within => 3..64
  validates_length_of :email, :within => 5..128
  validates_length_of :password, :within => 4..20, :if => :password_required?
  validates_length_of :profile, :maximum => 1000

  def before_save
    self.hashed_password = User.encrypt(password) if !self.password.blank?
  end

  def password_required?
    self.hashed_password.blank? || !self.password.blank?
  end

  def self.encrypt(string)
    return Digest::SHA256.hexdigest(string)
  end
end
```

You will notice this is a little more complex than the Page model from Chapter 2. The basic validations are similar, but a number of extra interesting things are going on here. The attr_protected statement defines the model's attributes that are to be protected. This is very important to the security of your data, because it protects the named attributes from being set in mass assignments, such as those usually performed when you create a new model instance with new(attributes) or save with update_attributes(attributes). Instead, these variables have to be set directly, which protects sensitive attributes in your model from hackers attempting to inject data into your database.

The attr_accessor statement specifies the attribute password. You may have noticed that this doesn't actually exist as a field in the database migration. This declares that password is an attribute of the model even though it doesn't exist as a database field. The model will be able to use the data from this field to create the hashed_password field. You will notice that this is done by the before_save filter. This will simply set the hashed_password field to be a hash of the clear password which, as stated in our specification, we can compare to the stored hashed_password value to authenticate a user's login credentials.

You will notice that the validation of the password confirmation and the validation of the presence of the password and password_confirmation attributes have an extra :if parameter, which means that the validation will only be performed under certain circumstances. In this case, it is performed if no password is currently stored in the database, or if the user is trying to change their password.

All that is left is to add a way of checking a user's login credentials. Add the following method:

```
def self.authenticate(username, password)
  find_by_username_and_hashed_password_and_enabled(username,
     User.encrypt(password), true)
end
```

This defines a class method that takes the username and clear password, creates a hash of the password, attempts to find that user in the database, and returns that user object if it is found. Also, only users who have the enabled attribute set to true will be found, making it simple to disable user accounts.

The Session-Handling Library

Before you can create the controllers and view to use this User model, you must have a way of storing and accessing the session data needed to remember the user's state across pages. Building a module encapsulates the session handling code and makes your application more readable and maintainable.

Create a new file called login_system.rb in the lib directory of you application, and add the code shown in Listing 3-3.

Listing 3-3. *The Login System Module*

```
module LoginSystem
  protected

  def is_logged_in?
    @logged_in_user = User.find(session[:user]) if session[:user]
  end

  def logged_in_user
    return @logged_in_user if is_logged_in?
  end
```

```
  def logged_in_user=(user)
    if !user.nil?
      session[:user] = user.id
      @logged_in_user = user
    end
  end

  def self.included(base)
    base.send :helper_method, :is_logged_in?, :logged_in_user
  end
end
```

Before we go any further, we have to make sure that the application knows about this module. We do this by adding a line to the app/controllers/application.rb file. Open this file, and add the include statement shown in bold in Listing 3-4.

Listing 3-4. *The Modification to the application.rb File*

```
class ApplicationController < ActionController::Base
  # Pick a unique cookie name to distinguish our session data from others'
  session :session_key => '_railscoders_session_id'
  include LoginSystem
end
```

This module adds a number of methods that allow you to get and set the logged_in_user object, as well as to find out if a user is logged in at all with the is_logged_in? method.

As you can see, setting a session variable is as simple as setting a normal Ruby variable. The session object is reserved by Rails for this purpose. You can store any kind of Ruby object in a session variable, but session variables work best if you just use them for storing simple things like integers. In this case, I am simply storing the ID of the logged-in user.

If a user is logged in, the first method will retrieve their user model and store it in the variable @logged_in_user. If you subsequently make reference to logged_in_user, the details of the user have already been preloaded into the @logged_in_user variable, meaning that the application doesn't have to do another database lookup.

The session variable is set by the logged_in_user= method. When the user object is assigned to logged_in_user the id of the user is placed in the session variable, and the user object is stored in @logged_in_user.

The final method of this module makes the is_logged_in? and logged_in_user methods available as helper method to the views of your application. This is incredibly convenient, as you can directly use the logged_in_user object in the views or show only a section of a page if a user is logged in.

Using these methods, handling the sessions becomes almost transparent. You will see how to put them to use as you build the controllers.

Creating the Controllers

Now you can create the users and account controllers:

```
$ ruby script/generate controller Users index show new create edit update ➥
  destroy enable
$ ruby script/generate controller Account login authenticate logout
```

Since the users controller implements a RESTful resource, you need to tell Rails that it should treat it as one. As with the pages controller, this is done in the config/routes.rb file. Add the users resource mapping line to the routes.rb file as shown in Listing 3-5.

Listing 3-5. *The Update to the Routes File*

```
ActionController::Routing::Routes.draw do |map|
  ...
  map.resources :pages
  map.resources :users

  map.connect ':controller/:action/:id'
end
```

The Users Controller

Edit the app/controllers/users_controller.rb file, and edit the methods as shown in Listing 3-6.

Listing 3-6. *The Users Controller File*

```
class UsersController < ApplicationController
  def index
    @users = User.find(:all)
  end

  def show
    @user = User.find(params[:id])
  end

  def show_by_username
    @user = User.find_by_username(params[:username])
    render :action => 'show'
  end

  def new
    @user = User.new
  end
```

```ruby
  def create
    @user = User.new(params[:user])
    if @user.save
      self.logged_in_user = @user
      flash[:notice] = "Your account has been created."
      redirect_to index_url
    else
      render :action => 'new'
    end
  end

  def edit
    @user = logged_in_user
  end

  def update
    @user = User.find(logged_in_user)
    if @user.update_attributes(params[:user])
      flash[:notice] = "User updated"
      redirect_to :action => 'show', :id => logged_in_user
    else
      render :action => 'edit'
    end
  end

  def destroy
    @user = User.find(params[:id])
    if @user.update_attribute(:enabled, false)
      flash[:notice] = "User disabled"
    else
      flash[:error] = "There was a problem disabling this user."
    end
    redirect_to :action => 'index'
  end

  def enable
    @user = User.find(params[:id])
    if @user.update_attribute(:enabled, true)
      flash[:notice] = "User enabled"
    else
      flash[:error] = "There was a problem enabling this user."
    end
    redirect_to :action => 'index'
  end
end
```

This adds methods that are very similar to those in the page controller, except with a few changes specific to handling users. Since we want to be able to display a user's profile by specifying the username as the reference, we've added a `show_by_username` method. You can link this to a nice-looking URL by adding a suitable mapping toward the end of your `routes.rb` file as follows:

```
...
map.show_user '/user/:username',
              :controller => 'users',
              :action => 'show_by_username'

map.connect ':controller/:action/:id.:format'
map.connect ':controller/:action/:id'
end
```

Looking back in the controller file, you will notice that when a user creates an account, that user is automatically logged in using the new session handler by `self.logged_in_user = @user`. This calls the session-handling method `logged_in_user=` with the newly created user.

Now, if you need to find out who the currently logged in user is, simply use the `logged_in_user` object.

Because this controller follows the Rails REST conventions, the actions `create`, `update`, and `destroy` are protected from accidentally being called from an HTTP `GET` request. They must be called with an HTTP method of `POST`, `PUT`, and `DELETE` respectively. However, the new action `enable` isn't automatically protected in this way, since Rails doesn't know that this method needs protection from being accidentally called.

To declare to Rails that the `enable` method must only be called by an HTTP `PUT` method, you must alter the existing `users` mapping in the `routes.rb` file:

```
map.resources :users, :member => { :enable => :put }
```

This tells Rails that the users controller contains an extra action called `enable` that can only be called by an HTTP `PUT` method. If a user or a search bot tries to `GET` the URL `/users/<id>;enable`, it will not have any effect on the `user` object. It will only be affected if the request is made with `PUT`.

The Account Controller

The account controller provides actions for logging in and logging out. Since you are not creating a REST resource but simply providing actions for the web site, these do not have to be constrained to the REST actions. These actions can be called using the URL format `/<controller>/<action>/<id>`.

Edit the `app/controllers/accounts_controller.rb` file as shown in Listing 3-7.

Listing 3-7. *The Account Controller File*

```
class AccountController < ApplicationController
  def authenticate
    self.logged_in_user = User.authenticate(params[:user][:username],
        params[:user][:password])
```

```
      if is_logged_in?
        redirect_to index_url
      else
        flash[:error] = "I'm sorry; either your username or password was incorrect."
        redirect_to :action => 'login'
      end
    end

    def logout
      if request.post?
        reset_session
        flash[:notice] = "You have been logged out."
      end
      redirect_to index_url
    end
  end
end
```

The login view does not require an action in the controller, since it is simply an HTML form—nothing needs to be done by the controller, because the login.rhtml view will simply be rendered.

When the user submits the login form, it is sent to the authenticate action. The authenticate method then attempts to find the user. The authenticate method in the User model takes the username and password as parameters and will return the found user object or nil if no user matches the values passed. This result is assigned to self.logged_in_user, which, as you saw in the create method in the Users controller, will pass the user to the session-handling code and store the user's ID in the session.

This is checked by testing the is_logged_in? method, redirecting the users to the index page if they are logged in or adding a flash message and redirecting to the login view if not.

FLASH MESSAGES

Flash is a way of passing objects between actions. In this chapter, it is used to pass a text message of a notification or error to the next action and show the result of the previous action.

However, any object that you put into flash will be available to the next action. If you need to retain a flash beyond the next action, you can use flash.keep to keep it alive for another action.

Creating the User Account Views

We now need to create the view that corresponds to the actions we have created for the users and account controllers.

The New User View

We'll start off with the page where a user can sign up. As with the new page form created in the previous chapter, this is a form built using the Rails form_for helper.

Edit the file `app/views/users/new.rhtml`, and enter the view shown in Listing 3-8.

Listing 3-8. *The New User View*

```
<h2>Signup</h2>

<%= error_messages_for :user %>

<% form_for :user, :url => users_path do |f| -%>
  <p>Username:<br /><%= f.text_field :username, :size => 40 %></p>
  <p>Email:<br /><%= f.text_field :email, :size => 60 %></p>
  <p>Password:<br /><%= f.password_field :password, :size => 60 %></p>
  <p>Password Confirmation:<br />
    <%= f.password_field :password_confirmation, :size => 60 %></p>
  <p>Profile:<br /><%= f.text_area :profile, :rows => 6, :cols => 60 %></p>
  <%= submit_tag 'Sign Up' %>
<% end -%>
```

You will notice that this provides both the `password` and the `password_confirmation` parameters. If you think back on the User model, you should remember that neither of these fields actually exists in the database. Both are virtual attributes, meaning that they appear to be regular attributes from the controller's viewpoint, but their values are used either as part of the validation (as in the case of the `password_confirmation`) or to derive the value to be stored.

When the user submits information, the controller tries to create and save a new `user` object. If it fails because the input fails validation, the same view is shown again, but with the validation errors passed through. If the validation succeeds and the new User model is saved, the user is logged in and redirected to the index page. This could obviously be any page on the site—you may wish to create a welcome page for new members.

Before we take a look at this in the browser, we should add some links to the sidebar to make it easy for us to get to the signup and login screens.

Open the sidebar menu partial file, `app/views/layouts/_menu.rhtml`, and update the file as shown in Listing 3-9. This uses the user authentication module to check if the user is logged in or not. If not, login and signup links are shown. If a user is logged in, the username is shown in the sidebar along with a logout link.

Listing 3-9. *The Updated Sidebar Menu Partial File*

```
<ul>
  <li><%= link_to 'Home', index_url %></li>
  <li><%= link_to 'Edit Pages', pages_path %></li>

  <li><hr size="1" width="90%" align="left"/></li>

  <% if is_logged_in? %>
    <li>Logged in as: <i><%= logged_in_user.username %></i></li>
    <li><%= link_to 'Logout', {:controller => 'account', :action => 'logout'},
                        :method => :post %></li>
```

```
<% else %>
  <li><%= link_to 'Signup', :controller => 'users', :action => 'new' %></li>
  <li><%= link_to 'Login', :controller => 'account', :action => 'login' %></li>
<% end %>
</ul>
```

Now we can take a look at the user signup screen and try creating a new user. Make sure that your Rails application server is running, and go to http://localhost:3000/ in your browser.

Clicking the Signup link in the sidebar menu will show the user creation form shown in Figure 3-1.

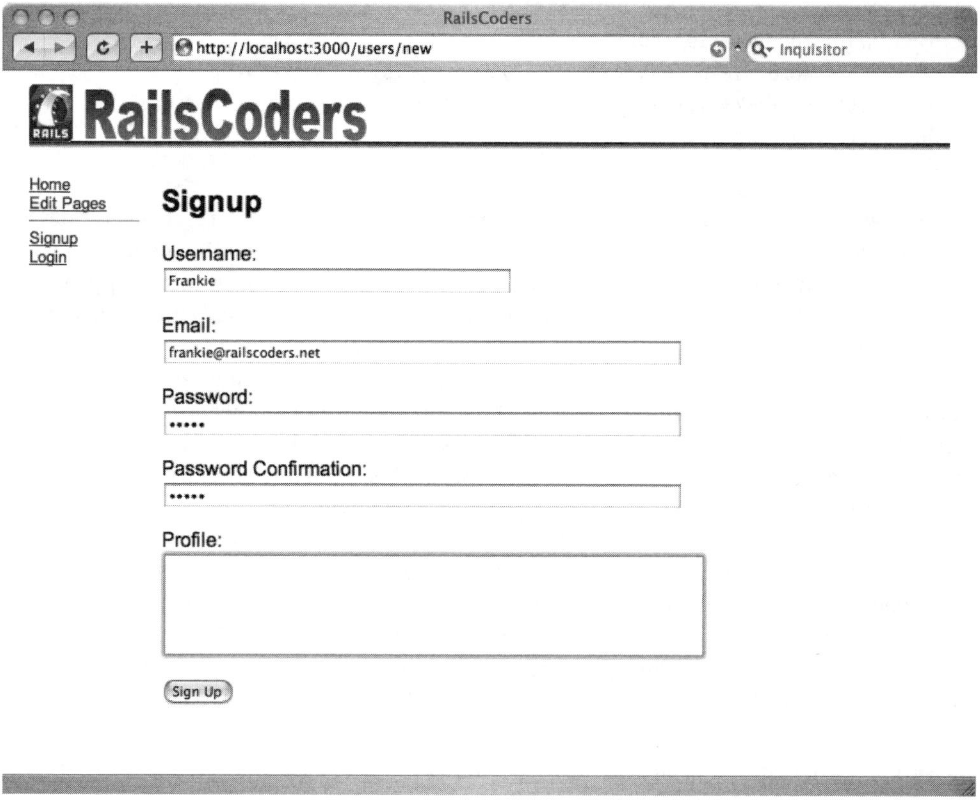

Figure 3-1. *The user signup form*

Try creating a new user and making sure that the flash message is shown, confirming the action you have just taken and that username is shown in the sidebar.

Log out of the site using the logout link in the sidebar—you will be returned to the home page, but the sidebar will change to show that you are not logged in any more, and you have the options of signing up or logging in.

You should also check the validations; for instance, try creating a user with an empty e-mail address or entering an incorrect password confirmation. The errors will be caught by the validation statements in the User model, and you will be sent back to the signup page with the error messages displayed.

Since we have not created the login page yet, we will do that now.

The Login View

Now that your users can create accounts, they need to be able to log in to the site. Open the app/views/account/login.rhtml file, and enter the code in Listing 3-10.

Listing 3-10. *The Login View*

```
<h2>Login</h2>

<% form_for :user, :url => {:action => 'authenticate'} do |f| -%>
  <p>Username:<br /><%= f.text_field :username, :size => 30 %></p>
  <p>Password:<br /><%= f.password_field :password, :size => 30 %></p>
  <%= submit_tag 'Login' %>
<% end %>
```

This simply accepts the user's username and password and then posts the info to the authenticate action.

■**Note** You may wish to change the code in Listing 3-10 to let the site authenticate users based on their e-mail addresses and passwords. Change the login, create views, and adapt the User model to your needs.

We can now try logging into the site using the previously created user. Make sure that the application server is running, and go to the site's homepage, http://localhost:3000, in the browser.

Click the Login link in the sidebar menu. You will now see the login form. Try entering an incorrect username or password to make sure that this is caught by the authentication checker, as shown in Figure 3-2.

Now try entering a correct username and password. You will be logged in and redirected to the home page, but the sidebar menu will show your username and a logout link.

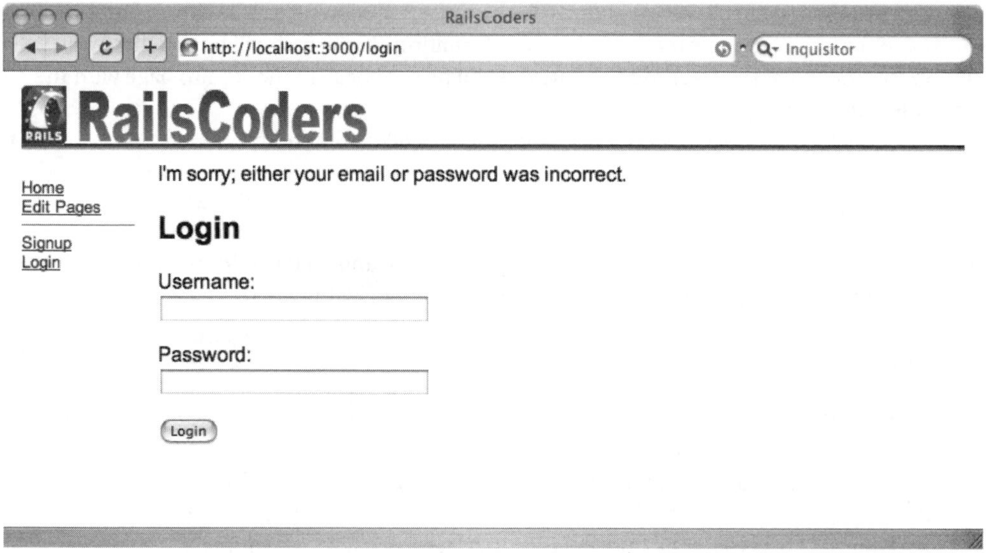

Figure 3-2. *The login screen showing an error message*

The Show User View

Next is the page that will display the profile of a given user. The show method in the users controller allows just that, but we also added the show_by_username method to allow searching based on the username rather than the user ID. The view code for both of these methods is the same. Edit the file app/views/users/show.rhtml, and enter the code in Listing 3-11.

Listing 3-11. *The User Show View File*

```
<h2>User: <%= @user.username %></h2>

<p>Member since <%= @user.created_at.to_s(:long) %></p>
<p><%= @user.profile %></p>
```

Listing 3-11 displays the username, when the user was created, and the user's profile. The created_at time and date are formatted using one of the Rails built-in date formatters. A number of date formats are built in, or you can create your own. The built-in formats include :db (a database-friendly timestamp), :short, and :long.

ADDING YOUR OWN DATE FORMATS

If you would like to display dates and times in a format different from one of the built-in Rails formats, you can easily define your own date display formats. All you have to do is add a data format string to the Time::DATE_FORMATS hash and use the to_s(format) method of the Time class.

You can take a look at the existing formats by opening a Rails console and displaying the DATE_FORMATS hash:

```
>> Time::DATE_FORMATS
=> {:short=>"%d %b %H:%M", :rfc822=>"%a, %d %b %Y %H:%M:%S %z", :long=>"%B %d,
   %Y %H:%M", :db=>"%Y-%m-%d %H:%M:%S"}
```

You can add your own format to these as follows:

```
>> Time::DATE_FORMATS[:time] = "%H:%M:%S"
=> "%H:%M:%S"
```

You can now call the to_s method with the format of :time as follows:

```
>> Time.now.to_s(:time)
=> "18:54:28"
```

To use this format anywhere in your application, add this new format declaration at the end of your config/environment.rb file.

You can also try viewing the profile of any user by going to either the show method specifying the user's ID (for example http://localhost:3000/users/2) or by using the show_by_username method that is mapped to the /user/<username> URL, for instance, http://localhost:3000/user/alan.

The profile view is shown in Figure 3-3.

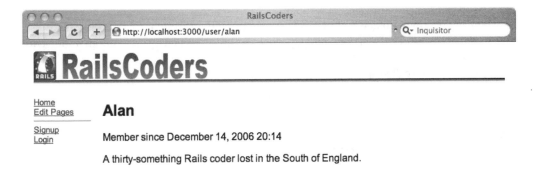

Figure 3-3. *The user show page*

Adding Administration Views

So far, we have concentrated on user-centric views. We need to add a few more views for administering users on the site.

Listing All Users in the Index View

The index action will list all of the users in the system. Later in this chapter, we will make this accessible by only the administrators of the site. It will list all of the usernames and allow an administrator to enable or disable an account.

To display a user information table, the markup of the actual user information lines will be in a partial file, similar to one we used to separate the menu sidebar from the layout—except this time, we will pass a collection of objects to the partial, and it will render the partial for each object in the collection.

Open app/views/users/index.rhtml, and enter the code shown in Listing 3-12.

Listing 3-12. *The Users Index View*

```
<h2>All users</h2>

<table id="users">
  <tr>
    <th>Username</th>
    <th>Email</th>
    <th>Enabled?</th>
    <th>Roles</th>
  </tr>
  <%= render :partial => 'user', :collection => @users %>
</table>
```

The collection of objects called @users is told to render through a partial file called _user.rhtml. As you saw with the sidebar, partial files are identified by prefixing an underscore to the partial name.

So create a file called app/views/users/_user.rhtml, and add the code in Listing 3-13.

Listing 3-13. *The User Partial View*

```
<tr class="<%= cycle('odd', 'even') -%>">
  <td><%= user.username -%></td>
  <td><%= user.email -%></td>
  <td><%= user.enabled ? 'yes' : 'no' -%>
  <% unless user == logged_in_user -%>
    <% if user.enabled -%>
      [<%= link_to('disable', user_url(user.id), :method => :delete) %>]
    <% else -%>
      [<%= link_to('enable', enable_user_url(user.id), :method => :put) %>]
    <% end -%>
  <% end -%>
  </td>
</tr>
```

This partial will be used to render the entire collection of user objects in the collection @users. It will display a disable or enable link, depending on the current state of that user's enabled flag.

The view also prevents users from disabling their own accounts by checking that the user rendered is not the currently logged in user. When this page is only accessible by the administrator, this will ensure that the administrator cannot accidentally disable the administrator account.

Before we take a look at the user index view, we should make it accessible from the sidebar menu and add some styling to the CSS file to make the table easier to read.

Open the sidebar menu file, app/views/layouts/_menu.rhtml, and add a link to the index action of the users controller for logged in users, along with a link to edit your own profile, as shown in Listing 3-14.

Listing 3-14. *Modification to the Sidebar Menu*

```
...
<% if is_logged_in? %>
    <li>Logged in as: <i><%= logged_in_user.username %></i></li>
    <li><%= link_to 'My Profile',
                    edit_user_path(logged_in_user) %></li>
    <li><%= link_to 'Administer Users', users_path %></li>
    <li><%= link_to 'Logout', {:controller => 'account', :action => 'logout'},
                              :method => :post %></li>
<% else %>
    <li><%= link_to 'Signup', :controller => 'users', :action => 'new' %></li>
    <li><%= link_to 'Login', :controller => 'account', :action => 'login' %></li>
<% end %>
</ul>
```

Now open the application's CSS file, public/stylesheets/main.css, and add the following CSS to the end of the file:

```
/* User table styling */
table#users { width: 100%;}
table#users th { font-size: 95%; }
table#users td { font-size: 90%; }
```

Go to the site in your browser, and log in via the sidebar Login link. Click the Administer Users link in the sidebar menu to display the list of users registered on the system, as shown in Figure 3-4. You can try disabling and re-enabling some users.

Before you can try editing your profile, we need to add the edit user view.

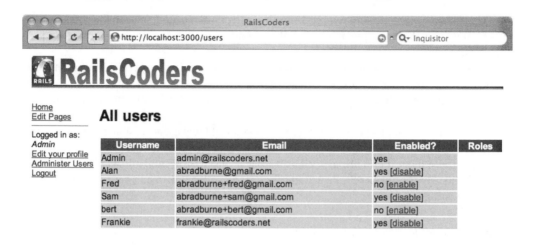

Figure 3-4. *The users index view allowing users to be enabled and disabled*

Editing a User with edit.rhtml

To allow users to change their details, an edit form is needed. This will be somewhat similar to the new user form, except that users will not be allowed to change their usernames. The users will be allowed to change their passwords if they enter new passwords and password confirmations. If they leave both of these fields blank, the password validation will not be used because of the condition that we set in the User model.

Edit the app/views/users/edit.rhtml file as shown in Listing 3-15.

Listing 3-15. *The User Edit View File*

```
<h2>Edit your account</h2>

<p><%= link_to 'Show my profile', user_path(@user) %></p>

<%= error_messages_for :user %>

<% form_for :user,
            :url => user_url(@user),
            :html => { :method => :put } do |f| -%>
  <p>Email:<br /><%= f.text_field :email, :size => 60 %></p>
  <p>Password:<br /><%= f.password_field :password, :size => 60 %></p>
  <p>Password Confirmation:<br />
    <%= f.password_field :password_confirmation, :size => 60 %></p>
  <p>Profile:<br /><%= f.text_area :profile, :rows => 6, :cols => 60 %></p>
  <%= submit_tag 'Save' %>
<% end -%>
```

The form is submitted with the HTTP PUT method. Since this is a Rails resource, this request will automatically be routed to the update method.

Now try logging into the site and editing your profile to change both your profile and your password. If you don't enter anything into the password or password confirmation boxes, your password will not be changed.

If you want to change your password, you have to enter your new choice of password into both the password and password confirmation boxes.

Testing

Of course, manually clicking around to test that the application is doing what you expect is useful, but it will not catch more subtle problems. Writing tests is vital to ensuring that your code performs exactly as expected.

Unit Testing

As with the page tests that were written in the previous chapter, the test cases should attempt both positive and negative tests.

First of all, create a user fixture in test/fixtures/users.yml; in this case, create a regular valid user:

```
valid_user:
  id: 1
  username: joe
  email: joe@example.com
  hashed_password: 5994471abb01112afcc18159f6cc74b4f511b99806da59b3caf5a9c173cacfc5
    # clear password = 12345
  profile: Just a regular Joe
  created_at: <%= 1.days.ago.to_s(:db) %>
```

You can now use this user to test for validation, like trying to create another user with a duplicate username or e-mail address. You will notice that in the fixture, we are using a Rails view helper to enter the created_at field.

Now create a test to ensure that creating a new user works OK. Edit test/unit/user_test.rb, and add a test as shown in Listing 3-16.

Listing 3-16. *The User Unit Test File*

```
require File.dirname(__FILE__) + '/../test_helper'

class UserTest < Test::Unit::TestCase
  fixtures :users

  def test_create_valid_user
    user = User.new(:username => 'fred', :email => 'fred@example.com',
        :password => 'abc123', :password_confirmation => 'abc123',
        :profile => 'A regular guy')
    assert user.save
  end
end
```

Before we run this test, we have to bring the test database schema up to date. Enter the rake command:

```
$ rake db:test:prepare
```

Now try running this test from the command prompt with the following command:

```
$ ruby test/unit/user_test.rb
```

```
Loaded suite test/unit/user_test
Started
.
Finished in 0.188329 seconds.

1 tests, 1 assertions, 0 failures, 0 errors
```

You can also use the rake helper tasks to either run all of your unit tests or just the tests that you have recently updated; or if you are using Subversion as a version repository, you can test any changes you have made since you last checked in your code. To see all of the available rake test helpers, type rake -T.

Now try adding a test to attempt creating a user with the same username as the user fixture:

```
def test_invalid_duplicate_username
  user = User.new(:username => 'joe', :email => 'fred@example.com',
      :password => 'abc123', :password_confirmation => 'abc123',
      :profile => 'A regular guy')
  assert !user.save
end
```

When you try running this test, it should fail, since the validations in your model prevent duplicate users. We could expand these unit tests to ensure that the other validations are working as expected, such as attempting to create a user with a duplicate e-mail address, an empty e-mail field, incorrect password confirmation, and so on.

Functional Testing

So far, we have added only unit tests. These tests prove that the model is working as expected, but they don't test the actual usage of the web site. To test that the site works as you expect, you need to add functional tests. Functional tests allow you to test the actions of a particular controller and ensure that it responds correctly. Functional tests perform actions as if they came from a user's interaction with a browser.

Testing users_controller

To test the login system's functionality, you need to add tests to the test/functional/ users_controller_test.rb file.

Once you have opened this file, you will notice that a setup method is defined; it is run before a test is performed and creates an instance of the controller under test, along with request and response instances. The request and response objects allow Ruby to perform the tests without actually having to start up a web server or a browser: the request instance acts like a browser, and the response instance acts as the server.

Add a simple test to check that the signup page is returned correctly, as shown in Listing 3-17.

Listing 3-17. *The Users Controller Functional Test File*

```
require File.dirname(__FILE__) + '/../test_helper'
require 'users_controller'

# Re-raise errors caught by the controller.
class UsersController; def rescue_action(e) raise e end; end

class UsersControllerTest < Test::Unit::TestCase
  def setup
    @controller = UsersController.new
    @request    = ActionController::TestRequest.new
    @response   = ActionController::TestResponse.new
  end

  def test_signup_page
    get :new
    assert_response :success
  end
end
```

This test simulates an HTTP GET of the new action and checks that a page is successfully returned.

You can now run the users_controller functional tests with the following command:

```
$ ruby test/functional/users_controller_test.rb
```

This will produce a normal test output detailing the status of the test result.

```
Loaded suite test/functional/users_controller_test
Started
.
Finished in 0.24553 seconds.

1 tests, 1 assertions, 0 failures, 0 errors
```

Now you need to add some more functional tests to ensure that the act of creating a user works as expected. Add the following test:

```
def test_valid_signup_and_redirect
  post :create, :user => {:username => 'fred',
                          :email => 'fred@example.com',
                          :password => 'abc123',
                          :password_confirmation => 'abc123',
                          :profile => 'A regular guy'}
  assert_response :redirect
end
```

This test posts a new user signup to the create action and checks to make sure that the response given is an HTTP redirect. In this case, it will redirect the user to the index page. If the signup had failed with a validation error, the response would have been a success—it would return a page rather than redirecting the user to the page containing the signup page again and showing the validation error messages. You can also check the contents of the instance variable created in the action. In this case, you can test the errors related to this object and ensure that the errors are related to the test being performed.

Now, add the following test:

```
def test_invalid_signup_dupe_username
  post :create, :user => {:username => 'joe',
                          :email => 'fred@example.com',
                          :password => 'abc123',
                          :password_confirmation => 'abc123',
                          :profile => 'A regular guy'}
  assert assigns(:user).errors.on(:username)
  assert_response :success
  assert_template 'users/new'
end
```

This test will attempt to create another user with a duplicate username as the user fixture. The first assertion checks the instance variable user to make sure that there is an error raised on the username attribute.

The assert_response checks that the action returns a page, and the assert_template checks to make sure that the correct view template is being rendered; in this case, the new user page is rendered again.

Run the tests again. This time, try running all of the tests you have written so far with the following command:

```
$ rake test
```

All of the tests should pass as expected. You may now wish to add some more tests to check that other validation errors are caught correctly.

Testing account_controller

When you are happy that the signup procedure is tested thoroughly, you need to test the account controller to make sure that the login procedures work as expected.

Edit the test/functional/account_controller_test.rb file, and add the positive test shown in Listing 3-18.

Listing 3-18. *The Account Controller Functional Test File*

```ruby
require File.dirname(__FILE__) + '/../test_helper'
require 'account_controller'

# Re-raise errors caught by the controller.
class AccountController; def rescue_action(e) raise e end; end

class AccountControllerTest < Test::Unit::TestCase
  fixtures :users

  def setup
    @controller = AccountController.new
    @request    = ActionController::TestRequest.new
    @response   = ActionController::TestResponse.new
  end

  def test_valid_login_and_redirect
    post :authenticate, :user => {:username => 'joe', :password => '12345'}
    assert session[:user]
    assert_response :redirect
  end
end
```

This test will attempt to log in with the user specified in the fixture using the correct username and password. The test then checks to make sure that a session variable is set and that an HTTP redirect is sent to the user. In this case, the user is redirected to the index page.

Now you should try the following negative test to make sure that attempting to log in with an incorrect username and password combination will fail:

```ruby
def test_invalid_login
  post :authenticate, :user => {:username => 'joe', :password => 'abc'}
  assert !session[:user]
  assert_response :redirect
  assert_redirected_to :action => 'login'
  assert flash.has_key?(:error)
end
```

When this test is executed, the code attempts a login that we know will fail. The test then checks to make sure that there is no session variable called user set. The response is checked to make sure that users are redirected and that they are redirected to the correct page.

A test also makes sure that the flash error message is set. If any of these assertions fail, the test will fail.

You should also check that when a user logs out, their session is destroyed correctly. A test_logout method could be written like this:

```
def test_logout
  post :authenticate, :user => {:username => 'joe', :password => '12345'}
  assert session[:user]
  post :logout
  assert !session[:user]
  assert_response :redirect
end
```

When the test is executed, this code logs a user in as before and checks to make sure that the session variable is set. Next, the test attempts to log out by making a POST to the logout action. If this is successful, the user's session will be cleared, and the user will be redirected to the index page. The test checks for this.

Again, you should add as many tests as you can to ensure that all aspects of the controllers are tested. The more tests that you have, the more confident you can be of your application being reliable.

Adding Roles

At the moment, all actions are available to all users. Obviously, this is unsuitable for a production site. We need to add some permissions to the actions so that only administrators are able to create and edit pages and view and disable user accounts.

This could be achieved in a number of ways, but the most flexible solution is to add the concept of roles. By adding user roles such as administrator or moderator, you can allow particular users access to different controllers or actions on the site. For example, you might want to allow trusted users to have moderation rights for forums or an editor to be able to update pages.

Creating the Role Model and Join Table

The first step is to create a Role model:

```
$ ruby script/generate model Role
```

Next, edit the migration script, db/migrate/03_create_roles.rb, to create the required database field for the roles table, as shown in Listing 3-19.

Listing 3-19. *The Roles Table Migration File*

```
class CreateRoles < ActiveRecord::Migration
  def self.up
    create_table :roles do |t|
      t.column :name, :string
    end
    Role.create(:name => 'Administrator')
  end
```

```
  def self.down
    drop_table :roles
  end
end
```

This creates a new database table called `roles` and an administrator role.

Now the application needs a way to associate the roles with users. There are two ways of doing this in Rails: `has_and_belongs_to_many` associations (commonly referred to as HABTM), or `has_many :through` associations. HABTM suits our needs best here.

We need to specify that each user can have many different roles and that roles can belong to many different users, so, in the `app/models/user.rb` file, add the `has_and_belongs_to_many` line as follows:

```
require 'digest/sha2'
class User < ActiveRecord::Base
  attr_protected :hashed_password, :enabled
  attr_accessor :password
  ...
  has_and_belongs_to_many :roles

  def before_save
  ...
```

In the `app/models/role.rb` file, add the reciprocal HABTM statement:

```
class Role < ActiveRecord::Base
  has_and_belongs_to_many :users
end
```

Next, we need to create the `roles_users` join table as discussed in the specification. Create a new database migration using the following line:

```
$ ruby script/generate migration CreateRolesUsersJoin
```

Edit the migration file `db/migrate/04_create_roles_users_join.rb`, and enter the code shown in Listing 3-20.

Listing 3-20. *The roles_users Table Migration File*

```
class CreateRolesUsersJoin < ActiveRecord::Migration
  def self.up
    create_table :roles_users, :id => false do |t|
      t.column :role_id, :integer, :null => false
      t.column :user_id, :integer, :null => false
    end
```

```
    admin_user = User.create(:username => 'Admin',
                             :email => 'admin@railscoders.net',
                             :profile => 'Site Administrator',
                             :password => 'admin', :password_confirmation => 'admin')
    admin_role = Role.find_by_name('Administrator')
    admin_user.roles << admin_role
  end

  def self.down
    drop_table :roles_users
    User.find_by_username('Admin').destroy
  end
end
```

This creates a simple database join table called `roles_users`. Because you have already specified that the two models are related with the HABTM statements, Rails will automatically use a table named after the two models.

The migration also creates a new user called Admin. The administrator role that was created by the previous migration is then assigned to the new Admin user.

We have also added a statement to the `self.down` method of the migration file. The down method is executed whenever the database is migrated to an earlier version of the schema. This method has to reverse any actions that have been taken in the up method. Since we have created a user called "Admin" as part of the up method, we need to make sure that we destroy this user if the down method is executed.

Now, run the migrations using `rake db:migrate`, and check your database to ensure that the new user is created and that a new record is created in the `roles_users` table.

Checking a User's Roles

Now that the application has more than one type of user, the application needs a way to check the roles of a user, and we need a way to specify which actions are to be restricted to administrators.

Add the following simple method to the `User` class in the `app/models/user.rb` model file:

```
def has_role?(rolename)
  self.roles.find_by_name(rolename) ? true : false
end
```

This method gives us an easy way of checking if a user object instance has a particular role or not. Check if a user has been given the administrator role with `user.has_role?('Administrator')`.

Now we need to use this to develop a way to add checks for specific actions. The Rails `before_filter` statement easily allows you to run a method either before all actions in a controller or specific actions. First, add the following methods to the `LoginSystem` module defined in the `lib/login_system.rb` file:

```ruby
def check_role(role)
  unless is_logged_in? && @logged_in_user.has_role?(role)
    flash[:error] = "You do not have the permission to do that."
    redirect_to :controller => 'account', :action => 'login'
  end
end


def check_administrator_role
  check_role('Administrator')
end
```

Now edit the app/controllers/users_controller.rb file by adding the before_filter at the top of the class:

```ruby
class UsersController < ApplicationController
  before_filter :check_administrator_role,
                :only => [:index, :destroy, :enable]
  ...
```

If one of the specified actions is requested, the check_administrator_role method will be called. If this returns false, a flash message is set; the user is redirected to the login page; and execution of the rest of the code is halted.

We should add this check to the pages controller from the previous chapter, so that users without the administration role cannot create and edit pages in the content management system. Open app/controllers/pages_controller.rb, and add the following check:

```ruby
class PagesController < ApplicationController
  before_filter :check_administrator_role, :except => :show
  ...
```

Notice that this time we are specifying the actions to leave unprotected using :except. If you don't specify any actions, all actions in this controller will be protected.

It would also be useful to be able to protect certain actions from users who are not logged in and redirect them to the login page with a message asking them to log in.

To allow us to check for this, add the following method to the lib/login_system.rb file:

```ruby
def login_required
  unless is_logged_in?
    flash[:error] = "You must be logged in to do that."
    redirect_to :controller => 'account', :action => 'login'
  end
end
```

We can now use this by adding the appropriate before_filter to app/controllers/users_controller.rb as follows:

```
class UsersController < ApplicationController
  before_filter :check_administrator_role,
                :only => [:index, :destroy, :enable_toggle]
  before_filter :login_required, :only => [:edit, :update]

  def index
    ...
```

Now try going to a protected page such as `http://localhost:3000/users/1;edit` while logged out. You will be redirected to the login page and shown a message asking you to log in.

Administering Roles

Now that users can have different roles, the application needs a way of administering these roles and allowing an administrator to assign or revoke roles from users.

As we defined in the specification, we will build a controller called `roles_controller` that is a nested resource—the roles controller can only be accessed with a specified user ID.

To configure this nested resource mapping, edit your `config/routes.rb` file as follows:

```
map.resources :users, :member => { :enable => :put } do |users|
  users.resources :roles
end
```

You can now access the `roles` resource using the URL /users/<user_id>/roles. We now need to create a new controller called app/controllers/roles_controller.rb. Create this file, and enter the code in Listing 3-21 to this file.

Listing 3-21. *The Roles Controller File*

```
class RolesController < ApplicationController
  before_filter :check_administrator_role

  def index
    @user = User.find(params[:user_id])
    @all_roles = Role.find(:all)
  end

  def update
    @user = User.find(params[:user_id])
    @role = Role.find(params[:id])
    unless @user.has_role?(@role.name)
      @user.roles << @role
    end
    redirect_to :action => 'index'
  end
```

```
  def destroy
    @user = User.find(params[:user_id])
    @role = Role.find(params[:id])
    if @user.has_role?(@role.name)
      @user.roles.delete(@role)
    end
    redirect_to :action => 'index'
  end
end
```

When accessed, because of the nested route mapping, the URL parameters will contain a user_id parameter. This parameter can now be used to create or destroy roles for this user. The index view will list of the assigned and available roles. You first need to create the views directory for this controller: app/views/roles. Then create the file app/views/roles/index.rhtml, and edit it as shown in Listing 3-22.

Listing 3-22. *The Roles Index View*

```
<h1>Roles for <%= @user.username %></h1>

<h2>Roles assigned:</h2>
<ul><%= render :partial => 'role', :collection => @user.roles %></ul>

<h2>Roles available:</h2>
<ul><%= render :partial => 'role', :collection => (@all_roles - @user.roles) %></ul>
```

You will see that this creates two lists, one showing the roles that this user has been assigned and another showing the possible roles that could be assigned to this user. You now need to create the partial view for the role, app/views/roles/_role.rhtml:

```
<li>
  <%= role.name %>
  [<% if @user.has_role?(role.name) %>
    <%= link_to 'remove role',
                role_url(:id => role.id, :user_id => @user.id),
                :method => :delete %>
  <% else %>
    <%= link_to 'assign role',
                role_url(:id => role.id, :user_id => @user.id),
                :method => :put %>
  <% end %>]
</li>
```

This uses the has_role? method of the User model to check if the user already has the role, in which case it shows a remove role link; if not, it shows an add role link.

Because the controller is a REST resource, you do not have to link to the actual methods; instead, you use the HTTP DELETE or PUT method to route to the correct request. The DELETE method will remove the role from the specified use; the PUT method will call the update action and add the role to the user.

When the roles are changed for the user, that user is redirected to the list of all roles, which shows the newly updated info.

Since there is currently only one role in the system, there will only be the one role available to assign or revoke. It is also now possible to remove the administrator role from the Admin user. You could add a test to make sure that it is not possible to remove the administration rights of all of the administrators by checking the number of users using `Role.find_by_name('Administrator').users.count`. If this is equal to 1, you could prevent the delete action from continuing.

To make life easier for the administrator, you should add a link to the roles manager in the user partial file for the index page, `app/views/users/_user.rhtml`, by adding an extra column to the table:

```
<tr class="<%= cycle('odd', 'even') %>">
  <td><%= user.username %></td>
  ...
  <% end %>
  </td>
  <td>[<%= link_to 'edit permissions', roles_url(user) %>]</td>
</tr>
```

We also need to modify the sidebar menu to move the Administer Users link so that it is only shown for the administrator user.

Open the sidebar partial file, `app/views/layouts/_menu.rhtml`, create a new section that is only shown for the Admin user, and move the Edit Pages and Administer Users links to this section, as shown in Listing 3-23.

Listing 3-23. *The Updated Sidebar Menu Partial File*

```
<ul>
  <li><%= link_to 'Home', index_url %></li>
  <li><hr size="1" width="90%" align="left"/></li>

  <% if is_logged_in? %>
    <li>Logged in as: <i><%= logged_in_user.username %></i></li>
    <li><%= link_to 'My Profile', edit_user_path(logged_in_user) %></li>
    <li><%= link_to 'Logout', {:controller => 'account', :action => 'logout'},
                            :method => :post %></li>
  <% else %>
    <li><%= link_to 'Signup', :controller => 'users', :action => 'new' %></li>
    <li><%= link_to 'Login', :controller => 'account', :action => 'login' %></li>
  <% end %>

  <% if logged_in_user and logged_in_user.has_role?('administrator') %>
    <li><hr size="1" width="90%" align="left"/></li>
    <li><b>Admin Options</b></li>
    <li><%= link_to 'Administer Users', users_path %></li>
    <li><%= link_to 'Edit Pages', pages_path %></li>
  <% end %>
</ul>
```

Try using this in your browser. Open your browser to the application's home page, and log in as the Admin user. The sidebar will now show two administrator only options, Administer Users and Edit Pages. Click on the Administer Users link, and click the Edit Permissions link of a user other than the Admin user.

As shown in Figure 3-5, this will show the only currently available role, Administrator, as being available but not assigned to this user. You can click the Assign Role link to make this user an administrator of the site.

We will be adding more roles to the site in Chapters 4 and 5.

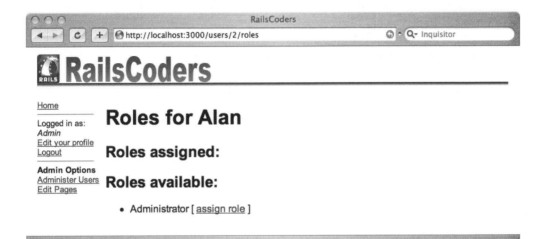

Figure 3-5. *Assigning Roles to a User*

Testing the Roles Functionality

As usual, you should spend some time planning the test cases to make sure that the roles functionality works as planned.

Before we write the tests, make sure that the test database, `railscoders_test`, is updated with the latest schema. Do this with the following command:

```
$ rake db:test:prepare
```

Previously, we used functional tests to test the individual actions in the controllers. However, now we want to test actions across multiple controllers. To do this, Rails has another type of testing baked right in called integration testing. This allows you to build stories that describe a series of actions that might be performed by a typical user.

Integration tests are created in the `test/integration` directory. Create a new integration test file called `test/integration/login_stories_test.rb`, and enter the code in Listing 3-24.

Listing 3-24. *The Login Stories Integration Test File*

```ruby
require "#{File.dirname(__FILE__)}/../test_helper"

class LoginStoriesTest < ActionController::IntegrationTest
  fixtures :users, :pages

  def test_valid_login
    get edit_user_url(1)
    assert_response :redirect
    follow_redirect!
    assert_response :success
    assert_template 'account/login'

    go_to_login

    login :user => {:username => 'joe', :password => '12345'}

    get edit_user_url(1)
    assert_response :success
    assert_template 'users/edit'
  end

  private

    def go_to_login
      get 'account/login'
      assert_response :success
      assert_template 'account/login'
    end

    def login(options)
      post 'account/authenticate', options
      assert_response :redirect
    end
end
```

Here, we have defined a simple DSL for logging into the system. The go_to_login and login methods can be reused throughout this integration test.

In this simple integration test, an attempt is made to get the edit user page, a page that cannot be viewed by a logged-out user. A check is made to ensure that the user is redirected to the login page. Then the user is logged into the site, and another attempt is made to get the edit user page. Since a user is now logged in, the page is successfully returned.

You can build any number of integration tests to test typical user actions through your site. Integration tests specifically test the flow of control throughout the site, ensuring that your controllers interact correctly.

You should try adding some more integration tests for other actions. You could check that only the Admin user has access to the index, disable, and enable user account actions. You should also test assigning and revoking the administrator role to another user.

Extending the User Management System

This user management system provides the basic features required, but you may wish to develop the system further.

At the moment, there is no facility to deal with users that have forgotten their passwords. You could add a feature to allow users to reset their passwords by sending a reset-password link for their accounts to their registered e-mail addresses.

You may also wish to consider integrating OpenID into the user accounts system, allowing users to log in with their existing OpenID identity. OpenID is an open, decentralized system allowing people to sign on to multiple web sites using the same identity. For more information, go to `http://openid.net`. If you are interested in it, there is a Rails plug-in that allows you to easily integrate with OpenID servers. See `http://identity.eastmedia.com/identity/show/ Consumer+Plugin` for more details.

Summary

In this chapter, we have added a user management system and a role management system. The user accounts system allows new users to the site to quickly sign up for accounts, while providing validation checks on the users' names and e-mail addresses and ensuring that the users enter known passwords by forcing them to confirm their passwords.

Existing users of the site can now log in and edit their accounts. This allows them to modify their profile messages and change their passwords. Again, the password change forces the users to confirm their passwords before saving.

We also developed a role management system that allows you to partition off certain aspects of the site to users with specific privileges. We created the first role on the site, called administrator. This superuser has the power to disable and re-enable user accounts and to assign or revoke roles for users. As we add other roles to the system, such as moderator privileges, role management will become more important.

In the next chapter, you will add another role to the system as well as content creators and editors to contribute and maintain news stories.

CHAPTER 4

■■■

Building a News Blog with RSS Feeds and an API

In Chapter 2, we set up a system to allow an administrator to edit single pages. While this is helpful and allows you to set up the basic pages of a site, it would be much more interesting to have up-to-date news items showing on the front page, along with an archive of the news articles. Of course, it is up to you to actually add the news items, but doing so will help keep the site fresh.

In this chapter, we will examine how we can build a rolling news list to be shown as the site's front page. This will be extended to provide RSS and Atom feeds of the news, along with providing an API to the news feature. The RSS and Atom feeds will allow users to subscribe to the news feed with an RSS newsreader and be automatically notified when a new article is posted.

Specifying the Feature Requirements

As always, the first step is understanding the feature, specifically what you require the feature to do, what the interfaces to the feature will be, and how the design should be implemented.

The basic functionality of the News module will be to allow administrator users or editors to create news stories to be shown on the site. They can then be checked and edited by other Admin users or editors before going live on the site.

I also want to allow the editors to be able to add markup without having to write HTML in the articles. This could be done using a WYSIWYG editor, but I want to use a textual markup system called Textile.

A category can be set for each article. These categories can be created and maintained through a web interface. This will be useful to allow you to separate articles about new features, events, downtime or maintenance issues, or just general news about what's going on at your site.

A new role will be created to allow creation and editing of articles. This will allow the site administrator to give permission to certain users to create and edit articles without giving them access to editing other parts of the site.

Textile Markup

Textile is a lightweight markup language originally developed by Dean Allen. It is billed as a "humane web text generator," meaning that rather than having to mark up your documents in HTML tags, with Textile you can use simple text shorthand to change and add styles, create lists and tables, insert links, and automatically convert special characters to HTML-safe entities.

For example, to add the HTML class `<strong>` to a word or phrase, simply surround it with asterisks *like so*. To underline a word, use the underscore character. For a full list of the syntax along with examples, see `http://hobix.com/textile/`.

The Ruby port of Textile is called RedCloth and is easily installed as a Ruby gem.

To display the rendered XHTML on a page instead of the Textile version, you simply use the helper method called `textilize` in your views.

A similar markup system called Markdown is also implemented by the RedCloth gem. You can find out more about Markdown at `http://daringfireball.net/projects/markdown/`.

The Article Model

The individual news articles will use a model called Article. The necessary fields to implement its functionality are shown in Table 4-1.

Table 4-1. *The Database Fields Required for the Articles Model*

Field Name	Field Type	Description
id	integer	The primary key.
user_id	integer	The id of the user who created the article. This will link the article to the User model.
title	string	The title of the article.
synopsis	text	A short synopsis of the article that will be shown in a list of articles. This should not be too long but will probably be longer than 255 characters, so a text field type with maximum length of 1,000 characters should be used.
body	text	The text of the article itself. Articles may be very long, so if a maximum article length is defined, it should be high. I will use a maximum length of 20,000 characters.
published	boolean	Articles can be saved and edited before being published on the site, so this states whether or not the article is published. This will default to false.
created_at	datetime	The date and time the article was created.
updated_at	datetime	The date and time that the article was last updated.
published_at	datetime	The date and time that the article was published. Since it is possible to create an article as a draft and then publish it later, the creation date might not be the same time as the article's publication date. Therefore, this field will be updated whenever the article is saved and the published field is set to true.
category_id	integer	This specifies a category for this article. This will link to the Category model, which is described in the next section.

Since we want to record which user created the article by storing the user's id, the User model needs to be updated to specify that each user can have many articles.

Defining the Category Model

Each article can belong to only one category. To do this, there needs to be a model for the categories.

The Category model consists of the fields specified in Table 4-2.

Table 4-2. *The Database Fields Required for the Category Model*

Field Name	Field Type	Description
id	integer	The primary key
name	string	The name of the category, which should have a limit of 80 characters

In this case, each story can belong to only one category, so a one-to-many relationship needs to be defined—each category can have many articles. In order to store this relationship, you need to ensure that a category_id field is part of the Article database table and that a belongs_to relationship is set in the Article model. Figure 4-1 shows the relationships among the article, category, and user models.

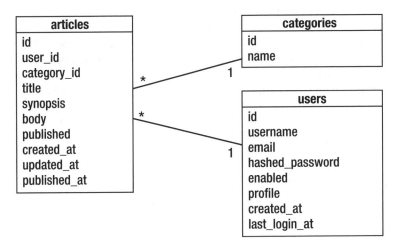

Figure 4-1. *Entity relationship diagram for the Article and Category models*

The Editor Role

Since the task of writing and editing news articles may be done by a user who does not need to have full administrator privileges, we should create a new role called "editor." A user will need to have this permission in order to create new or edit existing articles on the site.

This will involve creating a new permission in the database and adding methods to check that the currently logged-in user has the editor role as one of their permissions.

The Articles Controller

This controller will provide the normal REST create, read, update, and delete (CRUD) actions. The new, create, edit, update, and destroy actions are needed for the user who has the editor permission.

Since articles can belong to a category, the code should be designed to allow browsing of articles that are in a specific category. Since the articles are effectively children of a category, they should be accessible by URLs such as /categories/2/articles, which returns all of the articles with category ID 2.

We should also add a simple index view for the editors that shows a full list of all articles, published and draft. It should also show links for an editor to quickly add a new article or edit an existing one.

The Categories Controller

The categories controller will provide the usual CRUD actions for the Category model, allowing a user with the relevant permissions to add or edit categories. If an editor user tries to delete a category that has articles, the application should delete the category and reset the category_id of any related articles to null rather than deleting them. You might wish to change this behavior so that the delete fails and the user is informed that the category cannot be deleted until all of the articles in that category are changed to a different category.

If a user invokes the index action of the categories controller, a list of all categories together with the number of articles in each category is shown. Clicking a category will take the user to the list of articles within that category. Therefore, the show action of the categories controller simply redirects to the index action of the articles controller with the category's id as a parameter.

In addition to the regular CRUD actions, we need to create a new action that allows an editor user to view the categories together with links to create, edit, and delete categories. To do this, we will define an extra collection method in the resource mapping of the category resource.

Installing the RedCloth Gem

Before we can use the Textile markup system from within Rails, we need to install the RedCloth gem.

■**Note** If you are using Locomotive with OS X, this gem is already installed, so you can skip this section. Don't worry though; attempting to reinstall it will not cause any problems.

To install RedCloth, open a command window, and enter the following command:

```
$ gem install redcloth
```

To check that the gem is installed, you can list the details of an installed gem on your system using the following command:

```
$ gem list redcloth
```

```
*** LOCAL GEMS ***

RedCloth (3.0.3)
    RedCloth is a module for using Textile and Markdown in Ruby. Textile
    and Markdown are text formats.  A very simple text format. Another
    stab at making readable text that can be converted to HTML.
```

You can list all gems installed on your machine using the following command:

```
$ gem list
```

Creating the Article and Category Models

Now that we know the requirements and what needs to be developed, we can start developing the code. Both the Article and Category models are very straightforward.

Writing the Database Migrations

First of all, create the Article model using the script/generate tool:

```
$ ruby script/generate model Article
```

```
    exists  app/models/
    exists  test/unit/
    exists  test/fixtures/
    create  app/models/article.rb
    create  test/unit/article_test.rb
    create  test/fixtures/articles.yml
    exists  db/migrate
    create  db/migrate/005_create_articles.rb
```

Within the migration script db/migrate/005_create_articles.rb, edit the self.up method as follows:

```
def self.up
  create_table :articles do |t|
    t.column :user_id, :integer
    t.column :title, :string
    t.column :synopsis, :text, :limit => 1000
    t.column :body, :text, :limit => 20000
    t.column :published, :boolean, :default => false
    t.column :created_at, :datetime
    t.column :updated_at, :datetime
    t.column :published_at, :datetime
    t.column :category_id, :integer
  end
end
```

There should not be any surprises here. Now, you should create the Category model:

```
$ ruby script/generate model Category
```

```
      exists  app/models/
      exists  test/unit/
      exists  test/fixtures/
      create  app/models/category.rb
      create  test/unit/category_test.rb
      create  test/fixtures/categories.yml
      exists  db/migrate
      create  db/migrate/006_create_categories.rb
```

Edit the `self.up` and `self.down` methods of the migration script, db/migrate/006_create_categories.rb, to add the necessary fields and a default category for new articles:

```
def self.up
  create_table :categories do |t|
    t.column :name, :string
  end
  news_category = Category.create(:name => 'Site News')
  change_column :articles, :category_id, :integer, :default => news_category
end

def self.down
  change_column :articles, :category_id, :integer, :default => 0
  drop_table :categories
end
```

The default category is set by changing the table created in the `create_articles` migration using the `change_column` transformation. If the database is rolled back and the `down` method is executed, this column is reset so that it does not reference a nonexistent category.

Defining the Relationships Among Models

Now, you need to define the relationships among the users, articles, and categories. As specified earlier, each article belongs to a user (the user who created it), and consequently, each user can have many articles. Edit the app/models/user.rb file by adding the following relationship inside the User class:

```
has_many :articles
```

In the app/models/article.rb file, add the reciprocal relationships inside the Article class:

```
belongs_to :user
```

Now you can simply refer to the articles belonging to a user with `user.articles` and, conversely, refer to the author of an article using `article.user`.

You need to do the same with the article-category relationship. Still editing the app/models/
article.rb file, add the following relationship statement:

```
belongs_to :category
```

Finally, add the following relationship to the app/models/category.rb file:

```
has_many :articles
```

Defining the Validations

Now is a good time to add the basic validations to your models. Go back to the app/models/
article.rb file, and add the following validations to match the specification described earlier
in this chapter:

```
validates_presence_of :title
validates_presence_of :synopsis
validates_presence_of :body
validates_presence_of :title
validates_length_of :title, :maximum => 255
validates_length_of :synopsis, :maximum => 1000
validates_length_of :body, :maximum => 20000
```

Add the following validation to the app/models/category.rb model file:

```
validates_length_of :name, :maximum => 80
```

As you saw earlier with the validations for the Page and User models, these validations will
be performed whenever an attempt is made to save the model.

Automatically Nullifying category_id on Deletion

Our specification states that if a category is deleted, any articles that are assigned to that category need to have their category_id reset to null. Rails provides a very easy way of doing this.
In the model definition, when a has_many relationship is defined, you can instruct Rails what to
do to dependent records on a deletion.

We can either delete or nullify dependent records. Since we want to set any dependent
articles to have a null category, we use the nullify option. Edit the app/models/category.rb
model file again to change the has_many :articles line to the following:

```
has_many :articles, :dependent => :nullify
```

If you wanted Rails to automatically delete the articles if a category is deleted, you would
use :dependent => :destroy instead.

Automatically Updating the published_at Field

In the Article model, the published_at field is used to record the time and date that the article
was actually published to the site rather than the time that it was created. This is important
because the news blog is shown in reverse chronological order—if the blog was ordered using

the `created_at` field, a news item written as a draft and published later would be shown before a newly created news item that was published immediately.

We will use a `before_save` callback to ensure that the `published_at` field is updated automatically whenever the article is saved and that the `published` attribute is set to `true`.

Add this callback to the `app/models/article.rb` file:

```
before_save :update_published_at

def update_published_at
  self.published_at = Time.now if published == true
end
```

Adding the Editor Role

Before we work on the controllers, we should create a migration to add the new editor role to the database. We do not need to alter the structure of the database, but we can use a migration to add a new field to the `Roles` table.

Create a new migration file using the `generate` script:

```
$ ruby script/generate migration AddEditorRole
```

```
    exists  db/migrate
    create  db/migrate/007_add_editor_role.rb
```

Open the generated migration script, and edit the `self.up` method to create the field and the `self.down` method to remove it. Making sure that the `self.down` method returns the database to the same state as before the migration ensures that you can always roll back the database. As part of the migration, we should also add the editor role to our existing Admin user.

Edit the file as show in Listing 4-1.

Listing 4-1. *Migration to Add the Editor Role*

```
class AddEditorRole < ActiveRecord::Migration
  def self.up
    editor_role = Role.create(:name => 'Editor')
    admin_user = User.find_by_username('Admin')
    admin_user.roles << editor_role
  end

  def self.down
    editor_role = Role.find_by_name('Editor')
    admin_user = User.find_by_username('Admin')
    admin_user.roles.delete(editor_role)
    editor_role.destroy
  end
end
```

Go ahead and run the `rake` migration task to create the article and category tables, and add the new `editor` role.

```
$ rake db:migrate
```

```
== CreateArticles: migrating ====================================================
-- create_table(:articles)
   -> 0.1043s
== CreateArticles: migrated (0.1083s) ===========================================

== CreateCategories: migrating ==================================================
-- create_table(:categories)
   -> 0.0066s
== CreateCategories: migrated (0.0118s) =========================================

== AddEditorRole: migrating =====================================================
== AddEditorRole: migrated (0.1621s) ============================================
```

You should take a look at the contents of your database using either MySQL's command line or a graphical interface. You will notice that, along with the new tables, the editor role has been added to the Admin user in the `roles_users` table.

Now that the models are finished, we need to add the controllers.

Creating the Articles Controller and Views

We can now create the article and category controllers along with the relevant views. We also need to add the mapping of the routes to the controllers, since they are implementing a REST resource.

Mapping the REST Resources

Before we write the code for the controllers and design the views, we should add the mapping to the routes. This will allow us to easily access the controllers as REST resources.

Edit the `config/routes.rb` file, adding the following mappings:

```
map.resources :articles, :collection => {:admin => :get}

map.resources :categories, :collection => {:admin => :get} do |categories|
  categories.resources :articles, :name_prefix => 'category_'
end
```

This provides two ways of accessing the articles, either by the `/articles` URL or by specifying a specific category, such as `/categories/1/articles`. To stop the two named routes from clashing, I have specified a different name prefix for the articles when referenced with a category. By adding the name prefix of `category_` in the controllers and views, the route shortcuts in Table 4-3 become available.

Table 4-3. *REST Routes Added When a Name Prefix Is Specified*

Route Shortcut	URL Path
category_articles_path(category_id)	/categories/category_id/articles
category_article_path(category_id, article_id)	/categories/category_id/articles/article_id
category_new_article_path(category_id)	/categories/category_id/articles/new
category_edit_article_path(category_id, article_id)	/categories/category_id/articles/article_id;edit

You will notice that an extra method called admin is defined in the resource mapping of the categories and articles resources. This is defined with the parameter :collection => {:admin => :get}. This specifies that this is a method that applies to a collection of categories (in the same way as the index action) as opposed to a member (as in the case of the show or edit actions). It also specifies that the admin action responds to an HTTP GET request. This will automatically add the shortcut admin_categories_path to the list of available shortcuts for the categories resource and admin_articles_path for the articles resource. These can be accessed directly with the URLs /categories;admin and /articles;admin.

The Articles Controller

Create the articles controller using the Rails generate command:

```
$ ruby script/generate controller Articles index show new create edit update ➡
destroy admin
```

```
    exists  app/controllers/
    exists  app/helpers/
    create  app/views/articles
    exists  test/functional/
    create  app/controllers/articles_controller.rb
    create  test/functional/articles_controller_test.rb
    create  app/helpers/articles_helper.rb
    create  app/views/articles/index.rhtml
    create  app/views/articles/show.rhtml
    create  app/views/articles/new.rhtml
    create  app/views/articles/create.rhtml
    create  app/views/articles/edit.rhtml
    create  app/views/articles/update.rhtml
    create  app/views/articles/destroy.rhtml
    create  app/views/articles/admin.rhtml
```

The articles controller will follow the same pattern as our pages and users controllers but with some enhancements.

Edit the app/controllers/articles_controller.rb file's index method:

```
def index
  if params[:category_id]
    @articles_pages, @articles = paginate(:articles,
      :include => :user,
      :order => 'published_at DESC',
      :conditions => "category_id=#{params[:category_id].to_i} AND published=true")
  else
    @articles = Article.find_all_by_published(true)
    @articles_pages, @articles = paginate(:articles,
      :include => :user,
      :order => 'published_at DESC',
      :conditions => "published = true")
  end
  respond_to do |wants|
    wants.html
    wants.xml  { render :xml => @articles.to_xml }
    wants.rss  { render :action => 'rss.rxml', :layout => false }
    wants.atom { render :action => 'atom.rxml', :layout => false }
  end
end
```

Pagination

The first thing to notice is that rather than using a regular find to get a collection of articles, this method uses the paginate helper. The paginate helper allows you to easily paginate a large number of items, automatically creating page links and returning information such as the total number of items and number of pages of items.

The paginator in the index action returns just the articles that have the published attribute set to true. The paginator is instructed to order them by the published_at date and will supply the default ten items per page. This can be overridden if you wish by changing the parameters of the paginate commands. By specifying a :limit parameter you can change the number of items shown on a page.

The helper returns the specified collection of articles, along with an instance of the Paginator class. From this class instance, you can retrieve information about the current page and the size of the pagination collection. This will be used to create the links to the other pages of the collection.

The paginate method also specifies an :include parameter of :user. This instructs ActiveRecord to automatically retrieve any User models that are referenced by the Article objects found. It does this by constructing a SQL statement joining the tables and performs just one SQL query to retrieve both tables. If the :include parameter were not used, the database would have to be queried whenever the code tries to reference the user specified in an Article instance. If you have a number of different users who have created articles, this would result in a number of database queries rather than just one, as when :include is used. Since we know that whenever we display an article the user's name will be shown, it makes sense to include this now.

Returning XML Data

The index method uses the Rails REST web service support to automatically return XML data if the client requests XML rather than HTML. The request for XML can be specified either by the client's HTTP Accept header or by simply adding .xml to the end of the URL. In this case, http://localhost:3000/articles.xml would return the list of articles in XML rather than rendering the HTML layout.

This provides the beginnings of an API with very little work. Adding this API support to all of our methods means that our site becomes truly open and that it can interface with and respond to other applications or web sites. You can write desktop or web applications that can easily interface with the site, and other Rails sites can simply use Rail's ActiveResource module to access the site without any extra coding at all.

RSS and Atom Feeds

Along with providing XML output, the index method also responds to requests for RSS or Atom results. However, the XML for these formats is not already defined in Rails, so we need to specify it in an .rxml file. RXML files are similar to the RHTML files that make up all of the other view files, except they define an XML structure instead of HTML.

To make it easier to produce XML documents, Rails employs a Ruby library called Builder. This library provides a simple way of creating valid XML files using just Ruby code without having to check that all of your XML is valid and formed correctly. Also, it is a lot easier to read an RXML file than an ERb file of XML markup and embedded Ruby code.

To build the RSS feed, create an RXML file, app/views/articles/rss.rxml, and add the code in Listing 4-2.

Listing 4-2. *The rss.rxml File, Specifying an RSS Feed of Articles*

```
xml.instruct!

xml.rss "version" => "2.0", "xmlns:dc" => "http://purl.org/dc/elements/1.1/" do
  xml.channel do

    xml.title       "News Feed "
    xml.link        articles_url
    xml.pubDate     CGI.rfc1123_date @articles.first.published_at if @articles.any?
    xml.description "News about the RailsCoders"

    @articles.each do |article|
      xml.item do
        xml.title       article.title
        xml.link        article_url(article)
        xml.description article.body
        xml.pubDate     CGI.rfc1123_date article.published_at
        xml.guid        article_url(article)
        xml.author      "#{article.user.email} (#{article.user.username})"
      end
```

```
        end

    end
end
```

You will notice that this looks rather less complex than an XML file scattered with Ruby code to insert the necessary data. The Builder library allows you to simply use Ruby to iterate through a collection, creating the XML output as we go.

The Ruby CGI library provides a method to format dates to the RFC1123 style expected in RSS feeds.

Along with an RSS output, we can add the Atom feed output too. Create the file app/views/atom.rxml, and add the code in Listing 4-3.

Listing 4-3. *The atom.rxml File, Specifying an Atom Feed of Articles*

```
xml.instruct!

xml.feed "xmlns" => "http://www.w3.org/2005/Atom" do

  xml.title   "RailsCoders News"
  xml.link    "rel" => "self", "href" => articles_url
  xml.link    "rel" => "alternate", "href" => articles_url
  xml.id      articles_url
  if @articles.any?
    xml.updated @articles.first.updated_at.strftime "%Y-%m-%dT%H:%M:%SZ"
  end
  xml.author  { xml.name "RailsCoders Site" }

  @articles.each do |article|
    xml.article do
      xml.title   article.title
      xml.link    "rel" => "alternate", "href" => article_url(article)
      xml.id      article_url(article)
      xml.updated article.updated_at.strftime "%Y-%m-%dT%H:%M:%SZ"
      xml.author  { xml.name article.user.username }
      xml.summary article.synopsis
      xml.content "type" => "html" do
        xml.text! textilize(article.body)
      end
    end
  end

end
```

This works in the same way as the RSS feed, except with different formatting. It is up to you to decide if you want to provide an RSS or Atom feed or both. Most, if not all, newsreaders can parse both RSS and Atom feeds, so for the remainder of the book I will work only with RSS feeds. However, if you prefer Atom, you can use that instead.

Now that we have an RSS feed for the list of articles, we need to publicize the feed. To do this, we need to add an extra XHTML tag to the <head> section of our web page, specifying that there is an alternate version of the page available as an RSS XML feed. Since the feed is available at exactly the same URL (but accessed by using a different MIME type), this tag would be as follows:

```
<link href="http://localhost:3000/articles" rel="alternate" title="RSS"
    type="application/rss+xml" />
```

Rails handily provides a helper function to automatically create this link tag, auto_discovery_link_tag. By adding this to an ERb file, the relevant link tag is generated.

We only want this tag to be generated for the article's index view. However, we need to place this link into the <head> section of the page. If you look back at the application.rhtml layout file, you will notice that within the <head> section, there is a yield :head statement. This allows us to insert extra data at this point by specifying the extra data within a content_for :head block in a view file.

Open the app/views/articles/index.rhtml file. At the top of the file, insert the following code:

```
<% content_for :head do %>
  <%= auto_discovery_link_tag %>
<% end %>
```

Now, whenever this page is rendered, the link generated by the auto_discovery_link_tag helper will be inserted into the <head> tag of the layout template. Try it now—reload the page http://localhost:3000/articles, and view the source of the page. You will see the extra link tag at the expected position in the page source. If you are using Firefox or Safari, you will notice that there is an option for subscribing to or viewing the feed in the browser's location bar, normally shown as an orange feed icon or as an RSS icon.

You can use this technique to insert data at other parts of a layout template. You may wish to add extra sidebar menu options for particular pages, for instance. You may also wish to add a text or graphic link to the RSS feed to the sidebar too.

The Remaining Article Controller Actions

We should now go back to the app/controllers/articles_controller.rb file and edit the rest of the methods:

```
def show
  if is_logged_in? && @logged_in_user.has_role?('Editor')
    @article = Article.find(params[:id])
  else
    @article = Article.find_by_id_and_published(params[:id], true)
  end
  respond_to do |wants|
    wants.html
    wants.xml { render :xml => @article.to_xml }
  end
end
```

```ruby
def new
  @article = Article.new
end

def create
  @article = Article.create(params[:article])
  @logged_in_user.articles << @article
  respond_to do |wants|
    wants.html { redirect_to admin_articles_url }
    wants.xml  { render :xml => @article.to_xml }
  end
end

def edit
  @article = Article.find(params[:id])
end

def update
  @article = Article.find(params[:id])
  @article.update_attributes(params[:article])
  respond_to do |wants|
    wants.html { redirect_to admin_articles_url }
    wants.xml  { render :xml => @article.to_xml }
  end
end

def destroy
  @article = Article.find(params[:id])
  @article.destroy
  respond_to do |wants|
    wants.html { redirect_to admin_articles_url }
    wants.xml  { render :nothing => true }
  end
end

def admin
  @articles_pages, @articles = paginate(:articles, :order => 'published_at DESC')
end
```

At the moment, all of the actions are open to any user, logged in or not. To secure them so that only the editors can perform the create, edit, and destroy actions, we need to add a before_filter to check for the editor role at the top of the articles_controller.rb file:

```ruby
class ArticlesController < ApplicationController
  before_filter :check_editor_role, :except => [:index, :show]
  ...
```

Of course, we now need to write the check_editor_role method inside our lib/login_system.rb file. It is a good idea to put the method after the check_administrator_role method to keep the file tidy and easy to maintain:

```
def check_editor_role
  check_role('Editor')
end
```

The Article Views

All that's left for the articles now is to write the views to go along with the action methods. Edit the file app/views/articles/index.rhtml, replacing the generated view with the ERb in Listing 4-4.

Listing 4-4. *View for the Articles Index Action*

```
<% content_for :head do %>
  <%= auto_discovery_link_tag %>
<% end %>


<h2>News Articles</h2>

<% if @articles_pages.page_count > 1 %>
  <p class="pagination">Pages: <strong>
    <%= pagination_links @articles_pages, :params => params %>
  </strong></p>
<% end %>


<% @articles.each do |article| %>
  <div class="article">
    <h3><%= article.title %></h3>
    <% if article.category %>
      <p class="category">
        Category: '<%= link_to article.category.name,
                       category_articles_path(article.category) %>'
      </p>
    <% end %>

    <p>
      <%= article.created_at.to_s(:short) %> by <%= article.user.username %><br />
      <%= article.synopsis %><br />
      <%= link_to 'Read the full article', article_url(article) %>
    </p>
  </div>
<% end %>
```

You will notice that this view uses the pagination_links helper method to automatically display the links to each of the pages of articles, if there is more than one page. Any parameters that are currently set are passed on to the pagination links, allowing you to add, filter, or sort parameters in the view later.

There is also a link to view each article in full, which is a link to the article's controller show action.

If a category is set, a link to the articles of that category is shown along with each article title.

The Show Article View

Now we can write the show article view. Edit app/views/articles/show.rhtml to display the full article by adding the view code in Listing 4-5.

Listing 4-5. *The Show Article View*

```
<h2><%= @article.title %></h2>

<% if @article.category %>
  <p class="category">
    Category: '<%= link_to @article.category.name,
                    category_articles_path(@article.category) %>'
  </p>
<% end %>

<p>
  <%= @article.created_at.to_s(:short) %><br />
  <%= textilize(@article.body) %><br />
</p>
<p><%= link_to 'Back to article list', articles_url %></p>
```

This will also display the category and a link to the list of articles for that category if one is set for this article.

The New Article View

Now add the form to create a new article in app/views/articles/new.rhtml. Edit this file by adding the view code in Listing 4-6.

Listing 4-6. *The New Article View*

```
<h2>Create Article</h2>
<% form_for :article,
            :url => articles_url,
            :html => { :method => :post } do |f| -%>
  <p>Title:<br /><%= f.text_field :title, :size => 60 %></p>
  <p>Synopsis:<br /><%= f.text_area :synopsis, :rows => 4, :cols => 60 %></p>
  <p>Body:<br /><%= f.text_area :body, :rows => 20, :cols => 60 %></p>
  <p>Category:<br />
    <%= f.collection_select :category_id, Category.find(:all), :id, :name %></p>
  <p>Published? <%= f.check_box :published %></p>
  <%= submit_tag 'Save' %> or <%= link_to 'cancel', articles_url %>
<% end -%>
```

The Edit Article View

The form to edit an article is very similar, except it is submitted to a different URL using HTTP PUT rather than POST. Add the code in Listing 4-7 to app/views/articles/edit.rhtml.

Listing 4-7. *The Edit Article View*

```
<h2>Edit Article</h2>
<% form_for :article,
            :url => article_url(@article),
            :html => { :method => :put } do |f| -%>
  <p>Title:<br /><%= f.text_field :title, :size => 60 %></p>
  <p>Synopsis:<br /><%= f.text_area :synopsis, :rows => 4, :cols => 60 %></p>
  <p>Body:<br /><%= f.text_area :body, :rows => 20, :cols => 60 %></p>
  <p>Category:<br />
    <%= f.collection_select :category_id,
        Category.find(:all), :id, :name, :include_blank => true %></p>
  <p>Published? <%= f.check_box :published %></p>
  <%= submit_tag 'Save' %> or <%= link_to 'cancel', articles_url %>
<% end -%>
```

Note that this form has to specify that it sends its information using the HTTP PUT method to ensure that the update action will process it.

The helper collection_select is used to automatically create a drop-down select box from a list of categories. Since it is possible for an article to have a null category_id, the option :include_blank is set to true to instruct collection_select to include a blank option in the list.

The Articles Admin View

The admin view for the articles is similar to the index view, except that it includes a link to the Article resource create action.

Listing 4-8. *The Articles Admin View*

```
<h2>Edit Articles</h2>

<p><%= link_to 'Create New Article', new_article_path %></p>

<% if @articles_pages.page_count > 1 %>
  <p class="pagination">Pages: <strong>
    <%= pagination_links @articles_pages, :params => params %>
  </strong></p>
<% end %>
```

```
<ul>
<% @articles.each do |article| %>
  <li>
    <%= link_to article.title, article_url(article) %>
    [<%= link_to 'Edit', edit_article_path(article) %>]
    [<%= link_to 'Delete', article_path(article), :method => :delete,
              :confirm => 'Are you sure you wish to delete this article?' %>]

  </li>
<% end %>
</ul>
```

Using the Articles Feature

You can now start the Rails server and try creating, viewing, and editing a few articles. Since this can be performed only by a user with the editor role, you should make sure that you log in as the Admin user.

To create a new article, go to `http://localhost:3000/articles/new`, and enter some data. Try entering text marked up with Textile in the body of the article. Make sure you click the "published" check box to ensure that the article is viewable.

View the complete list of articles at `http://localhost:3000/articles`. If you create more than twenty articles, the pagination links will be shown.

Testing the XML API

You should now try requesting XML output for the actions that support it. As I mentioned earlier, you can do this either by appending `.xml` to the URL or by specifying that you require XML in the HTTP `Accept` header. Try requesting the XML for the list of articles through your browser by entering the URL `http://localhost:3000/articles.xml`. If you are using Internet Explorer or Firefox, the XML will be shown in the browser itself.

In order to investigate how this could be used by another application by requesting and sending XML, try accessing the articles through the command line. In real-world use, applications would construct XML programmatically, but the easiest way for us to test the XML API is to use the cURL utility.

■**Note** cURL is a handy open source tool for accessing anything that has a URL, such as web pages, files stored on a server, or REST resources. You can download it and read more about it at `http://curl.haxx.se`.

You can specify HTTP headers in cURL using the `-H` switch. Enter the command:

```
$ curl -H 'Accept: application/xml' http://localhost:3000/articles
```

```xml
<?xml version="1.0" encoding="UTF-8"?>
<articles>
  <article>
    <body>anybody listening?</body>
    <category-id type="integer"></category-id>
    <created-at type="datetime">2006-11-07T16:17:52+00:00</created-at>
    <id type="integer">1</id>
    <published type="boolean">true</published>
    <published-at type="datetime">2006-11-08T16:17:52+00:00</published-at>
    <synopsis>another article</synopsis>
    <title>Hello world</title>
    <updated-at type="datetime">2006-11-08T16:17:52+00:00</updated-at>
    <user-id type="integer">1</user-id>
  </article>
  <article>
    <body>Welcome to the RailsCoders community.</body>
    <category-id type="integer"></category-id>
    <created-at type="datetime">2006-11-07T22:22:27+00:00</created-at>
    <id type="integer">2</id>
    <published type="boolean">true</published>
    <published-at type="datetime">2006-11-08T18:02:39+00:00</published-at>
    <synopsis>abc</synopsis>
    <title>testing</title>
    <updated-at type="datetime">2006-11-08T18:02:39+00:00</updated-at>
    <user-id type="integer">1</user-id>
  </article>
</articles>
```

You can also request a single article using the URL for an individual article:

```
$ curl -H 'Accept: application/xml' http://localhost:3000/articles/1
```

```xml
<?xml version="1.0" encoding="UTF-8"?>
<article>
  <body>anybody listening?</body>
  <category-id type="integer"></category-id>
  <created-at type="datetime">2006-11-07T16:17:52+00:00</created-at>
  <id type="integer">1</id>
  <published type="boolean">true</published>
  <published-at type="datetime">2006-11-08T16:17:52+00:00</published-at>
  <synopsis>another article</synopsis>
  <title>Hello world</title>
  <updated-at type="datetime">2006-11-08T16:17:52+00:00</updated-at>
  <user-id type="integer">1</user-id>
</article>
```

Adding HTTP Authentication for the API

While providing a simple XML API works great for accessing the public actions, to perform the
create, edit, or destroy actions, you must be logged in to the site as an editor. However, if you
are using the API programmatically, as demonstrated with the curl command-line tool, you
cannot deal with being redirected to a login page. An API should be able to send the authentication details together with the request.

To solve this, we can use HTTP's own built-in authentication methods that use the HTTP
headers to pass the login details. You will no doubt have seen this in action on some web sites;
it is commonly used to protect directories of files on web servers. We can also use the same
method to allow an API call to perform authentication, allowing the actions that require a user
to be logged in to be called programmatically.

A little bit of work is required to integrate this method into our existing login system, but
once we do, our site can easily be accessed either via the Web or via API calls without any other
code being changed.

Go back to the lib/login_system.rb that we created in the previous chapter, and add the
following method to retrieve the login credentials from the HTTP headers if they are present.
This private method should be added as the last method in the file:

```
private
  def get_http_auth_data
    username, password = nil, nil
    auth_headers = ['X-HTTP_AUTHORIZATION', 'Authorization', 'HTTP_AUTHORIZATION',
      'REDIRECT_REDIRECT_X_http_AUTHORIZATION']
    auth_header = auth_headers.detect { |key| request.env[key] }
    auth_data = request.env[auth_header].to_s.split

    if auth_data && auth_data[0] == 'Basic'
      username, password = Base64.decode64(auth_data[1]).split(':')[0..1]
    end
    return [username, password]
  end
```

Because various web servers pass the HTTP authentication headers to Rails in differing
ways, this method checks a number of types of headers and if it finds one, it extracts the username and password and returns them both in an array.

Now that we have an easy way of checking the HTTP authentication data, we can change
the is_logged_in? method to check the session variable for web logins and HTTP authentication for API calls. To do this, change the is_logged_in? method in the lib/login_system.rb file
to the following:

```
def is_logged_in?
  username, password = get_http_auth_data
  @logged_in_user = User.find(session[:user]) if session[:user]
  @logged_in_user = User.authenticate(username, password) if username && password
  @logged_in_user ? @logged_in_user : false
end
```

Also, the `login_required` and `check_role` methods should be changed to correctly respond with HTTP status messages, rather than sending a web page back:

```ruby
def login_required
  unless is_logged_in?
    respond_to do |wants|
      wants.html do
        flash[:error] = "You must be logged in to do that."
        redirect_to :controller => 'account', :action => 'login'
      end
      wants.xml do
        headers["Status"]           = "Unauthorized"
        headers["WWW-Authenticate"] = %(Basic realm="Web Password")
        render :text => "Could't authenticate you",
               :status => '401 Unauthorized',
               :layout => false
      end
    end
  end
end

def check_role(role)
  unless is_logged_in? && @logged_in_user.has_role?(role)
    respond_to do |wants|
      wants.html do
        flash[:error] = "You do not have the permission to do that."
        redirect_to :controller => 'account', :action => 'login'
      end
      wants.xml do
        headers['Status']           = 'Unauthorized'
        headers['WWW-Authenticate'] = %(Basic realm="Password")
        render :text => "Insuffient permission",
               :status => '401 Unauthorized',
               :layout => false
      end
    end
  end
end
```

Testing the API Authentication

You can test this out by using `curl` again. The `curl -u` switch allows you to specify a username and password to be sent as login credentials. Since only certain methods are protected by passwords, you will need to try accessing one of those actions.

Because `curl` allows us to send an HTTP POST request, we can try adding a new article using only the API method and `curl`. This emulates how another application would talk to your site. To do this, you are going to have to write a `curl` command that sends XML data in an HTTP POST request to your site.

We have to tell the server that we are sending XML, so another HTTP header, `Content-Type`, is used to specify this.

Carefully enter the following `curl` command:

```
$ curl -u admin:admin -H 'Accept: application/xml' ➥
-H 'Content-Type: application/xml' -d '<article><title>testing</title> ➥
<synopsis>this is a test</synopsis><body>This is really a test</body> ➥
<category_id>1</category_id><published>true</published></article>' ➥
http://localhost:3000/articles
```

You will notice that the username and password are being sent, along with the required HTTP headers. Since we are specifying data to be sent with the `-d` switch, `curl` automatically sends the request as an HTTP POST, rather than an HTTP GET, request.

We send the request to the articles controller, and in return, we get the new article in XML format, similar to the following:

```
<?xml version="1.0" encoding="UTF-8"?>
<article>
  <body>This is really a test</body>
  <category-id type="integer">1</category-id>
  <created-at type="datetime">2006-11-09T03:23:38+00:00</created-at>
  <id type="integer">5</id>
  <published type="boolean">false</published>
  <published-at type="datetime"></published-at>
  <synopsis>this is a test</synopsis>
  <title>testing</title>
  <updated-at type="datetime">2006-11-09T03:23:38+00:00</updated-at>
  <user-id type="integer"></user-id>
</article>
```

Creating the Categories' Controller and Views

We should now create the controller and views for the categories. The categories controller again follows the basic CRUD pattern following the REST principles. It will look similar to the articles controller.

The Categories Controller

First of all, generate the skeleton controller using the generate script:

```
$ ruby script/generate controller Categories index show new create edit ➥
update destroy admin
```

```
exists  app/controllers/
exists  app/helpers/
create  app/views/categories
exists  test/functional/
create  app/controllers/categories_controller.rb
create  test/functional/categories_controller_test.rb
create  app/helpers/categories_helper.rb
create  app/views/categories/index.rhtml
create  app/views/categories/show.rhtml
create  app/views/categories/new.rhtml
create  app/views/categories/create.rhtml
create  app/views/categories/edit.rhtml
create  app/views/categories/update.rhtml
create  app/views/categories/destroy.rhtml
create  app/views/categories/admin.rhtml
```

Now open the app/controllers/categories_controller.rb file, and edit the class as shown in Listing 4-9:

Listing 4-9. *The Categories Controller File*

```
class CategoriesController < ApplicationController
  before_filter :check_editor_role, :except => [:index, :show]

  def index
    @categories = Category.find(:all)
    respond_to do |wants|
      wants.html
      wants.xml { render :xml => @categories.to_xml }
    end
  end

  def show
    @category = Category.find(params[:id])
    respond_to do |wants|
     wants.html { redirect_to category_articles_url(:category_id => @category.id) }
     wants.xml { render :xml => @category.to_xml }
    end
  end

  def new
    @category = Category.new
  end
```

```
  def create
    @category = Category.create(params[:category])
    respond_to do |wants|
      wants.html { redirect_to admin_categories_url }
      wants.xml { render :xml => @category.to_xml }
    end
  end

  def edit
    @category = Category.find(params[:id])
  end

  def update
    @category = Category.find(params[:id])
    @category.update_attributes(params[:category])
    respond_to do |wants|
      wants.html { redirect_to admin_categories_url }
      wants.xml { render :xml => @category.to_xml }
    end
  end

  def destroy
    @category = Category.find(params[:id])
    @category.find(params[:id]).destroy
    respond_to do |wants|
      wants.html { redirect_to admin_categories_url }
      wants.xml { render :nothing => true }
    end
  end

  def admin
    @categories = Category.find(:all)
    respond_to do |wants|
      wants.html
      wants.xml { render :xml => @categories.to_xml }
    end
  end
end
```

This controller limits everything except the index and show actions from being accessed by anyone except a user with the editor role. All of the categories will be returned. As before, XML will be returned if the client requests it. Since numerous categories are unlikely, there is no need to add pagination.

If the user requests to view a specific category, the browser is redirected to show all of the articles in that category.

The admin action provides the same information as the index action, except it uses a view that provides links to allow an administrator to create new categories or edit existing ones.

The Category Views

Since users are going to be redirected to the articles if they try to view an individual category, we only need to write views for the index, new, and edit actions.

The Category Index View

Edit the app/views/categories/index.rhtml file, adding the code shown in Listing 4-10.

Listing 4-10. *The Categories Index View*

```
<h2>Categories</h2>
<ul>
<% @categories.each do |category| %>
  <li>
    <%= link_to category.name, category_articles_url(:category_id => category) %>
  </li>
<% end %>
</ul>
```

This will show a list of the available categories and a link to a view of the articles in that category.

The New Category View

Now edit the app/views/categories/new.rhtml file as shown in Listing 4-11.

Listing 4-11. *The Category Create View*

```
<h2>Create a New Category</h2>
<%= error_messages_for :category %>
<% form_for(:category, :url => categories_path) do |f| -%>
  <p>Name:<br /><%= f.text_field :name, :size => 60 %></p>
  <%= submit_tag 'Save' %> or <%= link_to 'cancel', admin_categories_url %>
<% end %>
```

This simply provides a form to create a new category.

The Edit Category View

The app/views/categories/edit.rhtml file is very similar and is shown in Listing 4-12.

Listing 4-12. *The Category Edit View*

```
<h2>Edit a Category</h2>
<%= error_messages_for :category %>
<% form_for(:category,
            :url => category_path(@category),
            :html => {:method => :put}) do |f| -%>
  <p>Name:<br /><%= f.text_field :name, :size => 60 %></p>
  <%= submit_tag 'Save' %> or <%= link_to 'cancel', admin_categories_url %>
<% end %>
```

The Admin View

The admin view of the categories, providing links to allow an administrator to create new categories or edit existing ones is shown in Listing 4-13. Edit the file app/views/categories/admin.rhtml by adding the code shown.

Listing 4-13. *The Admin View of Categories*

```
<h2>Edit Categories</h2>

<p><%= link_to 'Create New Category', new_category_path %></p>

<ul>
<% @categories.each do |category| %>
  <li>
    <%= link_to category.name, category_articles_url(:category_id => category) %>
    [<%= link_to 'Edit', edit_category_path(category) %>]
    [<%= link_to 'Delete', category_path(category), :method => :delete,
                :confirm => 'Are you sure you wish to delete this category?' %>]
  </li>
<% end %>
</ul>
```

Adding a Link from the Sidebar Menu

To make it easy to access the news articles, we should add a link to the menu sidebar. Open the partial view file app/views/layouts/_menu.rhtml, and add a link to the news index action as follows:

```
<ul>
  <li><%= link_to 'Home', index_url %></li>
  <li><%= link_to 'News', articles_path %></li>

  <li><hr size="1" width="90%" align="left"/></li>

  <% if is_logged_in? %>
  ...
```

We should also add a link to allow editors to easily create a new news article and edit the categories. Add the following to the end of the _menu.rhtml file:

```
<% if is_logged_in? and logged_in_user.has_role?('editor') %>
  <li><hr size="1" width="90%" align="left" /></li>
  <li><b>Editor Options</b></li>
  <li><%= link_to 'News Articles', admin_articles_path %></li>
  <li><%= link_to 'News Categories', admin_categories_path %></li>
<% end %>
```

Manually Testing the News Blog System

We can now run through the whole news blog feature and check that it works as expected. Make sure that the Rails application server is running, and go to the application homepage, http://localhost:3000/. Now log in as the Admin user. The sidebar menu will show the new administration links, News Articles and News Categories.

First, try creating a new news category. Click the News Categories link. Since we created a default category called Site News in the migration, this will be shown. Try creating a new category, renaming it, and deleting it to make sure that it works as expected.

Next, we can try creating a new news article. Click the News Articles link, which will show us a list of current articles. Since there are no articles yet, it will be empty. Click the Create a New Article link at the top of the page, and enter an article, making sure to check the "published" box. When you save this, you will be returned to the list of articles, now showing your newly created article.

If you view this article, you will see how the article is displayed along with the category. If you then click the category, you will see all articles within that category. You should try creating a number of articles with an assortment of categories to check that this category viewing works correctly.

Testing the News Blog

It is now time to write some tests. We have previously added unit tests, functional tests, and integration tests. Here, I am just going to concentrate on functional and integration tests.

As before, you should expand these tests to add a collection of unit, functional, and integration tests to cover all the features that you have added.

Before we can perform functional tests on actions that require administrator or editor roles, we need to add those roles and users with those roles to the existing set of fixtures that we have defined.

Add the administrator and editor roles to the test/fixtures/roles.yml file:

```
admin:
  id: 1
  name: Administrator
editor:
  id: 2
  name: Editor
```

Edit the test/fixtures/users.yml file, adding the following two users to the existing fixture:

```
admin_user:
  id: 2
  username: admin
  email: admin@example.com
  hashed_password: 5994471abb01112afcc18159f6cc74b4f511b99806da59b3caf5a9c173cacfc5
  created_at: <%= 1.days.ago.to_s(:db) %>
```

```
editor_user:
  id: 3
  username: editor
  email: editor@example.com
  hashed_password: 5994471abb01112afcc18159f6cc74b4f511b99806da59b3caf5a9c173cacfc5
  created_at: <%= 1.days.ago.to_s(:db) %>
```

The hashed_password fields are equal to a clear text password of 12345.

Now, we need to create a new fixtures file, test/fixtures/roles_users.yml, to store the relationships among the users and roles, giving the relevant roles to the right users.

```
admin:
  role_id: 1
  user_id: 2
editor:
  role_id: 2
  user_id: 3
```

We also need to create fixtures for the categories and articles. First, define two category fixtures: one the default Site News and another for Rails News.

To do this, open the categories fixtures file, app/test/fixtures/categories.yml, and add the following YAML:

```
site_news:
  id: 1
  name: Site News
gossip:
  id: 2
  name: Rails News
```

We need to create some articles within these categories. We will create two article fixtures, one in each category. Open the article fixtures file, app/test/fixtures/articles.yml, and add the following fixtures:

```
good_news:
  id: 1
  user_id: 1
  title: Exciting news
  synopsis: New Feature.
  body: We have added a new features for you to enjoy.
  published: true
  created_at: <%= Time.now.to_s :db %>
  updated_at: <%= Time.now.to_s :db %>
  published_at: <%= Time.now.to_s :db %>
  category_id: 1
```

```
some_gossip:
  id: 2
  user_id: 1
  title: Rails Updated
  synopsis: A new update to Rails was released
  body: Time to update, folks!
  published: true
  created_at: <%= Time.now.to_s :db %>
  updated_at: <%= Time.now.to_s :db %>
  published_at: <%= Time.now.to_s :db %>
  category_id: 2
```

We can now use these fixtures to write functional and integration tests.

Functional Tests

Whenever you use a generator to create a controller, Rails creates a skeleton functional test file
for this controller. Open the test file test/functional/articles_controller_test.rb, delete
the automatically generated test_truth test, and add the real tests shown in Listing 4-14.

Note that, by default, the generated test class only loads the fixtures for the model relevant
to the controller being tested (specified by the line fixtures :articles). Since we want to test
using not just the article fixtures but also the users and roles, we need to specify the additional
fixtures that need to be loaded into the database before running these tests. The new fixtures
line at line 7 loads the articles, users, roles, and roles_users fixtures.

Listing 4-14. *The Functional Tests for the Articles Controller*

```
require File.dirname(__FILE__) + '/../test_helper'
require 'articles_controller'

class ArticlesController; def rescue_action(e) raise e end; end

class ArticlesControllerTest < Test::Unit::TestCase
  fixtures :articles, :users, :roles, :roles_users

  def setup
    @controller = ArticlesController.new
    @request    = ActionController::TestRequest.new
    @response   = ActionController::TestResponse.new
  end

  def test_index
    get :index
    assert_response :success
    assert_not_nil assigns(:articles)
  end
```

```
def test_index_as_xml
  @request.env['HTTP_ACCEPT'] = 'application/xml'
  get :index
  assert_response :success
  assert_not_nil assigns(:articles)
end

def test_show
  get :show, :id => 1
  assert_response :success
  assert_not_nil assigns(:article)
end

def test_create_article_with_http_auth_and_xml
  old_count = Article.count
  @request.env['HTTP_ACCEPT'] = 'application/xml'
  @request.env['Authorization'] = 'Basic ' + Base64::b64encode('editor:12345')

  post :create, :article => { :title => 'New article', :synopsis => 'Just a test',
    :body => 'Nothing to see here', :published => true }

  assert_response :success
  assert_equal old_count + 1, Article.count
  assert_not_nil assigns(:article)
end

def test_rest_routing
  with_options :controller => 'articles' do |test|
    test.assert_routing 'articles', :action => 'index'
    test.assert_routing 'articles/1', :action => 'show', :id => '1'
  end
end
end
```

There are a number of interesting tests performed here. In the test test_index, we are performing an HTTP GET request on the index action and checking that a page is successfully returned with the correct information by performing the assert_not_nil check on the assigns object. Whenever you perform a request in a functional test, any instance variables that are set in the code are passed back to the test as assigns. So by performing this test, we are checking that @articles has data in it after the method has been called.

The test_index_as_xml test performs the same test, except it requests the data in XML by adding the relevant HTTP header.

The test_show test simply performs a similar test to test_index, except that it requests one specific article. Again, both a successful page return is checked for along with a test to make sure that @article is not nil.

`test_create_article_with_http_auth_and_xml` tests the create article method, but it does so by using the newly added HTTP authentication. In order to do this, we have to construct a valid authentication header by encoding the username and password in base 64 and prefixing it with the type of HTTP authentication we are using, namely `Basic`.

Next, the test performs a `POST` request containing a new article and checks to make sure the request was a success. The number of articles in the database before and after the `create` action are compared to make sure that an article was successfully added to the database.

Finally, we perform a test to make sure that the REST mappings are set up and that the correct actions are performed when a REST URL is requested.

You can keep adding tests to cover other cases such as editing or deleting an article, along with negative tests to make sure that a nonauthenticated user cannot perform destructive actions.

Before you try running your tests, you will have to get the structure of your test database up to date. Run the `rake` task to rebuild the test database from the new schema by entering:

```
$ rake db:test:prepare
```

```
(in /Users/alan/Projects/rails/railscoders)
```

You can now try running your tests by either running all the functional tests with the command `rake test:functionals` or by invoking just this test file with the following command:

```
$ ruby test/functional/articles_controller_test.rb
```

```
Loaded suite test/functional/articles_controller_test
Started
ZWRpdG9yOjEyMzQ1
.....
Finished in 3.333111 seconds.

5 tests, 15 assertions, 0 failures, 0 errors
```

Categories should be tested in a similar way to ensure that only administrators or editors can create categories and that the correct list of articles is returned when a category is specified.

Integration Tests

As you have previously seen, integration tests are designed for when you need to test across multiple controllers. Since the articles feature utilizes the articles and categories controllers, there are a number of things we can test.

The categories resource is used in conjunction with the articles resource when a reader wants to look at all of the articles in just one category. To do this, they access a version of the articles resource nested beneath the categories resource.

We will now create the integration test to test these controllers using the fixtures created earlier. Create the file `app/test/integration/articles_stories_test.rb`, and add the code shown in Listing 4-15.

Listing 4-15. *The Articles Integration Test*

```
require "#{File.dirname(__FILE__)}/../test_helper"

class ArticlesStoriesTest < ActionController::IntegrationTest
  fixtures :users, :articles, :categories

  def test_view_all_articles
    get articles_url
    assert_response :success
    assert_template 'articles/index'
    assert_equal assigns['articles'].length, 2
  end

  def test_view_one_category
    get category_articles_url(:category_id => 1)
    assert_response :success
    assert_template 'articles/index'
    assert_equal assigns['articles'].length, 1
  end
end
```

As you can see, this contains two tests. The test_view_all_articles test checks that when the articles resource is accessed without specifying a category, all of the articles are returned. The test_view_one_category test requests the article's index action through the categories resource, specifying category number 1. Since in our fixtures we created one article within category 1, we know that one category will be returned. This is checked with the assert_equal statement.

Try running these tests now:

```
$ ruby test/integration/articles_stories_test.rb
```

```
Loaded suite test/integration/articles_stories_test
Started
..
Finished in 1.75416 seconds.

2 tests, 6 assertions, 0 failures, 0 errors
```

We can see that these tests pass successfully. You may wish to expand these integration tests further to incorporate creating, editing, and deleting articles and categories to make sure that the code meets our specifications.

Further Development of the News System

This news article feature could be extended in many ways. At the moment, only one category can be set per article. You may wish to think about how you could change the feature to allow multiple categories to be set for a new article. This would involve changing the relationship between articles and categories to be a one-to-many relationship.

You may also wish to improve the administration interface, allowing the editor of the article to preview the article easily before publishing. You may also wish to add a field in the Article model to allow the editors to create notes about the article, viewable only by other administrators or editors.

If you wish, you can go back to the page management system developed in Chapter 2 and add an API to that; Rails makes it so simple to add API functionality that it is as easy to add it as not to.

Summary

In this chapter, we added a rolling news blog that we can use to keep our users informed of developments at the site as well as keeping the site fresh and up to date. We created RSS feeds of the news articles to allow users to subscribe to the news feeds using their RSS aggregators. We also added an administration interface, allowing editors to create and edit articles. These editors do not have full administrator privileges, just the facility to create and edit news articles.

We looked at how this news blog system can then be extended to provide a full API to the feature. We also looked at how you can test the API through functional testing.

Through the Rails module ActiveRecord, it is very simple to integrate any other Rails sites with your site, which will allow your community to extend beyond the boundaries of your web site.

In the next chapter, we will build a discussion forum. This is often the center of a community site, so we want to make it as easy to use as possible.

CHAPTER 5

■■■

Building a Discussion Forum

In this chapter, we will look at how we can build a discussion forum for our community site. This will allow our users to discuss various aspects of Ruby and Rails development. We will also use the forum to talk about this book and allow users to discuss the code or sites that they have developed using this book.

The premise of the forum is that an administrator user will create a number of forums. Within each of these forums, users can create topics. Each topic then has any number of posts within it about that topic. There are already a number of open source forum implementations on the Web, of which the PHP-based phpBB and PunBB are the most popular. We can easily build similar functionality in Rails very quickly and have it fully integrated into our site.

To build this functionality, we will use the Rails generator script to create basic controllers, models, views, and tests for the relevant resources and adapt this scaffolding code to our needs. Then I will show how you can easily develop this scaffolding code to support nested resources.

Specifying the Discussion Forum Requirements

Before we dive into the code, we should establish the structure and design of the discussion forum. The application will allow for a moderator user to create a number of forums along with a description of the forum. This will allow for forums to be set up for different conversations on different topics. Within each forum, any logged-in user can create a new topic, which will consist of a number of posts.

This tells us that we are going to need three models: Forum, Topic, and Post. A forum can have many topics, and a topic, many posts.

For these models, we are going to make use of counter caches. A counter cache does exactly what it says—it keeps a cache of a counter. For instance, we'll display the number of topics in a given forum. While performing a count of the number of topics in a forum is not an especially taxing database query, if the application has to show the number of topics for each forum, an extra database query has to be done for each forum. Implementing a counter cache is trivial in Rails and can save your application making unnecessary database queries. While the Rails community generally advocates optimizing only when necessary, if you know you will need to show this counter, it is worth adding it now. We will use counter caches for the topics-per-forum counter and the posts-per-topic counter.

Since the topic counter is on a per-forum basis, including it necessitates an extra field in the `forums` database table. Keeping with the Rails conventions, this field should be called `topics_count`. You are free to rename this to something else, but you have to specify the field name in the `belongs_to` statement in the model when you set up the counter cache. However, it is much easier if you stick to conventions and use `topics_count`.

Defining the Forum Model

The Forum model will consist of simply a name and a description. Forums can be created, edited, and deleted only by a moderator or administrator.

Since we are using a counter cache to store the number of topics per forum, a `topics_count` field is added to each row. Table 5-1 shows the complete structure of the Forum model's database.

Table 5-1. *The Forum Model Database Structure*

Field Name	Field Type	Description
id	integer	The primary key
name	string	The forum name
description	text	Description of the forum
created_at	datetime	The date and time that the forum was created
updated_at	datetime	The date and time that the forum was last edited
topics_count	integer	The topic counter cache

Defining the Topic Model

The Topic model has the topic name along with the `user_id` of the user who created the topic. Any logged-in user can create a new topic, but only moderators can edit or delete topics. Deleting a topic will delete all of the posts within that topic.

Since we need a counter cache to store the number of posts per topic, a `posts_count` field has been added. The Topic model's database structure is show in Table 5-2.

Table 5-2. *The Topic Model Database Structure*

Field Name	Field Type	Description
id	integer	The primary key
forum_id	integer	The `id` of the forum that this topic belongs to
user_id	integer	The `id` of the user who created the topic
name	string	The subject of the topic
created_at	datetime	The date and time that the topic was created
updated_at	datetime	The date and time that the topic was last updated
posts_count	integer	The posts counter cache

Defining the Post Model

Each post has a body, a text field containing the body of the post, and the `user_id` of the user who created the post. Any logged-in user can create a post; only moderators can edit or delete. Table 5-3 shows the Post model's database structure.

Table 5-3. *The Post Model Database Structure*

Field Name	Field Type	Description
id	integer	The primary key
topic_id	integer	The id of the topic that this post belongs to
user_id	integer	The id of the user who created this post
body	text	The body of the post
created_at	datetime	The date and time that the post was created
updated_at	datetime	The date and time that the post was last edited

Figure 5-1 shows the relationships among the Forum, Topic, and Post models.

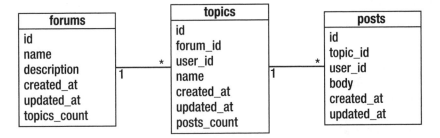

Figure 5-1. *Entity relationship diagram for the Forum, Topic, and Post models*

The Moderator Role

Since the task of moderating a busy discussion forum is too much for one administrator to handle, we will create a new user role to allow other nonadministrative users to be given the right to edit or remove forum posts. This user role will be called "moderator."

Since we built the role management system in Chapter 3, it will be very simple for the site administrator to assign this role to trusted users who can actively monitor and moderate the forums.

The Forum, Topic, and Post Controllers

The forum, topic, and post controllers will all be standard REST-style controllers. However, since each topic belongs to a particular forum, and each post belongs to a particular topic, these resources need to be nested.

The topics resource will be nested beneath a forum resource, assessable via URLs such as /forums/1/topics and /forums/1/topics/2.

The posts resource will be nested beneath a topic resource and, in turn, a forum resource. Therefore, the posts resource is assessable via URLs such as /forums/1/topics/2/posts and /forums/1/topics/2/posts/3.

Building the Forum

In the previous chapters, we used the generate script to create skeleton controllers and models and then wrote all the code ourselves. In this chapter, we are going to use the scaffold_resource generator. This automatically generates a controller, a model, and views for a given resource name. The generated code implements the basic CRUD functions of a REST resource. Doing this gives us a basic skeleton of a controller, speeding up our development process.

Building the Forum, Topic, and Post Models

The forums consist of three models: Forum, Topic, and Post. A forum has many topics, which in turn have many posts. In addition to this, each topic and each post belong to the user who created them.

To create these models, we are going to use the scaffold_resource generator to build the scaffolding code for the forum resources and edit the generated code to fit our needs. First, let's create the forum resource:

```
$ ruby script/generate scaffold_resource Forum
```

```
      exists  app/models/
      exists  app/controllers/
      exists  app/helpers/
      create  app/views/forums
      exists  test/functional/
      exists  test/unit/
      create  app/views/forums/index.rhtml
      create  app/views/forums/show.rhtml
      create  app/views/forums/new.rhtml
      create  app/views/forums/edit.rhtml
      create  app/views/layouts/forums.rhtml
   identical  public/stylesheets/scaffold.css
      create  app/models/forum.rb
      create  app/controllers/forums_controller.rb
      create  test/functional/forums_controller_test.rb
      create  app/helpers/forums_helper.rb
      create  test/unit/forum_test.rb
      create  test/fixtures/forums.yml
      exists  db/migrate
      create  db/migrate/008_create_forums.rb
       route  map.resources :forums
```

Next, we'll create the Topic model:

```
$ ruby script/generate scaffold_resource Topic
```

```
      exists  app/models/
      exists  app/controllers/
      exists  app/helpers/
      create  app/views/topics
...
      create  db/migrate/009_create_topics.rb
       route  map.resources :topics
```

and finally, the Post model:

```
$ ruby script/generate scaffold_resource Post
```

```
      exists  app/models/
      exists  app/controllers/
      exists  app/helpers/
      create  app/views/posts
...
      create  db/migrate/010_create_posts.rb
       route  map.resources :posts
```

Model Relationships

Before working on the migration scripts, we should work on the model files to make sure that we have the necessary database fields to support the relationships among the models.

First, open the model file forum.rb, and add the relationship statements as shown in Listing 5-1.

Listing 5-1. *The Forum Model File*

```
class Forum < ActiveRecord::Base
  has_many :topics, :dependent => :delete_all
  has_many :posts, :through => :topics
end
```

This model uses a relationship that you might not have encountered before—has_many :through. This specifies an intermediate object that sits between one object and another. In this case, it allows us to access all of the posts in a forum, irrespective of the topic.

You will also notice that the has_many :topics statement includes an extra parameter that states what should happen to dependent objects should this object be deleted. In this case, we want all dependents of this object to be deleted, meaning that if you delete a forum, all the topics in that forum will be deleted.

Add the relationships for the topic.rb model as shown in Listing 5-2.

Listing 5-2. *The Topic Model File*

```
class Topic < ActiveRecord::Base
  belongs_to :forum, :counter_cache => true
  belongs_to :user
  has_many :posts, :dependent => :delete_all
end
```

You will notice that here we are setting up the counter cache described earlier.

This model also declares that all dependents should be deleted in the case of this object being deleted, in the same way as the forum deletes the dependent topics if it is deleted. Now, if a forum is deleted, all of the topics and all the posts within those topics will be deleted, keeping the database clean.

Finally, add the relationships for the post.rb model as shown in Listing 5-3.

Listing 5-3. *The Post Model File*

```
class Post < ActiveRecord::Base
  belongs_to :topic, :counter_cache => true
  belongs_to :user, :counter_cache => true
end
```

There should be no surprises here. Again, this model uses a counter cache, this time for the number of posts in a given topic. This means that a posts_count integer field needs to be added to the topics database table.

This also adds a counter cache to the User model. This will allow the application to easily display and cache the number of posts made in the forum by a particular user.

Model Validations

Since we are already working on the models, we should add some basic validations to them.

The Forum model has two attributes that we should validate: name and description. The name field must be filled in; having a forum with an empty name is not helpful. We will also set a maximum of 255 characters for this field, enabling us to use a database string type rather than a text type. The forum names should be a short title, not a lengthy description.

The description field obviously needs to be longer but should still be kept within sensible limits. Also, some sites may decide not to fill in the description field; the name may be enough. Therefore, we do not have to test for the presence of this field.

To perform these validations, add the following to the forum.rb model file:

```
validates_presence_of :name
validates_length_of :name, :maximum => 255
validates_length_of :description, :maximum => 1000
```

For the Topic model, there is only one field that we need to validate—the name field. Since this is intended to be a simple description of the topic in discussion, it makes sense to keep this reasonably short. We will use a database string type, so we should validate that the text entered is 255 characters or less.

Also, we want each topic to have a name; having a blank topic name isn't useful to anyone visiting the site, so we will check that the field is not empty.

Edit the `topic.rb` model file, and add the following validations:

```
validates_presence_of :name
validates_length_of :name, :maximum => 255
```

The Post model also has only one field that is entered by a user and needs to be validated: the body field.

Since this is the actual meat of the discussion, we don't want to limit the size of the post too much. However, it is a good idea to place some limit on the size, albeit a high one. Again, we don't want this field to be empty.

Add the validations to the `post.rb` model file:

```
validates_presence_of :body
validates_length_of :body, :maximum => 10000
```

Migration Scripts

We can now build the migration scripts for these models. Edit the `self.up` method in the `008_create_forums.rb` file to simply create the necessary fields as follows:

```
def self.up
  create_table :forums do |t|
    t.column :name, :string
    t.column :description, :text
    t.column :created_at, :datetime
    t.column :updated_at, :datetime
    t.column :topics_count, :integer, :null => false, :default => 0
  end
end
```

The `009_create_topics.rb` migration file adds the necessary files along with adding a database index for this `forum_id` field. This will speed up the database queries for retrieving the list of topics in a given forum. Edit the `self.up` method as shown:

```
def self.up
  create_table :topics do |t|
    t.column :forum_id, :integer
    t.column :user_id, :integer
    t.column :name, :string
    t.column :created_at, :datetime
    t.column :updated_at, :datetime
    t.column :posts_count, :integer, :null => false, :default => 0
  end
  add_index :topics, :forum_id
end
```

Edit the `self.up` method in the `010_create_posts.rb` file to add the fields necessary for the posts table. Again, this creates a database index to speed up the database queries.

```
def self.up
  create_table :posts do |t|
    t.column :topic_id, :integer
    t.column :user_id, :integer
    t.column :body, :text
    t.column :created_at, :datetime
    t.column :updated_at, :datetime
  end
  add_index :posts, :topic_id
end
```

We also want to cache the number of posts by a given user. To do this, the users table will need to be modified and a posts_count integer field added to it; create a migration for this:

```
$ ruby script/generate migration AddUserPostsCount
```

```
    exists  db/migrate
    create  db/migrate/011_add_user_posts_count.rb
```

Edit the migration file to add the necessary up and down methods to add or remove the column as shown in Listing 5-4.

Listing 5-4. *Migration to Add a Posts Counter Cache to the Users Model*

```
class AddUserPostsCount < ActiveRecord::Migration
  def self.up
    add_column :users, :posts_count, :integer, :null => false, :default => 0
  end

  def self.down
    remove_column :users, :posts_count
  end
end
```

Before you run the migrations, we should create the new role called Moderator, and add this role to the roles of the Admin user. Of course, you can add the role to any other users that you wish to give forum moderator permissions.

Create a new migration script with the following command:

```
$ ruby script/generate migration AddModeratorRole
```

```
    exists  db/migrate
    create  db/migrate/012_add_moderator_role.rb
```

Edit the generator migration script as shown in Listing 5-5.

Listing 5-5. *Migration to Add the Moderator Role*

```
class AddModeratorRole < ActiveRecord::Migration
  def self.up
    moderator_role = Role.create(:name => 'Moderator')
    admin_user = User.find_by_username('Admin')
    admin_user.roles << moderator_role
  end

  def self.down
    moderator_role = Role.find_by_name('Moderator')
    admin_user = User.find_by_username('Admin')
    admin_user.roles.delete(moderator_role)
    moderator_role.destroy
  end
end
```

As in the previous chapter, this simply creates a new role, finds the existing user with the username Admin, and adds the new role to this user's list of roles.

You should now run these migrations, creating the database tables necessary for the forum:

```
$ rake db:migrate
```

```
(in /Users/alan/Projects/rails/railscoders)
== CreateForums: migrating ======================================================
-- create_table(:forums)
   -> 0.0105s
== CreateForums: migrated (0.0112s) =============================================

== CreateTopics: migrating ======================================================
-- create_table(:topics)
   -> 0.4358s
-- add_index(:topics, :forum_id)
   -> 0.2001s
== CreateTopics: migrated (0.6372s) =============================================

== CreatePosts: migrating =======================================================
-- create_table(:posts)
   -> 0.0743s
-- add_index(:posts, :topic_id)
   -> 0.0178s
== CreatePosts: migrated (0.0934s) ==============================================

== AddUserPostsCount: migrating =================================================
-- add_column(:users, :posts_count, :integer, {:default=>0, :null=>false})
   -> 0.1475s
== AddUserPostsCount: migrated (0.1481s) ========================================
```

```
== AddModeratorRole: migrating ===================================================
== AddModeratorRole: migrated (0.2128s) =========================================
```

Checking a User's Roles for Moderator Rights

First of all, we should add code to allow us to easily check if a user has moderator access, in the same way as we did for the administrator and editor roles.

Open the `lib/login_system.rb` module, and add the `check_moderator_role` method before the private methods:

```
def check_moderator_role
  check_role('Moderator')
end
```

This allows you to simply add `before_filter :check_moderator_role` for any controllers or actions that should be protected from unauthorized users.

Adding the Nested Resource Route Mappings

Before we work on the code, we should add the URL mappings to the `config/routes.rb` file.

You will notice that the generation script added basic resource mappings for forums, topics, and posts. However, for the forums, we are going to use nested routes: posts belong to a topic, and topics belong to a forum. Remove the following automatically generated resource mappings from the routes file:

```
map.resources :topics
map.resources :forums
map.resources :posts
```

Replace them with the nested routes for the resources:

```
map.resources :forums do |forum|
  forum.resources :topics do |topic|
    topic.resources :posts
  end
end
```

This tells Rails the structure of the resources in relation to their URLs. This means that you cannot reference a post simply with /post/<id>; it must be accessed with /forum/<forum_id>/topics/<topic_id>/posts/<post_id>.

Modifying the Layout Template and Style Sheet

By modifying the default templates and adding some simple markup to our style sheet, we can improve the look of our forum and make the pages much easier to read and follow. The styles can be changed and improved later, but adding some sensible defaults makes our lives a little easier.

Removing the Generated Layouts

Take a look in the /app/views/layouts directory. You will notice that the generate command has created layout files called forums.rhtml, posts.rhtml, and topics.rhtml, corresponding to the resources that were scaffolded.

Rails will automatically use a layout file matching the name of the controller if one is present. Since we are using a common layout file for our application, you should remove these files, leaving just the application.rhtml layout file that you created.

Adding CSS for the Forum Tables

All of the forums data is displayed using HTML tables. We can greatly improve the look of the default tables by adding some table styling to our CSS file.

Open the public/stylesheets/main.css file, and add the styles for the forum tables:

```
/* Forum styling */

table#forums { width: 100%; background-color: #fff; border: 1px solid #c33; }
table#forums td.name  { width: 60% }
table#forums td.topic { width: 20%; text-align: center; }

table#topics { width: 100%; background-color: #fff; border: 1px solid #000; }
table#topics td.name   { width: 60% }
table#topics td.reply  { width: 20%; text-align: center; }
table#topics td.author { width: 20%; text-align: center; }

table#posts { width: 100%; background-color: #fff; border: 1px solid #000; }
table#posts td.author { width: 20%; vertical-align: top; }
table#posts td.body   { width: 80% }

.forumname { font-size: 1.1em; }
.forumdescription { font-size: 0.7em; padding-top: 0.4em; }
```

The Forums Controller and Views

Now it is time to work on the action methods. Because the controllers were created with the scaffold_resource generation script, they are already prepopulated with code to provide basic REST services. If you open the controllers and take a look at the generated code, you will see that it is similar to the code that you wrote for all of the existing REST resource controller files. We can now use this as a basis for our forum.

The top level of the forum feature, the forums resource, does not require many changes. Most of the actions already work as we want them with the generated code. However, there are a few changes that should be made and the views need to be modified to suit our needs.

The Forum Index Action

The generated index action method for the forums controller just retrieves all of the forum objects. Since we want to display all of the forums on the forum index page, we do not have to change this.

The Forum Index Page

Open the generated app/views/forums/index.rhtml. While this provides a simple table of the forum data, we want to improve on this, adding extra information and formatting. Also, we do not want the Create New Forum, Edit Forum, or Delete Forum links being available to nonmoderator users.

The new index.rhtml is shown in Listing 5-6.

Listing 5-6. *The Forum Index View*

```
<h2>Forums</h2>

<% if is_logged_in? and logged_in_user.has_role?('Moderator') %>
  <p><%= link_to 'Create New Forum', new_forum_path -%></p>
<% end %>

<table id="forums">
  <tr>
    <th class="name">Forum name</th>
    <th class="topic">Topics</th>
  </tr>
  <% @forums.each do |forum| -%>
  <tr class="<%= cycle('odd', 'even') %>">
    <td class="name">
      <div class="forumname">
        <%= link_to forum.name, topics_path(:forum_id => forum) -%>
      </div>

      <div class="forumdescription">
        <%= forum.description -%>
      </div>

      <% if is_logged_in? and logged_in_user.has_role?('Moderator') -%>
        <br />
        <small>
          <%= link_to 'edit', edit_forum_path(forum) %>
          <%= link_to 'delete', forum_path(forum), :method => :delete,
                :confirm => 'Are you sure? This will delete this entire forum.' -%>
        </small>
      <% end -%>
    </td>
    <td class="topic"><%= forum.topics_count %></td>
  </tr>
  <% end -%>
</table>
```

This view makes the table view a little more interesting by adding classes to the table cells, allowing us to use CSS to style the table. The class of the table row uses the cycle helper to alternate between rows with the classes odd and even, allowing us to style alternating table rows with different colors or backgrounds to make the table a little easier to read.

The Create New Forum, Edit Forum, and Delete Forum links are shown only for users with moderator permissions by using the has_role method of the user object. The view also shows the number of topics within each forum using the topics_count counter cache attribute that is defined in the model.

The Show Action

In our design, the topics are subsets of a forum, and posts are subsets of a topic. This means that if you request a forum, the list of topics should be returned rather than just the details of the forum. Using the generated response would just display the name and description of a forum, rather than the topics within that forum. To show the topics, we can just forward the request of one particular forum to the topics path for that forum. The URL /forums/4 would be forwarded to /forums/4/topics.

We should do the same for any requests for a specific topic, forwarding the request to the list of posts for that topic. The URL /forums/4/topics/3 becomes /forums/4/topics/3/posts.

Open app/controllers/forums_controller.rb. To forward the show request as described previously, change the show method as follows:

```
def show
  redirect_to topics_path(:forum_id => params[:id])
end
```

Since this means that the app/views/forums/show.rhtml view file will not be used, you can delete this file.

Creating a New Forum

When a moderator creates a new forum, we should redirect the moderator back to the list of forums rather than going to the topic list view that will be empty. To do this, alter the create method in the forums_controller.rb file, and change the redirect on a successful create action:

```
def create
  ...
  if @forum.save
    flash[:notice] = 'Forum was successfully created.'
    format.html { redirect_to forums_path }
    format.xml  { head :created, :location => forum_path(@forum) }
  else
  ...
end
```

The Forum New and Edit Pages

Both the new.rhtml and edit.rhtml pages can be viewed only by moderator users, and both of the pages contain almost the same form. We can place the common parts of the form into a partial and include that partial in both the new and edit pages.

To do this, first create a new partial file app/views/forums/_form.rhtml, and add the inner code for a form:

```
<p>Forum Name:<br /><%= f.text_field :name, :size => 40 -%></p>
<p>Description:<br /><%= f.text_area :description, :rows => 4, :cols => 60 -%></p>
```

Next, edit the app/views/forums/new.rhtml file, add the code to create the form, and render the form partial by creating a form_for block and passing the form object to the partial. The new.rhtml page is shown in Listing 5-7.

Listing 5-7. *The Forum New View*

```
<h2>New forum</h2>
<%= error_messages_for :forum %>
<% form_for(:forum, :url => forums_path) do |f| %>
  <%= render :partial => 'form', :locals => {:f => f} -%>
  <%= submit_tag "Create" %>
<% end %>
<%= link_to 'Back', forums_path %>
```

The edit.rhtml page is almost the same, using the same way of including the form partial, except the form_for block that is created must use HTTP PUT. This is how Rails differentiates this as an object edit action rather than a create action. The new edit view is shown in Listing 5-8.

Listing 5-8. *The Forum Edit View*

```
<h2>Edit forum</h2>
<%= error_messages_for :forum %>
<% form_for(:forum,
            :url => forum_path(@forum),
            :html => { :method => :put }) do |f| %>
  <%= render :partial => 'form', :locals => {:f => f} -%>
  <%= submit_tag "Update" %>
<% end %>
<%= link_to 'Show', forum_path(@forum) %> |
<%= link_to 'Back', forums_path %>
```

Creating forms using partials can save you a lot of time if you have large forms. Keeping the form in a separate file also means that if the form is changed, you only have to change one file rather than two.

The Delete Forum Action

If the moderator chooses to delete an entire forum, the destroy action is invoked. Since the generated action does just this, we can leave it exactly as it is.

Manually Testing the Forums Controller

You can now start the Rails server and try creating a new forum. Of course, you will have to log in as the Admin user to see the create, edit, and delete links. Remember that in the migrations we gave the Admin user the moderator role.

After you have logged in as Admin, go to http://localhost:3000/forums/new. Try creating a new forum and saving it. You will be returned to the list of available forums, as shown in Figure 5-2.

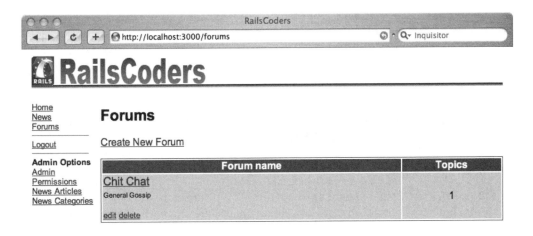

Figure 5-2. *The forum index action showing the list of available forums*

The Topics Controller and Views

We now need to develop the next level of the forum data—the topics. As we stated in the specifications, each topic belongs to a specific Forum object. When a forum is selected, the topics in this forum are listed, and new topics can be created by users of the site.

The Topic Index Action

The generated topics index action currently just retrieves all topics. Since we want to see topics only for a given forum, we need to change this behavior. Also, since the number of topics is likely to be large, we should paginate the topic list. To do this, we will use the Rails paginator helper as we did in Chapter 4.

Open the topics controller file, `app/controllers/topics_controller.rb`, and change the index action as follows:

```
def index
  @forum = Forum.find(params[:forum_id])
  @topics_pages, @topics = paginate(:topics,
      :include => :user,
      :conditions => ['forum_id = ?', @forum],
      :order => 'topics.updated_at DESC')

  respond_to do |format|
    format.html # index.rhtml
    format.xml  { render :xml => @topics.to_xml }
  end
end
```

As you can see, this first retrieves the `forum` object and uses the `paginate` helper to create `@topics_pages` and `@topics`, which will be passed to the view.

The Topic Index Page

The topic index is a list of topics for a given forum. This is similar in structure and markup to the forum index, except that obviously the table columns are different. The option to create a new topic is available to all logged-in users, not just moderators. If a user isn't logged in, a link to the login page is shown instead of the Create New Topic link.

Each topic in the table should also show edit and delete links for moderator users. The delete link should ask for the moderator to confirm that he or she wishes to delete the entire topic.

The `app/views/topics/index.rhtml` page should be edited as shown in Listing 5-9.

Listing 5-9. *The Topic Index View*

```
<h2>Forum : <%= @forum.name -%></h2>

<h3>Topics</h3>

<p>
<% if is_logged_in? -%>
  <%= link_to 'Post New Topic', new_topic_path(:forum_id => @forum) -%>
<% else -%>
  <%= link_to 'Login to post a new topic', :controller => 'account',
                                           :action => 'login' -%>
<% end -%>
</p>

<% if @topics_pages.page_count > 1 %>
  <p class="pagination">Pages: <strong>
    <%= pagination_links @topics_pages, :params => params %>
  </strong></p>
<% end %>
```

```
<table id="topics">
  <tr>
    <th class="name">Topics</th>
    <th class="reply">Posts</th>
    <th class="author">Author</th>
  </tr>
  <% @topics.each do |topic| -%>
    <tr class="<%= cycle('odd', 'even') %>">
      <td class="name">
        <%= link_to topic.name, posts_path(:forum_id => @forum,
                                          :topic_id => topic) -%>
      <% if is_logged_in? and logged_in_user.has_role?('moderator') -%>
        <br />
        <small>
          <%= link_to 'delete', topic_path(:forum_id => @forum,      :id => topic),
                 :method => :delete,
                 :confirm => 'Are you sure? This will delete this entire topic.' -%>
          <%= link_to 'edit', edit_topic_path(:forum_id => @forum, :id => topic) -%>
        </small>
      <% end -%>
      </td>
      <td class="reply"><%= topic.posts_count %></td>
      <td class="author"><%= link_to topic.user.username,
                            user_path(:id => topic.user) %></td>
    </tr>
  <% end -%>
</table>

<% if @topics_pages.page_count > 1 %>
  <p class="pagination">Pages: <strong>
    <%= pagination_links @topics_pages, :params => params %>
  </strong></p>
<% end %>
```

As you can see, each topic is linked to the show action for a given topic. The posts_count cache is used to display the number of posts without having to perform another database query.

Creating a New Topic

All logged-in users are allowed to create new topics. In our forum, a topic cannot exist without any posts belonging to it. Therefore, we must change the behavior of the topics' create action, so that creating a new topic creates a first post too. This stops empty topics appearing on the site and improves the usability—when the users create new topics, it's almost certain that they will want to create posts about those topics.

Take a look at the existing new and create actions in the topics_controller.rb file. At the moment, they simply create a new topic without specifying a forum that the topic belongs to, and obviously, create does not create a post for the topic.

Change the new method to instantiate a post object as well as a topic object:

```
def new
  @topic = Topic.new
  @post = Post.new
end
```

The view file for this method needs to allow the user to enter a topic name and a message. Edit the app/views/topics/new.rhtml file as shown in Listing 5-10.

Listing 5-10. *The New Topic View*

```
<h2>New Topic</h2>
<% form_for :topic, :url => topics_path do |f| -%>
  <p>Subject:<br /><%= f.text_field :name, :size => 40 -%></p>
  <p>First Post:<br /><%= text_area :post, :body, :rows => 8, :cols => 60 -%></p>
  <%= submit_tag 'Save' %>
<% end -%>
```

You will notice that the post body field is specified using a regular text_area helper, rather than the form block f. Even though the form is a new topic form and will be posted to the topic controller, we can still add fields for other objects.

Now take a look at the following create method that this form will be posted to. As discussed, this method creates not only a new topic but also a new post belonging to this topic. We also need to make sure that the topic is created with the relevant forum_id filled in from the parameter passed to the action via the URL.

```
def create
  @topic = Topic.new(:name => params[:topic][:name],
                     :forum_id => params[:forum_id],
                     :user_id => logged_in_user.id)
  @topic.save!
  @post = Post.new(:body => params[:post][:body],
                   :topic_id => @topic.id,
                   :user_id => logged_in_user.id)
  @post.save!
  respond_to do |format|
    format.html { redirect_to posts_path(:topic_id => @topic,
      :forum_id => @topic.forum.id) }
    format.xml  { head :created, :location => topic_path(:id => @topic,
      :forum_id => @topic.forum.id) }
  end
rescue ActiveRecord::RecordInvalid
  respond_to do |format|
    format.html { render :action => 'new' }
    format.xml  { render :xml => @post.errors.to_xml }
  end
end
```

As you can see, the topic and post are both created with the user_id of the logged-in user and the relevant forum and topic ids. If either of the objects is reported as invalid by ActiveRecord, this will be caught by the rescue exception handler, and the new view will be re-rendered with the appropriate error messages, or an XML error message will be returned.

If there is no problem, the user is either redirected to the list of posts for this new topic or the relevant XML response is sent.

Editing a Topic

Editing a topic can be performed only by a moderator user and allows only the topic name to be changed. The generated code is almost what we need; we just need to change a few things for it to work exactly as we want.

First of all, edit the topics_controller.rb file to change the redirection on a successful topic update. Because we are using nested routes, we need to include the forum id as part of the redirection and change it to show the list of posts, as follows:

```
def update
  @topic = Topic.find(params[:id])

  respond_to do |format|
  if @topic.update_attributes(params[:topic])
    flash[:notice] = 'Topic was successfully updated.'
    format.html { redirect_to posts_path(:topic_id => @topic,
                                :forum_id => @topic.forum) }
    format.xml  { head :ok }
  else
      format.html { render :action => "edit" }
      format.xml  { render :xml => @topic.errors.to_xml }
    end
  end
end
```

We also need to edit the app/views/topics/edit.rhtml topic view file to add the field that we want to allow to be edited. Also, the URL that the edit form posts to needs to be amended to include the forum id along with the topic id that is being edited. Edit the form section of the file to match the following:

```
<h1>Editing topic</h1>

<%= error_messages_for :topic %>

<% form_for(:topic, :url => topic_path(:id => @topic, :forum_id => @topic.forum),
          :html => { :method => :put }) do |f| %>
  <p>Subject:<br /><%= f.text_field :name, :size => 40 -%></p>
  <p>
    <%= submit_tag "Update" %>
  </p>
<% end %>
```

Deleting a Topic

The autogenerated `destroy` action simply destroys a given topic. We could just destroy the topic, which would automatically delete all the posts within this topic because of the dependency `delete_all` statement in the Topic model. However, since we are using a counter cache to keep track of the number of posts by a given user, we need to delete each post in turn. This isn't the most efficient method, but since deleting a topic is something that is going to be performed seldom and only by a moderator, it is acceptable.

Also, currently the method redirects to `topics_path` but does not specify the forum id. We need to change this and add the `forum_id` parameter to the redirection, as follows:

```
def destroy
  @topic = Topic.find(params[:id])
  @topic.posts.each { |post| post.destroy }
  @topic.destroy

  respond_to do |format|
    format.html { redirect_to topics_path(
                    :forum_id => params[:forum_id]) }
    format.xml  { head :ok }
  end
end
```

The Topic Show Action

We should also edit the `show` action to redirect the browser to the `index` action of the posts controller. Edit the `show` action of the `topics_controller` file as follows:

```
def show
  redirect_to posts_path(:forum_id => params[:forum_id], :topic_id => params[:id])
end
```

The Posts Controller and Views

All that is left is to adapt the posts controller code to work with the forum and topics.

The Posts Index Page

The posts `index` method lists all of the posts in a given topic. This requires us to change the `index` action to find the current topic and then retrieve all the posts within this topic, along with paginating the posts. We will use the default value of ten posts per page.

Edit the `app/controllers/posts_controller.rb` file, changing the `index` action as follows:

```
def index
  @topic = Topic.find(params[:topic_id], :include => :forum)
  @posts_pages, @posts = paginate(:posts,
      :include => :user,
      :conditions => ['topic_id = ?', @topic])
```

```
  respond_to do |format|
    format.html # index.rhtml
    format.xml  { render :xml => @posts.to_xml }
  end
end
```

Because of the extra find parameter :include => :user, ActiveRecord automatically joins the posts and users tables in one SQL query. Since we would otherwise have to perform a query to display the username of each post author, this greatly reduces the amount of database requests needed.

The posts index.rhtml file is again similar to the previous controllers' index files. We just want to display each post along with the author's username, the date they joined the site, and the number of posts that user has made.

Edit app/views/posts/index.rhtml, replacing the autogenerated view with the view code shown in Listing 5-11.

Listing 5-11. *The Posts Index View*

```
<h2><%= @topic.name -%></h2>

<h3>
  <%= link_to 'Forums', forums_path -%> >
  <%= link_to @topic.forum.name, forum_path(@topic.forum) -%> >
  <%= @topic.name -%>
</h3>

<p>
<% if is_logged_in? -%>
  <%= link_to 'Post Reply', new_post_path(:forum_id => @topic.forum,
                                          :topic_id => @topic) -%>
<% else -%>
  <%= link_to 'Login to post a reply', :controller => 'account',
                                       :action => 'login' -%>
<% end -%>
</p>

<% if @posts_pages.page_count > 1 %>
  <p class="pagination">Pages: <strong>
    <%= pagination_links @posts_pages, :params => params %>
  </strong></p>
<% end %>

<table id="posts">
  <tr>
    <th class="author">Author</th>
    <th class="post">Message</th>
  </tr>
  <% @posts.each do |post| -%>
```

```
    <tr class="<%= cycle('odd', 'even') %>">
      <td class="author">
        <%= link_to  post.user.username, user_path(post.user) -%><br />
        <small>
          Member since <%= post.user.created_at.to_s(:short) %><br />
          <%= pluralize(post.user.posts_count, 'post') -%>
        </small>
        <% if is_logged_in? and logged_in_user.has_role?('Moderator') -%>
          <br />
          <small>
            <%= link_to 'Edit', edit_post_path(:id => post,
                  :topic_id => @topic, :forum_id => @topic.forum) -%>
          <br />
            <%= link_to 'Delete', post_path(:id => post, :topic_id => @topic,
                  :forum_id => @topic.forum), :method => :delete,
                  :confirm => 'Are you sure you wish to delete this post?' -%>
          </small>
        <% end -%>
      </td>
      <td class="post"><%= textilize(post.body) -%></td>
    </tr>
  <% end -%>
</table>

<% if @posts_pages.page_count > 1 %>
  <p class="pagination">Pages: <strong>
    <%= pagination_links @posts_pages, :params => params %>
  </strong></p>
<% end %>
```

Creating a New Post

Creating a new post that is simply a reply to an existing topic is similar to the previous create topic method, except that we retrieve a topic and then add a new post to it. Again, we need to make sure that the currently logged-in user's id is saved with the post.

We also need to change the redirection targets, showing the list of posts for the current topic and forum on a successful post create. The XML response to post creation is simply the new post data, not the list of topics, so this can be left unchanged.

Open the app/controllers/posts_controller.rb file, and edit the create method as follows:

```
def create
  @topic = Topic.find(params[:topic_id])
  @post = Post.new(:body => params[:post][:body],
                   :topic_id => @topic.id,
                   :user_id => logged_in_user.id)
```

```
  respond_to do |format|
    if @post.save
      flash[:notice] = 'Post was successfully created.'
      format.html { redirect_to posts_path(:forum_id => @topic.forum_id,
                                            :topic_id => @topic) }
      format.xml  { head :created, :location => post_path(@post) }
    else
      format.html { render :action => "new" }
      format.xml  { render :xml => @post.errors.to_xml }
    end
  end
end
```

The view for the Create New Post action is a very simple form with a text_area for the post body. The form is sent to the posts_path with the relevant forum_id and topic_id.

Edit app/views/posts/new.rhtml to replace the generated form with the code in Listing 5-12.

Listing 5-12. *The New Post View*

```
<h2>New Post</h2>
<%= error_messages_for :post -%>

<h3>Topic: <%= @topic.name %></h3>

<% form_for :post, :url => posts_path(:forum_id => @topic.forum,
                                      :topic_id => @topic) do |f| -%>
  <p>Message:<br /><%= f.text_area :body, :rows => 8, :cols => 60 -%></p>
  <%= submit_tag 'Save' -%> or
  <%= link_to 'Cancel', topics_path(:id => @topic, :forum_id => @topic.forum) -%>
<% end -%>
```

Since this form expects the current topic object to be available as @topic, we need to edit the new method in posts_controller.rb to retrieve the specified topic:

```
def new
  @topic = Topic.find(params[:topic_id], :include => :forum)
  @post = Post.new
end
```

By including the forum in the Topic.find method, we save an extra query to the database when the new post form uses the forum variable.

Editing a Post

The edit post form is very similar to the new post form. We need to change posts_controller.rb to also include the topic and forum data when it retrieves the post to be edited, reducing the number of database queries.

Change the edit method as follows:

```
def edit
  @post = Post.find(params[:id], :include => { :topic => :forum })
end
```

The post edit view is similar to the new post form, except that the post URL is different, as it's sending the data as an HTTP PUT to the individual post URL. Edit the view at app/views/posts/edit.rhtml by replacing the generated form with the code in Listing 5-13.

Listing 5-13. *The Edit Post View*

```
<h2>Edit Post</h2>
<%= error_messages_for :post -%>
<h3>Topic: <%= @post.topic.name %></h3>
<% form_for :post, :url => post_path(:id => @post, :topic_id => @post.topic,
                                     :forum_id => @post.topic.forum),
                   :html => {:method => :put} do |f| -%>
  <p>Message:<br /><%= f.text_area :body, :rows => 8, :cols => 60 -%></p>
  <%= submit_tag 'Save' -%> or
  <%= link_to 'Cancel', topics_path(:id => @post.topic,
                                    :forum_id => @post.topic.forum) -%>
<% end -%>
```

The update method of the controller needs to be changed to include the forum id and topic id for the redirect to the list of posts.

Edit the update method of the posts_controller.rb file:

```
def update
  @post = Post.find(params[:id])

  respond_to do |format|
    if @post.update_attributes(params[:post])
      flash[:notice] = 'Post was successfully updated.'
      format.html { redirect_to posts_path(
                    :forum_id => params[:forum_id],
                    :topic_id => params[:topic_id]) }
      format.xml  { head :ok }
    else
      format.html { render :action => "edit" }
      format.xml  { render :xml => @post.errors.to_xml }
    end
  end
end
```

Deleting a Post

The destroy action for a post does exactly what we need; it simply destroys a given post. However, we still need to change the redirection path to include the forum_id and topic_id.

Edit the successful redirection for the destroy method of posts_controller.rb:

```
def destroy
  @post = Post.find(params[:id])
  @post.destroy

  respond_to do |format|
    format.html { redirect_to posts_path(:forum_id => params[:forum_id],
                  :topic_id => params[:topic_id]) }
    format.xml  { head :ok }
  end
end
```

Adding a Link to the Sidebar Menu

We should also add a direct link to the forums from the RailsCoders sidebar menu. Open the menu partial file, app/views/layouts/_menu.rhtml, and add the forum link as follows:

```
<ul>
  <li><%= link_to 'Home', index_url %></li>
  <li><%= link_to 'News', articles_path %></li>
  <li><%= link_to 'Forums', forums_path %></li>

  <li><hr size="1" width="90%" align="left"/></li>

  <% if is_logged_in? %>
  ...
```

Testing the Topics and Posts

You can now try manually testing the forum with your browser. Go to the forums index at http://localhost:3000/forums or by clicking the Forums link in the sidebar menu. You can now click the forum that you created earlier to see the list of topics. Obviously, this list is empty at the moment, so you should try creating a new topic and making sure that a new topic is created with a first post.

After creating the topic, you will be redirected to the list of posts within this topic. Try replying to this topic to make sure that you can add new posts to a topic.

The result of creating a new topic and adding another post is shown in Figure 5-3.

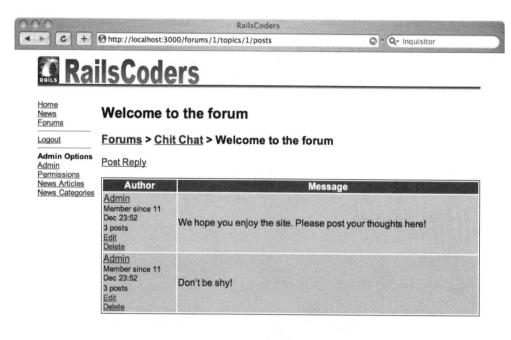

Figure 5-3. *The posts index action, showing the list of posts for a topic*

Restricting Actions to Moderators

At the moment, all users can perform all the actions, including destructive ones, because even if the links aren't shown on the page, users can still access the destructive actions by entering the correct URL. Obviously, this is not good, so we should add a before filter to make sure that only moderator users can create, edit, and delete forums.

Add the before filter at the top of the `forums_controller.rb`, specifying that regular users can run only the `index` and `show` methods:

```
class ForumsController < ApplicationController
  before_filter :check_moderator_role, :except => [:index, :show]
  ...
```

For the topics controller, we should ensure that a user is logged in to create a new topic and that only moderators can edit or destroy topics. Add the following before filters to the `topics_controller.rb` file:

```
class TopicsController < ApplicationController
  before_filter :check_moderator_role,
                :only => [:destroy, :edit, :update]
  before_filter :login_required, :except => [:index, :show]
  ...
```

The same permissions should be used for creating, editing, and destroying posts. Add the before filters to `posts_controller.rb`:

```
class PostsController < ApplicationController
  before_filter :check_moderator_role,
                :only => [:destroy, :edit, :update]
  before_filter :login_required, :except => [:index, :show]

  # GET /posts
  # GET /posts.xml
  def index
  ...
```

Testing the Forum

The `scaffold_resource` generator also creates a selection of functional tests for you. If you take a look in the `tests/functional/` directory, you will see `forums_controller_test.rb`, `topics_controller_test.rb`, and `posts_controller_test.rb`. These would be fine for testing a simple resource, but since we have made these actions require an authenticated user and created nested resources, the default tests will not work.

Before you write any tests, make sure that your test database structure is up to date. Run the following command to load the latest version of your schema into the test database:

```
$ rake db:test:prepare
```

```
(in /Users/alan/Projects/rails/railscoders)
```

Creating Test Fixtures

Before we adapt these tests to suit our code, we should first create some fixtures. We also need to add the moderator role to the `roles` fixtures along with a user who has that role.

Open `test/fixtures/roles.yml`, and add the moderator role to the end of the file:

```
moderator:
  id: 3
  name: Moderator
```

Next, open the `users` fixtures file, `test/fixtures/users.yml`, and add a moderator user:

```
moderator_user:
  id: 4
  username: moderator
  email: moderator@example.com
  hashed_password: 5994471abb01112afcc18159f6cc74b4f511b99806da59b3caf5a9c173cacfc5
  created_at: <%= 1.days.ago.to_s(:db) %>
```

Add the `moderator` role to the moderator user's permissions by adding the following to test/fixtures/roles_users.yml:

```
moderator:
  role_id: 3
  user_id: 4
```

We will now create valid fixtures for the forum, topic, and post tests. In the test/fixtures/forums.yml file, add the following fixture:

```
valid_forum:
  id: 1
  name: Forum 1
  description: Just a test forum
```

Add the following valid topic fixture to test/fixtures/topics.yml:

```
valid_topic:
  id: 1
  forum_id: 1
  user_id: 1
  name: we have a forum
  created_at: <%= 1.days.ago.to_s(:db) %>
```

Then add a post fixture to test/fixtures/posts.yml:

```
valid_post:
  id: 1
  topic_id: 1
  user_id: 1
  body: we have a forum
  created_at: <%= 1.days.ago.to_s(:db) %>
```

Creating the Functional Tests

If you take a look at the functional tests, you will see that they test all of the actions in each of the controller files. Since our application requires a moderator to be logged in to create or edit forums and topics and a regular user to create posts, we need to add code to our tests to handle basic authentication within a functional test.

When a user is logged in, we simply assign the user's id to a session variable and give the user a cookie with a reference to that session variable. Since this session variable is stored on the server, not on the client, we can simply set the relevant session variable within our functional tests to simulate a user being logged in. This is done by setting @request.session[:user] to the id of the user we wish to be logged in.

Since we're always looking for ways to make our code easier to read and understand, we can put this in the test_helper.rb file, allowing us to easily simulate the user login procedure for any test.

Open the test/test_helper.rb file. Add a helper function called login_as toward the end of the file, where the comments direct you to insert your helper methods:

```
  # Add more helper methods to be used by all tests here...
  def login_as(user)
    @request.session[:user] = users(user).id
  end
end
```

Whenever you use this in a functional test, you need to make sure that the users fixtures are loaded for that functional test file.

The Forums Functional Tests

Now take a look at the forums_controller_test.rb functional test file. The test_should_get_index test should work fine without any changes since it does not require a user to be logged in and it is the top level of our resource hierarchy and does not require any other parameters.

In order for the test_should_get_new test to work, we need to use the login_as function, since only moderators can access the new forum page.

Before we can use the login_as function, we have to ensure that the users, roles, and roles_users fixtures are loaded and available to the tests in this file. Near the top of the class, add the necessary fixtures to the forums fixtures already there:

```
class ForumsControllerTest < Test::Unit::TestCase
  fixtures :forums, :users, :roles, :roles_users
```

Now you can use the login_as method as follows:

```
def test_should_get_new
  login_as(:moderator_user)
  get :new
  assert_response :success
end
```

The login_as method identifies the moderator user by the fixture name of the user we require.

Add the same login_as(:moderator_user) statement at the top of all of the actions that require a moderator user to be logged in: test_should_create_forum, test_should_get_edit, test_should_update_forum, and test_should_destroy_forum.

We also need to update some of the tests to submit valid data. The test test_should_create_forum needs to create a valid new forum for the assertions to be valid. Also, on the successful creation of a new forum, the user is returned to the forum's index action, rather than the single forum view in the generated test. Edit the test as follows:

```
def test_should_create_forum
  login_as(:moderator_user)
  old_count = Forum.count
  post :create, :forum => { :name => 'testing',
                            :description => 'just a test'}
  assert_equal old_count+1, Forum.count
  assert_redirected_to forums_path
end
```

The test test_should_show_forum also needs to be changed to expect a different response. Our application performs a redirection to the list of topics when a user requests to view a particular forum, so we need to change the assertion. Change the test_should_show_forum test to the following:

```
def test_should_show_forum
  get :show, :id => 1
  assert_redirected_to :controller => 'topics', :action => 'index',
                       :forum_id => 1
end
```

This now tests to make sure that the user is redirected to the list of topics.

The submitted data in test_should_update_forum also needs to be changed to send valid data to the controller. Edit the test by changing the data submitted by the put command as follows:

```
def test_should_update_forum
  login_as(:moderator_user)
  put :update, :id => 1, :forum => { :name => 'testing', :description => 'a test'}
  assert_redirected_to forum_path(assigns(:forum))
end
```

Now try running these tests. From the command line, run just the functional tests for the forums controller:

```
$ ruby test/functional/forums_controller_test.rb
```

```
Loaded suite test/functional/forums_controller_test
Started
.......
Finished in 0.712121 seconds.

7 tests, 14 assertions, 0 failures, 0 errors
```

The Topics Functional Tests

You have to make sure that all the required fixtures are loaded and available for the tests to work. This time, we have to add the fixtures for the forums too.

All of the tests need to be altered since each action in the topic controller requires the forum id to be specified. We also need to add the login_as(:moderator_user) statement where it is required.

Open the topics controller's functional tests, test/functional/topics_controller_test.rb, and edit as shown in Listing 5-14.

Listing 5-14. *The Topics Controller Functional Tests*

```
require File.dirname(__FILE__) + '/../test_helper'
require 'topics_controller'

# Re-raise errors caught by the controller.
class TopicsController; def rescue_action(e) raise e end; end

class TopicsControllerTest < Test::Unit::TestCase
  fixtures :topics, :forums, :users, :roles, :roles_users

  def setup
    @controller = TopicsController.new
    @request    = ActionController::TestRequest.new
    @response   = ActionController::TestResponse.new
  end

  def test_should_get_index
    get :index, {:forum_id => 1}
    assert_response :success
    assert assigns(:topics)
  end

  def test_should_get_new
    login_as(:moderator_user)
    get :new, {:forum_id => 1}
    assert_response :success
  end

  def test_should_create_topic
    login_as(:moderator_user)
    old_count = Topic.count
    post :create, {:forum_id => 1,
                   :topic => { :name => 'a test topic' },
                   :post => { :body => 'and the message'} }
    assert_equal old_count+1, Topic.count
    assert_redirected_to posts_path(:forum_id => 1, :topic_id => assigns(:topic))
  end

  def test_should_show_topic
    get :show, { :id => 1, :forum_id => 1 }
    assert_redirected_to :controller => 'posts', :action => 'index',
                         :forum_id => 1, :topic_id => 1
    assert_redirected_to posts_path(:forum_id => 1, :topic_id => 1)
  end
```

```
  def test_should_get_edit
    login_as(:moderator_user)
    get :edit, { :id => 1, :forum_id => 1 }
    assert_response :success
  end

  def test_should_update_topic
    login_as(:moderator_user)
    put :update, {:id => 1, :forum_id => 1, :topic => { :name => 'a test' } }
    assert_redirected_to :controller => 'posts', :action => 'index',
                         :forum_id => 1, :topic_id => 1
  end

  def test_should_destroy_topic
    login_as(:moderator_user)
    old_count = Topic.count
    delete :destroy, { :id => 1, :forum_id => 1 }
    assert_equal old_count-1, Topic.count
    assert_redirected_to topics_path(:forum_id => 1)
  end
end
```

The tests test_should_get_index, test_should_get_new, and test_should_get_edit simply require the forum id to be added to the page request.

The test_should_show_topic, test_should_update_topic, and test_should_destroy_topic tests also need the forum id added to the request, but these expect different redirections than the generated tests.

If you think back to the Create New Topic page, you will remember that the create action expects not only a topic name but also the body of a post, which will become the first post in that topic. The test to create a new topic needs to make sure that a post is sent along with the topic and forum_id, as you can see from test_should_create_topic in Listing 5-14.

You should now run the tests and make sure that all the tests pass as expected:

```
$ ruby test/functional/topics_controller_test.rb
```

```
Loaded suite test/functional/topics_controller_test
Started
.......
Finished in 1.970497 seconds.

7 tests, 14 assertions, 0 failures, 0 errors
```

The Posts Controller Functional Tests

In order to perform functional tests on the posts controller, we have to make changes similar to those we made to the topics controller, since the posts resource is nested beneath the topic and forum resources. You cannot specify a post without giving the topic id and forum id.

Open the posts functional tests file, test/functional/posts_controller_test.rb. For these tests, we will add the required fixtures as for the previous functional tests, this time adding the posts fixtures.

Creating a new post requires a valid user to be logged in but does not require moderator privileges. To do this, we can use the user fixture :valid_user.

Edit the generated tests to match Listing 5-15. These tests use the necessary forum and topic ids, along with logging in the required user.

Listing 5-15. *The Posts Controller Functional Tests*

```ruby
require File.dirname(__FILE__) + '/../test_helper'
require 'posts_controller'

# Re-raise errors caught by the controller.
class PostsController; def rescue_action(e) raise e end; end

class PostsControllerTest < Test::Unit::TestCase
  fixtures :posts, :topics, :forums, :users, :roles, :roles_users

  def setup
    @controller = PostsController.new
    @request    = ActionController::TestRequest.new
    @response   = ActionController::TestResponse.new
  end

  def test_should_get_index
    get :index, {:forum_id => 1, :topic_id => 1}
    assert_response :success
    assert assigns(:posts)
  end

  def test_should_get_new
    login_as(:valid_user)
    get :new, {:forum_id => 1, :topic_id => 1}
    assert_response :success
  end

  def test_should_create_post
    login_as(:valid_user)
    old_count = Post.count
    post :create, {:forum_id => 1, :topic_id => 1,
                   :post => { :body => 'test message' } }
    assert_equal old_count+1, Post.count
    assert_redirected_to posts_path(:forum_id => 1, :topic_id => 1)
  end
```

```
  def test_should_show_post
    get :show, {:id => 1, :forum_id => 1, :topic_id => 1}
    assert_response :success
  end

  def test_should_get_edit
    login_as(:moderator_user)
    get :edit, :id => 1
    assert_response :success
  end

  def test_should_update_post
    login_as(:moderator_user)
    put :update, {:forum_id => 1, :topic_id => 1, :id => 1,
                  :post => { :body => 'test message'} }
    assert_redirected_to posts_path(:forum_id => 1, :topic_id => 1)
  end

  def test_should_destroy_post
    login_as(:moderator_user)
    old_count = Post.count
    delete :destroy, :id => 1, :forum_id => 1, :topic_id => 1
    assert_equal old_count-1, Post.count
    assert_redirected_to posts_path(:forum_id => 1, :topic_id => 1)
  end
end
```

Run the tests to ensure that they work as expected:

```
$ ruby test/functional/posts_controller_test.rb
```

```
Loaded suite test/functional/posts_controller_test
Started
.......
Finished in 2.144483 seconds.

7 tests, 13 assertions, 0 failures, 0 errors
```

Further Development of the Discussion Forum

The code in this chapter provides a working discussion forum, but you may wish to adapt it or extend it for your own needs.

If you take a look at the application logs while using the forum, you will notice that the check to see if the user is a moderator is performed for each line of the table. This involves performing two database queries. However, the result of this test is obviously going to be the same for each row of the table. Therefore, you could check to see if the user is a moderator at the top of the view file and store it in a variable. You could then reference the result throughout the view without querying the database.

You should also think about how you could add more tests to the functional tests, especially adding negative tests to ensure that a user who is not logged in cannot post a new message and that nonmoderator users cannot edit or delete topics and forums.

Since forums are targets for spammers, depending on your site, you may wish to think about adding a security feature called CAPTCHA. This ensures that the person posting a message is a real user, not a computer program, but requires the user to type the letters shown in a distorted image. Since it is somewhat difficult for a computer to interpret the image, it can catch a large portion of automated spam bots.

■**Note** There is a handy Rails plug-in called `validates_captcha` that allows you to easily add CAPTCHAs to your site. You can get the plug-in and read the documentation at `http://dev.2750flesk.com/validates_captcha`.

You may also wish to build extra moderation tools, such as allowing your moderators to quickly check the latest posts without having to look at each forum and topic in turn.

Some users may wish to subscribe to an RSS feed of a forum or topic; you could adapt the RSS code from the previous chapter to provide an RSS XML response to the forum and topic models.

Summary

In this chapter, we built a discussion forum with multiple forums for different types of discussion and moderation features allowing moderators to remove or edit posts.

To build this, we used the Rails `scaffold_resource` feature and then used the generated scaffolding code to build the forums. We looked at how the forums, topics, and posts resources can be nested and how they are related using the ActiveRecord `belongs_to` and `has_many` relationships. We also looked at how counter caches can be used to speed up your database queries.

In the next chapter, we will add user-created blogs to the system, allowing all of your users to create their own blogs and create personalized templates for their blog pages using the liquid templates plug-in.

■■■

## CHAPTER 6

Building a Blogging Engine with Web Services Support

In this chapter, we will build a blogging service for the site, allowing each user to create a blog (a reverse chronological list of journal entries). Each blog entry allows comments to be left by other members of the community. In the future, this could be extended to allow guest visitors to the site to leave comments, too.

A large number of bloggers use desktop blogging tools rather than an in-browser form, making the writing and editing of blog posts easier and faster than a web application. These desktop blogging clients use one of a number of established blog APIs. Our blog service will implement some of the features of these APIs, making it possible to use a desktop application to add blog entries.

Specifying the Blog Engine Requirements

The blogging system will allow each user to create a number of blog entries and each entry can have a number of comments. We will create two models, Entry and Comment.

Attributes common to an entire blog, such as its name and whether commenting should be enabled, will belong to the User model. A user's profile should show the three latest blog entries that a user has made, along with a direct link to the user's blog.

The Entry Model

Each blog entry will belong to a user, with each entry consisting of a title and the body text. There will be a flag defining whether the post has been published or if it is just a draft. The creation and last-update time of the entry will also be stored.

As we saw with the forum feature, we can use a counter cache to keep a record of how many objects belong to another object. In this case, since we know that each entry object can have many comments, we will use a counter cache to keep track of how many comments there are for each entry.

The database fields necessary for the entry model are shown in Table 6-1.

Table 6-1. *The Database Fields Required for the Entry Model*

Field Name	Field Type	Description
id	integer	The primary key
user_id	integer	The id of the user to whom the entry belongs
title	string	The title of the blog entry
body	text	The body text of the blog entry
comments_count	integer	The counter cache of the number of comments for this entry
created_at	datetime	The date and time this entry was created
updated_at	datetime	The date and time this entry was last updated

The Comment Model

The Comment model simply holds the details of the comments left for each blog entry. Since we only allow registered users of the site to leave comments, we simply store the user_id of the user who left the comment along with details of the comment including which entry the comment refers to, the body text, and when it was created.

The fields required for this model are shown in Table 6-2.

Table 6-2. *The Database Fields Required for the Comment Model*

Field Name	Field Type	Description
id	integer	The primary key
entry_id	integer	The id of the entry that this comment belongs to
user_id	integer	The id of the user who created this comment
body	text	The body text of the comment
created_at	datetime	The date and time that this comment was created

The User Model

We also need to update the User model to add a number of fields to support the blogging features. Users can set titles for their blogs and enable or disable commenting on their blogs. Also, we will add a counter cache to keep track of the number of entries that a user has created in the blog. The additional fields required for the existing user model are shown in Table 6-3.

Table 6-3. *The Additional Database Fields Required for the User Model*

Field Name	Field Type	Description
entries_count	integer	The counter cache of the number of entries created by this user.
blog_title	string	The title of the user's blog.
enable_comments	boolean	Are blog comments enabled or not?

The Entries Controller

The entries controller provides access to the user's blog. Since each collection of entries belongs to a specific user, this will be nested within the users resource via URLs such as /users/8/entries and /users/8/entries/12.

We will, therefore, use a standard REST-style controller. The index method will provide the standard blog view, and the show method will display a specific entry along with all comments left for that entry.

The new, create, edit, update, and destroy methods will only be accessible by the owner of the blog, allowing that user to maintain and post to the personal blog.

We will only implement the HTML-accessible version for the moment. We will not provide a REST XML interface, since we will be creating an API using one of the standardized blogging APIs.

The Comments Controller

Since the entries controller's show method will display all of the comments for a specified entry, and we do not have a requirement to just show one specific comment, we do not have to implement the index or show methods.

Also, we do not have any support to allow users to edit their comments, so we do not need the edit or update methods.

The new comment form will be displayed on the entry show view, so we do not require a new method, but we do require a create method to actually save a new comment.

We must also implement the destroy method to allow the owner of a blog to delete any comments if he or she wishes.

The Blogs Controller

To provide an entry portal to the blogs hosted by RailsCoders, we will create a blogs controller. This will implement just one method, index. This method will list the ten most recently updated blogs.

Blogging APIs

While it would be much simpler for us to define a new API for our blogging system using the RESTful resources, there are a number of established APIs used for posting to blogs; for example, Blogger, MetaWeblog, Movable Type, LiveJournal, and the Atom API. Some of these APIs have been around since the first blogging communities started.

The Blogger API was the first standardized API but is lacking in many features, so it has been mostly replaced by a combination of the MetaWeblog and Movable Type APIs. These three APIs are generally complementary, and each provides a set of method calls to add certain extra features. All three are implemented as XML-RPC (XML-Remote Procedure Call protocol) web services.

Since these APIs have been around for a number of years and are very well established, we should not define our own REST API; we'll choose, instead, to implement one or more of the existing APIs to allow existing blogging tools to work with our site's blogs.

Our site will implement a subset of the Blogger API, providing the basics of creating, editing, and publishing blog entries to the site. To do this, we will use part of Rails known as the ActiveWebService. These libraries enable us to create or use SOAP or XML-RPC web services.

Building the Blogging System

We can use the `generate` script to build scaffolding code for the resources required for the blog entries and comments. We will then build our blogging system on top of the generated code.

Before we add web service support, we should build the standard feature to be accessed through the web or via our own REST API. This is not too different from the other resources that we have built using resource scaffolding.

Generating the Blogging Scaffolding Code

Open a terminal window for your application, and run the generation script for each resource.

For the `Entry` resource, run the following:

```
$ ruby script/generate scaffold_resource Entry
```

```
     exists  app/models/
     exists  app/controllers/
     exists  app/helpers/
     create  app/views/entries
     exists  test/functional/
     exists  test/unit/
     create  app/views/entries/index.rhtml
     create  app/views/entries/show.rhtml
     create  app/views/entries/new.rhtml
     create  app/views/entries/edit.rhtml
     create  app/views/layouts/entries.rhtml
  identical  public/stylesheets/scaffold.css
     create  app/models/entry.rb
     create  app/controllers/entries_controller.rb
     create  test/functional/entries_controller_test.rb
     create  app/helpers/entries_helper.rb
     create  test/unit/entry_test.rb
     create  test/fixtures/entries.yml
     exists  db/migrate
     create  db/migrate/013_create_entries.rb
      route  map.resources :entries
```

For the comments resource, run this one:

```
$ ruby script/generate scaffold_resource Comment
```

```
     exists  app/models/
     exists  app/controllers/
     exists  app/helpers/
     create  app/views/comments
     exists  test/functional/
     exists  test/unit/
     create  app/views/comments/index.rhtml
     create  app/views/comments/show.rhtml
     create  app/views/comments/new.rhtml
     create  app/views/comments/edit.rhtml
     create  app/views/layouts/comments.rhtml
  identical  public/stylesheets/scaffold.css
     create  app/models/comment.rb
     create  app/controllers/comments_controller.rb
     create  test/functional/comments_controller_test.rb
     create  app/helpers/comments_helper.rb
     create  test/unit/comment_test.rb
     create  test/fixtures/comments.yml
     exists  db/migrate
     create  db/migrate/014_create_comments.rb
      route  map.resources :comments
```

We also need to add a migration to add the blog-specific settings— the blog title, a counter cache field for the number of entries, and a flag to set whether the user allows comments—to the User model.

Create a new migration to create these attributes in the User table:

```
$ ruby script/generate migration AddBlogSettingsToUser
```

```
     exists  db/migrate
     create  db/migrate/015_add_blog_settings_to_user.rb
```

We can also create the files for the blogs controller:

```
$ ruby script/generate controller Blogs
```

```
     exists  app/controllers/
     exists  app/helpers/
     create  app/views/blogs
     exists  test/functional/
     create  app/controllers/blogs_controller.rb
     create  test/functional/blogs_controller_test.rb
     create  app/helpers/blogs_helper.rb
```

Writing the Migrations

We can now write the database migrations to match the specification defined earlier.

The Entries Table

To edit the entries table, open db/migrate/013_create_entries.rb, and change the up method as shown in Listing 6-1.

Listing 6-1. *The Migration File to Create the Entries Table*

```
class CreateEntries < ActiveRecord::Migration
  def self.up
    create_table :entries do |t|
      t.column :user_id, :integer
      t.column :title, :string
      t.column :body, :text
      t.column :comments_count, :integer, :null => false, :default => 0
      t.column :created_at, :datetime
      t.column :updated_at, :datetime
    end
    add_index :entries, :user_id
  end

  def self.down
    drop_table :entries
  end
end
```

This provides the database fields necessary according to the feature specification. Since we will be accessing blog entries for a specific user, it is a good idea to create a database index for this table on the user_id field. This will speed up the database queries when retrieving a user's blog entries.

The Comments Table

The comments table is defined in db/migrate/014_create_comments.rb. Edit this file as shown in Listing 6-2.

Listing 6-2. *The Migration File to Create the Comments Table*

```
class CreateComments < ActiveRecord::Migration
  def self.up
    create_table :comments do |t|
      t.column :entry_id, :integer
      t.column :user_id, :integer
      t.column :guest_name, :string
      t.column :guest_email, :string
      t.column :guest_url, :string
```

```
      t.column :body, :text
      t.column :created_at, :datetime
    end
    add_index :comments, :entry_id
  end

  def self.down
    drop_table :comments
  end
end
```

Again, this migration adds an index, this time on the entry_id column. Comments will always be tied to a particular entry, so this will help speed up the database queries for retrieving comments.

The Blog Settings Migration

The settings for the blog will be stored within the User model. These columns are added through the migration db/migrate/015_add_blog_settings_to_user.rb. Open the migration file, and replace the generated code with the up and down migrations shown in Listing 6-3.

Listing 6-3. *The Migration to Add the Necessary Fields to the User Table*

```
class AddBlogSettingsToUser < ActiveRecord::Migration
  def self.up
    add_column :users, :entries_count, :integer, :null => false, :default => 0
    add_column :users, :blog_title, :string
    add_column :users, :enable_comments, :boolean, :default => true
  end

  def self.down
    remove_column :users, :entries_count
    remove_column :users, :blog_title
    remove_column :users, :enable_comments
  end
end
```

You can now run the database migration, creating the necessary tables, indexes, and additional columns by entering the following command:

```
$ rake db:migrate
```

```
== CreateEntries: migrating ====================================================
-- create_table(:entries)
   -> 0.0041s
-- add_index(:entries, :user_id)
   -> 0.1199s
== CreateEntries: migrated (0.1243s) ===========================================
```

```
== CreateComments: migrating ====================================================
-- create_table(:comments)
   -> 0.0044s
-- add_index(:comments, :entry_id)
   -> 0.0087s
== CreateComments: migrated (0.0134s) ==========================================

== AddBlogSettingsToUser: migrating ============================================
-- add_column(:users, :entries_count, :integer, {:default=>0, :null=>false})
   -> 0.0079s
-- add_column(:users, :blog_title, :string)
   -> 0.0088s
-- add_column(:users, :enable_comments, :boolean)
   -> 0.0085s
== AddBlogSettingsToUser: migrated (0.0257s) ===================================
```

The Models' Relationships and Validations

We now need to define the relationships and validations for each of the new models that we have created.

First of all, add the following has_many relationships to the list of relationships already present in the app/models/user.rb model file:

```
class User < ActiveRecord::Base
  ...
  has_and_belongs_to_many :roles
  has_many :articles
  has_many :entries
  has_many :comments
  ...
```

Now add the reciprocal relationship and the comments relationship to the app/models/entry.rb file. We can also add the validations for the title and body attributes.

```
class Entry < ActiveRecord::Base
  belongs_to :user, :counter_cache => true
  has_many :comments
  validates_length_of :title, :maximum => 255
  validates_length_of :body, :maximum => 10000
end
```

This also declares that the number of entries per user should use a counter cache.

Edit the Comment model at app/models/comment.rb, and add the relationships with the Entry and User models, along with a validation on the length of the body attribute:

```
class Comment < ActiveRecord::Base
  belongs_to :entry, :counter_cache => true
  belongs_to :user
  validates_length_of :body, :maximum => 1000
end
```

Creating the Resource Mapping

We now need to add the resource URL mappings to the routes configuration. Edit the config/
routes.rb file. You will need to delete the automatically generated map.resource statements for
entries and comments and add new mappings for both entries and comments nested under the
users resource. We also need to add the mapping for the blogs resource at the root level. These
changes are shown in Listing 6-4.

Listing 6-4. *The Mappings for the Entries, Comments, and Blogs Resources*

```
...
map.resources :pages
map.resources :blogs

map.resources :users, :member => { :enable => :put } do |users|
  users.resources :permissions
  users.resources :entries do |entry|
    entry.resources :comments
  end
end
...
```

The Blog Name Helper Method

In the migration, we defined a new field for the user model for the title or name of the blog.
When a new user signs up, this value is going to be null, so we need to make sure that we can
provide a default value to the entry views.

The simplest way to do this is to create a helper method. Since this will normally only be
used by the entry views, this should be placed in the app/helpers/entries_helper.rb file. If you
wanted the helper method to be available to all views, you should place the method in the
application_helper.rb file.

Open the entries_helper.rb file, and add a helper method called blog_title as shown in
Listing 6-5.

Listing 6-5. *The Entries Helper File*

```
module EntriesHelper
  def blog_title(user)
    user.blog_title ||= user.username
  end
end
```

This method takes a user object as a parameter and returns either the blog_title field from the database, if it is not null, or the user's username, if the blog_title field is null. The ||= in the method is simply a shorthand way of specifying this.

Adding the Blog Title to the Edit User Profile Page

To allow users to change the titles of their blogs, we need to add the blog title attribute to the edit user profile page.

Open the existing user profile, and edit the page app/views/users/edit.rhtml by adding the blog title field, as shown in Listing 6-6.

Listing 6-6. *Adding the Blog Title to the Edit User Profile Page*

```
<h2>Edit your account</h2>

<p><%= link_to 'Show my profile', user_path(@user) %></p>

<%= error_messages_for :user %>

<% form_for :user,
            :url => user_url(@user),
            :html => { :method => :put } do |f| -%>
  <p>Email:<br /><%= f.text_field :email, :size => 60 %></p>
  <p>Password:<br /><%= f.password_field :password, :size => 60 %></p>
  <p>Password Confirmation:<br />
    <%= f.password_field :password_confirmation, :size => 60 %></p>
  <p>Blog Title:<br /><%= f.text_field :blog_title, :size => 60 %></p>
  <p>Profile:<br /><%= f.text_area :profile, :rows => 6, :cols => 60 %></p>
  <%= submit_tag 'Save' %>
<% end -%>
```

We can try this out now by editing a user profile and ensuring that the new title is saved correctly.

Open a browser, and log into the application as a regular user. Click the My Profile link in the sidebar menu, and enter a title for your blog in the relevant field, as shown in Figure 6-1.

Save the changes to your profile, and check that the attribute has been changed in the database, either by checking the database using SQL, a database GUI tool, or the Rails console, as follows:

```
$ ruby script/console
```

```
Loading development environment.
```

```
>> User.find_by_username('alan').blog_title
```

```
=> "Alan's Rails Projects Blog"
```

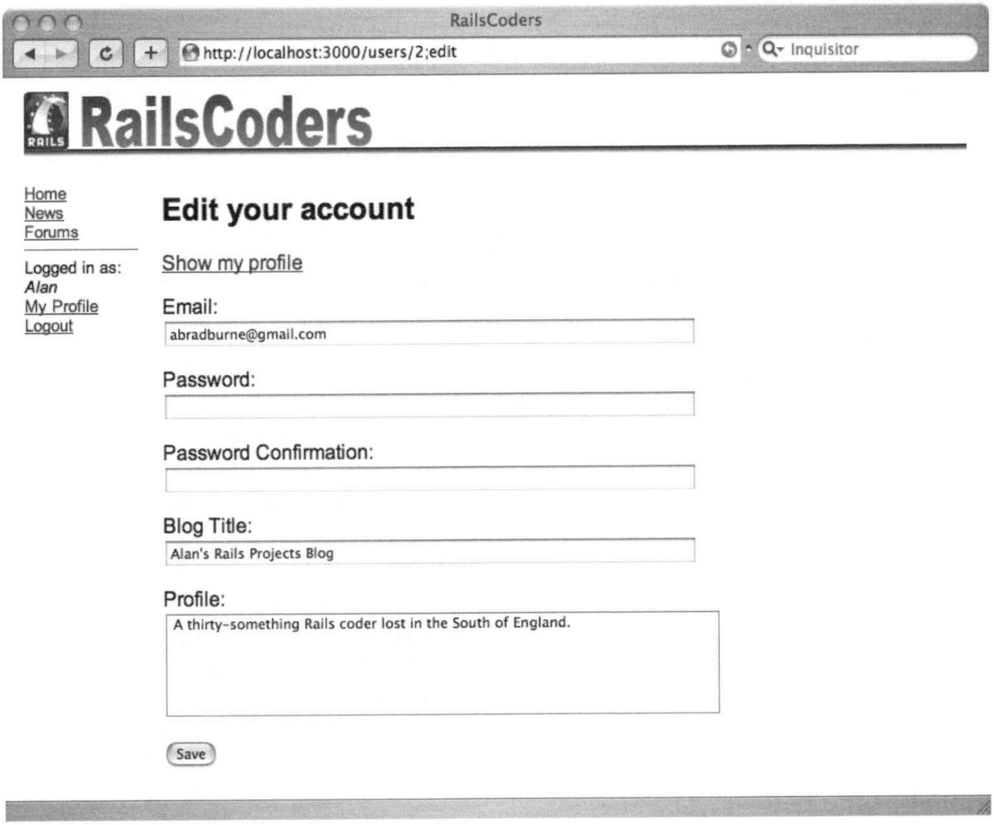

Figure 6-1. *Editing your blog title*

The Controllers and Views

Before we start thinking about the web services or custom templates, we should first build the controller code and some basic views that allow us to use the blog functionality and test that everything is working correctly. When we are happy with this, we can move on to building the web services feature.

Removing the Generated Layouts

First, delete the automatically generated layout templates. As you saw in the previous chapter, they allow you to define a different layout for each controller. Since we want to use the standard layout file for the whole site, delete the entries.rhtml and comments.rhtml files in app/views/layouts/.

The Entries Controller

The entries controller is a simple nested resource. When viewing a blog, we want to be able to view any user's blog index action and any show action, showing the entries of the user specified in the URL. However, when a user creates a new blog entry, it should be saved as belonging to the logged-in user, irrespective of the user id parameter.

We need to restrict all methods except index and show to logged-in users only. The code created by the scaffold_resource generator is a good starting point. Alter the app/controllers/ entries_controller.rb file as shown in Listing 6-7, creating, showing, and editing entries based on the user id and entry id. The index method uses the built-in Rails paginator, showing ten entries at a time.

Listing 6-7. *The Entries Controller File*

```ruby
class EntriesController < ApplicationController
  before_filter :login_required, :except => [:index, :show]

  def index
    @user = User.find(params[:user_id])
    @entry_pages = Paginator.new(self, @user.entries_count, 10, params[:page])
    @entries = @user.entries.find(:all, :order => 'created_at DESC',
                                  :limit => @entry_pages.items_per_page,
                                  :offset => @entry_pages.current.offset)
  end

  def show
    @entry = Entry.find_by_id_and_user_id(params[:id],
                                          params[:user_id],
                                          :include => [:user, [:comments => :user]])
  end

  def new
    @entry = Entry.new
  end

  def edit
    @entry = @logged_in_user.entries.find(params[:id])
  rescue ActiveRecord::RecordNotFound
    redirect_to :action => 'index'
  end

  def create
    @entry = Entry.new(params[:entry])
```

```
    if logged_in_user.entries << @entry
      flash[:notice] = 'Entry was successfully created.'
      redirect_to entry_path(:user_id => logged_in_user,
                             :id => @entry)
    else
      render :action => "new"
    end
  end

  def update
    @entry = @logged_in_user.entries.find(params[:id])

    if @entry.update_attributes(params[:entry])
      flash[:notice] = 'Entry was successfully updated.'
      redirect_to entry_path(logged_in_user.id, @entry)
    else
      render :action => "edit"
    end
  rescue ActiveRecord::RecordNotFound
    redirect_to :action => 'index'
  end

  def destroy
    @entry = @logged_in_user.entries.find(params[:id])
    @entry.destroy

    redirect_to entries_path
  rescue ActiveRecord::RecordNotFound
    redirect_to :action => 'index'
  end
end
```

If you look in the show method, you will see that I have specified a number of models within the :include parameter. This tells ActiveRecord that I will need to access the user that belongs to the entry, along with all of the comments and the user models that belong to these comments. This will generate a complex SQL query that retrieves all of the related models at once.

You should take a look at the Rails development log that the SQL generated if you want to understand the SQL query that ActiveRecord generates. Try comparing this with a query that does not use the include statement to see the database access that would be made otherwise.

The New Entry View

When a user creates a new blog entry, we simply want to offer a very simple form to allow entry of the title and the body text.

Open app/views/entries/new.rhtml, and modify the generated view as shown in Listing 6-8.

Listing 6-8. *The New Blog Entry View File*

```
<h1>New Blog Entry</h1>

<%= error_messages_for :entry %>

<% form_for(:entry, :url => entries_path) do |f| %>
  <p>Title:<br /><%= f.text_field :title, :size => 40 -%></p>
  <p>Blog Entry:<br /><%= f.text_area :body, :rows => 10, :cols => 60 -%></p>
  <p><%= submit_tag "Create" %></p>
<% end %>

<%= link_to 'Back', entries_path %>
```

Before we can take a look at this, we should create the show view, which the controller redirects the user to after creating a blog entry.

The Entries Show View

The show method should show just the one entry and list all of the comments, along with the user who left each comment, the time and date it was left, and the body text.

We will also include the new comment form on this page. It allows a visitor to the blog to quickly add a comment without having to navigate to another page.

Open the show action view at app/views/entries/show.rhtml, and edit it as shown in Listing 6-9.

Listing 6-9. *The Show Blog Entry View File*

```
<h1>
  <%= link_to blog_title(@entry.user), entries_path(:user_id => @entry.user) %>
</h1>

<h2><%= @entry.title %></h2>

<p><%= textilize(@entry.body) %></p>

<h3>Comments</h3>
<% @entry.comments.each do |comment| -%>
  <div class="comment">
    <p class="commentfrom">At <%= comment.created_at.to_s(:short) %>,
      <%= comment.user.username %> said:</p>
    <p class="commentbody"><%=h comment.body %></p>
  </div>
<% end -%>
```

```
<h3>Leave a comment</h3>
<%= error_messages_for :comment %>
<% form_for(:comment, :url => comments_path(:user_id => @entry.user,
            :entry_id => @entry)) do |f| -%>
  <p><%= f.text_area :body, :rows => 4, :cols => 40 %></p>
  <p><%= submit_tag 'Save Comment' -%></p>
<% end -%>
```

Since we have not yet created the comments controller, we cannot actually add comments to the entry, but we can try out the entry creation. Adding a link to the sidebar menu directing users to the entry creation page will make it quick and easy for users to add blog entries. We will also add a link to the blogs controller, which we will develop later in this chapter.

Open the sidebar menu partial view file, app/views/layouts/_menu.rhtml, and add the link to the section shown only to logged-in users and the link to the blogs controller as shown in Listing 6-10.

Listing 6-10. *The Create New Blog Post Link in the Menu Partial File*

```
<ul>
  <li><%= link_to 'Home', index_url %></li>
  <li><%= link_to 'News', articles_path %></li>
  <li><%= link_to 'Forums', forums_path %></li>
  <li><%= link_to 'Blogs', blogs_path %></li>

  <li><hr size="1" width="90%" align="left"/></li>

  <% if is_logged_in? %>
    <li>Logged in as: <i><%= logged_in_user.username -%></i></li>
    <li><%= link_to 'My Profile', edit_user_path(logged_in_user) -%></li>
    <li>
      <%= link_to 'New Blog Post', new_entry_path(
            :user_id => logged_in_user) -%>
    </li>
    <li><%= link_to 'Logout', {:controller => 'account', :action => 'logout'},
                        :method => :post %></li>
  <% else %>
    <li><%= link_to 'Signup', :controller => 'users', :action => 'new' %></li>
    <li><%= link_to 'Login', :controller => 'account', :action => 'login' %></li>
  <% end %>
  ...
```

Now, we'll try creating a blog entry using this link and ensure that it displays correctly with the show method.

Make sure that you application is running and log into the site as a regular user. Click the New Blog Post link in the sidebar menu. You will be prompted to create a new blog post, as shown in Figure 6-2.

Figure 6-2. *Creating a new blog post*

Enter the content of a new blog post, remembering that you can use Textile markup to add markup to the entry. For instance, you can markup using *bold text*, _italicized text_, or add links like "this":http://railscoders.net.

Saving the entry will redirect you to the show method, displaying the new blog entry along with a comment entry box, as shown in Figure 6-3.

We can now add the views for the other methods in the entries controller.

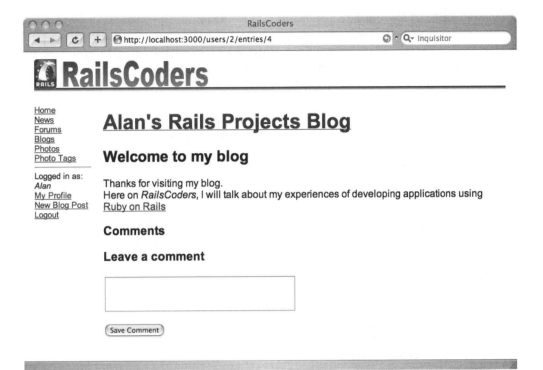

Figure 6-3. *A blog entry*

The Entries Index View

The index action simply finds the latest ten entries for the specified user (or ten entries with an offset if a page number is specified). So for the index page, we simply want to cycle through the entries, showing the title, the body of the entry, and the number of comments that have been left. We also need to provide links to view the comments and to edit or delete the entry if the user that is logged in is viewing their own blog.

Open app/views/entries/index.rhtml, and edit it as shown in Listing 6-11.

Listing 6-11. *The Entries Index View*

```
<h1><%= link_to blog_title(@user), entries_path(:user_id => @user.id) %></h1>

<% @entries.each do |entry| -%>
  <div class="blogentry">
    <h2><%= link_to entry.title,
               entry_path(:user_id => entry.user, :id => entry) %></h2>
```

```
<% if is_logged_in? and logged_in_user.id == @user.id -%>
  <div clas="blogoptions">
    <%= link_to 'Edit', edit_entry_path(:user_id => entry.user, :id => entry) %>
    <%= link_to 'Destroy', entry_path(:user_id => entry.user, :id => entry),
                          :confirm => 'Are you sure?', :method => :delete %>
  </div>
<% end -%>

  <div class="blogentrybody">
    <%= textilize(entry.body) %>
  </div>

  <div class="blognumcomments">
    <p><%= link_to pluralize(entry.comments_count, 'comment'),
                 entry_path(:user_id => entry.user, :id => entry) -%></p>
  </div>
 </div>
<% end -%>

<% if @entry_pages.page_count > 1 %>
  <p class="pagination">Pages: <strong>
    <%= pagination_links @entry_pages, :params => params %>
  </strong></p>
<% end %>
```

For each entry, the number of comments for that entry is also shown. This uses the `pluralize` helper to automatically display the plural form of the word "comment" if there is more than one comment. The number of comments is cached in the `comments_count` attribute of the entry's database record, saving us a large number of database queries. This is linked to the `show` method of the entry, as this method displays the list of comments for that entry.

Obviously, since we haven't written the comments controller yet, there is no way to add comments to an entry.

The pagination links are shown if there is more than one page of articles.

You can now take a look at the index view by clicking on the title of the blog on the show entry page. You should try adding a few extra articles to check that all of the entries are shown correctly, along with pagination when needed.

The Edit Entry View

Editing an entry is almost identical to the new entry view except that the form is posted with different parameters and with an HTTP PUT rather than a POST.

Open `app/views/entries/edit.rhtml`, and edit as shown in Listing 6-12.

Listing 6-12. *The Entry Edit View File*

```
<h1>Editing entry</h1>

<%= error_messages_for :entry %>

<% form_for(:entry,
            :url => entry_path(:user_id => logged_in_user.id, :id => @entry),
            :html => { :method => :put }) do |f| %>
  <p>Title:<br /><%= f.text_field :title, :size => 40 -%></p>
  <p>Blog Entry:<br /><%= f.text_area :body, :rows => 10, :cols => 60 -%></p>
  <p><%= submit_tag "Save" %> or <%= link_to 'cancel', entries_path %></p>
<% end %>
```

You can now try editing an existing blog entry by clicking on the edit link from the index and altering the entry. Click Save Comment to save the updated entry, and check that the content has changed on the show entry page.

Testing the Entries Controller

At this point, we can automate the testing of the entries controller. As before, we should create a fixture to test with. Open test/fixtures/entries.yml, remove the generated empty fixtures, and add the following entry fixture:

```
valid_entry:
  id: 1
  user_id: 1
  title: first post
  body: blah blah
  created_at: <%= 1.days.ago.to_s(:db) %>
  updated_at: <%= 1.days.ago.to_s(:db) %>
```

We simulate a login by a user where necessary to perform the relevant tests. Open test/functional/entries_controller_test.rb, and replace it with the code in Listing 6-13.

Listing 6-13. *The Entries Controller Functional Tests File*

```
require File.dirname(__FILE__) + '/../test_helper'
require 'entries_controller'

# Re-raise errors caught by the controller.
class EntriesController; def rescue_action(e) raise e end; end

class EntriesControllerTest < Test::Unit::TestCase
  fixtures :entries, :users
```

```ruby
def setup
  @controller = EntriesController.new
  @request    = ActionController::TestRequest.new
  @response   = ActionController::TestResponse.new
end

def test_should_get_index
  get :index, {:user_id => 1}
  assert_response :success
  assert assigns(:entries)
end

def test_should_get_new
  login_as(:valid_user)
  get :new, {:user_id => 1}
  assert_response :success
end

def test_should_create_entry
  login_as(:valid_user)
  old_count = Entry.count
  post :create, :entry => {:title => 'test entry', :body => 'a blog entry'}
  assert_equal old_count+1, Entry.count
  assert_redirected_to entry_path(:user_id => 1, :id => assigns(:entry))
end

def test_should_show_entry
  get :show, {:user_id => 1, :id => 1}
  assert_response :success
end

def test_should_get_edit
  login_as(:valid_user)
  get :edit, {:user_id => 1, :id => 1}
  assert_response :success
end

def test_should_update_entry
  login_as(:valid_user)
  put :update, {:user_id => 1, :id => 1,
                :entry => {:title => 'test entry', :body => 'a blog entry'} }
  assert_redirected_to entry_path(:user_id => 1, :id => 1)
end
```

```
  def test_should_destroy_entry
    login_as(:valid_user)
    old_count = Entry.count
    delete :destroy, {:user_id => 1, :id => 1}
    assert_equal old_count-1, Entry.count
    assert_redirected_to entries_path
  end
end
```

Before running these tests, bring the test database schema up to date with the following command:

```
$ rake db:test:prepare
```

Now, run the functional tests:

```
$ ruby test/functional/entries_controller_test.rb
```

```
Loaded suite test/functional/entries_controller_test
Started
.......
Finished in 0.829253 seconds.

7 tests, 13 assertions, 0 failures, 0 errors
```

Great, our tests pass! You should consider adding some negative tests to make sure that users cannot edit or delete another user's blog entries.

Now that we have the blog entries working, we can add code to save and manage comments for the entries.

Creating and Testing the Comments Controller

If you look back at our specification and how we want the comments feature to work, it is actually very straightforward. We need to create a comment only on submission of the new comment form, which we have already added to the show entry view.

Adding the Comments Controller

We do not need to edit existing comments, so the edit and update methods are not necessary. Also, since we show all of the comments on the entry view page, we do not need to implement the index method. We should keep the destroy method and allow only the owner of the entry to delete a comment.

Therefore, we only really need to implement the create and destroy methods. Open the comments controller, app/controllers/comments_controller.rb, and edit the generated controller as shown in Listing 6-14.

Listing 6-14. *The Comments Controller File*

```
class CommentsController < ApplicationController
  before_filter :login_required

  def create
    @entry = Entry.find_by_user_id_and_id(params[:user_id],
                                           params[:entry_id])
    @comment = Comment.new(:user_id => @logged_in_user.id,
                           :body => params[:comment][:body])

    if @entry.comments << @comment
      flash[:notice] = 'Comment was successfully created.'
      redirect_to entries_path(:user_id => @entry.user,
                               :entry_id => @entry)
    else
      render :controller => 'entries', :action => 'show',
             :user_id => @entry.user, :entry_id => @entry
    end
  end

  def destroy
    @entry = Entry.find_by_user_id_and_id(@logged_in_user.id,
                                          params[:entry_id],
                                          :include => :user)
    @comment = @entry.comments.find(params[:id])
    @comment.destroy

    redirect_to entry_path(:user_id => @entry.user.id,
                           :id => @entry.id)
  end
end
```

Since both of these methods redirect or show a view from the entries controller as a response, we do not need to create or edit any views for the comments controller.

However, we should add a link to the comment's delete action from the show entry page. This will enable blog owners to easily delete any comments they do not wish to be shown on their blogs.

Go back to `app/views/entries/show.rhtml`, and add the bold code in Listing 6-15 to the view file. The Delete this Comment link will only be shown if the user viewing the entry is the owner of the blog. Even if you did try to delete a comment that didn't belong to your blog, you couldn't, because the comments controller's `destroy` method only allows you to delete comments that belong to your blog.

Listing 6-15. *Modification to the Entry Show View to Add the Delete Link*

```
<h3>Comments</h3>
<% @entry.comments.each do |comment| -%>
  <div class="comment">
    <p class="commentfrom">At <%= comment.created_at.to_s(:short) %>,
      <%= comment.user.username %> said:</p>
    <% if is_logged_in? and logged_in_user.id == @entry.user.id -%>
      <p class="commentdelete">
        <%= link_to 'Delete this comment',
              comment_path(
                :user_id => @entry.user,
                :entry_id => @entry.id,
                :id => comment.id),
              :confirm => 'Are you sure?',
              :method => :delete -%>
      </p>
    <% end -%>
    <p class="commentbody"><%=h comment.body %></p>
  </div>
<% end -%>
```

Now, when the entry page is displayed for the owner of the blog, a Delete link is shown by each comment.

Try this out by creating a new comment in your blog. Open a blog entry from the index view by clicking either the entry title or the "0 comments" link.

On the entry view page, leave a comment in the text box, and click the Save Comment button. The comment will be saved and the article redisplayed along with the new comment.

Click the blog title to return to the blog index view. The number of comments shown along with the list of blog entries will now show that a comment has been left on the relevant entry, as shown in Figure 6-4.

Figure 6-4. *The blog entries index view*

Testing the Comments Controller

As before, try using the feature through your browser, adding comments both as yourself and as other users. Next, try deleting comments from your blog.

To automate this testing, add a comment fixture to the file test/fixtures/comments.yml:

```
valid_comment:
  id: 1
  entry_id: 1
  user_id: 2
  body: a quick comment
  created_at: <%= 1.days.ago.to_s(:db) %>
```

Create the functional tests as in the previous chapters. This time, we only have to build tests for the index, create, and destroy actions. Open test/functionals/comments_controller_test.rb, and replace the generated code with the required functional tests as shown in Listing 6-16.

Listing 6-16. *The Comments Functional Tests*

```
require File.dirname(__FILE__) + '/../test_helper'
require 'comments_controller'

# Re-raise errors caught by the controller.
class CommentsController; def rescue_action(e) raise e end; end

class CommentsControllerTest < Test::Unit::TestCase
  fixtures :comments, :users, :entries
```

```
def setup
  @controller = CommentsController.new
  @request    = ActionController::TestRequest.new
  @response   = ActionController::TestResponse.new
end

def test_should_create_comment
  login_as(:valid_user)
  old_count = Comment.count
  post :create,{:user_id => 1, :entry_id => 1,
                :comment => {:body => 'that is great'}}
  assert_equal old_count+1, Comment.count
  assert_redirected_to entry_path(:user_id => 1, :id => 1)
end

def test_should_destroy_comment
  login_as(:valid_user)
  old_count = Comment.count
  delete :destroy, :user_id => 1, :entry_id => 1, :id => 1
  assert_equal old_count-1, Comment.count
  assert_redirected_to entry_path(:user_id => 1, :id => 1)
end
end
```

Now, run your functional tests along with all of the functional tests for the application using the rake command:

```
$ rake test:functionals
```

```
Started
...ZWRpdG9yOjEyMzQ1
.........................................
Finished in 1.388685 seconds.

49 tests, 102 assertions, 0 failures, 0 errors
```

This should give you some confidence that everything is still working as expected in the application and that nothing has been broken with our new code.

Adding the Latest Blog Entries to User Profiles

We can now add code to show the last three entries to a user's blog on the profile page. To do this, we simply need to update the show method of the users controller to retrieve the latest entries and add code to display them in the profile view.

Open the file app/controllers/users_controller.rb, and modify the show method as follows:

```
def show
  @user = User.find(params[:id])
  @entries = @user.entries.find(:all, :limit => 3,
                                :order => 'created_at DESC')
end
```

To display these on the profile along with a link to the user's blog page, open the corresponding view file, app/views/users/show.rhtml, and add the necessary view code as follows:

```
<h2><%= @user.username %></h2>
<p>Member since <%= @user.created_at.to_s(:long) %></p>
<p><%= @user.profile %></p>

<h3>Blog Entries</h3>
<ul id="entries">
  <% for entry in @entries %>
    <li>
      <%= link_to entry.title,
                  entry_path(:user_id => @user, :id => entry) %>
    </li>
  <% end %>
</ul>
<p>
  <%= link_to "See all of #{@user.username}'s blog",
              entries_path(:user_id => @user) %>
</p>
```

Now log into the application, and take a look at your profile page by clicking the My Profile link followed by "Show my profile". The last three blogs posts are now shown on your profile page.

The Blogs Controller

We now need to create the blogs controller, giving us a portal into the blogs hosted by the site. We will retrieve the ten most recent blog entries and show links to view the blogs, along with the name of the blog author, the title of the latest blog entry, and when the entry was posted.

Open the generated blogs controller file, app/controllers/blogs_controller.rb, and replace the generated code with that shown in Listing 6-17.

Listing 6-17. *The Blogs Controller File*

```
class BlogsController < ApplicationController
  def index
    @entry_pages = Paginator.new(self, Entry.count, 10, params[:page])
    @entries = Entry.find(:all,
                          :limit => @entry_pages.items_per_page,
                          :offset => @entry_pages.current.offset,
                          :order => 'entries.created_at DESC',
                          :include => :user)
  end
end
```

This retrieves the ten latest entries using the Rails paginator, allowing us to use the pagination links to navigate through the entries.

Next, create the index view file, `app/views/blogs/index.rhtml`, and enter the code in Listing 6-18.

Listing 6-18. *The Blogs Index View File*

```
<h2>Recently updated blogs</h2>

<% @entries.each do |entry| %>
  <p>
    <%= link_to entry.user.username, entries_url(:user_id => entry.user) %><br />
    '<%= entry.title %>' was posted <%= time_ago_in_words(entry.created_at) %> ago
  </p>
<% end %>

<% if @entry_pages.page_count > 1 %>
  <p class="pagination">Pages: <strong>
    <%= pagination_links @entry_pages, :params => params %>
  </strong></p>
<% end %>
```

Now take a look at this view in the application. Click the Blogs link in the sidebar to see the list of the latest blog entries, as shown in Figure 6-5.

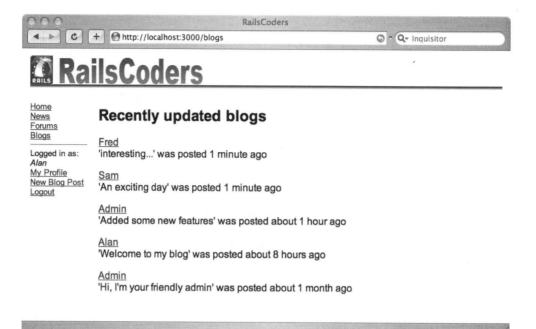

Figure 6-5. *The blogs index view*

Creating an XML-RPC Blogging Interface

As discussed in the specification, we need to create a number of API methods to allow other existing applications to interface with our blogging system. The methods that we need to implement in order to provide basic blogging support are shown in Table 6-4.

Table 6-4. *The Blogger API Methods*

Method	Description
blogger.getUsersBlogs(appkey, username, password)	Returns information about the blogs this user is able to publish to; necessary for some blogging clients
blogger.getUserInfo(appkey, username, password)	Returns information about a specific user
blogger.getPost(appkey, postid, username password)	Returns the content of a specific blog post
blogger.getRecentPosts(appkey, blogid, username, password, number_of_posts)	Returns a list of the most recent blog posts in a particular blog
blogger.newPost(appkey, blogid, username, password, content, publish)	Creates a new post on a particular blog
blogger.editPost(appkey, postid, username, password, content, publish)	Changes the content of a blog post

Some of these parameters do not apply directly to our blogging feature, but we can adapt them to make sure that our API responds in an applicable manner. For example, in our system, each user can have only one blog, but the Blogger API makes it possible for one user to have many different blogs with the same username and password. We will use the user's `id` value as the blog `id` to prevent duplicates.

Also, as part of the API calls, the Blogger API needs you to send an attribute called `appkey`. This is normally a unique string for each application that wants to use the API; it helps the service keep track of users of the system. However, we will ignore this value.

Action Web Service

Action Web Service (AWS) provides Rails with support for SOAP and XML-RPC web services, allowing you to easily implement web services as part of your application. To allow you to implement multiple APIs in your application, different methods of dispatching the web service request are possible within Rails. The method you chose depends on the nature of the API that you are implementing.

■**Note** In future releases of Rails, Action Web Service will be removed from the Rails core codebase and be made available as a plug-in.

Since the Blogger API is just one of the possible blogging APIs in common use, and it is commonly used in conjunction with the other blogging APIs, the method names are prefixed with the name of the service, as in `blogger.newPost`. The MetaWeblog API methods are named using the MetaWeblog service name, as in `metaWeblog.newMediaObject`. These multiple APIs are always accessed through a common endpoint.

The various Rails dispatching methods allow you to use either multiple endpoint URLs for each API or one endpoint that can delegate different API methods to various controllers. Specifically, the AWS layered dispatch method allows multiple APIs to use one endpoint, indicating the name of the API as a prefix to the method name, providing the facilities we need to correctly implement the Blogger API.

Generating the Web Service Code

When creating an XML-RPC or SOAP web service in Rails, there is a generator available to help you get started. In a terminal window, enter the following command from the application's root directory:

```
$ ruby script/generate web_service Backend
```

```
    exists  app/apis/
    exists  app/controllers/
    exists  test/functional/
    create  app/apis/backend_api.rb
    create  app/controllers/backend_controller.rb
    create  test/functional/backend_api_test.rb
```

As you can see, this generates a number of files for you, allowing you to start to build your own web service.

Defining the API Method Calls

In the `app/apis/` directory, we define the API calls that can be made to our application. The generator script created an API definition file called `app/apis/backend_api.rb`. But since we will be using the layered dispatch method, we need an API definition file to correspond to `blogger_api` rather than the generated `backend_api`. Therefore, you can delete the `app/apis/backend_api.rb` file.

Within the API definition files, we define the API calls that can be made, along with the parameters that they expect and what they return.

In the case of the `getUsersBlogs` call, we need to return a `struct` containing data about the user and the blog. This `struct` is simply an XML data structure. Since we need to tell Rails that we will be returning this particular data structure, we need to define it within our application.

Create a new directory called `app/apis/blogger_structs`, and within it, create a new file called `blog.rb` to define the blog `struct` that we need to return. In `app/apis/blogger_structs/blog.rb`, add the following `struct` definition:

```
module BloggerStructs
  class Blog < ActionWebService::Struct
    member :url,      :string
    member :blogId,   :string
    member :blogName, :string
  end
end
```

Next, create the definition of a user `struct` by creating the file `app/apis/blogger_structs/user.rb` and adding the following definition:

```
module BloggerStructs
  class User < ActionWebService::Struct
    member :userId, :string
    member :username, :string
    member :email, :string
    member :url, :string
  end
end
```

Create a blog post `struct` definition, `app/apis/blogger_structs/post.rb`, and add the following:

```
module BloggerStructs
  class Post < ActionWebService::Struct
    member :userId,      :string
    member :postId,      :string
    member :dateCreated, :string
    member :content,     :string
  end
end
```

We now need to define the API methods themselves. Create the file app/apis/blogger_api.rb, and add the code shown in Listing 6-19.

Listing 6-19. *The Blogger API Definition File*

```
class BloggerAPI < ActionWebService::API::Base
  inflect_names false

  api_method :getUsersBlogs,
    :expects => [ {:appkey => :string}, {:username => :string},
                  {:password => :string} ],
    :returns => [[BloggerStructs::Blog]]

  api_method :getUserInfo,
    :expects => [ {:appkey => :string}, {:username => :string},
                  {:password => :string} ],
    :returns => [BloggerStructs::User]

  api_method :getPost,
    :expects => [ {:appkey => :string}, {:postid => :string},
                  {:username => :string}, {:password => :string} ],
    :returns => [BloggerStructs::Post]

  api_method :getRecentPosts,
    :expects => [ {:appkey => :string}, {:blogid => :string},
                  {:username => :string}, {:password => :string},
                  {:numberOfPosts => :integer} ],
    :returns => [[BloggerStructs::Post]]

  api_method :newPost,
    :expects => [ {:appkey => :string}, {:blogid => :string},
                  {:username => :string}, {:password => :string},
                  {:content => :string}, {:publish => :boolean} ],
    :returns => [:int]

  api_method :editPost,
    :expects => [ {:appkey => :string}, {:postid => :string},
                  {:username => :string}, {:password => :string},
                  {:content => :string}, {:publish => :boolean} ],
    :returns => [:boolean]
end
```

The inflect_names false statement means that the Rails Inflector is turned off for the method names of this interface and will not try to change the method names from their camel case naming.

For each API method, we simply define the parameters that we expect and the parameters that we will return, including structs. For example, in the case of getUsersBlogs, we are returning the blog struct that we have defined.

Writing the Blogging API Method Code

When an API method is called, it is handled by the app/controllers/backend_controller.rb file. Since we are using layered dispatching, this is where we declare which web services we are implementing and which dispatch method we are using.

Open the app/controllers/backend_controller.rb file, and edit it as shown in Listing 6-20.

Listing 6-20. *The Backend Controller File*

```
class BackendController < ApplicationController
  web_service_scaffold 'invoke'
  web_service_dispatching_mode :layered
  web_service :blogger, BloggerService.new
end
```

This states that the web services prefixed with blogger. will be handled by the BloggerService.

You will notice that, at the top of the file, I have used the statement web_service_scaffold. This is a handy scaffolding tool in Rails that allows us to easily test our new web service using a web browser. This creates an action called invoke that gives us a simple web interface to run our API calls.

The BloggerService class that this back-end controller passes the blogger requests to is created in the controllers' directory, app/controllers/blogger_service.rb. Create this file, shown in Listing 6-21, to actually implement the web service API methods.

Listing 6-21. *The Blogger Web Service File*

```
class BloggerService < ActionWebService::Base
  web_service_api BloggerAPI

  def getUsersBlogs(appkey, username, password)
    if @user = User.authenticate(username, password)
      [BloggerStructs::Blog.new(
        :url => "http://localhost:3000/users/#{@user.id}/entries",
        :blogId => @user.id,
        :blogName => @user.blog_title ||= @user.username
      )]
    end
  end

  def getPost(appkey, postid, username, password)
    if @user = User.authenticate(username, password)
      entry = @user.entries.find(postid)
      BloggerStructs::Post.new(
        :userId => @user.id,
        :postId => entry.id,
        :dateCreated => entry.created_at.to_s(:db),
        :content => [entry.body]
      )
    end
  end
end
```

```ruby
  def getRecentPosts(appkey, blogid, username, password, numberofposts)
    if @user = User.authenticate(username, password)
      @user.entries.find(:all,
                          :order => 'created_at DESC',
                          :limit => numberofposts).collect do |entry|
        BloggerStructs::Post.new(
          :userId => entry.user_id,
          :postId => entry.id,
          :dateCreated => entry.created_at.to_s(:db),
          :content => entry.body
        )
      end
    end
  end

  def getUserInfo(appkey, username, password)
    if @user = User.authenticate(username, password)
      BloggerStructs::User.new(
        :userId => @user.id,
        :username => @user.username,
        :url => "http://localhost:3000/users/#{@user.id}/entries"
      )
    end
  end

  def newPost(appkey, blogid, username, password, content, publish)
    if @user = User.authenticate(username, password)
      entry = Entry.new
      entry.title = "New entry"
      entry.body = content.to_s
      entry.user = @user
      entry.save
      return entry.id
    end
  end

  def editPost(appkey, postid, username, password, content, publish)
    if @user = User.authenticate(username, password)
      entry = @user.entries.find(postid)
      entry.body = content
      entry.save
      return true
    end
  end
end
```

If you look at the code for each API method, you will see that each method tests to make sure that the login credentials specified are correct and then performs the actions, returning the data specified in the Blogger API documentation.

Testing the Web Services

We can perform manual testing of these web services using the web service scaffolding feature. You will need to restart your Rails server before this will work, however.

Open your browser, and go to `http://localhost:3000/backend/invoke`. You will see a list of the available API methods, as shown in Figure 6-6.

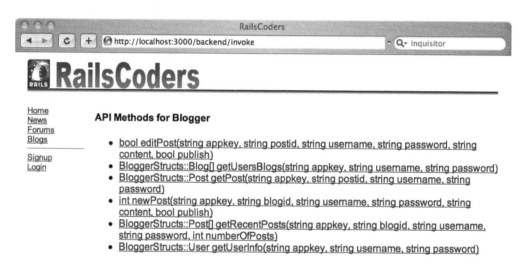

Figure 6-6. *The ActionWebService test scaffold page*

Click the `getUsersBlogs` method, fill in the parameters on the form, and submit the form to make the API call using the XML-RPC protocol. As I mentioned earlier, we'll ignore the `appkey` variable, so you can leave this blank. This will simulate an API call, and you will be shown the XML that would be sent to perform the call and the XML that the server returns.

Try testing the other method calls to make sure that they perform as expected.

Testing Using a Desktop Blogging Client

We should also manually test using a desktop blogging client. I am going to use Ecto, a fully featured blogging client application available for Windows and Mac. Go to `http://ecto.kung-foo.tv/` to download a trial version. I will be using the Mac version, but the Windows version works in the same way.

Ensure that the Rails application is running, and start Ecto. If you have not run Ecto before, you will be prompted to create a new profile. Enter the address of your weblog as `http://localhost:3000/users/<your user id>/entries`, and click Next.

You will be prompted to enter the type of API that your blog uses along with the Access Point or Endpoint, which is the URL that the XML-RPC API is available at.

Select Other as the System type and Blogger as the API type. Enter the XML-RPC endpoint of `http://localhost:3000/backend/api` in the Access Point field, and click Next. The `api` method of the back-end controller is automatically made available by Rails.

You will now be prompted to enter your username and password for the account on RailsCoders. Enter the username and password that corresponds to the user `id` that you entered as the blog URL, and click Next.

Enter a name for this blog profile, which can be anything you like. I have used "RailsCoders Blog." When you save this profile, Ecto will retrieve the most recent blog posts for the specified user and show them, as in Figure 6-7.

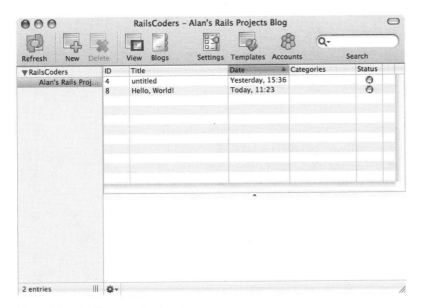

Figure 6-7. *The Ecto entries window*

Now try creating an entry using the Ecto New Post window. Click the New icon in the Ecto toolbar; enter the content of a new blog post; and click the Publish icon. This will create a new blog post in the RailsCoders application and update the list of blog entries in the Ecto main window.

You can also try editing an entry to ensure that the content on the server is updated by sending an entry edit call.

Since XML-RPC is the normal protocol used for the Blogger API, we have just used the XML-RPC endpoint, that is, the `/api` method of the back-end controller. If we were to need SOAP access to a web service that we built, it would be available by appending `/service.wsdl` to the controller. Therefore, the Blogger API would be available at `http://localhost:3000/backend/service.wsdl`. This URL provides an XML document that gives details of all of the methods available and the parameters that they expect and return.

It is also very easy to call another application's web service from Rails's using the ActionWebService tools. The Rails API documentation provides details of how this is done.

Automated Testing of the Blogging API

We can now automate the API testing. Since we are testing the functionality of a controller, the automated tests will be functional ones. The generate command created the skeleton of the functional test that we need. Open this file, test/functional/backend_api_test.rb, and modify it as shown in Listing 6-22.

Listing 6-22. *The Back-end Functional Tests*

```
require File.dirname(__FILE__) + '/../test_helper'
require 'backend_controller'

class BackendController; def rescue_action(e) raise e end; end

class BackendControllerApiTest < Test::Unit::TestCase
  fixtures :users, :entries

  def setup
    @controller = BackendController.new
    @request    = ActionController::TestRequest.new
    @response   = ActionController::TestResponse.new
  end

  def test_get_users_blogs
    blogs = invoke_layered :blogger, :getUsersBlogs, '', 'joe', '12345'
    assert_equal '1', blogs[0]['blogId']
  end

  def test_get_post
    entry = invoke_layered :blogger, :getPost, '', '1', 'joe', '12345'
    assert_equal '1', entry['postId']
  end

  def test_get_recent_posts
    entries = invoke_layered :blogger, :getRecentPosts, '', '1', 'joe', '12345', '1'
    assert_equal 1, entries.size
    assert_equal '1', entries[0]['postId']
  end

  def test_new_post
    blogs = invoke_layered :blogger, :getUsersBlogs, '', 'joe', '12345'
    new_post = invoke_layered :blogger, :newPost, '', blogs[0]['blogId'],
      'joe', '12345', 'New Post', true
    assert new_post.is_a?(Integer)
  end
```

```
  def test_new_and_edit_post
    blogs = invoke_layered :blogger, :getUsersBlogs, '', 'joe', '12345'
    new_post = invoke_layered :blogger, :newPost, '', blogs[0]['blogId'],
      'joe', '12345','New Post', true
    result = invoke_layered :blogger, :editPost, '', new_post, 'joe', '12345',
      'Edited Post', true
    assert_equal true, result
  end
end
```

To test the API methods through the layered dispatch process, we use the invoke_layered command and pass in the service name, the method name, and the method parameters. We can then perform assertions on the data returned to make sure that the API is working as expected. Run these tests with the following command:

```
$ ruby test/functional/backend_api_test.rb
```

```
Loaded suite test/functional/backend_api_test
Started
.....
Finished in 0.247508 seconds.

5 tests, 6 assertions, 0 failures, 0 errors
```

You could expand these tests and add negative tests to make sure that we cover all eventualities and perform extra assertions to make sure that the methods are working exactly as they should.

Further Development of the Blogging System

This blogging system could easily be developed further. Since a user might want to draft articles before publishing them, we could add a draft flag, similar to the one in the Article model developed in Chapter 4. The Blogger API supports this flag, so it would be easy to integrate.

You could also look at developing other API interfaces. The Blogger API is reasonably limited in what external applications can do, but the MetaWeblog API provides more possibilities for development. Since the web services controller with layered dispatching allows for overlapping APIs, it is simple to add other web services to the same endpoint.

Summary

In this chapter, we developed a blogging engine for the users of the RailsCoders site, allowing them to create entries and allowing visitors to easily add comments to blog entries. Blog owners can edit their blogs and have the capability to remove comments. We also added users' latest entries to their profile pages along with links to their blogs.

We have implemented the Blogger API over XML-RPC, allowing existing third-party applications to talk directly to our application to create and edit entries. We demonstrated this using the Ecto desktop blogging client.

In the next chapter, we implement file uploading to the server. This will allow users to send their own files, such as images, to the server. We will build a simple photo gallery for the site using the file upload feature.

CHAPTER 7

■■■

Building a Photo Gallery

In this chapter, we will build an online photo gallery, allowing users to upload their photos from their PCs to their profiles on RailsCoders. While this is a nice way for us to encourage our users to get involved on the site and to make it more personal, it could also become the basis for a community built around photo sharing such as Flickr, Fotolog, or Phlog.

Working with files uploaded by users can be a little tricky and time-consuming, so we will use the `attachment_fu` plug-in to make our lives a little easier and enable us to work with files without having to perform manual file management.

Since we want to make it easy for visitors to browse photos, the site should show thumbnailed versions of the photos, so we will look at how you can resize images using ImageMagick and the RMagick plug-in.

Working with Uploaded Files

Before we start defining our feature, there are a number of issues that we need to consider when dealing with files uploaded by users.

First, there is the issue of file size. Image files from a digital camera can easily be 2MB or 3MB in size. While this isn't a problem if you are only dealing with a small number of files, if you have thousands of users who upload hundreds of photographs each, you will need to have either a very generous hosting provider or a dedicated server with a large amount of online storage. This also has an effect on the bandwidth that the site will consume. Almost certainly, however you end up hosting your site—with a shared host, a virtual private server (VPS), or a dedicated machine at a colocation—you will have an allocated amount of upload and download bandwidth. If you start hosting gigabytes of images, you will quickly burn through your allocated bandwidth and end up paying your hosting provider high rates for extra bandwidth.

Also, there are some security concerns. If you allow users to upload any file, store it, and allow others to download it without checking the file size or file type to make sure it is a valid image, it is possible that some malicious users will take advantage of your generous nature to store other types of files, or worse still, attempt to hack or break your site by uploading illegal or malicious files.

While Rails provides a number of useful methods for dealing with files uploaded from a web form, they are reasonably basic, so we have to manually deal with all of the necessary actions: handling the uploaded file, examining the file to make sure it is an image, processing the image to create the thumbnails, and storing the image.

Since working with uploaded files is a pretty common task, as you might expect, a number of Rails developers have produced plug-ins and gems to simplify the task of working with files uploaded by users.

The most popular plug-ins for this are `file_column`, `acts_as_attachment`, and `attachment_fu`. We are going to use `attachment_fu`.

`attachment_fu` is a rewrite of `acts_as_attachment` that is written in a more modular way to make extending it much easier. Both `acts_as_attachment` and `attachment_fu` are written by Rick Olson, a member of the Rails core development team.

ALTERNATIVE METHODS OF WORKING WITH UPLOADS

Although `attachment_fu` provides us with very simple and easy ways of working with uploaded files, you may wish to perform some actions outside of the scope of the plug-in. The Rails wiki provides details on how to work with uploaded files at `http://wiki.rubyonrails.org/rails/pages/HowtoUploadFiles`.

The `file_column` plug-in was the first popular plug-in to attempt to simplify the uploading process and is still used by some developers. You can read more about this plug-in at `http://www.kanthak.net/opensource/file_column`.

Development of the `acts_as_attachment` plug-in has now been abandoned in favor of `attachment_fu`.

The attachment_fu Plug-in

The `attachment_fu` plug-in automatically recognizes file types and can be configured to automatically create different sizes of thumbnails for images. You can also configure several methods of storing the uploaded data. By default, it stores uploaded files in the database, but you can easily change it to store data in the file system or in Amazon Web Service's Simple Storage Service (AWS S3 or just S3). Because of the modular nature of the plug-in, it is easy to add different storage mechanisms if you have different requirements.

THE AMAZON SIMPLE STORAGE SERVICE

AWS S3 is a web service provided by Amazon.com that allows you to store any data files in a personal data "bucket" on Amazon's servers.

You can upload any type of file to the service using a simple API. You can set permissions on the uploaded files, allowing them to be downloaded by either anyone who knows the URL or only users or applications providing a password.

Amazon charges for the amount of data stored and the amount of upload and download bandwidth used, but it is very cheap compared to the cost of traditional hosting. File serving is also very fast and reliable because the file is stored on Amazon's distributed file servers.

To find out more, visit `http:/aws.amazon.com/s3`.

Marcel Molina Jr. has developed a library to make it easy to use S3 in Rails. You can find more information at `http://amazon.rubyforge.org`.

To use `attachment_fu`, simply add a `has_attachment` statement in the model that you wish to use to store file uploads. You can specify options for the storage mechanism, the size of thumbnails (if required), and constraints on the files that can be uploaded (such as restricting to files below a certain size or only allowing certain file types).

You must also ensure that the database fields shown in Table 7-1 are added to the model that you are using with file uploads.

Table 7-1. *Additional Database Fields Required by Models Using the attachment_fu Plug-in*

Field Name	Field Type	Description
content_type	string	The MIME type of the uploaded file.
filename	string	The original file name of the uploaded file.
size	integer	The size of the uploaded file in bytes.
parent_id	integer	If file is a thumbnail, the id of the parent file.
thumbnail	string	If file is a thumbnail, the name of the size of thumbnail as specified in the has_attachment statement (e.g., thumb or tiny).
width	integer	If file is an image, the width in pixels.
height	integer	If file is an image, the height in pixels.
db_file_id	integer	If the database is used to store the uploaded files, this is the id of the file's object; otherwise, it's optional.

If you choose to use the database to store the uploaded files, you will also require another database table called `db_files`. The required database fields for this table are shown in Table 7-2.

Table 7-2. *Database Fields Required for the db_files Table*

Field Name	Field Type	Description
id	integer	Primary key and id of the file
data	binary	Data of the uploaded file

Using the database as a storage system has a number of advantages and disadvantages. If we use the database, every file that is requested will have to be retrieved from the database and sent by the Rails application server. This has the advantage of allowing us to create a finely grained permissions system, if need be—we could restrict downloads to specific users or users with certain permissions. However, this would be rather slow. A traditional web server such as Apache or lighttpd can serve a binary file faster and with a much lower CPU load than a Rails application server. To speed this up, we could develop a way to cache these files and a method of instructing the web server to serve a file from a cache.

Also, you can easily scale a database across multiple servers and automatically fail over to a backup if a machine fails.

Using the file system is obviously the simplest and fastest method. The uploaded files will automatically be stored in the `public/` directory, meaning that in a production environment, they are served directly by the web server. This is very quick, as it means that serving a file does not require processing by the Rails application server. However, you have no dynamic control over who has access to the files; they are all available to all visitors to the site.

To upload a file, you must create a web form with the form multipart option set to true. This enables a form `POST` request to be sent with file attachments. Next, you add a `file_field` tag to your form with the attribute name of `uploaded_data`. When you submit a form with this tag, `attachment_fu` will do the rest of the work.

`attachment_fu` adds a number of class methods, including a number of callbacks, meaning that you can perform extra processing on uploaded files at different points during the uploading process.

A number of instance methods are also added to any models specified as having attachments. These instance methods allow us to work with the uploaded file, process the file if it is an image, and fetch information about the file and how it can be retrieved.

The Photo Gallery Requirements

From a user's perspective, the gallery feature should allow each user of the site to upload image files from his or her computer to the RailsCoders site. The latest photos from a user will then be displayed on the profile page with a link to view more photos. This link will then take the visitor to a gallery page, showing all of the user's photos with the latest photo first. These photos will be thumbnailed versions of the uploaded photos, so clicking them will show the full-size version of the photo.

We also want to be able to view all photos on the site, irrespective of the user.

So that our server doesn't explode by trying to host hundreds of gigabytes of other people's images, we are going to resize all incoming photos to 640×480 pixels. This will keep the file size reasonably small. If the photo gallery proves to be a success and we wish to store larger photos or the original files, we can revisit this later.

Along with storing the 640×480 versions, we need to be able to show the photos as thumbnails. Having made a quick sketch of how the page will be laid out, we calculate that 160×120 pixels should be a good size for our thumbnails. Also, since we will develop a mobile version of our site in Chapter 13, we want a smaller thumbnail to show on a cell phone screen. An image with a width of 50 pixels should look fine on a 2-inch screen.

To show the latest photos and order the gallery in reverse chronological order, we need to record the upload date and time. As usual, we can use the automatically updated attribute `created_at`.

Along with the upload time, we want to allow the user to enter a title and a description for each photo. Both of these fields will be optional.

Since we are going to use the `attachment_fu` plug-in, recall that we need to define a storage mechanism for the files. The plug-in currently supports storing in the database, the file system, or S3. Since we do not require the features of using the database, we are going to use the file system. If the site grows quickly and we need to store a significant amount of data, we could easily move the data over to S3. We can deal with this scaling issue if and when it happens.

Defining the Photo Model

As we have already discussed, we need to add certain fields to the Photo model to use the attachment_fu plug-in. In addition to these, we require the fields specified in Table 7-3.

Table 7-3. *The Database Fields Required for the Photo Model*

Field Name	Field Type	Description
id	integer	The primary key
title	string	The title of the photo
body	text	A longer description of the photo
created_at	datetime	The date and time the photo was uploaded

The Photos Controllers

Since we want to be able to display the photos from a specific user or for the entire site, we will create two controllers:

- To view all photos on the site, we will create a controller that will be accessed at the root level, that is, /photos. This resource only needs to implement the index action, since the show, new, create, edit, update, and delete actions need to be accessed via a nested resource.

- To view photos belonging to a specific user and to allow the photo owners to edit their photos, we will create a nested resource called user_photos. This will be accessed via URLs such as /users/1/photos and /users/1/photos/2. This controller will provide the usual REST CRUD actions. As we only want logged-in users to upload files or edit the attributes of an existing image, the new, create, edit, update, and destroy actions should require a user to be logged in.

Installing ImageMagick, RMagick, and attachment_fu

To be able to process the images to create thumbnails, we need two libraries installed: namely ImageMagick and RMagick. ImageMagick is an open source set of general-purpose image processing libraries. These libraries can be used by other applications or via command-line tools. If you use Linux, you may have come across the convert command, which is part of ImageMagick, for resizing images. You can find out more about ImageMagick at http://www.imagemagick.org.

RMagick is a Ruby interface to the ImageMagick libraries. Using RMagick, you can easily resize, crop, and rotate images, along with applying special effects such as blur and sharpen and producing composite images. To learn more about RMagick, visit http://rmagick.rubyforge.org, or you can read the online documentation at http://www.simplesystems.org/RMagick/doc/index.html.

Installing on Windows

If you are running Instant Rails on Windows, the easiest method of installing ImageMagick and RMagick is to install the Windows binary version of RMagick, which includes the necessary ImageMagick libraries.

Go to the RMagick RubyForge page at `http://rubyforge.org/projects/rmagick`, and click the download link for the `rmagick-win32` binary gem. From there, select the latest zip file of the binary RMagick gem, such as `RMagick 1.14.1 binary gem for Ruby 1.8.5`.

When the zip file has downloaded, unzip the file into a temporary directory and carefully follow the instructions in the included `README.html` file, ensuring that you uninstall any earlier versions of RMagick that you may have installed before you begin.

You first need to install ImageMagick using the installer file included in the package. After that, install the included gem using the command line by changing to the directory created when you unzipped the RMagick package and entering the following command:

```
$ gem install rmagick --local
```

Once that is installed, you need to restart Instant Rails for it to pick up the changes.

Installing on OS X

If you are running Locomotive on OS X, there is a ready-made bundle containing ImageMagick and the RMagick plug-in available on the Locomotive site. Go to the Locomotive bundles download page at `http://locomotive.raaum.org/bundles/index.html`, and download the RMagick bundle. Uncompress the bundle, and copy the contents into the `Locomotive/Bundles/` folder where you have installed Locomotive.

Restart Locomotive, and select your Rails application in the main Locomotive window. Click the information icon at the top of the window, and select the RMagick bundle from the Web Framework options. You can close this window and start your application. You now have the RMagick plug-in installed.

Installing on Linux

To install on Ubuntu Linux, first install the ImageMagick libraries using the command:

```
$ sudo apt-get install libmagick9-dev
```

Next, install the RMagick gem using the following command:

```
$ sudo gem install rmagick
```

You are now ready to work with the RMagick libraries in your Rails application.

Installing the attachment_fu Plug-in

To install the `attachment_fu` plug-in, enter the following command:

```
$ ruby script/plugin install \
http://svn.techno-weenie.net/projects/plugins/attachment_fu/
```

```
+ ./attachment_fu/README
+ ./attachment_fu/Rakefile
+ ./attachment_fu/amazon_s3.yml.tpl
+ ./attachment_fu/init.rb
+ ./attachment_fu/install.rb
...
+ ./attachment_fu/test/test_helper.rb
+ ./attachment_fu/test/validation_test.rb
attachment-fu

=====================
```

This copies the latest version of the plug-in into the vendor/plugins/ directory of your application's root directory.

Building the Photo Gallery

Now that we understand the requirements of the photo gallery and have installed the necessary libraries and plug-in, we can begin to develop the code.

Generating the Scaffolding Code

As in previous chapters, we are going to use the scaffold_resource generator to produce scaffolding code for the resource.

```
$ ruby script/generate scaffold_resource Photo
```

```
     exists  app/models/
     exists  app/controllers/
     exists  app/helpers/
     create  app/views/photos
     exists  test/functional/
     exists  test/unit/
     create  app/views/photos/index.rhtml
     create  app/views/photos/show.rhtml
     create  app/views/photos/new.rhtml
     create  app/views/photos/edit.rhtml
     create  app/views/layouts/photos.rhtml
  identical  public/stylesheets/scaffold.css
     create  app/models/photo.rb
     create  app/controllers/photos_controller.rb
     create  test/functional/photos_controller_test.rb
     create  app/helpers/photos_helper.rb
     create  test/unit/photo_test.rb
     create  test/fixtures/photos.yml
     exists  db/migrate
     create  db/migrate/016_create_photos.rb
      route  map.resources :photos
```

Since we do not need this photo resource to implement any actions other than the index action, delete the following files:

```
app/views/photos/show.rhtml
app/views/photos/new.rhtml
app/views/photos/edit.rhtml
```

We will simply create the necessary view file for the user_photo resource. We do not require a separate model for creating the user_photo resource, as it simply uses the Photo model created with the previous generator.

Writing the Migration

As I discussed earlier, any models that are to be used to store attachments require certain database columns to be added.

Along with these, we need to store the id of the user to whom the image belongs, the time and date when the image is uploaded, and a title specified by the user.

Edit the create database migration file db/migrate/016_create_photos.rb to match the migration shown in Listing 7-1.

Listing 7-1. *Migration Script for the Photos Table*

```ruby
class CreatePhotos < ActiveRecord::Migration
  def self.up
    create_table :photos do |t|
      t.column :user_id, :integer
      t.column :title, :string
      t.column :body, :text
      t.column :created_at, :datetime

      # the following columns are required for attachment_fu
      t.column :content_type, :string, :limit => 100
      t.column :filename, :string, :limit => 255
      t.column :path, :string, :limit => 255
      t.column :parent_id, :integer
      t.column :thumbnail, :string, :limit => 255
      t.column :size, :integer
      t.column :width, :integer
      t.column :height, :integer
    end
    add_column :users, :photos_count, :integer
  end

  def self.down
    drop_table :photos
    remove_column :users, :photos_count
  end
end
```

We can now run the migration to add the photos table to the database. To do this, enter the following command:

```
$ rake db:migrate
```

```
(in /Users/alan/Documents/Projects/Rails/railscoders)
== CreatePhotos: migrating =====================================================
-- create_table(:photos)
   -> 0.6035s
== CreatePhotos: migrated (0.6232s) ============================================
```

Creating the Photo Model and Its Relationships

In the Photo model file, we need to specify that this model is going to store uploaded files. This is also where we configure how the files will be stored, what thumbnails we want to create, and any constraints we want to place on the uploaded files.

We also need to add the user-photo relationship to the User model.

Create the Photo Model

Open the Photos model file app/models/photos.rb, and edit it as shown in Listing 7-2.

Listing 7-2. *The Photo Model*

```
class Photo < ActiveRecord::Base
  has_attachment :storage => :file_system,
                 :resize_to => '640x480',
                 :thumbnails => { :thumb => '160x120', :tiny => '50>' },
                 :max_size => 5.megabytes,
                 :content_type => :image,
                 :processor => 'Rmagick'
  validates_as_attachment
  belongs_to :user
end
```

This specifies that the model will have attached uploaded files. As defined in the specification, we will resize all uploaded photos to fit within 640×480 pixels.

We will also create two thumbnails, one named thumb, which will be 160×120 pixels, and one named tiny, which has been specified as 50> (this means that the image will be resized with the width set to 50 pixels while keeping the aspect ratio of the original image). You can also specify image dimensions as an array, such as ['640', '480'].

The has_attachment statement also specifies that only file types that are images will be accepted and that the maximum size of an uploaded file will be 5MB.

The model also uses a new validation introduced by the plug-in, validates_as_ attachment. This ensures that the attachment meets the requirements of being a file: having a size, a content type, and a file name.

The relationship with the User model is also stated.

Adding the Users Relationship

Since we have specified that each photo will belong to a user, we need to add the reciprocal relationship to the User model.

Open the User model file app/models/user.rb, and add the has_many relationship as shown:

```
require 'digest/sha2'
class User < ActiveRecord::Base
  ...
  has_many :comments
  has_many :photos

  def before_save
  ...
```

Mapping the Photos Resource

We now need to create the mapping of the photos resources.

The photos resource is created at the root level. The user_photos resource must be nested below the users resource, since we will access all photos by specifying both the user and the photo id.

Edit the config/routes.rb file by adding the photos resource mapping nested within the users resource as follows:

```
map.resources :photos
map.resources :users, :member => { :enable => :put } do |users|
  users.resources :roles
  users.resources :entries do |entries|
    entries.resources :comments
  end
  users.resources :photos, :name_prefix => 'user_',
                           :controller => 'user_photos'
end
```

This nested mapping allows us to access the user_photos_controller via URLs such as /users/1/photos. To use the path shortcuts in the controllers and views, we have specified that we will use the name prefix of user_, meaning that we can use shortcuts such as user_photos_path(:user_id => 1) or user_edit_photo_path(:user_id => 1, :id => 2).

The Photos and User Photos Controllers

We can now work on the photos controller and the user photos controller.

The photos_controller file only needs to implement the index action. Edit the generated file app/controllers/photos_controller.rb as shown in Listing 7-3.

Listing 7-3. *The Photos Controller File*

```
class PhotosController < ApplicationController
  def index
    photos_count = Photo.count(:conditions => 'thumbnail IS NULL')
    @photo_pages = Paginator.new(self, photos_count, 9, params[:page])
    @photos = Photo.find(:all,
                          :conditions => 'thumbnail IS NULL',
                          :order => 'created_at DESC',
                          :limit => @photo_pages.items_per_page,
                          :offset => @photo_pages.current.offset)
  end
end
```

Now, let's move on to the user_photos controller. Create the file app/controllers/
user_photos_controller.rb file, and add the code shown in Listing 7-4.

Listing 7-4. *The User Photos Controller File*

```
class UserPhotosController < ApplicationController
  before_filter :login_required, :except =>  [:index, :show]


  def index
    @user = User.find(params[:user_id])
    @photo_pages = Paginator.new(self, @user.photos.count, 9, params[:page])
    @photos = @user.photos.find(:all, :order => 'created_at DESC',
                                :limit => @photo_pages.items_per_page,
                                :offset => @photo_pages.current.offset)
    respond_to do |format|
      format.html # index.rhtml
      format.xml  { render :xml => @photos.to_xml }
    end
  end

  def show
    @photo = Photo.find_by_user_id_and_id(params[:user_id],
                                          params[:id],
                                          :include => :user)

    respond_to do |format|
      format.html # show.rhtml
      format.xml  { render :xml => @photo.to_xml }
    end
  end

  def new
    @photo = Photo.new
  end
```

```ruby
  def edit
    @photo = @logged_in_user.photos.find(params[:id])
  rescue ActiveRecord::RecordNotFound
    redirect_to :action => 'index'
  end

  def create
    @photo = Photo.new(params[:photo])

    respond_to do |format|
    if @logged_in_user.photos << @photo
        flash[:notice] = 'Photo was successfully created.'
        format.html { redirect_to(user_photos_path(:user_id=>@logged_in_user.id)) }
        format.xml  { head :created,
          :location => user_photo_path(:user_id => @photo.user_id, :id => @photo)}
      else
        format.html { render :action => 'new' }
        format.xml  { render :xml => @photo.errors.to_xml }
      end
    end
  rescue ActiveRecord::RecordInvalid
    render :action => 'new'
  end

  def update
    @photo = @logged_in_user.photos.find(params[:id])

    respond_to do |format|
      if @photo.update_attributes(params[:photo])
        flash[:notice] = 'Photo was successfully updated.'
        format.html { redirect_to user_photo_path(:user_id => @logged_in_user,
                                                  :id => @photo) }
        format.xml  { head :ok }
      else
        format.html { render :action => "edit" }
        format.xml  { render :xml => @photo.errors.to_xml }
      end
    end
  rescue ActiveRecord::RecordNotFound
    redirect_to :action => 'index'
  end

  def destroy
    @photo = @logged_in_user.photos.find(params[:id])
    @photo.destroy
```

```
    respond_to do |format|
      format.html { redirect_to user_photos_path }
      format.xml  { head :ok }
    end
  rescue ActiveRecord::RecordNotFound
    redirect_to :action => 'index'
  end

end
```

You should find that most of the code is familiar from the previous controllers that we have developed. You will see that the `index` actions in both controllers make use of the paginator helper that we used in the entries controller.

The `show` action uses the `:include` option to preload the `user` object that is associated with the specified photo, saving us one database query.

Notice that the `create` action, which receives the file posted from the web form, is very simple; all of the file handling is performed by the plug-in. The action instantiates a new Photo model from the form parameters and saves this model by associating it with the logged-in user. As long as the file field in the web form is called `uploaded_data`, the file will automatically be validated as specified in the model, the image resized, and the thumbnails created and saved.

The Photo Views

We can now create the corresponding views for the photos and user photos controllers. But before we do, we should remove the generated layout file of the `photos` resource, since we want to use the standard `application.rhtml` layout file. Delete this file, `app/views/layouts/photos.rhtml`.

The New Photo View

We should create the view for the new action. Create the file and directory `app/views/user_photos/new.rhtml`, and replace the generated view with the view in Listing 7-5.

Listing 7-5. *View File for the New Photo Action*

```
<h2>Upload a new photo</h2>

<%= error_messages_for :photo %>

<% form_for(:photo,
            :url => user_photos_path(:user_id => @logged_in_user),
            :html => { :multipart => true }) do |f| %>
  <p>Select a photo to upload</p>
  <p>Title:<br /><%= f.text_field 'title' %></p>
  <p>Description:<br /><%= f.text_area 'body', :rows => 6, :cols => 40 %></p>
  <p>Photo:<br /><%= f.file_field 'uploaded_data' %></p>
  <p>
    <%= submit_tag 'Upload Photo' %> or
    <%= link_to 'cancel', user_photos_path(@logged_in_user) %>
  </p>
<% end %>
```

This is similar to a regular form, except that because we are uploading a file from the form, we have to add statement `:multipart => true` to the `form_for` method. Without this, the file attachment will not be received by the controller.

■**Note** Whenever you build a form that performs a file upload, you must specify `:multipart => true` in the form tag.

The Edit Photo View

The edit view is similar to the `new` view, except that there is no file form tag; just the title and description are editable. The thumbnail of the image is also shown on the page. Create the `app/views/user_photos/edit.rhtml` file now, and enter the view code in Listing 7-6.

Listing 7-6. *View File for the Edit Photo Action*

```
<h2>Edit photo details</h2>

<%= link_to image_tag(@photo.public_filename('thumb')),
          user_photo_path(:user_id => @photo.user, :id => @photo) %>

<%= error_messages_for :photo %>

<% form_for(:photo,
          :url => user_photo_path(:user_id => @photo.user, :id => @photo),
          :html => { :method => :put }) do |f| %>
  <p>Title:<br /><%= f.text_field 'title' %></p>
  <p>Description:<br /><%= f.text_area 'body', :rows => 6, :cols => 40 %></p>
  <p><%= submit_tag "Save" %> or <%= link_to 'cancel', user_photos_path %></p>
<% end %>
```

The Index Views

Since the `index` views for both controllers are very similar and both the pagination links and the thumbnailed photos use the same code, we can use partials to allow us to reuse code.

Create the user photos index view, `app/views/user_photos/index.rhtml`, and enter the view code in Listing 7-7.

Listing 7-7. *View File for the User Photos Index Action*

```
<h2><%= @user.username %>'s Photos</h2>

<% if is_logged_in? && logged_in_user == @user %>
  <p><%= link_to 'Upload a new photo', new_user_photo_path %></p>
<% end %>
```

```
<%= render :partial => 'photo/page_links' %>

<ul id="photos">
  <%= render :partial => 'photo/photo', :collection => @photos %>
</ul>

<%= render :partial => 'photo/page_links' %>
```

You will notice that this uses two partial views. The page_links partial contains the pagination links for the current page and the photo partial displays a thumbnail of an image. We will put both partials in the app/view/photos directory. Create this partial view file, app/views/photos/_page_links.rhtml, and add the following code:

```
<% if @photo_pages.page_count > 1 %>

  <% if @photo_pages.current.previous %>
    <%= link_to '&laquo; Previous', :page => @photo_pages.current.previous %>
  <% end %>

  <%= pagination_links @photo_pages, :params => params %>

  <% if @photo_pages.current.next %>
    <%= link_to 'Next &raquo;', { :page => @photo_pages.current.next } %>
  <% end %>

<% end %>
```

This uses the pagination_links helper method to produce the numeric pagination links. It also adds Next and Previous links to the next and previous pages if they are available. The next and previous page numbers are available using current.next and current.previous as shown.

The photo partial is a thumbnail of each photo, which is a link to the show action of that photo. Create this partial file now, app/views/photos/_photo.rhtml, and add the following view code:

```
<li>
    <%= link_to image_tag(photo.public_filename('thumb')),
            user_photo_path(:user_id => photo.user, :id => photo) %>
</li>
```

To display a thumbnail of each photo, we use the instance method public_filename, provided by the attachment_fu plug-in. This returns the path and file name of the requested file object as accessible from a URL. In this case, we are requesting the version of the file that has been saved with the thumbnail value of 'thumb'. As you will recall, this was specified in the has_attachment statement in the model – the 'thumb' thumbnail is a photo of size 160×120.

We can now easily create the view for the photos controller's index action using the same partials. Edit the file app/views/photos/index.rhtml by adding the view code shown in Listing 7-8.

Listing 7-8. *View File for the Photos Index Action*

```
<h2>All Photos</h2>

<%= render :partial => 'page_links' %>

<ul id="photos">
  <%= render :partial => 'photo', :collection => @photos %>
</ul>

<%= render :partial => 'page_links' %>
```

The Show Photo View

The only remaining view is the show action to display one individual photo with the title, body, time and date it was uploaded, and owner of the photo. We should also include a link back to see all of the photos of the user to whom the photo belongs.

We also need to allow the owner of the photo to edit and delete the photo, so we should add these options but show them only if the user viewing the page is logged in as the owner of the photo.

Create the show view file, app/views/user_photos/show.rhtml, and enter the view in Listing 7-9.

Listing 7-9. *View File for the Photo Show Action*

```
<h3>
  <%= link_to "#{@photo.user.username}'s Photos",
              user_photos_path(:user_id => @photo.user) %>
</h3>
<h2><%=h @photo.title %></h2>
<p><%=h @photo.body %>

<% if is_logged_in? && @photo.user_id == logged_in_user.id %>
  <p>
    <%= link_to 'Edit', user_edit_photo_path(:user_id=>@photo.user, :id=>@photo) %>,
    <%= link_to 'Delete', user_photo_path(:user_id => @photo.user, :id => @photo),
                                          :confirm => 'Are you sure?',
                                          :method => :delete %>
  </p>
<% end %>

<%= image_tag @photo.public_filename, :id => 'photo' %>
```

This uses the image_tag Rails helper to display the image by requesting the public_filename of the photo object, as in the index view. This time, we do not specify a thumbnail size, so we use the path to the parent file—in our case, the resized version of the uploaded file. If no resize was requested, or the uploaded file is not an image, this would be the public path to the original file.

Adding Links to the Gallery and New Photo Pages

To make uploading photos to the gallery easy for users, we should add a link to the logged-in users section of the sidebar menu. We should also add a link to the gallery showing all the uploaded photos.

Edit the sidebar menu partial, app/views/layouts/_menu.rhmtl. Add the links to the photos resource and new_photo_path for the logged-in user as shown below:

```
<ul>
  ...
  <li><%= link_to 'Blogs', blogs_path %></li>
  <li><%= link_to 'Photos', photos_path %></li>

  <li><hr size="1" width="90%" align="left"/></li>

  <% if is_logged_in? %>
    <li>Logged in as: <i><%= logged_in_user.username -%></i></li>
    <li><%= link_to 'My Profile', edit_user_path(logged_in_user) -%></li>
    <li>
      <%= link_to 'New Blog Post', new_entry_path(
            :user_id => logged_in_user) -%>
    </li>
    <li><%= link_to 'Upload Photo',
              user_new_photo_path(:user_id => logged_in_user) -%></li>
    <li><%= link_to 'Logout', {:controller => 'account', :action => 'logout'},
                        :method => :post %></li>
    ...
</ul>
```

Adding the Latest Photos to a User's Profile

On a user's profile page, along with a link to a user's gallery, we can show a few of the latest photos from that user. To do this, we need to add a find statement to the show action in the users controller file.

Edit the app/controllers/users_controller.rb file by adding the call to retrieve the latest three photos of the user to the show action as follows:

```
def show
  @user = User.find(params[:id])
  @entries = @user.entries.find(:all, :limit => 3, :order => 'created_at DESC')
  @photos = @user.photos.find(:all, :limit => 3,
                              :order => 'created_at DESC')
end
```

We now need to add the corresponding view code to the show view file. Add the following code to the end of the app/views/users/show.rhtml file:

```
<h3>Photos</h3>
<ul id="photos">
  <%= render :partial => 'photos/photo', :collection => @photos %>
</ul>
<p>
  <%= link_to "See all of #{@user.username}'s photos",
              user_photos_path(:user_id => @user) %>
</p>
```

This reuses the partial view created for the `index` action.

Styling for the Gallery

We should also add some simple styling to the gallery to put a small border around the images and to show the photos in a grid format. Add the following CSS to the end of the `public/stylesheets/main.css` file:

```
/* Photo gallery styling */

#photos ul { list-style: none; }

#photos li { display: inline; }

#photos li a img {
  margin: 10px;
  padding: 5px;
  background: #000;
}

#photo {
  margin-bottom: 20px;
  padding: 5px;
  background: #000;
}
```

Manually Testing the Gallery

We can now try running through the gallery manually to make sure everything works as expected. Make sure the Rails application server is running and log in to the application as a valid user via the page `http://localhost:3000/login`.

Click the Upload Photo link from the sidebar menu. From this upload page, enter a title and description, and select an image file from your computer to upload. Then click the Upload Photo button. The photo will be uploaded, and you will be forwarded to the gallery page for the logged-in user. Try uploading a number of photos to check that the pagination works. This is shown in Figure 7-1.

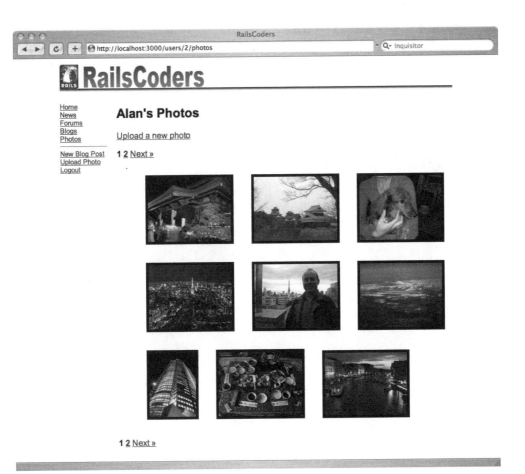

Figure 7-1. *The gallery index view for a user*

If you look in the `public/photos/` directory of your application, you will see a number of directories called 1, 4, 7, and so on. Each directory corresponds to a `photo` object's parent `id`. In our application, each parent has a resized original file and two thumbnails. If you look within one of these photo object directories, you will see a file with the original file name of the uploaded file and two files with the suffixes `_thumb` and `_tiny`.

Try clicking a photo and editing the title and description. Try deleting a photo. This will delete the database rows corresponding to the photo and the files within the `public/photos/` directory. This is automatically performed by the `attachment_fu` plug-in, using a callback.

You should also try logging in as a different user and uploading some more photos. If you then look at the photos `index` action at `http://localhost:3000/photos`, you will see all of the photos uploaded by both users.

Writing the Test Cases

Although we have manually checked that the gallery works, we should also write a collection of tests so that we can make sure that we have covered all possibilities and have more confidence in our code when it goes into production.

We should perform unit and functional testing, but since our gallery does not interact with any other controllers, we do not need to perform any integration testing.

Creating the Photo Fixtures

First of all, create some database fixtures for the Photo model. Open the file `test/fixtures/photos.yml`. Remove the fixture placeholders, and enter the following fixtures:

```
parent_photo:
  id: 1
  user_id: 1
  title: a test photo
  body: just a test
  content_type: image/jpeg
  filename: testimage.jpg
  size: 1000
  width: 640
  height: 480
  created_at: <%= 1.days.ago.to_s(:db) %>
thumb_photo:
  id: 2
  parent_id: 1
  width: 160
  height: 120
  filename: testimage_thumb.jpg
  thumbnail: thumb
  created_at: <%= 1.days.ago.to_s(:db) %>
tiny_photo:
  id: 3
  parent_id: 1
  width: 80
  height: 80
  filename: testimage_tiny.jpg
  thumbnail: tiny
  created_at: <%= 1.days.ago.to_s(:db) %>
```

Unit Testing

We should add some unit tests to test the operation of the Photo model to make sure that we can create new photos by uploading a file and that destroying a photo deletes all thumbnail database records along with deleting all the image files.

Open the photos unit test file, `test/unit/photo_test.rb`, and delete the generated `test_truth` test. Add the tests as shown in Listing 7-10.

Listing 7-10. *Unit Tests for the Photo Model*

```
require File.dirname(__FILE__) + '/../test_helper'

class PhotoTest < Test::Unit::TestCase
  fixtures :photos, :users

  def test_should_upload_photo_and_create_thumbnails
    photo_object = upload_file 'rails.png', users(:valid_user)
    assert_file_exists photo_object.id, "rails.png"
    assert_file_exists photo_object.id, "rails_thumb.png"
    assert_file_exists photo_object.id, "rails_tiny.png"
  end

  def test_should_delete_db_row_and_files
    photo_object = upload_file 'rails.png', users(:valid_user)
    photo_count = Photo.count

    assert_file_exists photo_object.id, "rails.png"
    Photo.destroy(photo_object.id)

    assert_equal photo_count-3, Photo.count
    assert_file_does_not_exist photo_object.id, "rails.png"
    assert_file_does_not_exist photo_object.id, "rails_thumb.png"
    assert_file_does_not_exist photo_object.id, "rails_tiny.png"
  end

  protected
    def upload_file(image_file, user)
      image_file = File.join(RAILS_ROOT, 'public', 'images', image_file)
      photo = user.photos.create(:filename => image_file,
                                 :content_type => 'image/png',
                                 :temp_path => image_file)
      assert_valid photo
      photo
    end

    def assert_file_exists(photo_id, image_file)
      file = File.join(RAILS_ROOT, 'public', 'photos',
                       "#{photo_id}", "#{image_file}")
      assert File.file?(file), "File not found: #{image_file}"
    end

    def assert_file_does_not_exist(photo_id, image_file)
      file = File.join(RAILS_ROOT, 'public', 'photos',
                       "#{photo_id}", "#{image_file}")
      assert !File.file?(file)
    end
end
```

For these tests, I am going to test uploading the Rails logo, rails.png, which can be found in the public/images/ directory of any generated application.

To upload files, I have added a number of helper methods. The upload_file method takes the file name of an image within the public/images/ directory and a user object as parameters and creates a new photo object belonging to that user. Since we are not performing an upload through a browser, we have to manually supply the filename and content_type attributes. This method returns the new photo object.

The assert_file_exists and assert_file_does_not_exist methods simply check for the presence (or not) of a photo file.

The unit test test_should_upload_photo_and_create_thumbnails performs a file upload using the helper and checks that the file has been uploaded and the two thumbnails, thumb and tiny, have been created.

The test test_should_delete_db_row_and_files again performs a file upload but destroys the object using the destroy method. This will perform any callbacks that are related to the Photo model and, therefore, it should delete the files. The test checks that the three database rows, relating to the parent and the two thumbnails, are deleted. It then checks that the three files have been deleted from the file system.

Before we can run the tests, we have to update the test database to include the changes made for the Photo model. Enter the following command:

```
$ rake db:test:prepare
```

Now try running the units tests by entering the following command:

```
$ ruby test/unit/photo_test.rb
```

```
Loaded suite test/unit/photo_test
Started
..
Finished in 1.389494 seconds.

2 tests, 10 assertions, 0 failures, 0 errors
```

This proves to us that the model is working correctly and that the correct files are being created and deleted.

Functional Tests

For our functional tests, we should attempt to log in as a valid user and perform all of the valid actions to confirm that they are completed correctly and that the resulting pages or redirections are successful.

Create the functional test file test/functional/user_photos_controller_test.rb, and replace the generated tests with the code in Listing 7-11.

Listing 7-11. *Functional Tests for the Photos Controller*

```ruby
require File.dirname(__FILE__) + '/../test_helper'
require 'user_photos_controller'

# Re-raise errors caught by the controller.
class UserPhotosController; def rescue_action(e) raise e end; end

class UserPhotosControllerTest < Test::Unit::TestCase
  fixtures :photos, :users

  def setup
    @controller = PhotosController.new
    @request    = ActionController::TestRequest.new
    @response   = ActionController::TestResponse.new
  end

  def test_should_get_index
    get :index, {:user_id => 1}
    assert_response :success
    assert assigns(:photos)
  end

  def test_should_get_new
    login_as(:valid_user)
    get :new, {:user_id => 1}
    assert_response :success
  end

  def test_should_create_photo
    login_as(:valid_user)
    old_count = Photo.count
    image_file = File.join(RAILS_ROOT, 'public', 'images', 'rails.png')

    post :create, :photo => {:title => 'test photo',
                             :body => 'a test image',
                             :temp_path => image_file,
                             :content_type => 'image/png',
                             :filename => 'rails.png'}

    assert_equal old_count+3, Photo.count
    assert_redirected_to user_photos_path(:user_id => 1)
  end

  def test_should_show_photo
    get :show, {:user_id => 1, :id => 1}
    assert_response :success
  end
```

```ruby
  def test_should_get_edit
    login_as(:valid_user)
    get :edit, {:user_id => 1, :id => 1}
    assert_response :success
  end

  def test_should_update_photo
    login_as(:valid_user)

    # upload a test image
    image_file = File.join(RAILS_ROOT, 'public', 'images', 'rails.png')
    post :create,
        :photo => {:title => 'test photo',
                   :body => 'a test image',
                   :temp_path => image_file,
                   :content_type => 'image/png',
                   :filename => 'rails.png'}

    put :update, {:user_id => assigns['photo'].user_id, :id => assigns['photo'].id,
        :photo => {:body => 'this has been edited' }}
    assert_redirected_to user_photo_path(:user_id => assigns['photo'].user_id,
                                         :id => assigns['photo'].id)
  end

  def test_should_destroy_photo
    login_as(:valid_user)

    # upload a test image
    image_file = File.join(RAILS_ROOT, 'public', 'images', 'rails.png')
    post :create,
        :photo => {:title => 'test photo',
                   :body => 'a test image',
                   :temp_path => image_file,
                   :content_type => 'image/png',
                   :filename => 'rails.png'}

    old_count = Photo.count
    delete :destroy, {:user_id => assigns['photo'].user_id,
                      :id => assigns['photo'].id}
    assert_equal old_count-3, Photo.count
    assert_redirected_to user_photos_path
  end
end
```

These functional tests should look familiar from previous chapters. We have modified them to work with our controller. To test the `create` action, we are using the same technique as the unit test.

You should run the functional tests by entering the following command:

```
$ ruby test/functional/user_photos_controller_test.rb
```

```
Loaded suite test/functional/user_photos_controller_test
Started
.......
Finished in 1.217765 seconds.

7 tests, 13 assertions, 0 failures, 0 errors
```

This shows that our controller is working as expected.

Further Development of the Photo Gallery

While the gallery we have developed is pretty simple, it can be very easily expanded and developed further. You may wish to try experimenting with different storage mechanisms, especially S3, as it provides a simple way for you to offer a very fast, large, and reliable file hosting system.

Depending on your community, you may also wish to offer hosting of other types of files. Using the `attachment_fu` plug-in, you can easily test for different file types if necessary.

In Chapter 4, we added an RSS feed of the RailsCoders news blog. Using a similar technique, you could easily add RSS feeds of each user's photo gallery or a feed of all photos posted to the site. Also, you may wish to consider allowing users to add comments to other's photos.

Summary

In this chapter, we created a photo gallery for users of the RailsCoders site. Users can upload any photos to their galleries, where photos will be displayed in a thumbnail view. To do this, we made use of the `attachment_fu` plug-in to automatically handle file management, image resizing, and thumbnail creation.

We also discussed how to configure `attachment_fu` to use different file storage mechanisms and the benefits of each method.

In the next chapter, we will implement an e-mail newsletter for our users, along with e-mail notifications of blog comments.

CHAPTER 8

■■■

Sending E-mail and Building a Newsletter Mailing List

In this chapter, we will add functionality to allow the RailsCoders site to send e-mail to our users. There are many instances where it is useful to be able to automatically send e-mails directly to users, such as sending a welcome mail when they sign up or mail to allow them to reset their passwords. In this chapter, we will create an automated mailer that will inform users when someone has left a new comment in their blogs, which will allow the blog's owner to quickly reply to the comment.

We will also build an e-mail newsletter feature. Instead of a being an automated mailer, this feature will allow the administrator of the site to easily create and send newsletters or notices to all users of the site.

Using ActionMailer

The Rails framework includes a module called ActionMailer. As you will guess by its name, it is designed to allow you to easily send and receive e-mails from a Rails application. It can send mails using either a Simple Mail Transfer Protocol (SMTP) server or a local sendmail application. ActionMailer uses ERb templates in the same way as the web templates we have used to build the web site.

To send e-mails from Rails, you need to create a type of model called a mailer. Mailers are special types of models that inherit from the `ActionMailer::Base` class. You can create methods within this model that are used to set items such as the recipient and the subject, along with variables in the e-mail templates that you have created. You can also add attachments or create multipart e-mails. These model files are placed in the usual model directory, `app/models/`.

The e-mail templates for the mailer methods you create are placed in the views directory corresponding to the model name. For example, if your mailer model is called `notifier`, the e-mail templates for this are placed in the directory `app/views/notifier/`.

Configuring ActionMailer

Before you send e-mails using ActionMailer, you will have to configure your application to work with either an SMTP server or a local sendmail application. This is done in the Rails configuration files in the `config/` directory.

We have talked before about the fact that Rails has three modes for running an application: development, test, and production. Since it is likely that the mail server settings will be different for an application running on your local development machine or remotely on a server, you can specify different ActionMailer configurations for each of the Rails run modes.

Within the `config/` directory, there is another directory called `environments/`. This has three configuration files, one for each mode: `development.rb`, `test.rb`, and `production.rb`.

The test mode is already set up not to actually deliver mails but to collect them in an array that is accessible by the test methods.

If you look at the `config/environments/test.rb` file, you will see that this is set by the following line:

```
config.action_mailer.delivery_method = :test
```

If you are using Linux or OS X, you may wish to use the sendmail application to send e-mails from your local machine. This requires very little configuration and is convenient for development mode.

To configure ActionMailer to use sendmail, edit the relevant configuration file, for example, `config/environments/development.rb`, by adding the following line:

```
config.action_mailer.delivery_method = :sendmail
```

For most purposes, configuring ActionMailer to use an SMTP sever is the best method. However, you will need to know the settings of your SMTP server. Most ISPs and hosting companies provide you with an SMTP server.

To configure your application to use SMTP, add the following line to the relevant environment configuration file, such as `config/environments/development.rb`:

```
config.action_mailer.delivery_method = :smtp
```

You also need to provide the details of the SMTP server. This is done in the `config/environment.rb` file. At the end of this file, add the following code, and replace the `address`, `user_name`, and `password` with your own settings:

```
ActionMailer::Base.smtp_settings = {
  :address => 'smtp.yourserver.com',    # default: localhost
  :port => '25',                        # default: 25
  :authentication => :plain,            # :plain, :login or :cram_md5
  :user_name => 'user',
  :password => 'pass'
}
```

Specifying the E-mail Feature Requirements

For many aspects of our application, sending e-mails to our users would be very useful, such as sending a welcome e-mail when they sign up or allowing them to receive recent news articles as e-mails.

In this chapter, we will add a facility so that new comments left on users' blogs are automatically sent to them as e-mails. Also, we want to be able to send an occasional newsletter to all users of the site.

E-mail Notifications of New Comments

When a new comment is left in response to a post on a user's blog, we want to notify the owner of the blog that someone has commented and provide a link to allow the user to easily see the comment. We can do this by adding code to the specific action where this event happens, that is, the comments controller's create action.

ActionMailer allows us to create e-mails based on an e-mail template, so we can write a generic e-mail that will be personalized for each outgoing e-mail with the user and comment details.

We want the mail to have both plain text and HTML parts, meaning that the mail will display as only plain text on text-based e-mail applications and as an HTML e-mail in applications that support it.

The e-mail should contain a link to the entry that has been commented on, allowing the user to quickly go to the entry and respond.

E-mail Newsletters

We want to be able to send a message to all registered users of the site. This could be used for newsletters or to notify users of upgrades or new features.

To respect your users' privacy, you should consider adding a user-settable option for whether they should receive bulk e-mails or not. In this chapter, we will not implement this, but it should be considered for a live site.

Sending an e-mail message to many users at once can put a strain on your server if you are running a local sendmail process. SMTP servers are generally limited to accept only a limited number of messages within a given time frame. This may be as little as a hundred e-mails per hour, depending on your SMTP server provider. Because we want to send a personalized e-mail message to each user, we cannot just specify a list of recipients on a BCC list.

Therefore, we need to work out a way of sending a large number of e-mails without overloading our system. Unsurprisingly, this problem has already been solved and built into a plug-in called ar_mailer. ar_mailer was developed by Eric Hodel, and you can find the documentation at http://dev.robotcoop.com/Tools/ar_mailer.

ar_mailer utilizes a database table to store all the to-be-sent e-mails, which are subsequently processed by a separate script, ar_sendmail. When the ar_sendmail script is executed, it will process each of the messages waiting to be sent in the database table, sending them with the SMTP settings set up for ActionMailer.

In order to allow newsletters to be created, stored, and edited before sending, we will also create a resource for the newsletters that we send to users. This model simply needs to store the e-mail subject, body text, and the time and date that it was created. The model should also store whether the newsletter has been sent or not and if so, the date and time that it was sent.

This database structure is shown in Table 8-1.

Table 8-1. *The Newsletter Database Structure*

Field Name	Field Type	Description
id	integer	The primary key
subject	string	The e-mail subject line
body	text	The body of the e-mail
sent	boolean	Whether this newsletter has been sent or not
created_at	datetime	The date and time that the newsletter was created

Along with the normal REST actions, the controller for the newsletter resource also needs to have an action that actually sends the newsletter out to the users. We will call this action sendmails.

■**Caution** Be careful when naming your actions, as you cannot use certain method names that are reserved by the system. For instance, you cannot use the name send for an action in a Rails controller.

Building the New Comment Notifier

To allow us to send e-mails on a specific event, we will have to create a Rails mailer together with the relevant views for this mailer.

We also need to call this mailer when a specific event occurs. We will do this from an existing controller.

Creating the Mailer

To create a Mailer model, we will use the Rails generate script. This will create a skeleton model, views directory, and test code.

Enter the following command:

```
$ ruby script/generate mailer Notifier
```

```
    exists  app/models/
    create  app/views/ notifier
    exists  test/unit/
    create  test/fixtures/ notifier
    create  app/models/notifier.rb
    create  test/unit/notifier_test.rb
```

If you open the Mailer model file, app/models/notifier.rb, you will notice that this class definition inherits from the ActionMailer class. Now, edit this file as shown in Listing 8-1.

Listing 8-1. *The Notifier Mailer Model*

```
class Notifier < ActionMailer::Base
  def new_comment_notification(comment)
    blog_owner = comment.entry.user
    recipients blog_owner.email_with_username

    from       "RailsCoders <system@railscoders.net>"
    subject    "A new comment has been left on your blog"
    body       :comment => comment,
               :blog_owner => blog_owner,
               :blog_owner_url => "http://railscoders.net/users/#{blog_owner.id}",
               :blog_entry_url =>
      "http://railscoders.net/users/#{blog_owner.id}/entries/#{comment.entry.id}"
  end
end
```

You will notice that the new_comment_notification method specifies the e-mail address of recipients, the e-mail address that the mail is to be sent from, and a subject for the message, and it passes an instance variable comment to the template. You can specify any number of variables here, which are all passed to the template and can be used in your e-mail.

For the recipient's e-mail address, we have used email_with_username. However, at the moment, no such attribute exists for the model. When specifying an e-mail address, you can use a friendly name and specify the e-mail address within < and >, as we did with the from address. To produce an e-mail address for a user, we will add a method called email_with_username to the User model.

To do this, open the User model file, app/models/user.rb. Add the following method near to the end of the file but within the User class:

```
...
  def email_with_username
    "#{username} <#{email}>"
  end
end
```

This will now return the user's username and e-mail in the desired format.

In the new_comment_notification method, you will notice that we create an instance variable called @blog_entry_url in the variables that are passed to the template. This is simply a string consisting of the URL of the entry. Notice here that we have to manually specify the site's hostname, railscoders.net, because when a mailer is executed, it has no knowledge about the request. A normal action method responds to an HTTP request, specifying the URL of the site along with the request. However, when a mailer is called from a controller, it does not have any context about the incoming request, so we have to specify the details ourselves.

We now need to create the view template that corresponds to the mailer method new_comment_notification. Create the file app/views/notifier/new_comment_notification.rhtml, and enter the e-mail template shown in Listing 8-2.

Listing 8-2. *The Comment Notification E-mail Template*

```
Hi <%= @blog_owner.username %>,

A new comment has been left on your blog at RailsCoders.net.

The comment was left by '<%= @comment.user.username %>' at ➥
<%= @comment.created_at.to_s(:short) %>.

To read the comment, go to <%= @blog_entry_url %>.

Cheers,
The RailsCoders Team
```

As you can see, this uses the instance variables set by the new_comment_notification method within the e-mail.

However, this e-mail seems a little old school, being only a plain text e-mail. Since there is a link to the blog entry with the new comment supplied in the e-mail, it would be nice to send the e-mail as an HTML e-mail.

Thankfully, ActionMailer allows us to easily create multipart e-mails, delivering an e-mail with a plain text part and an HTML part. E-mail readers are smart enough to know which parts they should display, depending on their configuration.

To do this, all we have to do is provide templates with certain names. Rails will automatically look for template names for the particular method with a content type specified before the .rhtml suffix. Therefore, files ending in .text.plain.rhtml, .text.html.rhtml, or .text.xml.rhtml will be rendered and attached to the e-mail as separate parts with the appropriate content type. A file ending in .text.html.rhtml will be sent with the content type of text/html.

Since the e-mail template we have already written is in plain text, rename that as new_comment_notification.text.plain.rhtml, keeping it within the same directory.

We can now create a HTML version of the same e-mail. Create the file app/views/notifier/new_comment_notification.text.html.rhtml, and enter the view shown in Listing 8-3.

Listing 8-3. *The HTML New Comment Notification E-mail Template*

```
<%= image_tag "http://railscoders.net/images/logo.png", :alt => "RailsCoders" %>

<p>Hi <%= @blog_owner.username %>,</p>

<p>A new comment has been left on your blog at RailsCoders.</p>

<p>The comment was left by <%= link_to @comment.user.username,
@blog_owner_url %> at <%= @comment.created_at.to_s(:short) %>.</p>

<p>To read the comment, go to <%= link_to @blog_entry_url, @blog_entry_url %></p>

<p>Cheers,<br />
<a href="http://railscoders.net">The RailsCoders Team</a></p>
```

Now we have made the e-mail a little more interesting by adding links to the comment author's profile and the entry for which the comment was made, along with including our logo.

Manually Testing E-mail Creation

Before we integrate the comment notification feature into our system, we can test it out manually, to check that the expected mail is composed by our notifier and templates. To do this, we are going to use the interactive features of Ruby, specifically the Rails console.

The Rails console allows you to interactively use your application using Ruby and Rails commands. This allows you to investigate inside your system rather than just using the web interface and looking at logs.

To start the Rails console, open a terminal window, and enter the following command:

```
$ ruby script/console
```

```
Loading development environment.
>>
```

The >> is a prompt for you to enter commands. Here, you can now run any Ruby or Rails commands and immediately see the result. You can also inspect and debug your code.

For instance, if you wanted to check that the new email_with_username method that we added to the User model earlier is working, try the following:

```
>> adminuser = User.find_by_username('admin')
```

```
#<User:0x33ea584 @attributes={"last_login_at"=>nil, "updated_at"=>"2007-01-10
05:55:00", "profile"=>"Site Administrator", "hashed_password"=>"8c6976e5b5410
415bde908bd4dee15dfb167a9c873fc4bb8a81f6f2ab448a918", "entries_count"=>"0",
"username"=>"Admin", "enable_comments"=>nil, "blog_title"=>nil, "enabled"=>"1",
"id"=>"1", "posts_count"=>"3", "created_at"=>"2006-12-11 23:52:23",
"email"=>"admin@example.com"}>
```

You can see from the result that Rails has executed the code that we entered. You can now use this instance of the User model, adminuser, as you would in your Rails code. For instance, to test the email_with_username method, enter the following:

```
>> adminuser.email_with_username
```

```
"Admin <admin@railscoders.net>"
```

This is exactly what we expected and wanted—the username together with the e-mail address enclosed in < and >.

We can now use this same method to manually test the e-mail creation. It is also a good idea to use this in conjunction with monitoring the Rails log files. When you enter a command, the log files will show any SQL queries that are executed and also the content of any e-mails that are generated by the system.

■Tip By default, Rails will attempt to deliver e-mails created in the development mode. If you wish to change this, add `config.action_mailer.delivery_method = :test` to your development mode configuration file, `config/environments/development.rb`.

To invoke a method in a mailer class, you simply prefix `deliver_` to the method name and call that as a class method of the mailer class. For example, to invoke the `new_comment_notification` method and deliver the e-mail, you would use `Notifier.deliver_new_comment_notification(comment)`, where `comment` is the comment object of the new comment that has been left on the blog.

We can try this now. First, make sure that you have a blog entry added for one of your users and that this blog entry has a comment added to it. For this example, I have an entry with id of 1, which has a comment with the comment id of 1.

To create an instance of this comment object, use the `find` command as follows:

```
>> comment = Comment.find(1)
```

```
#<Comment:0x3403430 @attributes={"updated_at"=>"2007-01-03 16:55:26",
"entry_id"=>"1", "body"=>"a comment!", "id"=>"1", "user_id"=>"2",
"created_at"=>"2007-01-03 16:55:26"}>
```

As you can see from the console output, we have successfully retrieved the `comment` object. If you look at the `development.log` file, you will see the SQL query that was performed:

```
Comment Columns (0.135616)    SHOW FIELDS FROM comments
Comment Load (0.043175)    SELECT * FROM comments WHERE (comments.id = 1)
```

You can now invoke the `deliver_new_comment_notification` method, creating and sending the e-mail to the blog owner:

```
>> mail = Notifier.deliver_new_comment_notification(comment)
```

```
#<TMail::Mail port=#<TMail::StringPort:id=0x19db598>
bodyport=#<TMail::StringPort:id=0x19da030>>
```

If you take a look at the `development.log` file now, you will see the entire e-mail, complete with the plain text and HTML parts:

```
Sent mail:
From: system@railscoders.net
To: Alan <abradburne@gmail.com>
Subject: A new comment has been left on your blog
Mime-Version: 1.0
Content-Type: multipart/alternative; boundary=mimepart_45bfd0d45013b_18d7118ba0152


--mimepart_45bfd0d45013b_18d7118ba0152
Content-Type: plain/text; charset=utf-8
Content-Transfer-Encoding: Quoted-printable
Content-Disposition: inline


Hi Alan,

A new comment has been left on your blog at RailsCoders.net.

The comment was left by 'Alan' at 03 Jan 16:55.

To read the comment, go to http://railscoders.net/users/2/entries/1

--mimepart_45bfd0d45013b_18d7118ba0152
Content-Type: plain/html; charset=utf-8
Content-Transfer-Encoding: Quoted-printable
Content-Disposition: inline


<img alt="RailsCoders" src="http://railscoders.net/images/logo.png" />

<p>Hi Alan,</p>

<p>A new comment has been left on your blog at RailsCoders.</p>

<p>The comment was left by <a href="http://railscoders.net/users/2">Alan</a> on
03 Jan 16:55.

To read the comment, go to <a href="http://railscoders.net/users/2/entries/1">
http://railscoders.net/users/2/entries/1</a>

Cheers,
<p><a href="http://railscoders.net">The RailsCoders Team</a></p>

--mimepart_45bfd0d45013b_18d7118ba0152--
```

This has created a new object called mail. You can also interrogate the mail object that you just created in the Rails console.

■**Tip** The Rails mailer uses a Ruby library called TMail to work with e-mails. You can find the TMail documentation at http://i.loveruby.net/en/projects/tmail/doc.

For example, to look at the addressee of the e-mail, type the following command:

```
>> mail.to
```

```
=> ["abradburne@gmail.com"]
```

Or to view the entire e-mail header, use this:

```
>> mail.header
```

```
{"message-id"=>#<TMail::MessageIdHeader "<45c1c6b631951_18d7118ba045@alans-
computer.local.tmail>">, "mime-version"=>#<TMail::MimeVersionHeader "1.0">,
"from"=>#<TMail::AddressHeader "system@railscoders.net">, "content-
type"=>#<TMail::ContentTypeHeader "multipart/alternative">,
"date"=>#<TMail::DateTimeHeader "Thu, 04 Jan 2007 10:53:42 +0000">,
"subject"=>#<TMail::UnstructuredHeader "A new comment has been left on your blog">,
"to"=>#<TMail::AddressHeader "\"Alan\" <abradburne@gmail.com>">}
```

To display the body of the text-only part of the e-mail, use this:

```
>> mail.parts.first.body
```

```
=> "Hi Alan,\n\nA new comment has been left on your blog at RailsCoders.net.\n\n
The comment was left by 'Alan' at 03 Jan 16:55.\n\nTo read the comment, go to
http://railscoders.net/users/2/entries/1"
```

Now that we can see that the e-mail created by our notifier method looks correct, we can integrate it with the necessary controller.

Calling the Mailer from the Comments Controller

This e-mail will be sent when a new comment is added to a blog. As you will remember from Chapter 6, new comments are created by the create action of the comments controller.

Open the comments controller, app/controllers/comments_controller.rb, and take a look at the create action. For reference, this is shown in Listing 8-4.

Listing 8-4. *The Comments Controller Create Action*

```
def create
  @entry = Entry.find_by_user_id_and_id(params[:user_id],
                                         params[:entry_id])
  @comment = Comment.new(:user_id => @logged_in_user.id,
                         :body => params[:comment][:body])

  if @entry.comments << @comment
    flash[:notice] = 'Comment was successfully created.'
    redirect_to entry_path(:user_id => @entry.user,
                           :id => @entry)
  else
    render :controller => 'entries', :action => 'show',
           :user_id => @entry.user, :entry_id => @entry
  end
end
```

We need to invoke the `deliver_new_comment_notification` method when we know that a comment has been successfully created and associated with an entry. Therefore, we need to add the invocation within the when-true execution path of the `if` statement, where the comment has successfully been saved and added to an entry.

Add the mailer delivery method as follows:

```
...
if @entry.comments << @comment
flash[:notice] = 'Comment was successfully created.'
Notifier.deliver_new_comment_notification(@comment)
redirect_to entry_path(:user_id => @entry.user, :id => @entry)
else
...
```

We can now try running this from within the application.

Testing the Mailer from Within the Application

Make sure that the Rails application server is running and that you are logged into the site as a regular user. Now, visit a blog on the site that already has a blog entry, and click the comments link beneath the entry to create a new comment.

You should watch the development log file, using either the command `tail -f log/development.log` if you are using OS X or Linux or a tail application if you are using Windows.

Create a new comment for this entry, and click save. The comment will be created, and your browser will be directed to the blog index view.

Take a look at your development log file. Scroll back to the beginning of the processing for this request, marked by the following line:

```
Processing CommentsController#create (for 127.0.0.1 at 2007-01-04 12:42:26) [POST]
```

Beneath this, you will see all of the SQL queries that were performed for this request, including the INSERT statement used to create the comment and the UPDATE statement that associates the comment with the entry.

After these, you will see the mail that was created and sent to the owner of the blog entry.

Automating the Mailer Tests

Of course, while manually testing the mailer is useful, we should write automated test cases too. We should develop both unit tests and functional tests.

The unit test cases will test the mailer on its own. We will use the fixtures that we have already created to make a new comment notification e-mail, which we will then test using some simple assertions that look for specific patterns in the created mail, such as the correct URL to the entry and the correct username of the comment poster.

The functional test cases will test that the right e-mail is sent at the right time. In our application, the new comment notification e-mail will be sent when a new comment is saved, so this is what we need to check.

Unit Tests

When you used the generate command to create a mailer, Rails also creates the skeleton file for your mailer. This is placed with the other unit tests in the test/unit/ directory. Open the test/unit/notifier.rb file now.

You will notice that this is similar to a normal unit test file, except that along with setting a few variables and including an ActionMailer class, a setup method and two private methods, read_fixture and encode, are provided.

Our unit test should simply retrieve one of our comment fixtures and create a new notification message based on that. We can then test that the dynamic text within that e-mail is correct by performing several assertions.

To add the test, edit the notifier.rb file as shown in Listing 8-5.

Listing 8-5. *Unit Test for the Comment Notification*

```
require File.dirname(__FILE__) + '/../test_helper'

class NotifierTest < Test::Unit::TestCase
  FIXTURES_PATH = File.dirname(__FILE__) + '/../fixtures'
  CHARSET = "utf-8"
  fixtures :entries, :comments, :users

  include ActionMailer::Quoting
```

```
  def setup
    ActionMailer::Base.delivery_method = :test
    ActionMailer::Base.perform_deliveries = true
    ActionMailer::Base.deliveries = []

    @expected = TMail::Mail.new
    @expected.set_content_type "text", "plain", { "charset" => CHARSET }
    @expected.mime_version = '1.0'
  end

  def test_comment_notify
    comment = Comment.find(1)
    response = Notifier.create_new_comment_notification(comment)
    assert_equal "A new comment has been left on your blog", response.subject
    assert_match /Hi #{comment.entry.user.username}/, response.body
    assert_match /The comment was left by '#{comment.user.username}' at ➥
#{comment.created_at.to_s(:short)}/, response.body
    assert_match /go to http:\/\/railscoders.net\/users\/1\/entries\/1/,
      response.body
  end

  private
    def read_fixture(action)
      IO.readlines("#{FIXTURES_PATH}/notifier/#{action}")
    end

    def encode(subject)
      quoted_printable(subject, CHARSET)
    end
end
```

You should now run this unit test as follows:

```
$ ruby test/unit/notifier_test.rb
```

```
Loaded suite test/unit/notifier_test
Started
.
Finished in 0.253968 seconds.

1 tests, 4 assertions, 0 failures, 0 errors
```

Functional Tests

To ensure that mail is sent at the right time, we should write functional tests to initiate sending a comment notification e-mail.

Since this is handled by the comments controller, we will add this functional test to the comments functional test file that we already created. Open `test/functional/comments_controller_test.rb` now. Add the following test to the end of this file, before the last end statement:

```
def test_send_notify_email
  num_deliveries = ActionMailer::Base.deliveries.size

  login_as(:valid_user)
  post :create,{:user_id => 1, :entry_id => 1,
                :comment => {:body => 'that is great'}}

  assert_equal num_deliveries + 1, ActionMailer::Base.deliveries.size
end
```

This test simply checks the number of e-mails to be delivered before and after a comment is created. After a new comment is created, there should be one extra message.

Run the comments controller functional tests again to check that this test passes:

```
$ ruby test/functional/comments_controller_test.rb
```

```
Loaded suite test/functional/comments_controller_test
Started
....
Finished in 0.313221 seconds.

4 tests, 9 assertions, 0 failures, 0 errors
```

Building the Newsletter Feature

The newsletter feature is a little more complex than the comment notification. First of all, we need some way of storing the newsletter. Since a newsletter is going to be different every time, we need a little more than just an ERb mail template.

Installing ar_mailer

As discussed earlier, we are going to use the Ruby gem `ar_mailer` to make it easier for us to send mail to a large number of users at the same time.

If we decide to use `ar_mailer`, we need to change the delivery method for the system. Rather than using the SMTP or sendmail settings shown at the beginning of the chapter, we tell ActionMailer to use ActiveRecord as the delivery method.

First of all, install the gem using the following command:

```
$ gem install ar_mailer
```

```
Successfully installed ar_mailer-1.1.0
Installing ri documentation for ar_mailer-1.1.0...
Installing RDoc documentation for ar_mailer-1.1.0...
```

■**Note** On Linux or OS X, you may need to prefix the gem install command with sudo.

The ar_mailer gem utilizes a database table to store all of the messages that it needs to send. We need to create a migration to add the necessary table to our database.

Create a new migration with the following command:

```
$ ruby script/generate model Email
```

```
exists  app/models/
exists  test/unit/
exists  test/fixtures/
create  app/models/email.rb
create  test/unit/email_test.rb
create  test/fixtures/emails.yml
exists  db/migrate
create  db/migrate/017_create_emails.rb
```

Edit the migration file db/migrate/017_create_emails.rb as shown in Listing 8-6. This will create a new table called emails to store the e-mails waiting to be sent.

Listing 8-6. *The ar_mailer Migration Script*

```
class CreateEmails < ActiveRecord::Migration
  def self.up
    create_table :emails do |t|
      t.column :from, :string
      t.column :to, :string
      t.column :last_send_attempt, :integer, :default => 0
      t.column :mail, :text
    end
  end

  def self.down
    drop_table :emails
  end
end
```

To use the `ar_mailer` code to deliver e-mails, we need to change the `Notifier` class to inherit from `ActionMailer::ARMailer` instead of `ActionMailer::Base`. Open the notifier, `app/models/notifier.rb`, and change the class definition line as follows:

```
class Notifier < ActionMailer::ARMailer
  def new_comment_notification(comment)
    blog_owner = comment.entry.user
    ...
```

We also need to change the delivery method in the Rails configuration files to deliver e-mails using ActiveRecord. We will change the delivery method for the development mode, since we are only working in development mode here. You should also make the same changes in the `production.rb` file if you are going to use `ar_mailer` in a production environment.

Open the Rails configuration file, `config/environments/development.rb`, and change the delivery method as follows:

```
config.action_mailer.delivery_method = :activerecord
```

Finally, we need to make sure that the correct paths are set for the `ar_mailer` to be loaded by Rails. Edit the file `config/environment.rb` by adding the following line to the end of the file:

```
require 'action_mailer/ar_mailer'
```

Creating the Skeleton Resource

To allow easy creation and editing of the newsletters, we will create a new resource, called `newsletters`, which is only accessible by the Admin user.

We will use the `scaffold_resource` generator to create the resource and modify the generated code to meet our requirements. We can add the attribute names and their database table types to the command, and they will be automatically added to the migration script:

```
$ ruby script/generate scaffold_resource Newsletter
```

```
    exists  app/models/
    exists  app/controllers/
    exists  app/helpers/
    create  app/views/newsletters
    exists  test/functional/
    exists  test/unit/
    create  app/views/newsletters/index.rhtml
    create  app/views/newsletters/show.rhtml
    create  app/views/newsletters/new.rhtml
    create  app/views/newsletters/edit.rhtml
    create  app/views/layouts/newsletters.rhtml
 identical  public/stylesheets/scaffold.css
    create  app/models/newsletters.rb
    create  app/controllers/newsletters_controller.rb
    create  test/functional/newsletters_controller_test.rb
    create  app/helpers/newsletters_helper.rb
```

```
create  test/unit/newsletters_test.rb
create  test/fixtures/newsletters.yml
exists  db/migrate
create  db/migrate/018_create_newsletters.rb
 route  map.resources :newsletters
```

We can now update the migration file to add the database columns detailed in the specification. Alter the migration file, db/migrations/018_create_newsletters.rb, as shown in Listing 8-7.

Listing 8-7. *The Migration File for the Newsletter*

```
class CreateNewsletters < ActiveRecord::Migration
  def self.up
    create_table :newsletters do |t|
      t.column :subject, :string
      t.column :body, :text
      t.column :sent, :boolean, :null => false, :default => false
      t.column :created_at, :datetime
      t.column :updated_at, :datetime
    end
  end

  def self.down
    drop_table :newsletters
  end
end
```

Now, run the migration:

```
$ rake db:migrate
```

```
(in /Users/alan/Documents/Projects/Rails/railscoders)
== AddArMailerTable: migrating ==================================================
-- create_table(:emails)
   -> 0.1708s
== AddArMailerTable: migrated (0.1709s) =========================================

== CreateNewsletters: migrating =================================================
-- create_table(:newsletters)
   -> 0.0045s
== CreateNewsletters: migrated (0.0047s) ========================================
```

Mapping the Newsletter Resource

The newsletter resource is not nested under any other resources, so a simple top-level mapping, as created by the generate script, is fine.

However, we have specified that we need an extra action for the newsletter resource, called `sendmails`. This will initiate the sending of a specific newsletter to all users. We need to declare this in the `routes.rb` file.

Since we want this action to be available only to members of the newsletter resource, we declare it with the parameter `:member`. If we wanted to declare an action that was available to a collection of newsletter resources as a whole, we would use the parameter `:collection`.

Open the `config/routes.rb` file now. You will see that the `generate` script has already created the line `map.resources :newsletters`. Modify this to include the `sendmails` action as follows:

```
map.resources :newsletters, :member => { :sendmails => :put }
```

This specifies that the `sendmails` action can only be accessed via an HTTP PUT request. This will ensure that the send action is not accidentally initiated by a web accelerator application.

The Newsletter Model

The Newsletter model needs to have the validations added to it. Since the newsletters are not related to any other models, there are no relationships to define.

Because the Newsletter model is very simple, the only two fields that are entered by a user, and therefore, the only two that require validating are the message subject and body. We should also use the `validates_presence_of` validation to test that neither field is left blank.

Open the newsletter model file, `app/models/newsletter.rb`, and add the validations shown in Listing 8-8.

Listing 8-8. *The Newsletter Model*

```ruby
class Newsletter < ActiveRecord::Base
  validates_presence_of :subject, :body
  validates_length_of :subject, :maximum => 255
  validates_length_of :body, :maximum => 10000
end
```

Writing the Newsletter Controller and Views

The newsletter controller is a simple resource, allowing an administrator user to create and edit newsletters, which can then be sent by clicking a button on the newsletter show screen.

The scaffolding code produced by the generator gives us a useful starting point, but we need to adapt it to our application. For simplicity, we will just implement a web version of the controller. If you wish to allow this to be accessed via an XML API, you can add the functionality as we have in earlier chapters.

Open the controller, `app/controllers/newsletters_controller.rb`, and edit it as shown in Listing 8-9.

Listing 8-9. *The Newsletters Controller*

```
class NewslettersController < ApplicationController
  before_filter :check_administrator_role

  # GET /newsletters
  def index
    @newsletters = Newsletter.find(:all)
  end

  # GET /newsletters/1
  def show
    @newsletter = Newsletter.find(params[:id])
  end

  # GET /newsletters/new
  def new
    @newsletter = Newsletter.new
  end

  # GET /newsletters/1;edit
  def edit
    @newsletter = Newsletter.find_by_id_and_sent(params[:id], false)
  end

  # POST /newsletters
  def create
    @newsletter = Newsletter.new(params[:newsletter])

    if @newsletter.save
      flash[:notice] = 'Newsletter was successfully created.'
      redirect_to newsletter_path(@newsletter)
    else
      render :action => "new"
    end
  end

  # PUT /newsletters/1
  def update
    @newsletter = Newsletter.find_by_id_and_sent(params[:id], false)

    if @newsletter.update_attributes(params[:newsletter])
      flash[:notice] = 'Newsletter was successfully updated.'
      redirect_to newsletter_path(@newsletter)
    else
      render :action => "edit"
    end
  end
```

```
# DELETE /newsletters/1
def destroy
  @newsletter = Newsletter.find_by_id_and_sent(params[:id], false)
  @newsletter.destroy

  redirect_to newsletters_path
end

# PUT /newsletters/1;send
def sendmails
  newsletter = Newsletter.find_by_id_and_sent(params[:id], false)
  users = User.find(:all)
  users.each do |user|
    Notifier.deliver_newsletter(user, newsletter)
  end
  newsletter.update_attribute('sent', true)
  redirect_to newsletters_path
end

end
```

We need to make sure that only administrator users can access this controller, so we will protect it using the before filter check_administrator_role.

The Index Action and View

The index action method simply returns all newsletters. This is fine, but we have modified the action method to order the newsletters by the last update time, showing the most recently updated item first.

For the view, we want to show the list of newsletters including the subjects, whether or not the newsletters have been sent, the times they were created and updated, along with links to show, edit, or delete newsletters. However, since we do not want an administrator user to edit an already sent newsletter, we should only show these links for newsletters that have not been sent. The sent Boolean field tells us if it has been sent or not. However, this will display true or false, whereas it would be more user friendly to display "yes" or "no." To do this, we will create a helper method to convert true to the string 'yes' and false to the string 'no'. Since this method might be useful for other views, not just the newsletter views, we will create it in the applicationwide helper file, app/helpers/application_helper.rb.

Open this file now, and edit it as shown in Listing 8-10.

Listing 8-10. *The Applicationwide Helper File*

```
module ApplicationHelper

  def yes_no(bool)
    if bool == true
      "yes"
```

```
    else
      "no"
    end
  end
end
```

Now, open the index view file, `app/views/newsletters/index.rhtml`, and enter the view shown in Listing 8-11.

Listing 8-11. *The Newsletter Index View*

```
<h1>Listing newsletters</h1>

<%= link_to 'Create new newsletter', new_newsletter_path %>

<table>
  <tr>
    <th>Subject</th>
    <th>Sent</th>
    <th>Created at</th>
    <th>Updated at</th>
  </tr>

<% for newsletter in @newsletters %>
  <tr>
    <td><%=h newsletter.subject %></td>
    <td><%= yes_no(newsletter.sent) %></td>
    <td><%=h newsletter.created_at %></td>
    <td><%=h newsletter.updated_at %></td>
    <% if !newsletter.sent %>
      <td><%= link_to 'Show', newsletter_path(newsletter) %></td>
      <td><%= link_to 'Edit', edit_newsletter_path(newsletter) %></td>
      <td><%= link_to 'Destroy', newsletter_path(newsletter),
                :confirm => 'Are you sure?', :method => :delete %></td>
    <% end %>
  </tr>
<% end %>
</table>
```

Notice that we are using the yes_no helper method to show if the newsletter has been sent or not.

The Show Action

The show action should just display one newsletter, along with links to allow the user to edit the newsletter, initiate the sendmails action, or go back to the list of newsletters. If the newsletter has already been sent, the edit and sendmails links should not be shown.

Open the show view, `app/views/newsletters/show.rhtml`, and enter the code as shown in Listing 8-12.

Listing 8-12. *The Newsletter Show View*

```
<h2>Newsletter</h2>

<p>
  <b>Subject:</b> <%=h @newsletter.subject %>
</p>

<p>
  <b>Created at:</b> <%=h @newsletter.created_at %>
</p>

<p>
  <b>Updated at:</b> <%=h @newsletter.updated_at %>
</p>

<p>
  <b>Sent:</b> <%= yes_no(@newsletter.sent) %>
</p>

<p>
  <b>Body:</b>
  <br />
  <%=h @newsletter.body %>
</p>

<% if !@newsletter.sent %>
  <%= link_to 'Edit', edit_newsletter_path(@newsletter) %> |
  <%= link_to 'Send', sendmails_newsletter_path(@newsletter),
        :method => :put,
        :confirm => 'Are you sure you wish to send this newsletter?' %> |
<% end %>
<%= link_to 'Back', newsletters_path %>
```

Notice that we are using the yes_no helper method again.

The New Action

The new newsletter view should simply display a form for allowing an administrator user to write a new newsletter. Since the body of the newsletter will be parsed as an ERb template, the Admin user can enter embedded Ruby commands in the same was as any regular e-mail template. We should make the Admin user who is creating the e-mail aware of any objects that can be used in the e-mail, so we have added a note at the bottom of the form.

The page submits the form to the `newsletters_path` URL, which will be processed by the create action, as usual.

Open the new newsletter view `app/views/newsletters/new.rhtml`, and add the code shown in Listing 8-13.

Listing 8-13. *The New Newsletter View*

```
<h2>Create New Newsletter</h2>

<%= error_messages_for :newsletter %>

<% form_for(:newsletter, :url => newsletters_path) do |f| %>
  <p>
    <b>Subject</b><br />
    <%= f.text_field :subject, :size => 70 %>
  </p>

  <p>
    <b>Body</b><br />
    <%= f.text_area :body, :cols => 70, :rows => 25 %>
    <br />
    You can access the user model with @user. <br >
    e.g. &lt;%= @user.username %&gt; or &lt;%= @user.email %&gt;
  </p>

  <p>
    <%= submit_tag "Save draft" %> or <%= link_to 'Cancel', newsletters_path %>
  </p>
<% end %>
```

The Create Action

If you look at the `create` action in the controller, we have not made any changes from the version created by the generator. It simply creates a new newsletter object using the parameter passed by the form, if the parameters are valid. If not, the new view is shown again, together with any error messages.

The Edit Action

The `edit` action simply loads a specific newsletter and displays it in a form to allow the Admin user to edit it. However, since we do not allow editing of newsletters that have already been sent, the controller action has been modified to find newsletters based on an `id` and the `sent` field, where the `sent` field must be `false`.

The edit view is similar to the new newsletter view. Open the view file, `app/views/newsletters/edit.rhtml`, and edit as shown in Listing 8-14.

Listing 8-14. *The Newsletter Edit View*

```
<h1>Edit Newsletter</h1>

<%= error_messages_for :newsletter %>

<% form_for(:newsletter,
            :url => newsletter_path(@newsletter),
            :html => { :method => :put }) do |f| %>
  <p>
    <b>Subject</b><br />
    <%= f.text_field :subject, :size => 70 %>
  </p>

  <p>
    <b>Body</b><br />
    <%= f.text_area :body, :cols => 70, :rows => 25 %>
    <br />
    You can access the user model with @user. <br >
    e.g. &lt;%= @user.username %&gt; or &lt;%= @user.email %&gt;
  </p>

  <p>
    <%= submit_tag "Save draft" %> or <%= link_to 'Cancel', newsletters_path %>
  </p>
<% end %>
```

The Update Action

The generated controller update action has also been modified to save updates only to newsletters where the sent field is false.

The Destroy Action

Like the edit and update actions, the destroy method has also been modified so that it is impossible for an administrator user to delete a newsletter that has already been sent.

The Sendmails Action

When the user initiates the sendmails action, the method retrieves all of the users of the site and cycles through them, sending a message to each one in turn. The mail is sent by calling the deliver_newsletter method of the Notifier class. Recall from earlier that this means we need to create the method newsletter in our Notifier class, which we will do next.

After sending all of the mails, the sendmails action also updates the Newsletter object, setting the sent flag to true.

Creating the Newsletter Mailer

We now need to add the mailer method that the newsletter controller will use to send the messages to the users. We will add it to the existing `Notifier` mailer class.

Open the notifier mailer, `app/models/notifier.rb`. After the `new_comment_notification` method but before the closing `end` statement, add the method shown in Listing 8-15.

Listing 8-15. *The Newsletter Mailer Method*

```
def newsletter(user, newsletter)
  recipients user.email
  from       "RailsCoders <system@railscoders.net>"
  subject    newsletter.subject
  body       :body => newsletter.body, :user => user
end
```

We also need to add some simple mailer templates. Since we want to send just a text version of the mail, we will just create the template with the content type `text/plain`.

Create the file `app/views/notifier/newsletter.text.plain.rhtml`, and edit it as shown in Listing 8-16.

Listing 8-16. *The Plain Text Newsletter Template*

```
RailsCoders Newsletter

<%= render :inline => @body %>
```

Add the Newsletters to the Sidebar

Now let's add a link to the newsletter resource `index` action to the sidebar menu. We need to add this to the section that is only shown to administrator users.

Open the sidebar menu partial view file, `app/views/layouts/_menu.rhtml`, and add the following link:

```
...
<% if logged_in_user and logged_in_user.has_role?('administrator') %>
  <li><hr size="1" width="90%" align="left"/></li>
  <li><b>Admin Options</b></li>
  <li><%= link_to 'Admin Permissions', users_path %></li>
  <li><%= link_to 'Edit Pages', pages_path %></li>
  <li><%= link_to 'Newsletters', newsletters_path %></li>
<% end %>
...
```

We also need to remember to delete the layout file created by the Rails generator script, `app/views/layouts/newsletter.rhtml`. Do this now.

Testing the Newsletter Mailer

We can now try creating a newsletter to make sure that our newsletter feature works and see the effect of using `ar_mailer`. Open your browser, and go to the application's home page at `http://localhost:3000/`. Log in as the Admin user, and click the Newsletters link in the Admin section of the sidebar.

At the moment, since you haven't created any newsletters, the newsletter list is empty. Click the Create New Newsletter link. You will be presented with the newsletter creation screen, shown in Figure 8-1. Here, you can enter a subject for the mailing together with the body of the message. As reminded by the on-screen note, we can use the User model within the mail. So in your test message, try using this.

For instance, you might wish to start the message with a personalized greeting by entering a message such as:

```
Hello <%= @user.username %>!
```

As you know from the ERb templates that you have created for Rails view files, this will insert the username into the mailing.

Now save this newsletter by clicking the Save draft button. You will be redirected to the `show` action, displaying the new newsletter. Now click the Send link, and confirm that you wish to send the mail by clicking OK on the pop-up dialog. The `sendmails` action will then be invoked, and you will be returned to the list of newsletters.

Because we are using `ar_mailer`, this mail will not immediately be sent. It has been placed in a queue by `ar_mailer`, and we can take a look at the queue to find out what messages are waiting to be sent.

Open a command window. We will use the `ar_mailer` command `ar_sendmail` to inspect the queue. Enter the following command:

```
$ ar_sendmail --mailq
```

You will see a list of the messages waiting to be sent, one for each of the registered users on your site. It will look similar to the following:

```
-Queue ID- --Size-- ----Arrival Time---- -Sender/Recipient-------
        1    713              Unknown   system@railscoders.net
                                        abradburne@gmail.com

        2    722              Unknown   system@railscoders.net
                                        abradburne+fred@gmail.com

        3    716              Unknown   system@railscoders.net
                                        abradburne+joe@gmail.com
```

This shows the sender, recipient, and size of each message.

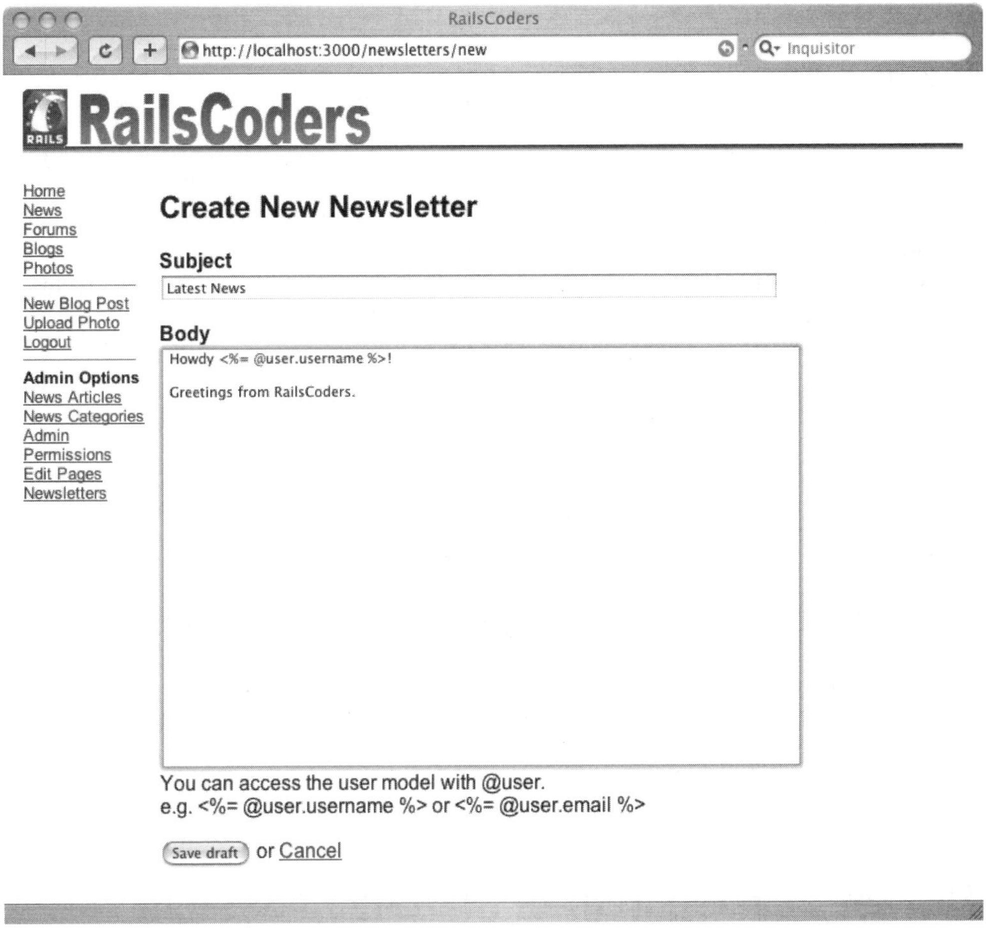

Figure 8-1. *The Create New Newsletter screen*

If you manually take a look at the `emails` table in your database, you can check to see the contents of each e-mail. If we look at the `mail` field for record 3, we can see the full mail that will be sent:

```
From: RailsCoders <system@railscoders.net>
To: abradburne+joe@gmail.com
Subject: Latest News
Mime-Version: 1.0
Content-Type: multipart/alternative; boundary=mimepart_45c7aa0d6fd36_4d9719659f64c5


--mimepart_45c7aa0d6fd36_4d9719659f64c5
Content-Type: text/plain; charset=utf-8
Content-Transfer-Encoding: Quoted-printable
Content-Disposition: inline
```

```
RailsCoders Newsletter

Howdy Joe!

--mimepart_45c7aa0d6fd36_4d9719659f64c5--
```

As you can see, the embedded Ruby code to insert the user's name has been parsed and the correct text, in this case "Joe," has been inserted into the mail.

In order to actually send the mail, you should check that your SMTP server is correctly configured in the config/environment.rb file and run the following command:

```
$ ar_sendmail
```

> **Note** ar_mailer requires that you specify your SMTP login username using the parameter :user rather than :user_name. You should add this to your SMTP config in the environment.rb file.

ar_mailer will then process all of the messages in the emails database table, sending them via your SMTP server.

Depending on the configuration of your SMTP server, you can adjust how many e-mails ar_mailer will send in a batch by adding the switch --batch-size <batch-size>.

Obviously, you do not want to have to run ar_sendmail by hand every time that your application creates an e-mail, so you can configure ar_sendmail to run as a daemon, or you could add it to a scheduler, such as cron.

Further Development of the E-mail System

Since some of your users will not want to have e-mail notifications or newsletters delivered to their inboxes, it would be a good idea to add a preference that can be set by users allowing them to turn e-mail notifications on or off.

Also, there are many other parts of the site that could benefit from having e-mail notifications added. As mentioned previously, you may wish to send users welcome messages when they join the site, or you could add a system for them to reset their passwords where the reset link is sent to their registered e-mail addresses.

You could also add an interface to make it easy for the administrator to send e-mails to specific users of the site, without having to look up their e-mail addresses.

Summary

In this chapter, we added e-mail functionality to the RailsCoders site, allowing the site to respond to events with e-mails and allowing personalized mass e-mails to be sent to all registered users of the site at once.

We developed an e-mail notifier using ActionMailer to automatically send e-mails triggered by a specific event, in our case when a blog comment is created. In order to allow us to send many e-mails at once, we also used the Ruby gem `ar_mailer` to queue all outgoing e-mails in a database table, freeing the application from having to wait for a remote SMTP server. The database table is then processed by a separate application, `ar_sendmail`.

In the next chapter, we will allow each user to add a number of friends to his or her profile. This will allow users to easily check on their friends' blogs, photos, and forum posts. We will also look at how we can display these friendships using the XFN microformat.

CHAPTER 9

■■■

Adding Friends with XFN Details

In this chapter, we will add friends to user profiles. This will allow users to add other users to a friends list. This friends list can then be viewed by any user, but most importantly, it will allow you to keep up to date with your friends by displaying your friends' latest activities on the site. Since we don't want to cause privacy concerns, this will be limited to showing only simple information about particular actions, such as if they have uploaded a new photo or posted a new entry to a blog.

When adding a friend to the friends list, you will be able to set attributes specifying the type of relationship you have with the user. These attributes will then be rendered as part of the friends list, allowing users, browsers, and other applications to understand the relationships of users.

Microformats and XFN

When displaying a link to a user, either a friend or yourself, we can add extra information about your relationship to this user with a microformat called XHTML Friends Network (XFN).

Microformats are simple, open data formats that allow you to add semantic information to XHTML documents and allow users and applications to extract meaning from that page based on the markup. Microformats build on existing standards rather than trying to develop a whole new markup system. They are designed to address small, specific uses or sections of markup, such as contact details or calendar entries. By default, they do not change the way the page is shown in your browser, but the extra information that they provide makes it very easy for software to understand the data on your page. However, it is possible to enhance the rendered page using CSS or JavaScript, which we will do later in this chapter.

You can find out a lot more information about what microformats are, what microformats have been defined, and how you apply them at `http://microformats.org`.

XFN is simply a type of microformat that allows you to embed information about your relationships into the `rel` attribute of an HTML or XHTML anchor tag, adding a human element into the link rather than just a pointer to a URL.

For instance, if you link to my profile on RailsCoders, are my friend, and have met me, you would specify the `rel` attribute as follows:

```
<a href="http://railscoders.net/users/2" rel="friend met">Alan</a>
```

This information can then be displayed alongside the links using CSS, or it could be used by other applications to map your friendships with other users on both RailsCoders and other social networking sites. Since the markup is very simple and easily understood by both humans and applications, it is very simple for new applications to be developed using this information.

Within the `rel` attribute you can specify a number of types of relationship, separated by spaces.

- *Friendships*: You can specify at most one of these:

  - `contact`: Someone you know how to get in touch with

  - `acquaintance`: Someone you have exchanged greetings with

  - `friend`: Someone who you call a friend

- *Physical*

  - `met`: Someone you have met in person.

- *Professional*: You can specify neither, either, or both of these:

  - `co-worker`: Someone you work with or who works at the same organization as you

  - `colleague`: Someone who works in the same field as you

- *Geographical*: You can specify at most one of these:

  - `co-resident`: Someone who lives at the same address as you

  - `neighbor`: Someone who lives near you

- *Family*: You can specify at most one of these:

  - `child`: Your child

  - `parent`: One of your parents

  - `sibling`: A brother or sister

  - `spouse`: Someone you are married to

  - `kin`: Another relative

- *Romantic*: You can specify as many of these as you wish:

  - `muse`: Someone who brings you inspiration

  - `crush`: Someone you have a crush on

  - `date`: Someone you are dating

  - `sweetheart`: Someone you are intimate with and committed to

- *Identity*

  - `me`: Yourself!

Because the `rel` attribute is just part of the normal anchor tag, it is very simple to implement and is transparent to the user. However, it can be used to style the rendered page using CSS or JavaScript if you wish.

XFN was developed by Matthew Mullenweg, Eric Meyer, and Tantek Çelik. The full XFN specification, background to its development, and more information can be found at its home page at `http://www.gmpg.org/xfn`.

The Friends Feature Requirements

The RailsCoders friends feature requires two parts:

- First, we need a way to create and modify our friends list. We will do this by creating a new resource called friends. Since each user has a unique friends list, this resource should be nested beneath the users controller.

- We also need to add code to store the last action and the date and time of that action with each user. This is so that the friends list can easily show a list of your friends' latest actions. If the `index` action had to query each of the tables to look for what action a user performed last, the query could take a very long time, especially if it had to do this for a large number of users.

The Friends Resource

We will create a new resource called friends. Since each user has a unique friends list, this resource should be nested beneath the users controller, accessible through URLs like `/users/4/friends` and `/users/4/friends/9`.

This resource should provide a number of functions through the regular CRUD interface. The `index` method should allow us to view a list of all of our friends, showing both their names and a link to their profiles, and also our relationships with those users according to the XFN specification. This page should also show when a friend was last active on RailsCoders and the latest activity performed, such as posting on a forum or uploading a photo.

The link to the profile will display a friend page view, the `show` action of the friends resource. This redirects to the user profile view, showing the user's latest blog posts and photos but also providing the facility to edit the relationship to the user.

The `new` and `edit` actions of the friends resource allow you to set the friendship attributes according to the XFN specification. The new friendship page will be accessible by a link on a user's profile page. Since we need to be able to specify the `id` of this user to create a friendship with them, the `id` of the person you wish to add as a friend will be passed as a URL parameter.

As you would expect, the `destroy` action will remove a friendship.

In order to store the friendships and the information about the relationships among users, we are going to use a join model called `Friendship`. Join models are exactly what you would think—they are models that join two other database tables together, while treating the relationship as a real model.

In the early releases of Rails, join tables (rather than models) would be specified in the related models as `has_and_belongs_to_many` (often referred to as HABTM by Rails developers). This would then use a table to store the `ids` of the two objects being joined. It was possible to add extra attributes to this association. However, this was not the most elegant of Rail's features, and it treated those attributes as just some extra attributes to an association, rather than treating the relationship and the relationship's attributes as a real model.

Rails 1.1 added the concept of join models. This significantly improved the has_and_belongs_to_many concept, making it possible to join multiple models together using another model. For instance, rather than just linking users together using a friends_users table (where friends was specified as just being a type of user model), we create a join model called Friendship. This model is then a first-class citizen of Rails, being able to use all of the features of Rails models. This model uses a database table called, of course, friendships.

Since we want to be able to store not only the ids of the two user objects that are friends but the details of their relationship, we will add attributes to the Friendship model for each of the XFN relationship values.

Some of the XFN relationship values are mutually exclusive; for instance, you cannot be a child and a parent of the same person. Since all access to the friendship object is performed through the Friendship model, we will use the model to validate and control what values can be set. In the database, we will just use Boolean values for each of the XFN values. All of the xfn_ fields will default to false.

The friendships database table schema is shown in Table 9-1.

Table 9-1. *The Friendships Database Schema*

Field Name	Field Type	Description
user_id	integer	The ID of the owner and creator of this friendship
friend_id	integer	The user to whom this friendship refers
xfn_friend	boolean	Refers to the XFN friend attribute
xfn_acquaintance	boolean	Refers to the XFN acquaintance attribute
xfn_contact	boolean	Refers to the XFN contact attribute
xfn_met	boolean	Refers to the XFN met attribute
xfn_coworker	boolean	Refers to the XFN co-worker attribute
xfn_colleague	boolean	Refers to the XFN colleage attribute
xfn_coresident	boolean	Refers to the XFN co-resident attribute
xfn_neighbor	boolean	Refers to the XFN neighbor attribute
xfn_child	boolean	Refers to the XFN child attribute
xfn_parent	boolean	Refers to the XFN parent attribute
xfn_sibling	boolean	Refers to the XFN sibling attribute
xfn_spouse	boolean	Refers to the XFN spouse attribute
xfn_kin	boolean	Refers to the XFN kin attribute
xfn_muse	boolean	Refers to the XFN muse attribute
xfn_crush	boolean	Refers to the XFN crush attribute
xfn_date	boolean	Refers to the XFN date attribute
xfn_sweetheart	boolean	Refers to the XFN sweetheart attribute

Showing Users' Latest Activities

To easily show what your friend's latest update is, we will keep a record of the last activity performed by each user. We can decide what activities get recorded by selectively choosing what to store and when to store it.

We can easily store and update this information by adding a few columns to the `users` database table and creating callback methods for the models that we wish to be able to update these columns. For instance, we would add an `after_save` callback for the forum's Post model, which updates the User model and stores the date and time and a string such as "Created Forum Post" in the User model.

We will add callbacks like this to the forum's Post model, the Photo model, and the blog's Entry model.

To store these details, we will add the fields shown in Table 9-2 to the `users` database table.

Table 9-2. *The Additional Fields for the users Table*

Field Name	Field Type	Description
last_activity	string	A description of the last activity performed by the user
last_activity_at	datetime	The time and date that this activity was performed

Building the Friends Resource

To build the friends feature, we have to create the necessary database migrations, and develop the Friendship join model and friends resource controller and views. We then need to update the models that will update the user's latest activity fields, the forum's Post model, the Photo model, and the blog's Entry model. This information will then be added to the friend view page.

Creating the Database Migrations

First of all, we will create the required join model called `Friendship`. Do this using the Rails generator script:

```
$ ruby script/generate model Friendship
```

```
      exists  app/models/
      exists  test/unit/
      exists  test/fixtures/
      create  app/models/friendship.rb
      create  test/unit/friendship_test.rb
      create  test/fixtures/friendships.yml
      exists  db/migrate
      create  db/migrate/019_create_friendships.rb
```

Now, we need to edit the generated migration file and create the `friendships` database table as specified earlier. Open the file `db/migrate/019_create_friendships.rb`, and enter the

migration as shown in Listing 9-1. This migration also creates an index based on the user_id
and the friend_id.

Listing 9-1. *The friendships Table Database Migration*

```
class CreateFriendships < ActiveRecord::Migration
  def self.up
    create_table :friendships do |t|
      t.column :user_id,          :integer, :null => false
      t.column :friend_id,        :integer, :null => false

      t.column :xfn_friend,       :boolean, :default => false, :null => false
      t.column :xfn_acquaintance, :boolean, :default => false, :null => false
      t.column :xfn_contact,      :boolean, :default => false, :null => false

      t.column :xfn_met,          :boolean, :default => false, :null => false

      t.column :xfn_coworker,     :boolean, :default => false, :null => false
      t.column :xfn_colleague,    :boolean, :default => false, :null => false

      t.column :xfn_coresident,   :boolean, :default => false, :null => false
      t.column :xfn_neighbor,     :boolean, :default => false, :null => false

      t.column :xfn_child,        :boolean, :default => false, :null => false
      t.column :xfn_parent,       :boolean, :default => false, :null => false
      t.column :xfn_sibling,      :boolean, :default => false, :null => false
      t.column :xfn_spouse,       :boolean, :default => false, :null => false
      t.column :xfn_kin,          :boolean, :default => false, :null => false

      t.column :xfn_muse,         :boolean, :default => false, :null => false
      t.column :xfn_crush,        :boolean, :default => false, :null => false
      t.column :xfn_date,         :boolean, :default => false, :null => false
      t.column :xfn_sweetheart,   :boolean, :default => false, :null => false
    end

    add_index :friendships, [:user_id, :friend_id]
  end

  def self.down
    drop_table :friendships
  end
end
```

Before we run the migration, we can create the migration file to add the necessary columns to the users database table. Create a new migration using the generate script:

```
$ ruby script/generate migration AddUsersLatestActivity
```

```
exists  db/migrate
create  db/migrate/020_add_users_latest_activity.rb
```

Now edit the generated migration script, db/migrate/020_add_users_latest_activity.rb, as shown in Listing 9-2.

Listing 9-2. *The Migration to Add Last Activity to the users Table*

```ruby
class AddUsersLatestActivity < ActiveRecord::Migration
  def self.up
    add_column :users, :last_activity, :string
    add_column :users, :last_activity_at, :datetime
  end

  def self.down
    remove_column :users, :last_activity
    remove_column :users, :last_activity_at
  end
end
```

We can now run the database migration task:

```
$ rake db:migrate
```

```
== CreateFriendships: migrating ================================================
-- create_table(:friendships)
   -> 0.0276s
-- add_index(:friendships, [:user_id, :friend_id], {:index_type=>:unique})
   -> 0.0195s
== CreateFriendships: migrated (0.0474s) =======================================

== AddUsersLatestActivity: migrating ===========================================
-- add_column(:users, :last_activity, :string)
   -> 0.3621s
-- add_column(:users, :last_activity_at, :datetime)
   -> 0.0849s
== AddUsersLatestActivity: migrated (0.4474s) ==================================
```

Building the Friends Resource

Create the friends resource controller file using the generator script:

```
$ ruby script/generate controller Friends
```

```
exists  app/controllers/
exists  app/helpers/
create  app/views/friends
exists  test/functional/
create  app/controllers/friends_controller.rb
create  test/functional/friends_controller_test.rb
create  app/helpers/friends_helper.rb
```

We now need to add the friends resource mapping. Open the file `config/routes.rb`, and add the friends resource nested within the users resource, as shown in Listing 9-3.

Listing 9-3. *The Friends Resource Mapping in the routes.rb File*

```
...
map.resources :users, :member => { :enable => :put } do |users|
  users.resources :roles
  users.resources :entries do |entries|
    entries.resources :comments
  end
  users.resources :friends
  ...
```

We now need to define the self-referential many-to-many relationship between users and other users (which will be known as friends), via the join model called Friendship.

Open the existing User model file, `app/models/user.rb`. We need to add two `has_many` statements: one stating that a user will have many friendships and the other stating that the user will have many friends using Friendships as a join model and that friends are actually instances of the User model.

Do this by adding the highlighted lines in Listing 9-4 to the existing relationship statements in the user model file.

Listing 9-4. *The Modifications to the User Model File*

```
...
has_many :comments
has_many :photos, :extend => TagCountsExtension

has_many :friendships
has_many :friends, :through => :friendships, :class_name => 'User'

def before_save
  ...
```

We now need to define the Friendship model. As we have stated in the User model, this belongs to two instances of the User model: one known as user, the other as friend. Therefore, we need to add the two `belongs_to` statements shown in Listing 9-5. Because the class name and database foreign key cannot be inferred from the model name in the case of the Friend model, we have to state the class name and foreign key explicitly. Open the Friendship model file `app/models/friendship.rb`, and edit as shown in Listing 9-5.

Listing 9-5. *The Friendship Model File*

```
class Friendship < ActiveRecord::Base
  belongs_to :user
  belongs_to :friend, :class_name => 'User', :foreign_key => 'friend_id'
end
```

We can now create and edit friendships for each user, with a friend of a user being directly accessible through user.friends or via the Friendship model, for instance, user.friendships[0]. friend. Of course, by accessing the Friendship model, you also have access to the XFN attributes, such as user.friendships[0].xfn_met.

■**Note** If you wish, you can try using this through the Rails interactive console.

Before we move onto building the corresponding controller, we should look more at the Friendship model. When we discussed XFN, we mentioned that some of the XFN attributes are mutually exclusive; for instance, you obviously cannot be a child and a parent of one person.

We need to improve our existing Friendship model to make it easier to set and retrieve the mutually exclusive attributes of the model. We will create three new accessors to the Friendship model, one for each of the groups of mutually exclusive attributes. To provide these accessors, we will write both attribute reader methods and attribute writer methods. Open the Friendship model file, `app/models/friendship.rb`, and update it as shown in Listing 9-6.

Listing 9-6. *The Updated Friendship Model File*

```
class Friendship < ActiveRecord::Base
  belongs_to :user
  belongs_to :friend, :class_name => 'User', :foreign_key => 'friend_id'

  def xfn_friendship=(friendship_type)
    self.xfn_friend = false
    self.xfn_acquaintance = false
    self.xfn_contact = false

    case friendship_type
    when 'xfn_friend' : self.xfn_friend = true
    when 'xfn_acquaintance' : self.xfn_acquaintance = true
    when 'xfn_contact' : self.xfn_contact = true
    end
  end
end
```

```ruby
  def xfn_friendship
    return 'xfn_friend' if self.xfn_friend == true
    return 'xfn_acquaintance' if self.xfn_acquaintance == true
    return 'xfn_contact' if self.xfn_contact == true
    false
  end

  def xfn_geographical=(geo_type)
    self.xfn_coresident = false
    self.xfn_neighbor = false

    case geo_type
    when 'xfn_coresident' : self.xfn_coresident = true
    when 'xfn_neighbor' : self.xfn_neighbor = true
    end
  end

  def xfn_geographical
    return 'xfn_coresident' if self.xfn_coresident
    return 'xfn_neighbor' if self.xfn_neighbor
    false
  end

  def xfn_family=(family_type)
    self.xfn_child = false
    self.xfn_parent = false
    self.xfn_sibling = false
    self.xfn_spouse = false
    self.xfn_kin = false

    case family_type
    when 'xfn_child' : self.xfn_child = true
    when 'xfn_parent' : self.xfn_parent = true
    when 'xfn_sibling' : self.xfn_sibling = true
    when 'xfn_spouse' : self.xfn_spouse = true
    when 'xfn_kin' : self.xfn_kin = true
    end
  end

  def xfn_family
    return 'xfn_child' if self.xfn_child
    return 'xfn_parent' if self.xfn_parent
    return 'xfn_sibling' if self.xfn_sibling
    return 'xfn_spouse' if self.xfn_spouse
    return 'xfn_kin' if self.xfn_kin
    false
  end
end
```

As you can see, this adds the attribute accessory methods xfn_friendship, xfn_geographical, and xfn_family. You can now set the XFN friendship type by calling the instance method xfn_friendship, for instance:

```
@user.friendships[0].xfn_friendship = 'xfn_contact'
```

Requesting the attribute xfn_friendship will return a string stating which of the XFN friendships attributes is set to true. For example:

```
@user.friendships[0].xfn_friendship
```

```
=> "xfn_contact"
```

This behavior is exactly what is required by the Rails radio_button helper. HTML radio buttons allow us to group a number of options together and allow only one of those options to be selected. By using the new accessor methods that we have just created, we can create a group of radio buttons for the friendships, geographical, and family accessors.

Updating the User's Latest Activity

In order to show each friend's latest activity on the friend's page, we will add after_save callbacks to the Post, Entry, and Photo models. Using after_save rather than before_save means that the User model will only be updated when the object has been successfully saved.

Open the forum's Post model, app/models/post.rb, and add the after_save callback method within the Post class, as shown in Listing 9-7.

Listing 9-7. *The Modifications to the Post Model*

```
...
validates_length_of :body, :maximum => 10000

def after_save
  self.user.update_attribute(:last_activity, "Posted in the forum")
  self.user.update_attribute(:last_activity_at, Time.now)
end
end
```

Now add a similar callback to the blog's Entry model, app/models/entry.rb, as shown in Listing 9-8.

Listing 9-8. *The Modifications to the Entry Model*

```
...
validates_length_of :body, :maximum => 10000

def after_save
  self.user.update_attribute(:last_activity, "Wrote a blog entry")
  self.user.update_attribute(:last_activity_at, Time.now)
end
end
```

Finally, add the after_save callback shown in Listing 9-9 to the Photo model, app/models/photo.rb.

Listing 9-9. *The Modifications to the Photo Model*

```
...
validates_as_attachment

def after_save
  if self.user
    self.user.update_attribute(:last_activity, "Uploaded a photo")
    self.user.update_attribute(:last_activity_at, Time.now)
  end
end
end
```

These callbacks specify the user to update simply by using the object self.user. We then update the attributes with the appropriate text and the current time and date. The Photo model checks to see if the user_id is set for this particular object, since three photo objects are created for each upload, one for each size, and the thumbnailed objects do not have a user_id set.

If you wish, you can try logging in to the site, creating new blog entries or forum posts or uploading some photos, and checking the users table of the database to see the changes to the last_activity and the last_activity_at columns.

The Friends Controller and Views

We can now build the friends resource controller file to allow a user to create, modify, and view friends through the web interface.

Open the generated controller file, app/controllers/friends_controller.rb, and enter the code shown in Listing 9-10.

Listing 9-10. *The Friends Controller File*

```
class FriendsController < ApplicationController
  before_filter :login_required, :except => [:index, :show]

  def index
    @user = User.find(params[:user_id], :include => [:friendships => :friend])
  end

  def show
    redirect_to user_path(params[:id])
  end
```

```ruby
def new
  @user = User.find(logged_in_user)
  @friend = User.find(params[:friend_id])
  unless @user.friends.include?(@friend)
    @friendship = @user.friendships.new(:friend_id => @friend.id)
  else
    redirect_to friend_path(:user_id => logged_in_user, :id => @friend)
  end
end

def edit
  @user = User.find(logged_in_user)
  @friendship = @user.friendships.find_by_friend_id(params[:id])
  @friend = @friendship.friend if @friendship
  if !@friendship
    redirect_to friend_path(:user_id => logged_in_user, :id => params[:id])
  end
end

def create
  @user = User.find(logged_in_user)
  params[:friendship][:friend_id] = params[:friend_id]
  @friendship = @user.friendships.create(params[:friendship])
  redirect_to friends_path(:user_id => logged_in_user)
rescue ActiveRecord::RecordInvalid
  render :action => 'new'
end

def update
  @user = User.find(logged_in_user)
  @friendship = @user.friendships.find_by_friend_id(params[:id])
  @friendship.update_attributes(params[:friendship])
  redirect_to friends_path(:user_id => logged_in_user)
rescue ActiveRecord::RecordInvalid
  render :action => 'edit'
end

def destroy
  @user = User.find(params[:user_id])
  @friendship = @user.friendships.find_by_friend_id(params[:id]).destroy
  redirect_to friends_path(:user_id => logged_in_user)
end
end
```

First, let's take a look at the index method and create a view.

The Index View

The index action method simply retrieves all of the friendships and friends for the specified user id. This then needs to be presented in a table, allowing the viewer to see the list of friends, along with the last activities (if any) and links to their profiles. However, we should show a slightly different view if the user is viewing his or her own friends list, adding a link to the edit page to allow the user to modify the friendship attributes for this particular friend or to remove that friend from the list.

To do this, we will use one index view but two partials. One partial, _friendship.rhtml, will simply show the view-only table row. The other, _friendship_with_edit.rhtml, will add a column to that table row with a link to edit the user.

The index view checks to see if the user is logged in and, if so, if that user is viewing his or her own friends page. Depending on this, the relevant partial file will be rendered. Doing this check in the index view rather than the partial view means that the conditional statement is only performed once, rather than for each user in the friends list.

First, create the index view file, app/views/friends/index.rhtml, and enter the code shown in Listing 9-11.

Listing 9-11. *The Friends Index View File*

```
<h2><%= @user.username %>'s Friends</h2>

<table>
  <% if is_logged_in? and logged_in_user == @user %>
    <%= render :partial => 'friendship_with_edit', :collection=>@user.friendships %>
  <% else %>
    <%= render :partial => 'friendship', :collection => @user.friendships %>
  <% end %>
</table>
```

Now, create the partial view without the edit link, app/views/friends/_friendship.rhtml, and enter the view code in Listing 9-12.

Listing 9-12. *The friendship Partial View*

```
<tr class="<%= cycle('odd', 'even') %>">
  <td id="friendname">
    <%= link_to friendship.friend.username,
                user_path(friendship.friend),
                :class => 'xfnRelationship',
                :rel => xfn_rel_tag(@user, friendship),
                :id => "friend-#{friendship.friend.id}" %>
  </td>
  <td id="activity">
    <% if friendship.friend.last_activity_at %>
      <%= friendship.friend.last_activity %>
      <%= time_ago_in_words(friendship.friend.last_activity_at) %> ago
    <% end %>
  </td>
</tr>
```

The app/views/friends/_friendship_with_edit.rhtml partial file is very similar; you're just adding an extra column. Open this file now, and enter the code in Listing 9-13.

Listing 9-13. *The friendship_with_edit Partial View*

```
<tr class="<%= cycle('odd', 'even') %>">
  <td id="friendname">
    <%= link_to friendship_with_edit.friend.username,
                user_path(friendship_with_edit.friend),
                :class => 'xfnRelationship',
                :rel => xfn_rel_tag(@user, friendship_with_edit),
                :id => "friend-#{friendship_with_edit.friend.id}" %>
  </td>
  <td id="activity">
    <% if friendship_with_edit.friend.last_activity_at %>
      <%= friendship_with_edit.friend.last_activity %>
      <%= time_ago_in_words(friendship_with_edit.friend.last_activity_at) %> ago
    <% end %>
  </td>
  <td id="editfriendship">
    [<%= link_to 'edit friendship',
                 edit_friend_url(:user_id => @user,
                                 :id => friendship_with_edit.friend) %>]
  </td>
</tr>
```

If you look at the link to the friend in both of these partials, you will see that the HTML rel tag of the link is set using :rel => xfn_rel_tag(@user, friendship). As we talked about in the introduction to XFN, the rel tag is used to define the attributes on the HTML page. We need to define a way of converting our XFN data stored in the database to an XFN rel tag, and we will write a Rails helper called xfn_rel_tag() to do this.

Since we may want use this helper across multiple resources, we will add it to the app/helpers/application_helper.rb file. Open this now, and add the helper method shown in Listing 9-14 within the module ApplicationHelper.

Listing 9-14. *The xfn_rel_tag Helper Method*

```
def xfn_rel_tag(user, friendship)
  rel_tag = []
  if user.id == friendship.friend.id
    # identity
    rel_tag << 'me'
  else
    # friendship
    rel_tag << 'friend' if friendship.xfn_friend
    rel_tag << 'acquaintance' if friendship.xfn_acquaintance
    rel_tag << 'contact' if friendship.xfn_contact
```

```
    # physical
    rel_tag << 'met' if friendship.xfn_met

    # professional
    rel_tag << 'co-worker' if friendship.xfn_coworker
    rel_tag << 'colleague' if friendship.xfn_colleague

    # geographical
    rel_tag << 'co-resident' if friendship.xfn_coresident
    rel_tag << 'neighbor' if friendship.xfn_neighbor

    # family
    rel_tag << 'child' if friendship.xfn_child
    rel_tag << 'parent' if friendship.xfn_parent
    rel_tag << 'sibling' if friendship.xfn_sibling
    rel_tag << 'spouse' if friendship.xfn_spouse
    rel_tag << 'kin' if friendship.xfn_kin

    # romantic
    rel_tag << 'muse' if friendship.xfn_muse
    rel_tag << 'crush' if friendship.xfn_crush
    rel_tag << 'date' if friendship.xfn_date
    rel_tag << 'sweetheart' if friendship.xfn_sweetheart
  end
  rel_tag.join(' ')
end
```

This helper method first checks to see if the user object id and the friend_id of the friendship object passed to it are the same; if so, the friend shown is yourself, and the XFN rel tag will simply be 'me'. Otherwise, the method creates an empty array and populates it with the relevant XFN attribute keywords based on the friendship object passed to it. These array values are joined together, separated by spaces, and the string is automatically returned. The string is then used to specify the rel tag of the friend link.

Before we can take a look at this in the browser, we need to add some friendships to our user. You could do this manually using the Rails console if you want to, but we will just build the view for the new action so that we can do it via the browser.

The New View

The friends new view has to provide an interface to easily allow a user to define the XFN relationship attributes for a new friend and post this to the friends controller.

We will build the interface using a combination of HTML radio buttons for the attributes that consist of groups of mutually exclusive characteristics and HTML check boxes for attributes that can be set independently of any other values.

Create and open the file app/views/friends/new.rhtml, and enter the view code in Listing 9-15.

Listing 9-15. *The New Friendship View File*

```
<h2>Add a new friend</h2>

<%= error_messages_for :friendship %>

<% form_for(:friendship,
            :url => friends_path(:user_id => @logged_in_user,
                                 :friend_id => @friend),
            :html => { :multipart => true }) do |f| %>
  <p>
    Define your relationship with <strong><%= @friend.username %></strong>
  </p>

  <p>
    <strong>Friendship</strong><br />
    <%= f.radio_button :xfn_friendship, :xfn_contact %> Contact
    <%= f.radio_button :xfn_friendship, :xfn_acquaintance %> Acquaintance
    <%= f.radio_button :xfn_friendship, :xfn_friend %> Friend
    <%= f.radio_button :xfn_friendship, false %> None
  </p>

  <p>
    <strong>Physical</strong><br />
    <%= f.check_box :xfn_met %> Met
  </p>

  <p>
    <strong>Professional</strong><br />
    <%= f.check_box :xfn_coworker %> Co-worker
    <%= f.check_box :xfn_colleague %> Colleague
  </p>

  <p>
    <strong>Geographical</strong><br />
    <%= f.radio_button :xfn_geographical, :xfn_coresident %> Co-resident
    <%= f.radio_button :xfn_geographical, :xfn_neighbor %> Neighbor
    <%= f.radio_button :xfn_geographical, false %> None
  </p>

  <p>
```

```
    <strong>Family</strong><br />
    <%= f.radio_button :xfn_family, :xfn_child %> Child
    <%= f.radio_button :xfn_family, :xfn_parent %> Parent
    <%= f.radio_button :xfn_family, :xfn_sibling %> Sibling
    <%= f.radio_button :xfn_family, :xfn_spouse %> Spouse
    <%= f.radio_button :xfn_family, :xfn_kin %> Kin
    <%= f.radio_button :xfn_family, false %> None
  </p>

  <p>
    <strong>Romantic</strong><br />
    <%= f.check_box :xfn_muse %> Muse
    <%= f.check_box :xfn_crush %> Crush
    <%= f.check_box :xfn_date %> Date
    <%= f.check_box :xfn_sweetheart %> Sweetheart
  </p>

  <%= f.hidden_field :friend_id %>
  <p>
    <%= submit_tag 'Save' %> or <%= link_to 'cancel', user_path(@friend) %>
  </p>
<% end %>
```

If we take a look at this page in the browser, we can see how this comes together. Make sure that you are logged in to the site and that there are at least two user accounts created. I will use user ids 1 and 2, and I will log in as user 1 (the Admin user). Go to http://localhost:3000/users/1/friends/new?friend_id=2 . This will open the "Add a new friend" page shown in Figure 9-1.

Set some relationship attributes for this user; for instance; assume that this person is a friend who the user has met and a neighbor. Then click Save.

This will create a new friendship object for the Admin user and redirect you to the friends index page for your user account, displaying the newly created friendship, as shown in Figure 9-2. If this friend has performed another action after you have added the callback that updates the last_activity attribute, the last activity performed will be shown. In testing, you should log in as the other user and carry out some actions such as posting in the forum or adding a blog entry to check that the callback is working correctly.

If you log out of the site and go back to the friends index page for the Admin user, you will see the same page, except that the edit link will not be present.

Now take a look at the source HTML of the index page (using the menu option View ➤ View Source in Safari, View ➤ Page Source in Firefox, and View ➤ Source option in Internet Explorer). If you look at the HTML code for the table around line 59, you will see the link to the friend including the XFN details in the rel attribute as follows:

```
<td id="friendname">
  <a href="/users/2" class="xfnRelationship" rel="friend met neighbor">Alan</a>
</td>
```

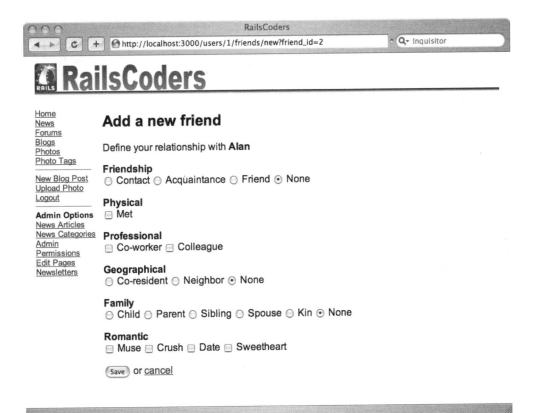

Figure 9-1. *The Add a new friend page*

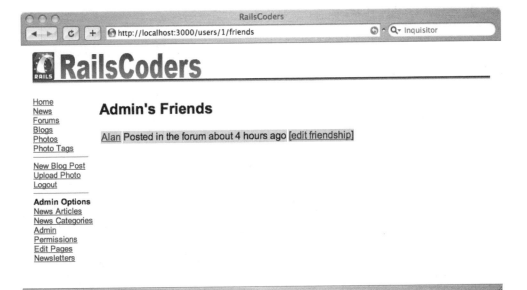

Figure 9-2. *The friends index page*

As you can see, the `rel` attribute is exactly as expected, showing the XFN attributes that have been set for this friendship.

Since the view for the `edit` action will be very similar to the `new` view, we can simply create that now.

The Edit View

Create the `edit` action view, `app/views/friends/edit.rhtml`, and add the code from Listing 9-16.

Listing 9-16. *The Friendship Edit View*

```
<h2>Edit a friend</h2>

<%= error_messages_for :friendship %>

<% form_for(:friendship,
            :url => friend_path(:user_id => @logged_in_user,
                                :friend_id => @friend),
            :html => { :multipart => true, :method => :put }) do |f| %>
  <p>
    Define your relationship with <strong><%= @friend.username %></strong>
  </p>

  <p>
    <strong>Friendship</strong><br />
    <%= f.radio_button :xfn_friendship, :xfn_contact %> Contact
    <%= f.radio_button :xfn_friendship, :xfn_acquaintance %> Acquaintance
    <%= f.radio_button :xfn_friendship, :xfn_friend %> Friend
    <%= f.radio_button :xfn_friendship, false %> None
  </p>

  <p>
    <strong>Physical</strong><br />
    <%= f.check_box :xfn_met %> Met
  </p>

  <p>
    <strong>Professional</strong><br />
    <%= f.check_box :xfn_coworker %> Co-worker
    <%= f.check_box :xfn_colleague %> Colleague
  </p>

  <p>
    <strong>Geographical</strong><br />
    <%= f.radio_button :xfn_geographical, :xfn_coresident %> Co-resident
    <%= f.radio_button :xfn_geographical, :xfn_neighbor %> Neighbor
    <%= f.radio_button :xfn_geographical, false %> None
  </p>
```

```
<p>
  <strong>Family</strong><br />
  <%= f.radio_button :xfn_family, :xfn_child %> Child
  <%= f.radio_button :xfn_family, :xfn_parent %> Parent
  <%= f.radio_button :xfn_family, :xfn_sibling %> Sibling
  <%= f.radio_button :xfn_family, :xfn_spouse %> Spouse
  <%= f.radio_button :xfn_family, :xfn_kin %> Kin
  <%= f.radio_button :xfn_family, false %> None
</p>

<p>
  <strong>Romantic</strong><br />
  <%= f.check_box :xfn_muse %> Muse
  <%= f.check_box :xfn_crush %> Crush
  <%= f.check_box :xfn_date %> Date
  <%= f.check_box :xfn_sweetheart %> Sweetheart
</p>

<p>
  <%= submit_tag 'Save' %> or <%= link_to 'cancel', user_path(@friend) %>
</p>
<p>
  <%= link_to 'Delete this friendship',
              friend_path(:user_id => @logged_in_user, :id => @friend),
              :method => :delete %>
</p>

<% end %>
```

As you will notice, the main form part of this page is identical to the new view, so you could move the form body to a partial view and include the partial in the new and edit pages.

The edit form submits the form with the HTTP method set to PUT, so the update action will be invoked rather then the new action.

We have also added a deletion link at the bottom of the page to allow a user to delete the relationship and remove the friend from the list.

You can now try clicking the "edit relationship" link on the friends index page, modifying the relationship, and saving it. Check the changed attributes by viewing the page source and checking the database attributes for the relevant friendship object.

Adding Friends Links to the Sidebar Menu

We should add a link to your personal friends list on the sidebar menu. Open the existing sidebar menu partial, app/views/layouts/_menu.rhtml, and edit as shown in Listing 9-17.

Listing 9-17. *The Updated Menu Partial File*

```
...
<li><hr size="1" width="90%" align="left"/></li>

<% if is_logged_in? %>
  <li>Logged in as: <i><%= logged_in_user.username -%></i></li>
  <li><%= link_to 'My Profile', edit_user_path(logged_in_user) -%></li>
  <li>
    <%= link_to 'My Friends', friends_path(:user_id => logged_in_user) %>
  </li>
  <li>
    <%= link_to 'My Photos', user_photos_path(:user_id => logged_in_user) -%>
  </li>
  <li><%= link_to 'Upload Photo',
           user_new_photo_path(:user_id => logged_in_user) -%></li>
  <li><%= link_to 'New Blog Post', new_entry_path(
          :user_id => logged_in_user) -%>
  </li>
  <li><%= link_to 'Logout', {:controller => 'account', :action => 'logout'},
                            :method => :post %></li>
<% else %>
  ...
```

We also want to make it very simple for someone to add a user as a friend, so we should add a link to each user profile page. This link will take you directly to the friendship creation page.

Open the user profile view page, app/views/users/show.rhtml. Add the link to the page as shown in Listing 9-18.

Listing 9-18. *The Update to the User View File*

```
...
  <%= render :partial => 'photos/photo', :collection => @photos %>
</ul>

<p>
  <% if is_logged_in? and @user.id != logged_in_user.id %>
    <% if logged_in_user.friends.include?(@user) %>
      <%= @user.username %> is your friend
    <% else %>
      <%= link_to "Add #{@user.username} as a friend",
                  new_friend_path(:user_id => logged_in_user,
                                  :friend_id=>@user) %>
    <% end %>
    <br />
  <% end %>
```

```
<%= link_to "See all of #{@user.username}'s photos",
            user_photos_path(:user_id => @user) %>
</p>
```

This will only show the add friend link if you are logged in and the other user is neither you nor already in your friends list. If you are logged in and the user is already on your friends list, the page displays a message stating that this member is already your friend.

Now try visiting some profiles on the site to check that this works under the right conditions.

Styling the Friends List

At the moment, the friends list is simply shown as a list of names. The XFN metadata is present in the source of the page and can be easily understood if you look at the source, but the relationship is not directly shown to the user. We could display these attributes as an extra text column, but it would be better to use the existing data in the rel attribute to change the rendered page.

Thankfully, CSS allows us to style elements of a page based on the rel attribute. However, note that this is does not work on Internet Explorer 6, but it does work fine on Firefox, Safari, Opera, and newer versions of Internet Explorer.

To style an element based on the rel attribute, we use CSS attribute selectors. For instance, to style a link that has the word met in the rel attribute, we would use the following selector:

```
a[rel~="met"]
```

We can then specify any CSS attributes to set for this selector, including adding images to the style.

A set of icons has been designed by Wolfgang Bartelme and Chris Messina to represent a number of the XFN attributes. These icons are shown in Figure 9-3 and can be downloaded from Messina's site at http://www.factorycity.net/projects/microformats-icons. A number of extra icons have been added by Jon Galloway, and they have been included in the set shown. You can download all of these from the RailsCoders site.

A repository of icons representing these and other microformat icons is kept at http://microformats.org/wiki/icons.

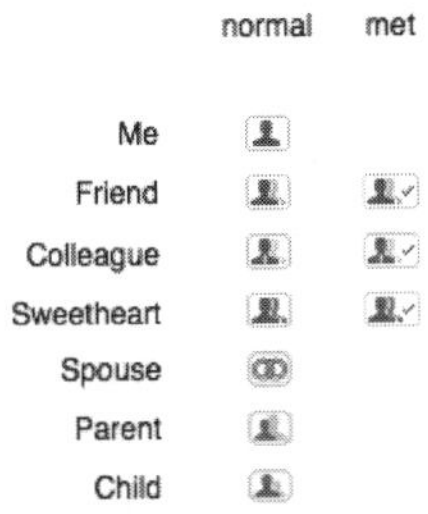

Figure 9-3. *Icons representing the XFN attributes*

In the friends list, we want to show the relevant icon next to each friend's name. The CSS to do this was written by Steve Harman (http://stevenharman.net) and adapted for the RailsCoders site.

First of all, download the XFN icons set from the Apress or the RailsCoders site and place the icon files into the public/images/ directory.

Next, open the application's style sheet, public/stylesheets/main.css, and add the CSS in Listing 9-19 to the end of the current CSS file.

Listing 9-19. *The CSS to Display the XFN Icons*

```
/* XFN Styling */
a.xfnRelationship {
  padding-right: 26px;
  background: url(/images/xfn-small.png) no-repeat right;
}

a.xfnRelationship[rel~="colleague"],
a.xfnRelationship[rel~="co-worker"] {
  padding-right: 21px;
  background: url(/images/xfn-colleague.png) no-repeat right;
}

a.xfnRelationship[rel~="colleague"][rel~="met"],
a.xfnRelationship[rel~="co-worker"][rel~="met"] {
  padding-right: 26px;
  background: url(/images/xfn-colleague-met.png) no-repeat right;
}

a.xfnRelationship[rel~="friend"] {
  padding-right: 21px;
  background: url(/images/xfn-friend.png) no-repeat right;
}

a.xfnRelationship[rel~="friend"][rel~="met"] {
  padding-right: 26px;
  background: url(/images/xfn-friend-met.png) no-repeat right;
}

a.xfnRelationship[rel~="sweetheart"] {
  padding-right: 21px;
  background: url(/images/xfn-sweetheart.png) no-repeat right;
}

a.xfnRelationship[rel~="sweetheart"][rel~="met"] {
  padding-right: 26px;
  background: url(/images/xfn-sweetheart-met.png) no-repeat right;
}
```

```
a.xfnRelationship[rel~="child"] {
  padding-right: 21px;
  background: url(/images/xfn-child.png) no-repeat right;
}

a.xfnRelationship[rel~="parent"] {
  padding-right: 21px;
  background: url(/images/xfn-parent.png) no-repeat right;
}

a.xfnRelationship[rel~="spouse"] {
  padding-right: 21px;
  background: url(/images/xfn-spouse.png) no-repeat right;
}

a.xfnRelationship[rel~="me"] {
  padding-right: 21px;
  background: url(/images/xfn-me.png) no-repeat right;
}
```

Now, go back to your friends view, and reload the page to refresh the CSS. The relevant XFN icon will be shown alongside each username, as shown in Figure 9-4.

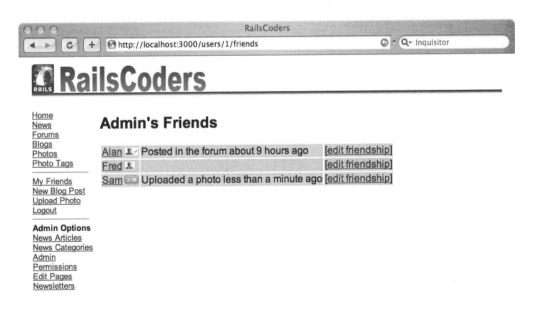

Figure 9-4. *Friends list showing the XFN icons*

Testing

We should write some functional tests for the friendship feature to ensure that it works as expected and so that we can continue to easily test the feature when we have made modifications.

First, create a simple fixtures file for the Friendship model called test/fixtures/ friendships.yml. Enter the fixture shown in Listing 9-20, where user id 2 is a friend of user id 1, with the xfn_met attribute set to true. All of the other attributes will default to false.

Listing 9-20. *The Friendship Fixtures File*

```
valid_friendship:
  id: 1
  user_id: 1
  friend_id: 2
  xfn_met: true
```

Open the generated friends functional test file, test/functional/friends_controller_ test.rb, and enter the code in Listing 9-21.

Listing 9-21. *The Friends Controller Functional Test File*

```
require File.dirname(__FILE__) + '/../test_helper'
require 'friends_controller'

# Re-raise errors caught by the controller.
class FriendsController; def rescue_action(e) raise e end; end

class FriendsControllerTest < Test::Unit::TestCase
  fixtures :friendships, :users, :roles, :roles_users

  def setup
    @controller = FriendsController.new
    @request    = ActionController::TestRequest.new
    @response   = ActionController::TestResponse.new
  end

  def test_should_get_index
    get :index, {:user_id => 1}
    assert_response :success
    assert assigns(:user)
  end

  def test_should_get_new
    login_as(:valid_user)
    get :new, {:user_id => 1, :friend_id => 3}
    assert_response :success
  end
```

```
def test_should_create_friendship
  login_as(:valid_user)
  old_count = Friendship.count
  post :create, {:user_id => 1, :friend_id => 3, :friendship =>{:xfn_met => true}}
  assert_equal old_count + 1, Friendship.count
  assert_redirected_to friends_path(:user_id => 1)
end

def test_should_get_edit
  login_as(:valid_user)
  get :edit, :user_id => 1, :id => 2
  assert_response :success
end

def test_should_update_friendship
  login_as(:valid_user)

  get :index, {:user_id => 1}
  assert_select "a#friend-2[rel~=crush]", false

  put :update, {:user_id => 1, :id => 2, :friendship => { :xfn_crush => true} }
  assert_redirected_to friends_path(:user_id => 1)

  get :index, {:user_id => 1}
  assert_response :success
  assert_select "a#friend-2[rel~=crush]", true
end

def test_should_destroy_friendship
  login_as(:valid_user)
  old_count = Friendship.count
  delete :destroy, :user_id => 1, :id => 2
  assert_equal old_count - 1, Friendship.count
  assert_redirected_to friends_path(:user_id => 1)
end
end
```

These functional tests perform the basic functions of the friends controller, ensuring that friends are listed, added, modified, and deleted as expected.

If you take a look at the test test_should_update_friendship, you will notice that this uses assert_select to check the rel attribute for a specific word. With assert_select, you can use CSS selectors to specify one particular element of a page, checking for particular content. In this case, we check for the XFN crush keyword in the rel attribute of the friend with the user id of 2. Since we have a unique id for each link, we can easily test the individual elements on the page. Before the update, it does not have the crush attribute set as set in the fixtures file. We then perform an update and recheck for the crush attribute, which we now expect to be set.

You can find a useful cheat sheet for `assert_select` at `http://blog.labnotes.org/2006/09/04/assert_select-cheat-sheet` and a tutorial on CSS selectors at `http://css.maxdesign.com.au/selectutorial`.

Before we run the tests, we need to make sure that the test database schema is up to date. Run the `db:test:prepare` rake task:

```
$ rake db:test:prepare
```

Now, run the functional tests:

```
$ ruby test/functional/friends_controller_test.rb
```

```
Loaded suite test/functional/friends_controller_test
Started
......
Finished in 0.473295 seconds.

6 tests, 16 assertions, 0 failures, 0 errors
```

You may wish to expand these tests to cover all of the XFN attributes and to add negative tests to ensure that users cannot modify other user's friendships.

Further Development of the Friendship Feature

There are a few ways you may wish to develop the friendship feature further:

- You could add a method to view the reciprocal friendships, that is, the people who have added you as a friend. You could also add notifications to let you know when someone new adds you to a friends list.

- You could also expand on the friends' list view idea, showing the latest uploaded photos of your friends or providing links to the latest entries of forum posts.

- It would also be possible to expand the list to provide details of friends of friends, allowing you to see who you are connected to through your network of friends.

- At the moment, you can add a friend without their permission, but you may wish to modify the feature to provide a system where the friend you are adding has to approve your friendship, in a similar way to sites like MySpace or LinkedIn.

- You may also wish to make use of the XFN data to enhance blog or forum posts to allow users to link to their friends, automatically adding the relevant `rel` attribute and displaying the XFN icons.

Summary

In this chapter, we have added a friendship system, allowing users to easily add other users to their friends list. From this list, users can quickly see the latest activities of their friends, so that they know if any friends have posted new photos or added entries to their blogs. This makes it easy for users to keep up to date with their friends' activities.

The friendships are enhanced by adding metadata based on the XFN microformat specification. This allows users and applications to easily understand the relationships among other users and their friends.

In the next chapter, we will add tags to the photo gallery we created in Chapter 7. This will allow users to tag their photos with keywords, making the galleries easily searchable or allow users to browse photos based on keywords.

■■■

## CHAPTER 10

Adding Tags to the Photo Gallery

In this chapter, we will extend the photo gallery to support tagging. Tags are simply keywords that are used to describe a particular object. Tagging has become hugely popular for social web applications and is a very useful way of categorizing items that makes it very easy for users to search and browse objects. Some of the most successful web sites that use tagging are Flickr.com, del.icio.us, and Amazon.com.

Along with being an incredibly useful way to allow searching of objects on the site, they also make for a fun browsing experience. Tag clouds are often shown, displaying the most popular tags as the largest, so you can quickly see the most popular topics. Tag clouds make a great starting point to allow people to discover new photos on your site.

To implement the tagging functionality, we are going to make use of a Rails plug-in. We will also use a Rails feature called Remote JavaScript (RJS) templates to implement Ajax effects, allowing the tag list to be dynamically updated on the photo edit page.

The Gallery Tagging Requirements

We will add tags to the RailsCoders photo galleries. Each photo on the site can be assigned a number of tags by the owner of the photo. Users can then browse the photo galleries using tag clouds.

Users of the site can view a tag cloud for all of the photos on the site or for one specific user. Clicking a tag within the tag cloud will show a paginated series of photos for that particular tag, again either showing all photos on the site with that tag or just those belonging to a specific user.

We will also need to add a way of adding tags to a photo. Since this can be performed only by the owner of a photo, we can simply add this to the photo edit page. We could implement this using just a standard text entry box, but to make it easier for the user to add and delete tags, we will implement it using an Ajax-based interface. This means that we will be able to add and delete tags from a tag list without having to reload the entire page; we can just update the specific part of the current page that has changed.

AJAX

Ajax (Asynchronous JavaScript and XML) is a technique that allows web applications to change only the relevant part of a web page, rather than forcing the browser to reload the entire page. This can greatly improve the usability of a web application if used properly. It also makes the application feel more responsive, since only a small amount of data is exchanged between the browser and web server.

The term Ajax was coined by Jesse James Garrett in 2005, but the technology has been around since 1998 when Microsoft released Internet Explorer 5, which included a technology called XMLHttpRequest. This allowed JavaScript on a web page to talk to the server in the background without having to reload a web page.

You could write your own JavaScript to make this happen, but Rails ships with the JavaScript libraries Prototype and script.aculo.us, which make it incredibly simple to implement Ajax features in your application in just a few lines of code.

Basically, a JavaScript action is tied to an event on your web page, such as a link or a button. When this event is triggered by the user, the JavaScript code is executed, which, in turn, sends a request to your application server. However, it does this asynchronously, allowing the user to continue using the page. The Rails application server sends back a snippet of JavaScript code, which updates a specific part of the current web page. The `id` and `class` tags in your XHTML code allow you to reference specific items or sections of the page.

To allow two ways to view the tag data—one for all users and one for a specific user—we will create two controllers.

To view tags by all users, the controller will be accessed by URLs such as `/tags` and `/tags/puppy`. We will create this to act as a normal REST resource, but we will not create a corresponding Tag model as we have with the other resources we have built; the retrieved tags are from the Photo model.

To view tags that only belong to one user, the controller will be accessed by URLs such as `/users/1/tags` and `/users/1/tags/puppy`. This will also act as a REST resource, but this time, it's nested beneath the users resource. We will create a second controller for this. We could handle both types of request with one controller, but we would require conditional statements to retrieve the correct data and render different views depending on the request. That would just complicate our code and make it harder for us to maintain and extend in the future.

We also need to add a way for a user to add and remove tags from a photo. Since tags are only accessible through the Photo model, this should be performed as an action of the photo controller. Therefore, we will add two methods to the existing `user_photo_controller` file: `add_tag` and `remove_tag`.

Tagging with Rails

Implementing our own tagging system from scratch would require some pretty complex SQL queries and take a significant amount of time to build and test properly. However, the Rails community has built a number of Rails extensions implementing tagging functionality. Which library you decide to use depends on your needs, since each library has different advantages.

The currently available libraries follow:

- `acts_as_taggable` *gem*: This was the first tagging library for Rails but is starting to show its age, and it is currently only available for Rails 1.1. However, it may still be useful if you are working with older Rails code. You can find out more at http://rubyforge.org/projects/taggable.

- `acts_as_taggable` *plug-in*: This plug-in was developed by David Heinemeier Hansson, the original creator of Rails. It was developed as a demonstration of the Rails `has_many :through` feature rather than a library intended for production use. Therefore, it is not fully featured and is not in active development. However, many people have modified it and are using it, even though the plug-in itself has not been updated. You can find out more information at http://wiki.rubyonrails.com/rails/pages/ActsAsTaggablePluginHowto.

- `acts_as_taggable_on_steroids` *plug-in*: This library is based on the `acts_as_taggable` plug-in but has been extended by Jonathan Viney to add tests, better tag assignment, and a feature to automatically perform tag cloud calculations. You can find more information about this plug-in at http://www.agilewebdevelopment.com/plugins/acts_as_taggable_on_steroids.

- `has_many_polymorphs` *ActiveRecord plug-in*: This is not a straightforward tagging plug-in; it basically allows you to define self-referential polymorphic associations in your models. It was developed by Evan Weaver and can be easily adapted to provide tagging facilities. You can find more information on how to use it to develop tagging features at http://blog.evanweaver.com/articles/2006/06/02/has_many_polymorphs.

For the RailsCoders site, we are going to use the `acts_as_taggable_on_steroids` plug-in. Currently, this is the most fully featured and easiest to use tagging library, providing us with a very simple way to add and edit tags and perform searches based on tags. It can also provide us with tag counts so that we can easily produce tag clouds.

The acts_as_taggable_on_steroids Plug-in

The `acts_as_taggable_on_steroids` plug-in, though based on the original `acts_as_taggable` plug-in, has been extended with improved tag assignment methods and tag cloud calculations. This makes it ideal for using on RailsCoders.

The plug-in also comes with a number of tests, meaning that you can easily test the plug-in's functionality to ensure it is working as you expect.

The library uses a Rails feature that allows you to relate two models through a third model. You do this by using the `has_many` statement and specifying a join model. For instance, with our tagging system, we will join the Photo model and the Tag model together using a join model called Tagging. We would specify that the photo has many tags, but to access these, the request must go through the Tagging model. The statement `has_many :tags, :through => :taggings` would tell ActiveRecord to do this. In turn, each tag has many taggings, meaning that you can find which objects have been tagged with a specific tag.

It also uses another interesting feature of ActiveRecord—polymorphic associations. This means that the join association is not limited to one particular model, it can be associated with any model, since the model name is stored in the join model itself.

To do this, we need to add a database column specifying the model type. The Tagging join model and the Tag model are defined within the acts_as_taggable_on_steroids plug-in, but we still have to create the database tables for the plug-in to be able to work. The plug-in requires two tables: one to store the tag names and one to store the relationships of the tags with other models.

The database table for the Tag model is shown in Table 10-1.

Table 10-1. *The Tags Table*

Field Name	Field Type	Description
id	integer	The primary key
name	string	The tag name

The database table for the Tagging model is shown in Table 10-2. We will never access this table directly; it is only used to associate one model with another. However, since it is a real model and not just a database table, we can add extra attributes or callbacks.

Because we are using polymorphic associations, this table includes the column taggable_type to store the model name as well as taggable_id to store the associated model ID.

Table 10-2. *The Tagging Database Table*

Field Name	Field Type	Description
id	integer	The primary key
tag_id	integer	The id of the tag
taggable_id	integer	The id of the taggable object
taggable_type	string	The model name of the taggable object
created_at	datetime	The time and date that this tagging was created

To use the tagging library with a particular model, you simply add the statement acts_as_taggable to a model class definition. Doing this adds a number of instance and class methods to the model, which are used to add tags to an object and to find objects that are tagged with particular tags.

To add tags to an object or list the tags that have been assigned to an object, you use the methods tag_list and tag_list=. These allow you to access a comma-separated list of the object's tags.

For example, if you have a photo object called @photo, you would assign tags with the following command:

```
@photo.tag_list = "puppy,dog,cute"
@photo.save
```

After you have saved the tagged object, you can access the tags for that object either with the `tag_list` instance method or by accessing the tag objects that belong to the object:

```
@photo.tags_list
```

```
=> "puppy, dog, cute"
```

```
@photo.tags
```

```
=> [#<Tag:0x3136034 @attributes={"name"=>"puppy", "id"=>"4"}>,
#<Tag:0x313600c @attributes={"name"=>"dog", "id"=>"5"}>,
#<Tag:0x3135fe4 @attributes={"name"=>"cute", "id"=>"6"}>]
```

In order to find objects that are tagged with a particular tag, we use the class method `find_tagged_with`, for instance:

```
@photos = Photo.find_tagged_with('puppy')
```

If you want to find objects with any one of multiple tags, you can just specify them as a list separated by commas:

```
@photos = Photo.find_tagged_with('puppy, dog')
```

To find objects that have all of the listed tags, use the `:match_all` parameter:

```
@photos = Photo.find_tagged_with('puppy, dog', :match_all => true)
```

You can also use regular find options such as `:order`, `:limit`, and `:offset` as part of the `find_tagged_with` method.

The plug-in also has a useful method that allows us to easily create tag clouds. A tag cloud is simply a list of tags, but the size of each tag is proportional to its popularity. In order to produce a tag cloud, we need to know the frequency of each tag's use. The plug-in provides an instance method `tag_counts` for the tagged model. It will return an array of hashes containing the tag name, ID, and the number of times that this tag has been used, for instance:

```
Photos.tag_counts
```

```
=> [#<Tag:0x30a2014 @attributes={"name"=>"puppy", "id"=>"4", "count"=>"1"}>,
#<Tag:0x30a1fec @attributes={"name"=>"dog", "id"=>"5", "count"=>"2"}>,
#<Tag:0x30a1fc4 @attributes={"name"=>"cute", "id"=>"6", "count"=>"4"}>]
```

If you wish to use this to find the frequency of use for tags belonging to a specific user, you must extend the `has_many` association of the user to the photos like this:

```
class User < ActiveRecord::Base
  has_many :photos, :extend => TagCountsExtension
end
```

You can then use the `tag_count` method for a specific user, for example:

```
User.find(1).photos.tag_counts
```

```
=> [#<Tag:0x30671bc @attributes={"name"=>"puppy", "id"=>"4", "count"=>"1"}>,
#<Tag:0x3067194 @attributes={"name"=>"dog", "id"=>"5", "count"=>"1"}>,
#<Tag:0x306716c @attributes={"name"=>"cute", "id"=>"6", "count"=>"2"}>]
```

`TagCountsExtension` should only be used on associations where you have declared the model to use `acts_as_taggable`.

Building the Photo Tagging Feature

We will need to update the Photo model to declare that it will use `acts_as_taggable`. We also need to extend the User model to use the `TagCountsExtension`.

We need to create two controllers. One will be accessed from the root path; we will call this simply `tags_controller`. The other will be nested beneath the user resource; we will call this `user_tags_controller`. We then need to create the relevant mappings for these controllers in the routes file.

However, first we need to install the `acts_as_taggable_on_steroids` plug-in.

Installing the acts_as_taggable_on_steroids Plug-in

The `acts_as_taggable_on_steroids` plug-in is distributed simply as a Rails plug-in. To install the plug-in, use the normal Rails `plugin` script. Enter the following command:

```
$ ruby script/plugin install ➥
  http://svn.viney.net.nz/things/rails/plugins/acts_as_taggable_on_steroids
```

```
+ ./acts_as_taggable_on_steroids/CHANGELOG
+ ./acts_as_taggable_on_steroids/MIT-LICENSE
+ ./acts_as_taggable_on_steroids/README
+ ./acts_as_taggable_on_steroids/Rakefile
+ ./acts_as_taggable_on_steroids/init.rb
+ ./acts_as_taggable_on_steroids/lib/acts_as_taggable.rb
+ ./acts_as_taggable_on_steroids/lib/tag.rb
+ ./acts_as_taggable_on_steroids/lib/tag_counts_extension.rb
+ ./acts_as_taggable_on_steroids/lib/tagging.rb
+ ./acts_as_taggable_on_steroids/test/abstract_unit.rb
+ ./acts_as_taggable_on_steroids/test/acts_as_taggable_test.rb
+ ./acts_as_taggable_on_steroids/test/database.yml
+ ./acts_as_taggable_on_steroids/test/fixtures/photo.rb
+ ./acts_as_taggable_on_steroids/test/fixtures/photos.yml
+ ./acts_as_taggable_on_steroids/test/fixtures/post.rb
+ ./acts_as_taggable_on_steroids/test/fixtures/posts.yml
+ ./acts_as_taggable_on_steroids/test/fixtures/taggings.yml
```

```
+ ./acts_as_taggable_on_steroids/test/fixtures/tags.yml
+ ./acts_as_taggable_on_steroids/test/fixtures/user.rb
+ ./acts_as_taggable_on_steroids/test/fixtures/users.yml
+ ./acts_as_taggable_on_steroids/test/schema.rb
+ ./acts_as_taggable_on_steroids/test/tag_test.rb
+ ./acts_as_taggable_on_steroids/test/tagging_test.rb
```

Creating the Database Tables

To create the database tables needed by the tagging plug-in, we will create a migration and add the changes to the database to that.

Create the migration file using the Rails generator script:

```
$ ruby script/generate migration AddTaggingSupport
```

```
      exists   db/migrate
      create   db/migrate/021_add_tagging_support.rb
```

Now, open the migration file db/migrate/021_add_tagging_support.rb, and add the migration code shown in Listing 10-1.

Listing 10-1. *The Migration to Add Tagging Support*

```ruby
class AddTaggingSupport < ActiveRecord::Migration
  def self.up
    create_table :tags, :force => true do |t|
      t.column :name, :string
    end

    create_table :taggings, :force => true do |t|
      t.column :tag_id, :integer
      t.column :taggable_id, :integer
      t.column :taggable_type, :string
      t.column :created_at, :datetime
    end

    add_index :tags, :name
    add_index :taggings, [:tag_id, :taggable_id, :taggable_type]
  end

  def self.down
    drop_table :tags
    drop_table :taggings
  end
end
```

This will create the necessary tables, along with instructing the database to create indexes based on the `tags.name` field and the `taggings.tag_id`, `taggable_id`, and `taggable_type` fields. Since all database queries will be based on these fields rather than the primary key, it makes sense to add these indexes now.

Next, run the `migrate` command to perform these changes to the database:

```
$ rake db:migrate
```

```
== AddTaggingSupport: migrating =================================================
-- create_table(:tags, {:force=>true})
   -> 0.1125s
-- create_table(:taggings, {:force=>true})
   -> 0.0070s
-- add_index(:tags, :name)
   -> 0.0157s
-- add_index(:taggings, [:tag_id, :taggable_id, :taggable_type])
   -> 0.0079s
== AddTaggingSupport: migrated (0.1240s) =======================================
```

Updating the Models

As we have discussed, we need to update both the Photo and User models. Open the Photo model file, `app/models/photo.rb`, and add the statement `acts_as_taggable` as shown in Listing 10-2.

Listing 10-2. *The Modification to the Photo Model*

```
class Photo < ActiveRecord::Base
  acts_as_taggable
  belongs_to :user
  ...
```

We now need to update the user file's relationship with the Photo model, adding the `TagCountsExtension`. Open the User model file, `app/models/user.rb`. Now modify the photo relationship as shown in Listing 10-3.

Listing 10-3. *The Modification to the User Model*

```
require 'digest/sha2'
class User < ActiveRecord::Base
  attr_protected :hashed_password, :enabled
  attr_accessor :password
  ...
  has_many :usertemplates
  has_many :comments
  has_many :photos, :extend => TagCountsExtension
  ...
```

Creating the Controllers

As we discussed in the requirements, we will create a controller for each different way of accessing the tags:

- To view all tags, via URLs such as /tags and /tags/tree, we will create and use a controller called tags_controller.rb.

- To view tags belonging to a specific user, via URLs such as /user/1/tags and /user/1/tags/tree, we will use a controller called user_tags_controller.rb.

We should create these controllers and add the relevant mappings to the routes file now. Create tags_controller.rb with the Rails generate command:

```
$ ruby script/generate controller Tags
```

```
    exists  app/controllers/
    exists  app/helpers/
    create  app/views/tags
    exists  test/functional/
    create  app/controllers/tags_controller.rb
    create  test/functional/tags_controller_test.rb
    create  app/helpers/tags_helper.rb
```

Next, create user_tags_controller.rb:

```
$ ruby script/generate controller UserTags
```

```
    exists  app/controllers/
    exists  app/helpers/
    create  app/views/user_tags
    exists  test/functional/
    create  app/controllers/user_tags_controller.rb
    create  test/functional/user_tags_controller_test.rb
    create  app/helpers/user_tags_helper.rb
```

Adding the Resource Mappings

We now need to map the URLs to the specific controllers in the routes file. Open the file config/routes.rb. Add the tags mapping, and modify the existing users mapping to add the nested tags. We can also add the new methods, add_tag and remove_tag, for the existing user_photos resource mapping. The add_tag method uses HTTP PUT, while the remove_tag method uses HTTP DELETE.

Edit the routes file as shown in Listing 10-4, adding the bold lines.

Listing 10-4. *Updates to the Route Mappings File*

```
map.resources :photos
map.resources :tags

map.resources :users, :member => { :enable => :put } do |users|
  users.resources :permissions
  users.resources :entries do |entries|
    entries.resources :comments
  end
  users.resources :tags, :name_prefix => 'user_',
                         :controller => 'user_tags'
  users.resources :photos, :name_prefix => 'user_',
                           :controller => 'user_photos',
                           :member => { :add_tag => :put,
                                        :remove_tag => :delete }
end
```

Writing the Controllers and Views

We can now write the code to actually perform the actions set up in the mappings.

The Tags Controller

The tag_controller.rb index method displays all of the tags that have been added to photos on the site, regardless of user. Since we want to display this as a tag cloud, we should retrieve the tags using the tag_counts method.

The show method will show all of the photos that match a particular tag. This is done simply with the method find_tagged_with.

Since it is not possible for a user to create, update, or delete tags through this resource, only as an update to a photo, we only have to create the index and show methods.

Open the app/controllers/tag_controller.rb file, and edit it as shown in Listing 10-5.

Listing 10-5. *The Tag Controller File*

```
class TagsController < ApplicationController

  def index
    @tags = Photo.tag_counts(:order => 'name')
  end

  def show
    @photos = Photo.find_tagged_with(params[:id])
  end

end
```

For the tag index action, we have requested that the tags be ordered alphabetically using the tag name. We now need to create the views for the index and show actions.

The Tag Index View

To create the tag cloud for the tag index view, we will create a helper method that takes the array of tags with usage counts and return a series of CSS class names that we can add to the displayed tags. The class names are assigned based on how common a tag is in relation to the other tags. This code is based on a Rails helper developed by Tom Fakes. You can find the original code at http://blog.craz8.com/articles/2005/10/28/acts_as_taggable-is-a-cool-piece-of-code.

First of all, we should add the tag_cloud helper to a helper file. Since we will use this helper from both the tags_controller and the user_tags_controller files, we should add the tag_cloud helper to the applicationwide helper file.

Open app/helpers/application_helper.rb, and add the new tag_cloud helper to the ApplicationHelper module as shown in Listing 10-6.

Listing 10-6. *The Tag Cloud Helper*

```
# Methods added to this helper will be available to all templates in
the application.
module ApplicationHelper
  def yes_no(bool)
    ...
  end

  def tag_cloud(tags, classes)
    max, min = 0, 0
    tags.each do |tag|
      max = tag.count if tag.count > max
      min = tag.count if tag.count < min
    end

    divisor = ((max - min) / classes.size) + 1

    tags.each do |tag|
      yield tag.name, classes[(tag.count - min) / divisor]
    end
  end
end
```

We can now create the index view file, app/views/tags/index.rhtml. Create this file, open it, and enter the code in Listing 10-7.

Listing 10-7. *The Tags Index View*

```
<h2>Most Popular Tags</h2>

<% tag_cloud @tags, %w(tag1 tag2 tag3 tag4 tag5) do |name, css_class| %>
  <%= link_to name, tag_path(name), :class => css_class %>
<% end %>
```

This passes the @tags array (which includes the count attribute) and an array of CSS class names to the tag_cloud helper. %w() is simply a quick way to create an array from a list of words in Ruby.

We use the returned data from the helper in a Ruby block, taking the name and calculated CSS class name and using them to generate a link. This links to the show action of the tag resource.

We now need to create the definitions of the CSS classes that the tag_cloud helper uses. Since we want the size of the text to be proportional to the tag's popularity, we will just set the font-size attribute for each of the classes.

Open the style sheet for the application, public/stylesheets/main.css, and add the CSS code shown in Listing 10-8 to the end of the file.

Listing 10-8. *The CSS Style Sheet for the Tag Cloud*

```
/* Tag cloud styling */
.tag1 { font-size: 100%; }
.tag2 { font-size: 120%; }
.tag3 { font-size: 140%; }
.tag4 { font-size: 160%; }
.tag5 { font-size: 170%; }
.tag6 { font-size: 180%; }
```

The Tag Show View

To create the view for the show action, we simply have to render the partial view that has already been created for the regular photo gallery. Create the show view file, app/views/tags/show.rhtml, and add the code in Listing 10-9.

Listing 10-9. *The Tags Show View File*

```
<h2>Photos Tagged: <%=h params[:id] %></h2>

<ul id="photos">
  <%= render :partial => 'photos/photo', :collection => @photos %>
</ul>
```

The User Tags Controller

The user_tags_controller is used in a similar way to tags_controller, except that it only shows tags and photos for a specific user. Like tags_controller, this controller also needs only the index and show actions, since tags are never edited through this controller.

Open the generated controller, app/controller/user_tags_controller.rb, and edit it as shown in Listing 10-10.

Listing 10-10. *The User Tags Controller File*

```
class UserTagsController < ApplicationController

  def index
    @user = User.find(params[:user_id])
    @tags = @user.photos.tag_counts(:order => 'name')
  end

  def show
    @user = User.find(params[:user_id])
    @photos = @user.photos.find_tagged_with(params[:id])
  end

end
```

You will notice that this is almost the same as the tags_controller, except that we first retrieve the user specified in the URL and then search for tags or photos with a specific tag within the scope of that user. This also means that the view files will also be very similar.

The User Tags Index View

We will use the same tag_cloud helper method as the tags_controller index view. Create the file app/views/user_tags/index.rhtml, and add the view code in Listing 10-11.

Listing 10-11. *The User Tags Index View*

```
<h2><%= @user.username %>'s Most Popular Tags</h2>

<p><%= link_to "Show all user's tags", tags_path %></p>

<% tag_cloud @tags, %w(tag1 tag2 tag3 tag4 tag5) do |name, css_class| %>
  <%= link_to name, tag_path(name), :class => css_class %>
<% end %>
```

Since we have retrieved the specified user's details, we can use that to display the user's name as the title of the page. We have also added a link to go to the root-level tag view, showing all of the tags on the site.

The User Tags Show View

This view, showing the user's photos tagged with a specific word, also makes use of the existing thumbnail partial view that we wrote for the photo gallery. Create the file app/views/user_tags/show.rhtml, and enter the code shown in Listing 10-12.

Listing 10-12. *The User Tags Show View*

```
<h2><%= @user.username %>'s Photos Tagged: <%=h params[:id] %></h2>

<p>
  <%= link_to "Show all photos tagged with #{h(params[:id])}", tag_path(h(params[:id])) %>
</p>

<ul id="photos">
  <%= render :partial => 'photos/photo', :collection => @photos %>
</ul>
```

Along with showing all the photos in the specified user's gallery tagged with the requested word, we have also included a link to show all photos on the site tagged with this word.

Adding Tags to a Photo

We need to develop the controller methods and interface to allow users to add tags to their photos.

In the routes file, we added mappings for two extra methods for the user_photo resource. Take another look at the mapping in the routes.rb file:

```
users.resources :photos, :name_prefix => 'user_', :controller => 'user_photos',
                         :member => { :add_tag => :put, :remove_tag => :delete }
```

This adds the actions add_tag and remove_tag to the nested resource, which is accessible through the URLs /user/1/photos/2;add_tag and /user/1/photos/2;remove_tag. We can use the shortcuts user_add_tag_photo_path and user_remove_tag_photo_path to access these in views and controllers. We also need to make sure that we specify the correct HTTP method to access these: PUT for add_tag and DELETE for remove_tag.

Allowing the User to Add Tags to a Photo

First of all, we will develop the code necessary to add tags to a photo object. We will just add this to the existing user_photos_controller file. Open the file app/controllers/user_photos_controller.rb. Within the UserPhotosController class, create the new action method shown in Listing 10-13.

Listing 10-13. *The add_tag Method*

```
def add_tag
  @photo = @logged_in_user.photos.find(params[:id])
  @photo.tag_list += ',' + params[:tag][:name]
  @photo.save
  @new_tag = @photo.reload.tags.last
end
```

The add_tag method is very simple. First, it retrieves the photo to which a tag is being added. This is found using the user_id of the currently logged-in user and the id parameter given in the URL.

As you will recall, we add tags to an object by specifying them as a comma-separated list in a string. Since we don't want to remove the tags that are already given for the tag, we just add the new tag, prefixed by a comma, to the end of the string. We then save the photo object.

Finally, we retrieve this new tag as a Tag model. This allows the view to access this new tag as it would any other tag, rather than having to deal with it as just a string.

Normally, we would then automatically render an HTML view or redirect to a different action. We could simply redirect to the edit action, which would reload the entire edit page in the user's browser. However, we are going to use Ajax techniques to update just the existing list of tags on the edit page.

To do this, we need to display the list of tags and add the form to enter a tag onto the photo edit page.

Edit the file app/views/user_photos/edit.rhtml as shown in Listing 10-14.

Listing 10-14. *The Updated user_photos Edit File*

```
<h2>Editing photo</h2>

<%= error_messages_for :photo %>

<%= link_to image_tag(@photo.public_filename('thumb')),
            user_photo_path(:user_id => @photo.user, :id => @photo) %>

<h3>Tags</h3>
<ul id="taglist">
  <%= render :partial => 'edit_tag', :collection => @photo.tags %>
</ul>

<% remote_form_for(:tag,
                   :url => user_add_tag_photo_path(:id => @photo),
                   :method => :put,
                   :complete => "Field.clear('tag-name')") do |f| %>
  <%= f.text_field :name, :id => 'tag-name' %>
  <%= submit_tag 'Add Tag' %>
<% end %>

<% form_for(:photo,
            :url => user_photo_path(:user_id => @photo.user, :id => @photo),
            :html => { :method => :put }) do |f| %>
  <p>Title:<br /><%= f.text_field 'title' %></p>
  <p>Description:<br /><%= f.text_area 'body', :rows => 6, :cols => 40 %></p>
  <p><%= submit_tag "Save" %> or <%= link_to 'cancel', user_photos_path %></p>
<% end %>
```

Here, we have added a list of the tags using the render :partial command, so we need to write this partial view. Create the file app/views/user_photos/_edit_tag.rhtml, and enter the partial view code in Listing 10-15. Since we will not use this partial in the photos controller, we should place it in the user_photos view directory.

Listing 10-15. *The edit_tag Partial View*

```
<li id="tag-<%= edit_tag.id %>">
  <span><%= edit_tag.name %></span>
</li>
```

Note that we are adding the id of the tag to the id attribute of the `<li>` tag. Although the `class` and `id` attributes of HTML objects are often used just for styling using CSS, we can also use them to find a specific part of the document. In this case, we will use this to allow us to delete a tag from the tag list by specifying exactly which page element we wish to remove.

We are using a Rails helper method `remote_form_for` to create the form where a user enters a new tag. This works in a similar way to the `form_for` helper that we have used in all of our `new` and `edit` views so far, except `remote_form_for` uses XMLHttpRequest to submit the form in the background rather than as a regular HTTP POST, which would force a page reload. This is achieved using a JavaScript library, which collects the form elements then submits them to our application. You can then process this in exactly the same way as you would a regular HTTP request. As you can see in the `add_tag` method, we still use `params[:tag][:name]` to access the form parameters.

The `remote_form_for` helper takes the same parameters as the `form_for` helper, so we still specify the destination URL and HTTP method. But we can also use special callbacks to perform JavaScript actions on the page. These callbacks are shown in Table 10-3.

Table 10-3. *The Ajax Callbacks*

Callback	Called When
`:loading`	The remote document is being loaded by the browser.
`:loaded`	The browser has finished loading the remote document.
`:interactive`	The user can interact, even if the document has not finished loading.
`:success`	The remote document has loaded and has a success HTTP Status code.
`:failure`	The remote document has loaded but does not have a success HTTP Status code.
`:complete`	The remote document has been completely loaded.

We are using the `:complete` callback to clear the tag name form field. This allows the user to enter a number of tags quickly, without having to manually clear the form field first.

So now that we have a form that can call the `add_tag` action in the background, we need to define what gets returned to the browser.

We have already seen how Rails can easily respond to different types of requests with the `respond_to` statement. This time, we will respond only to JavaScript requests.

The response that we want to send to the browser is a piece of JavaScript code that will instruct the browser to add the new tag to the end of the existing tag list. If we were sending an HTML page, we would write an `.rhtml` file. However, since we want to send JavaScript, Rails uses a different type of file to allow us to define a JavaScript response. These files are called Remote JavaScript (RJS) files.

RJS files work in a very similar way to an .rhtml or .rxml view file—you simply create a file with the same name as the action that you are responding to but with the suffix of .rjs.

Since our action method is called add_tag, create the corresponding RJS file, app/views/user_photos/add_tag.rjs. Enter the RJS code shown in Listing 10-16 to this file.

Listing 10-16. *The add_tag RJS File*

```
page.insert_html :bottom, 'taglist', { :partial => 'edit_tag',
                                        :locals => {:edit_tag => @new_tag} }
page.visual_effect :highlight, "tag-#{@new_tag.id}", :duration => 2
```

RJS files allow us to change data that is currently on the page. In this instance, we insert a new instance of the edit_tag partial at the bottom of the page element tag list. We need to set the new tag object, @new_tag, as a local variable to the partial.

We then call the visual effect method, telling it to highlight the newly created tag for a period of 2 seconds.

If we wanted to support browsers that were not capable of processing JavaScript, we could use the respond_to statement. If we wanted to support both JavaScript and HTML responses, we would add the following lines:

```
format.html
format.js
```

This renders the relevant template based on how the request was received.

RJS TEMPLATES

RJS template files are simply snippets of Ruby code that use a DSL to generate JavaScript code that is then sent to the requesting browser.

RJS relies on the Prototype and script.aculo.us JavaScript libraries that are shipped with Rails and should be included as part of the application layout with the tag `<%= javascript_include_tag :defaults %>`.

When you write an RJS file, you have access to an object called page, which is simply an instance of the Rails JavaScriptGenerator class. All the desired responses are made as method calls to the page object.

You can call a large number of available methods that allow you to change, remove, or add content to the page; make sections draggable; produce alert boxes; hide or display page elements; and so on.

To find out more about RJS, there is a very useful list of resources at the Ruby Inside blog http://www.rubyinside.com/16-rjs-resources-and-tutorials-for-rails-programmers-5.html.

For a more advanced reference to RJS templates, the e-book *RJS Templates for Rails* by Cody Fauser (O'Reilly, 2006) is a worthwhile purchase.

Before we try this out, we should add the delete_tag method and update the partial to allow us to easily delete tags.

Removing a Tag from a Photo Object

To give the users the option of removing a tag from one of their photo objects, we have to write the action method to remove the particular tag, write the response (in this case another RJS file), and add an option to the user interface to allow the users to perform this action easily.

Since we are using a partial to list the tags on the edit photo page, we can simply update this partial to show a delete link next to each tag.

Reopen this partial view file, `app/views/user_photo/_edit_tag.rhtml`, and edit it as shown in Listing 10-17 to add the delete link.

Listing 10-17. *Updated edit_tag Partial View*

```
<li id="tag-<%= edit_tag.id %>">
  <span><%= edit_tag.name %></span>
  <small>
    [<%= link_to_remote 'delete',
          :url => user_remove_tag_photo_path(:id => @photo.id,
                                              :tag_id => edit_tag.id),
          :method => :delete %>]
  </small>
</li>
```

This uses the Rails helper method `link_to_remote`. This works in the same way as the `remote_form_for` helper, making the remote request in the background without making the browser reload the whole page. This time, we have to specify the method to be `DELETE`, since we have specified in the routes file that the `remove_tag` action can only be accessed by the `DELETE` method. If you wished to perform other JavaScript actions before or after the `link_to_remote` method, you could also add the Ajax callbacks mentioned earlier. However, we do not require any callbacks to be executed.

We now need to write the `remove_tag` action method itself and the corresponding RJS file. Open the file `app/controllers/user_photos_controller.rb`, and add the `remove_tag` method shown in Listing 10-18 after the `add_tag` method but before the closing `end` statement.

Listing 10-18. *The remove_tag Action Method*

```
def remove_tag
  @photo = @logged_in_user.photos.find(params[:id])
  @tag_to_delete = @photo.tags.find(params[:tag_id])

  if @tag_to_delete
    @photo.tags.delete(@tag_to_delete)
  else
    render :nothing => true
  end
end
```

The method first retrieves the photo being modified. Since it only searches the photos within the scope of the `@logged_in_user`, it is impossible for someone who is not logged in as the photo owner to modify the photo's tags.

We then search the tags set for this photo for the tag specified in the request parameters. Only if this tag exists for this photo do we attempt to delete the tag and respond with the RJS file.

To delete the tag, we simply need to remove it from the tags associated with this photo. Since we already have the `@tag_to_delete` object, we simply call the `delete` method on `@photo.tags` to remove the specified `tag` object.

We now need to write the RJS template to define the response to this request. Create the file `app/views/user_photos/remove_tag.rjs`, and add the RJS code in Listing 10-19.

Listing 10-19. *The remove_tag RJS Template*

```
page.remove "tag-#{@tag_to_delete.id}"
page.visual_effect :highlight, 'taglist', :duration => 2
```

This RJS file simply removes the page element with the `id` of the tag that we are deleting. Since our page renders each tag with the tag object `id` prefixed with `tag-`, we can specify exactly which item in the list we wish to remove.

We then highlight the entire tag list for 2 seconds to show the user that the list has changed.

Linking to the Tag Browser

Finally, we should add some links to make it quick and easy for a visitor to browse the site using tags.

We should add a link to the menu sidebar, linking to the root-level tag `index` view, and we should also show all of the tags for a particular photo on the photo show page. We can also add a link to show users' tags from their profile pages.

Adding Tags to the Sidebar Menu

Open the sidebar menu partial file, `app/views/layouts/_menu.rhtml`, and add a link to the `tags_controller` index view as shown in Listing 10-20.

Listing 10-20. *Adding the Tag Index Link to the Sidebar Menu*

```
...
<li><%= link_to 'Blogs', all_blogs_path %></li>
<li><%= link_to 'Photos', photos_path %></li>
<li><%= link_to 'Photo Tags', tags_path %></li>

<li><hr size="1" width="90%" align="left"/></li>
...
```

Adding Tag Links to the Photo Show View

When a user views a particular photo, this is shown by the view `app/views/user_photos/show.rhtml`. Open this file now. Beneath the photo title and description, we will show the list of tags for this photo.

We could simply use the `tag_list` method, which would render a string listing all of the tags for this photo separated by commas. While this is fine, it would be much more useful to render each tag as a link, linking to the `user_tags` controller's `show` action. We will do this by cycling through the tags and creating a link for each tag.

Modify the file by adding the code as shown in Listing 10-21.

Listing 10-21. *The Updated user_photos Show View*

```
.. .
<p><%=h @photo.body %></p>

<p>Tags:
  <% @photo.tags.each do |tag| %>
    <%= link_to tag.name, user_tag_path(@photo.user, tag.name)%>
  <% end %>
</p>

<% if is_logged_in? && @photo.user_id == logged_in_user.id %>
...
```

Adding a Link on the Users Profile Page

Finally, we should add a link to the user's tag index page on their individual profile. Open the user profile's show view, app/views/users/show.rhtml, and add a link to the bottom of the page as shown in Listing 10-22.

Listing 10-22. *The Updated User Show View*

```
...
<p>
  <%= link_to "See all of #{@user.username}'s photos",
      user_photos_path(:user_id => @user) %>
</p>
<p>
  <%= link_to "#{@user.username}'s Tags",
      user_tags_path(:user_id => @user) %>
</p>
```

Now that all of the pieces are in place, we can run through the feature and manually test the functions.

Manually Testing

Fire up your browser, and go to the application home page, http://localhost:3000/. Log in to the site as one of the users you have created. Now, go to your photos page. If you have not uploaded any photos as this user, you should upload a few now.

View one of these photos by clicking on the photo itself. Since this photo belongs to you, the "edit" and "delete" links will be shown on this page. Click the "edit" link. This will show your photo along with edit boxes for the title and description, and a new text box allowing you to enter a tag.

Enter a tag that describes the picture, and press Return/Enter or click the Add Tag button. This new tag will appear in the tag list above the tag text entry box, as shown in Figure 10-1, and be highlighted briefly.

Figure 10-1. *The "Editing photo" screen with the tag entry box*

Do this with a number of photos, using the same tag and new tags. This will give us an interesting tag cloud view.

Next, click the Photo Tags link in the sidebar menu to display all of the tags added on the site with their popularity shown by the size of the font, as shown in Figure 10-2.

Now try clicking one of the tags to show all of the photos for that particular tag. You will notice that the tag being viewed is simply given as part of the URL.

Log out of the site and log in as a different user. Try adding some tags to photos owned by this other user, and take a look at the tag views for both the previous user and this new user—you will see that the tag clouds are unique for each user, as expected.

Figure 10-2. *The photos tag cloud*

Further Development of the Tagging System

This tagging feature can be extended further in a number of ways:

- Right now, the tag `index` action shows all tags. This is fine for a small site with a limited number of tags, but it will soon become excessive on a large-scale site. You could limit the number of tags shown by the `index` action to a hundred or so of the most popular tags, which should be about a page full of tags.

- Also, the pages showing all photos with a specific tag are not paginated. You should consider paginating them if you anticipate a large number of photos.

- When showing photos that are tagged with a keyword, you could retrieve other tags used to tag the same photos. This would produce a related tags list, allowing the users to browse the photo galleries easily.

- You could also show a list of users who have most frequently used a particular tag.

- You may also wish to add tags to other objects on the site, such as blog entries.

Summary

In this chapter, we have added a complete tagging system to the photo gallery. We used the `acts_as_taggable_on_steroids` plug-in to add tagging features to the Photo model and developed an interface for the user.

This involved developing an Ajax-based system to allow the tags to be added and deleted dynamically from the photo edit page. This used the `remote_form_for` and `remote_link_to` helpers and RJS templates to send the data and dynamically construct JavaScript from the Ruby RJS file.

We also created a tag cloud of all the tags on the site, allowing users to quickly see which tags are the most popular.

In the next chapter, we will look at how we can integrate with other web applications, in particular Google Maps and Flickr, by using their public APIs.

CHAPTER 11

■■■

Creating Mashups and Integrating with Web 2.0

In this chapter, we will integrate RailsCoders with some other web applications, creating what has become known as a mashup, which is simply using parts of existing web applications to build something new.

Many web applications now offer public APIs for free, meaning that it is very simple to retrieve or save data on the site using an application. Google has APIs for many of their applications, including Google Base, Search, Maps, Calendar, and Mail. Flickr offers access to virtually all the features of the web site through REST, XML-RPC, or SOAP interfaces. Amazon has many innovative APIs including access to product search and historical price data. These are only a few examples of the types of APIs available on the web. For an extensive list of sites that offer APIs, visit `http://www.programmableweb.com/apilist`. If you have a favorite web application, it is highly likely that they offer some form of API.

Unfortunately, since the requirements of each site differ, most APIs are implemented in different ways, either using SOAP, XML-RPC, or REST, but most Web 2.0 sites are moving toward REST architectures to offer very simple and lightweight interfaces to their data.

For the RailsCoders site, we will integrate with two of the most popular applications for creating mashups: Google Maps and Flickr. We will use Google Maps to allow users to add physical location data to their uploaded photographs. We will use the Flickr API to allow users to add their Flickr IDs to their profiles. User profile pages will then be able to show the users' latest Flickr photos along with their RailsCoders photos.

Integrating the Google Maps API

Google launched their mapping service early in 2005, and it quickly became a hugely popular service. Before Google Maps, all free online mapping services were rather awkward and only offered basic manipulation and search tools, but Google Maps opened up the possibilities of embedding interactive, scrollable maps to your own site. Google released a simple API to Google Maps in June 2005 and has continued to extend and improve its features. The API offers extensive control over how you want the map to look and allows you to add markers and information to it.

To display a map, we will use the Google Maps API. This API makes it easy to embed maps or satellite images on another web page. You can set the center point of the map, along with the zoom level, making it easy to show exactly the map you require. We will also make use of the marker feature, which enables us to create marker points on the displayed map.

■**Note** Full documentation for the Google Maps API is available at `http://www.google.com/apis/maps/documentation`.

The Google Maps API is very straightforward to use, but a number of useful Rails plug-ins have been created that act as a wrapper around it, allowing us to use syntax and commands familiar to us from Rails as an interface to the features of the API. This makes it even easier to create maps and add markers.

We are going to use a plug-in called YM4R/GM, an acronym for Yellow Maps For Rails using Google Maps. YM4R/GM is part of the YM4R collection of mapping tools for Ruby developed by Guilhem Vellut. You can find more information about the YM4R tools at `http://thepochisuperstarmegashow.com/projects/#ym4r` and `http://rubyforge.org/projects/ym4r/`.

The Google Maps API is a JavaScript API so you would normally need to use it by writing JavaScript, but as mentioned, we will be using the YM4R/GM plug-in. This acts as a wrapper around the JavaScript API, making it very easy to use Ruby to create and configure the map and any map markers.

Of course, if we need to add extra JavaScript code to perform actions outside of the scope of the plug-in, we can easily do that too.

■**Note** The documentation for YM4R/GM is available online at `http://www.thepochisuperstarmegashow.com/ProjectsDoc/ym4r_gm-doc/`.

The Mapping Feature Requirements

As part of the photo albums feature, we want to be able to store geographical coordinates for each picture if they are available and show the actual location of the photograph on a map on the photo's show page.

Obviously, the latitude and longitude of each photo will not always be available—not everyone carries a GPS around with them at all times. Therefore, we will add an embedded map to the photo's edit page, allowing the user to drag and zoom in on the map to select a point on the map to set the longitude and latitude.

To store the geographical location, we need to extend the Photo model, adding fields to store the location data and also a preference setting, which will be set if the user wants this location to be shown on the photo page. The required fields are shown in Table 11-1. As usual, we will add these through a database migration.

We then need to update the `user_photos` edit page, adding these fields to the list of editable fields. The Photo model file does not need to be changed.

Table 11-1. *The Extra Fields Required by the Photo Model for Mapping Data*

Field Name	Field Type	Description
geo_lat	float	The latitude of the photo's location
geo_long	float	The longitude of the photo's location
show_geo	boolean	A user-settable option to determine if the location data is displayed to others, with a default of true

Building the Mapping Feature

Now that we know the requirements of the RailsCoders mapping feature and the tools we will use to develop it, we can begin to implement the feature.

Getting a Google Maps API Key

Before we get started, we first need to obtain a Google Maps API key. This key is necessary if we want to use Google Maps on a production site. Google allows you to use the API for free as long as you agree to Google's terms and conditions. These are not restrictive, but there is a limit on the number of geocode queries (but not map requests) you can perform, and you must agree to make your application freely available. If you wish to use Google Maps in an enterprise environment, you can sign up for Google Maps for Enterprise. By requesting a key from Google, they can keep track of your requests to Google Maps to ensure that you are keeping within these limits.

To obtain a key from Google, simply go to http://www.google.com/apis/maps/signup.html, and enter the details of your site. You will receive a long string of characters that is the key you will need to use.

Installing the YM4R/GM Plug-in

We will use the Rails plug-in script to install the YM4R/GM plug-in. However, we need to install the Subversion source control software in order to access the repository where this plug-in is stored.

For Windows, download the Subversion client software from http://subversion.tigris.org/servlets/ProjectDocumentList?folderID=91. Download the file called svn-1.4.3-setup.exe, and run the installation program. You will then need to restart InstantRails and your console window to pick up the new path settings.

On Ubuntu Linux, simply enter the following command:

```
$ sudo apt-get install subversion
```

If you are running Mac OS X, download an installation package from http://www.codingmonkeys.de/mbo/articles/2007/01/25/subversion-1-4-3. Run the installation package, and follow the on-screen prompts.

Now that you have Subversion installed, install YM4R by entering the following command:

```
$ ruby script/plugin install ➥
svn://rubyforge.org/var/svn/ym4r/Plugins/GM/trunk/ym4r_gm
```

```
A    [...]/railscoders/vendor/plugins/ym4r_gm
A    [...]/railscoders/vendor/plugins/ym4r_gm/test
A    [...]/railscoders/vendor/plugins/ym4r_gm/test/gm_test.rb
A    [...]/railscoders/vendor/plugins/ym4r_gm/rakefile.rb
A    [...]/railscoders/vendor/plugins/ym4r_gm/init.rb
A    [...]/railscoders/vendor/plugins/ym4r_gm/tasks
A    [...]/railscoders/vendor/plugins/ym4r_gm/tasks/gm_tasks.rake
A    [...]/railscoders/vendor/plugins/ym4r_gm/javascript
A    [...]/railscoders/vendor/plugins/ym4r_gm/javascript/geoRssOverlay.js
A    [...]/railscoders/vendor/plugins/ym4r_gm/javascript/clusterer.js
A    [...]/railscoders/vendor/plugins/ym4r_gm/javascript/ym4r-gm.js
A    [...]/railscoders/vendor/plugins/ym4r_gm/javascript/wms-gs.js
A    [...]/railscoders/vendor/plugins/ym4r_gm/javascript/markerGroup.js
A    [...]/railscoders/vendor/plugins/ym4r_gm/lib
A    [...]/railscoders/vendor/plugins/ym4r_gm/lib/ym4r_gm.rb
A    [...]/railscoders/vendor/plugins/ym4r_gm/lib/gm_plugin
A    [...]/railscoders/vendor/plugins/ym4r_gm/lib/gm_plugin/map.rb
A    [...]/railscoders/vendor/plugins/ym4r_gm/lib/gm_plugin/geocoding.rb
A    [...]/railscoders/vendor/plugins/ym4r_gm/lib/gm_plugin/helper.rb
A    [...]/railscoders/vendor/plugins/ym4r_gm/lib/gm_plugin/control.rb
A    [...]/railscoders/vendor/plugins/ym4r_gm/lib/gm_plugin/overlay.rb
A    [...]/railscoders/vendor/plugins/ym4r_gm/lib/gm_plugin/key.rb
A    [...]/railscoders/vendor/plugins/ym4r_gm/lib/gm_plugin/point.rb
A    [...]/railscoders/vendor/plugins/ym4r_gm/lib/gm_plugin/mapping.rb
A    [...]/railscoders/vendor/plugins/ym4r_gm/lib/gm_plugin/layer.rb
A    [...]/railscoders/vendor/plugins/ym4r_gm/gmaps_api_key.yml.sample
A    [...]/railscoders/vendor/plugins/ym4r_gm/install.rb
A    [...]/railscoders/vendor/plugins/ym4r_gm/README
Exported revision 86.
```

As part of the plug-in installation procedure, the necessary JavaScript files are copied to the public/javascripts/ directory of your application and a configuration file for the Google Maps API, config/gmaps_api_key.yml, is created and placed inside the config/ directory. Open this file now.

You should obtain an API key for http://localhost, which you should insert into the file for the development and test modes and a key for the domain of your own site for the production mode. Enter these into the config/gmaps_api_key.yml as shown in Listing 11-1, replacing railscoders.net with your own domain name.

Listing 11-1. *The gmaps_api_key.rb Configuration File*

```
# Fill here the Google Maps API keys for your application
# In this sample:
# For development and test, we have only one possible host (localhost:3000), so
# there is only a single key associated with the mode.
# In production, the app can be accessed through 2 different hosts:
# thepochisuperstarmegashow.com and exmaple.com. There then needs a 2-key hash.
# If you deployed to one host, only the API key would be needed (as in development
# and test).

development:
  <API_key_for_localhost>

test:
  <API_key_for_localhost>

production:
  railscoders.net: <API_key_for_railscoders.net>
```

Adding the Geographical Fields to the Photo Schema

Before we can make use of the YM4R/GM plug-in to start displaying maps, we need to add location data to some photos to give us data to work with.

First, we need to create a migration file to add the necessary fields to the existing Photo model. Create a new migration file with the following command:

```
$ ruby script/generate migration AddGeoToPhotos
```

```
      exists  db/migrate
      create  db/migrate/022add_geo_to_photos.rb
```

Next, edit this generated migration file, db/migrate/022_add_geo_to_photos.rb. Update this file as shown in Listing 11-2. Note that the down method removes the fields created by the up method, ensuring that the database migration can be rolled back.

Listing 11-2. *Migration File to Add Geographical Coordinates to the Photo Model*

```
class AddGeoToPhotos < ActiveRecord::Migration
  def self.up
    add_column :photos, :geo_lat, :float
    add_column :photos, :geo_long, :float
    add_column :photos, :show_geo, :boolean, :default => true, :null => false
  end
```

```
    def self.down
      remove_column :photos, :geo_lat
      remove_column :photos, :geo_long
      remove_column :photos, :show_geo
    end
end
```

Now execute this migration:

```
$ rake db:migrate
```

```
== AddGeoToPhotos: migrating ====================================================
-- add_column(:photos, :geo_lat, :float)
   -> 0.0113s
-- add_column(:photos, :geo_long, :float)
   -> 0.0333s
-- add_column(:photos, :show_geo, :boolean, {:null=>false, :default=>true})
   -> 0.0116s
== AddGeoToPhotos: migrated (0.0567s) ===========================================
```

You may wish to check your database to make sure that the fields have been created correctly.

Adding the Geographical Fields to the Photo Edit and New Pages

We will now add these newly created fields to the photo edit page. Since this is accessed by user_photos_controller.rb, the file we need to edit is app/views/user_photos/edit.rhtml.

For the moment, we will just add simple text fields to the edit page, allowing the user to enter the latitude and longitude coordinates by hand. When we have added that and have the map displaying the location on the photo show page, we will then add a map to the edit page.

Open the file app/views/user_photos/edit.rhtml, and edit the form fields at the end of the file, as shown in Listing 11-3.

Listing 11-3. *Modifications to the user_photos Edit Page*

```
...
<% form_for(:photo,
            :url => user_photo_path(:user_id => @photo.user, :id => @photo),
            :html => { :method => :put }) do |f| %>
  <p>Title:<br /><%= f.text_field 'title' %></p>
  <p>Description:<br /><%= f.text_area 'body', :rows => 6, :cols => 40 %></p>
  <p>Latitude: <%= f.text_field 'geo_lat', :size => '8' %></p>
  <p>Longitude: <%= f.text_field 'geo_long', :size => '8' %></p>
  <p>Display Location Data? <%= f.check_box 'show_geo' %></p>
  <p><%= submit_tag "Save" %> or <%= link_to 'cancel', user_photos_path %></p>
<% end %>
```

Since these fields are just part of the model, we do not have to alter the controller file—the fields will automatically be saved when the edit form is submitted.

We should also add these fields to the photo upload form so that a user can enter the location data at the same time as uploading a new photo. Open the photo upload form, app/views/user_photos/new.rhtml, and add the new fields as shown in Listing 11-4.

Listing 11-4. *Modifications to the user_photos New Page*

```
<h2>Upload a new photo</h2>

<%= error_messages_for :photo %>

<% form_for(:photo,
            :url => user_photos_path(:user_id => @logged_in_user),
            :html => { :multipart => true }) do |f| %>
  <p>Select a photo to upload</p>
  <p>Title:<br /><%= f.text_field :title %></p>
  <p>Description:<br /><%= f.text_area :body, :rows => 6, :cols => 40 %></p>
  <p>Latitude: <%= f.text_field 'geo_lat', :size => '8' %></p>
  <p>Longitude: <%= f.text_field 'geo_long', :size => '8' %></p>
  <p>Display Location Data? <%= f.check_box 'show_geo' %></p>
  <p>Photo:<br /><%= f.file_field 'uploaded_data' %></p>
  <p>
    <%= submit_tag 'Upload Photo' %> or
    <%= link_to 'cancel', user_photos_path(@logged_in_user) %>
  </p>
<% end %>
```

Try adding location data now. If you don't know the latitude and longitude of any photos, just use the demonstration fields shown, or use Google Maps to find the latitude and longitude of the location where your photo was taken.

Log in to the site with a regular user, and select Upload Photo from the sidebar menu. Select a new photo to upload, and fill in the fields including the location data, as shown in Figure 11-1.

Now click the Upload Photo button to upload the photo to the site. The photo will be uploaded as expected. Of course, the location data will not yet be shown, as we haven't added this functionality to the site, but you should now try editing this photo to see that the latitude and longitude data has been added.

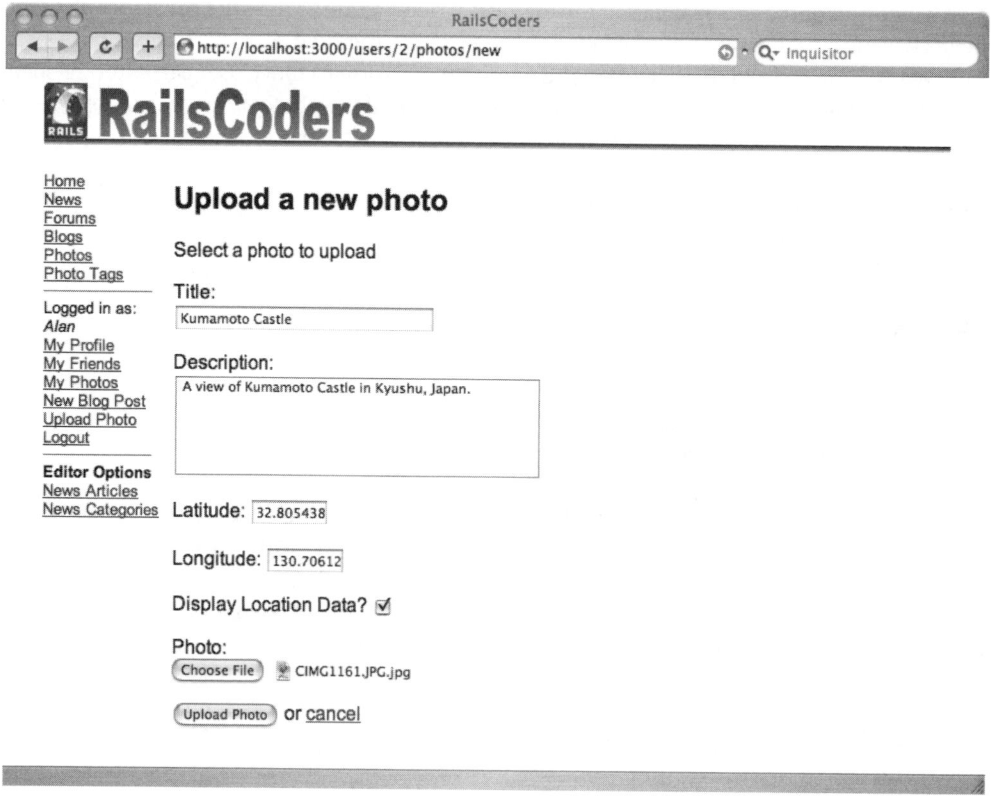

Figure 11-1. *Uploading a new photo with location data*

Displaying the Location Data as a Map

Now that we have a photo with location data, we can show it as a point on a map on the photo show page. To do this, we will use the YM4R/GM plug-in that we installed earlier. This involves three stages:

1. Edit the controller to create a new GMap object. This object is provided by the plug-in and is essentially a wrapper around the Google Maps JavaScript API.

2. Set various parameters of the GMap object, such as the center point of the map and the zoom level.

3. Embed the map on the view page by calling the to_html method of the GMap object.

Using the GMap method control_init, we can set the buttons that are shown overlaid on the map. The options :small_map, :large_map, :small_zoom, :scale, :map_type, and :overview_map are available.

We will center the map at the photo's coordinates and set a default zoom level using the method center_zoom_init. We can also add markers to the map. We need to create an instance of the GMarker object with the latitude and longitude of our photo, together with an optional title (shown when hovering the mouse over the marker) and informational window (shown after the user clicks on the marker). This marker is then added to the map as an overlay using the call @map.overlay_init method.

Open the app/controllers/user_photos_controller.rb file, and edit the show action method as shown in Listing 11-5.

Listing 11-5. *Update to the Show Action of user_photos_controller*

```
def show
  @photo = Photo.find_by_user_id_and_id(params[:user_id],
                                        params[:id],
                                        :include => :user)

  if @photo.show_geo && (@photo.geo_lat && @photo.geo_long)
    @map = GMap.new("map_div_id")
    @map.control_init(:map_type => false, :small_zoom => true)
    @map.center_zoom_init([@photo.geo_lat, @photo.geo_long], 8)

    marker = GMarker.new([@photo.geo_lat, @photo.geo_long],
                         :title => @photo.title,
                         :info_window => @photo.body)
    @map.overlay_init(marker)
  end

  respond_to do |format|
    format.html # show.rhtml
    format.xml  { render :xml => @photo.to_xml }
  end
end
```

You will notice that if the show_geo field is set to false or if either the geo_lat or geo_long field is empty, the @map object is not instantiated.

We can now create the map view using the methods provided by the plug-in. To display the map, we call the method @map.to_html. @map.div outputs the XHMTL <div> tags, which have been configured. You can pass in :width and :height to this method, allowing you to set the size of the map on the page.

We also need to make sure that the Google Maps JavaScript libraries are loaded by the user's browser by adding the helper method GMap.header to the <head> section of the page. You will remember that we can add extra code to the page's <head> by specifying content_for :head within our page view.

In the map section of the page, we have also used link_to_function helpers to display links that allow the user to hide and show the map; link_to_function allows you to specify a piece of JavaScript that will be executed when the link is clicked. In this case, each link simply calls Element.hide and Element.show with the respective ids of the map and the Show Map link.

Open the photo show page, app/views/user_photos/show.rhtml, and modify the file as shown in Listing 11-6.

Listing 11-6. *The Updated user_photos Show File*

```
<% content_for :head do %>
  <%= GMap.header %>
<% end %>


<h3>
  <%= link_to "#{@photo.user.username}'s Photos",
              user_photos_path(:user_id => @photo.user) %>
</h3>
<h2><%=h @photo.title %></h2>
<p><%=h @photo.body %></p>

<% if @photo.tags.any? %>
  <p>Tags:
    <% @photo.tags.each do |tag| %>
      <%= link_to tag.name, user_tag_path(@photo.user, tag.name)%>
    <% end %>
  </p>
<% end %>

<% if is_logged_in? && @photo.user_id == logged_in_user.id %>
  <p>
  <%= link_to 'Edit', user_edit_photo_path(:user_id => @photo.user, :id=>@photo) %>,
  <%= link_to 'Delete', user_photo_path(:user_id => @photo.user, :id => @photo),
                                        :confirm => 'Are you sure?',
                                        :method => :delete %>
  </p>
<% end %>


<% if @map %>
  <div id="gmap">
    <%= link_to_function 'Hide Map',
          "Element.hide('gmap'); Element.show('showmaplink')" %>
    <%= @map.to_html %>
    <%= @map.div(:width => 650, :height => 200) %>
    <br />
  </div>
  <%= link_to_function 'Show Map',
        "Element.show('gmap'); Element.hide('showmaplink')",
        :id => 'showmaplink',
        :style => 'display:none' %>
<% end %>

<%= image_tag @photo.public_filename, :id => 'photo' %>
```

You can now take a look at the photo page in your browser. The location that was set in the geo_lat and geo_long fields will now be displayed in the embedded map, as shown in Figure 11-2.

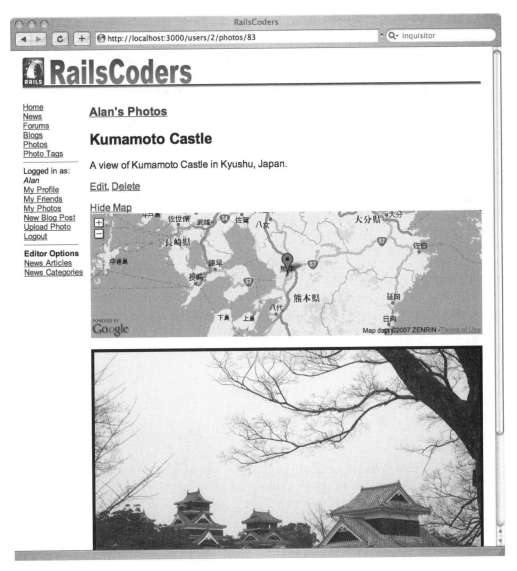

Figure 11-2. *The photo show page with embedded Google map*

Try moving the map around by clicking and dragging it. You can zoom in and out with the plus (+) and minus (–) buttons. You can hide the map with the Hide Map link and redisplay it with the Show Map link.

You should also try editing the latitude and longitude coordinates of the photo and reloading the photo page. The map will center on the new location of the photo.

Try deselecting the Display Location Data? check box on the edit page—the photo show page will not show any embedded map at all.

Selecting the Location Using the Map

As I mentioned earlier, asking the user to manually enter latitude and longitude coordinates is inconvenient and cumbersome. There are a number of ways that we could make it easier for a user to enter location data.

One method would be to let the user enter a real-world street address. This could be achieved by using the Google Maps Geocoder. A geocoder accepts an address and returns the coordinates of that point. This would be very useful, but requires the user to know the actual address. If photos have been taken on vacation or away from home, which is very likely, then the user might not know the address of the location where the photo was taken.

A much more intuitive method is to allow the user to simply move the map to the location that the photo was taken and click the point on the map. This is what we will implement.

To do this, we will have to add code to the edit action method to create a GMap object for the edit page, add the code to display this GMap object on the edit page, and write some JavaScript to add an event listener to the map, which will allow us to dynamically modify the page when the map is clicked.

First, edit the app/controllers/user_photos_controller.rb file. Modify the existing edit method as shown in Listing 11-7.

Listing 11-7. *Modification to the user_photos_controller Edit Method*

```
def edit
  @photo = @logged_in_user.photos.find(params[:id])

  @map = GMap.new("map_div_id")
  @map.control_init(:large_map => true)
  if @photo.geo_lat && @photo.geo_long
    @map.center_zoom_init([@photo.geo_lat, @photo.geo_long], 8)

    marker = GMarker.new([@photo.geo_lat, @photo.geo_long],
      :title => @photo.title, :info_window => @photo.body)
    @map.overlay_init(marker)
  else
    @map.center_zoom_init([25,0], 1)
  end

  @map.record_init @map.on_click(
    "function (overlay, point) { updateLocation(point); }")

rescue ActiveRecord::RecordNotFound
  redirect_to :action => 'index'
end
```

This method now instantiates a GMap object and sets the control buttons as before. If there are existing longitude and latitude coordinates for the @photo object, the map is centered on this point, and a marker is created. If no coordinates are set, a world map is shown.

We next create an on_click event for the @map object that calls a JavaScript function called updateLocation with the point that was clicked as a parameter. We will create this JavaScript function in a moment.

This event is given as a parameter to the @map.record_init method call—this outputs the given JavaScript in the load JavaScript function, meaning that it will be executed when the map is loaded.

To add a new JavaScript function to our application, we can simply add it to the file public/javascripts/application.js. This file is automatically loaded whenever you include the javascript_include_tag :defaults command in your application layout file, which we have already done when we created the app/views/layouts/application.rhtml file in Chapter 2.

Open the public/javascripts/application.js file, and add the function shown in Listing 11-8 to the end of this file.

Listing 11-8. *The application.js File*

```
function updateLocation(point) {
  document.getElementById('photo_geo_lat').value = point.y;
  document.getElementById('photo_geo_long').value = point.x;
  map.clearOverlays();
  map.addOverlay(new GMarker(new GLatLng(point.y, point.x)));
}
```

When this function is called, the function sets the value of the geo_lat and geo_long form fields on the page using the document.getElementById function. Then it clears the map's existing overlays (which would be a marker if the map already had coordinates set) and creates a new overlay, which consists of a marker at the point clicked on the map.

Finally, we have to actually add the map to the edit photo page. Open the file app/views/user_photos/edit.rhtml, and edit as shown in Listing 11-9.

Listing 11-9. *Modifications to the user_photos Edit Page*

```
<% content_for :head do %>
  <%= GMap.header %>
<% end %>

<h2>Edit photo details</h2>

<%= error_messages_for :photo %>

<%= link_to image_tag(@photo.public_filename('thumb')),
          user_photo_path(:user_id => @photo.user, :id => @photo) %>

<h3>Tags</h3>
<ul id="taglist">
  <%= render :partial => 'edit_tag', :collection => @photo.tags %>
</ul>
```

```
<% remote_form_for(:tag,
                    :url => user_add_tag_photo_path(:id => @photo),
                    :method => :put,
                    :complete => "Field.clear('tag-name')") do |f| %>
  <%= f.text_field :name, :id => 'tag-name' %>
  <%= submit_tag 'Add Tag' %>
<% end %>

<% form_for(:photo,
            :url => user_photo_path(:user_id => @photo.user, :id => @photo),
            :html => { :method => :put }) do |f| %>
  <p>Title:<br /><%= f.text_field 'title' %></p>
  <p>Description:<br /><%= f.text_area 'body', :rows => 6, :cols => 40 %></p>
  <p>Latitude: <%= f.text_field 'geo_lat', :size => '8' %></p>
  <p>Longitude: <%= f.text_field 'geo_long', :size => '8' %></p>
  <p>Display Location Data? <%= f.check_box 'show_geo' %></p>

  <div id="gmap">
    <%= @map.to_html %>
    <%= @map.div(:width => 650, :height => 300) %>
  </div>

  <p><%= submit_tag "Save" %> or <%= link_to 'cancel', user_photos_path %></p>
<% end %>
```

As you can see, we need to include the necessary mapping JavaScript with the GMaps.header statement. We add the map to the bottom of the form in the same way as we embedded a map on the photo show page.

Before we try this out, we should add the same functionality to the new method, allowing a user to set the location when uploading a photo.

Edit the app/controllers/user_photos_controller.rb file again by modifying the new method as shown in Listing 11-10.

Listing 11-10. *Update to the new Method of the user_photos_controller File*

```
def new
  @photo = Photo.new

  @map = GMap.new("map_div_id")
  @map.control_init(:large_map => true)
  @map.center_zoom_init([25,0], 1)
  @map.record_init @map.on_click(
      "function (overlay, point) { updateLocation(point); }")
end
```

Since there is no possibility of a new photo having an existing set of location coordinates, we just create a new map showing the world view without a marker.

Now update the new view by editing app/views/user_photos/new.rhtml as shown in Listing 11-11.

Listing 11-11. *Update to the user_photos New View*

```
<% content_for :head do %>
  <%= GMap.header %>
<% end %>

<h2>Upload a new photo</h2>

<%= error_messages_for :photo %>

<% form_for(:photo,
            :url => user_photos_path(:user_id => @logged_in_user),
            :html => { :multipart => true }) do |f| %>
  <p>Select a photo to upload</p>
  <p>Title:<br /><%= f.text_field :title %></p>
  <p>Description:<br /><%= f.text_area :body, :rows => 6, :cols => 40 %></p>
  <p>Latitude: <%= f.text_field 'geo_lat', :size => '8' %></p>
  <p>Longitude: <%= f.text_field 'geo_long', :size => '8' %></p>
  <p>Display Location Data? <%= f.check_box 'show_geo' %></p>
  <p>Photo:<br /><%= f.file_field 'uploaded_data' %></p>

  <div id="gmap">
    <%= @map.to_html %>
    <%= @map.div(:width => 650, :height => 300) %>
  </div>

  <p>
    <%= submit_tag 'Upload Photo' %> or
    <%= link_to 'cancel', user_photos_path(@logged_in_user) %>
  </p>
<% end %>
```

We can try using this now. Log in to the site, and try uploading a new photo. On the photo upload screen, there will now be a world map, as shown in Figure 11-3.

Select a photo to upload, and add a title and description for the photo. Now, instead of manually entering latitude and longitude values, zoom in on a location using the map, and scroll until you find the location where the photo was taken. Next, simply click the location on the map once. The latitude and longitude values will automatically be filled in with the coordinates of the location that you have clicked.

Now, click the Upload Photo button to upload the new photo with the specified coordinates. You will be taken to the thumbnail page showing all of your photos. Click the photo that you have just uploaded to show the photo in full along with the embedded Google map pinpointing the photo's location.

Try editing another photo to test the edit photo page. Use the Google map to select a different location, updating the values of the photo's latitude and longitude attributes. Save this photo, and reopen the photo by clicking it. Make sure that this now points to the newly saved location on the map.

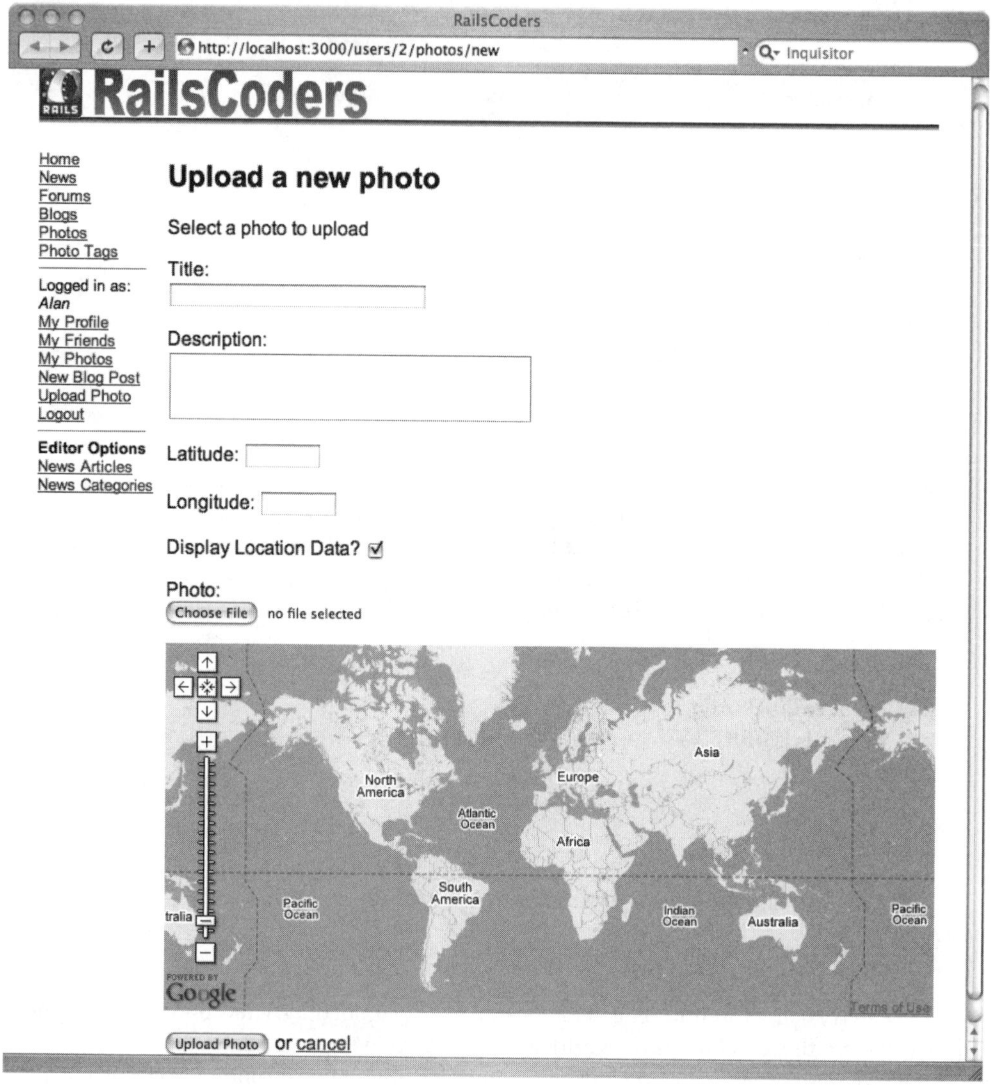

Figure 11-3. *The photo upload page with embedded Google map*

Integrating the Flickr API

Flickr is a very popular online photo-sharing site. It was originally developed by Ludicorp and released in February 2004 but has since been acquired by Yahoo! Flickr allows members to easily upload photos and tag them with metadata, in a similar way to our RailsCoders photo gallery.

Flickr has hundreds of millions of photographs online and many users have already invested a lot of time creating an archive of their photographs there, so we should allow our users to link to their existing Flickr galleries.

Flickr provides a very complete API available for noncommercial use. The complete Flickr API documentation is available online at `http://www.flickr.com/services/api`.

There are a number of libraries written for Rails that act as wrappers around the Flickr API, but since the API is incredibly easy to use, we will just build our own code to interface to Flickr.

If you don't already have a Flickr account, it would be a good idea to get one now so that you can follow along. To register for Flickr, you simply use an existing Yahoo! account or register a new account at Yahoo! if you don't already have one. Then go to `http://flickr.com`, and sign in to Flickr with your Yahoo! account details. You will be prompted to enter a username to use on Flickr. All Flickr usernames are unique. Once you log in, you will be able to upload photos to Flickr using either the web site or a number of desktop uploading tools.

The Flickr Feature Requirements

Since it is highly likely that many of our users will already have accounts on Flickr.com with a large number of photos stored there, we want to allow users to add their Flickr usernames to their profiles. When someone views a user profile, it will display a number of the latest photos uploaded to Flickr, along with a link to the user's Flickr home page.

To do this, we will have to store the user's Flickr username as part of the user details. However, when accessing Flickr via the API, you do not use the username of a member as the user key. Instead, Flickr assigns an `nsid` to each user, which is a unique ID similar to 35237095947@N01.

Since this ID will not be known by users, we will have to use the API to retrieve the `nsid`s by searching for usernames and storing both the `nsid`s and the Flickr usernames in our database.

The required database fields are shown in Table 11-2 and will be added to our existing database with a migration script.

Table 11-2. *Extra Fields Required for the Users Table*

Field name	Field type	Description
flickr_username	string	The Flickr username of the member
flickr_id	string	The Flickr nsid of the member

To allow users to enter their Flickr usernames, we will add a text field to the user profile edit page. We will then add a method call to the user's `before_save` callback, which retrieves the `nsid` from Flickr if the `flickr_username` field is not left blank and saves this `nsid` as part of the User model.

To obtain a user's latest photos, we can simply request an RSS feed of this Flickr member's photos. Since a Flickr feed then belongs to a user, we will simply add a method to the User model to retrieve and return the Flickr RSS feed for a user.

We will extend the show method of the users controller to assign this feed to an instance variable that can then be shown in the user's profile.

Building the Flickr Integration Feature

We can now go ahead and start building the Flickr integration feature. Similar to the Google Maps API, use of the Flickr API requires an API key, so we will have to obtain an API key first.

Obtaining a Flickr API Key

To make use of the Flickr API, we need to obtain a key from Flickr. Keys are free for noncommercial use. If the key is for commercial use, you can apply in the same way, but your request will be reviewed by Flickr before being assigned.

First, log in to your Flickr account using your Yahoo! login details. Then go to `http://www.flickr.com/services/api/keys/apply`. Make sure your name and e-mail address are correct, and select if your key is for noncommercial or commercial use. Enter a brief description of your site in the box provided; check the boxes to indicate that you agree with their conditions of use; then click Apply.

You will be provided with a key and asked to fill in the API Key Authentication Setup form. We will not need to provide user authentication for members, since we will just be working with read-only methods, but if you wanted to work with read-write API methods to allow the user to edit and post to a Flickr account, you would need to configure Flickr authentication.

Since we don't want to have to enter this key into our code every time we want to make a call to Flickr, it is best to define it as a constant in your `config/environment.rb` file. Open this now, and define the constant `FLICKR_API_KEY` at the end of this file as follows:

```
FLICKR_API_KEY = "<insert_your_key>"
```

Note that any changes to the `environment.rb` file require the application server to be restarted before they are picked up.

Creating the Flickr User Database Fields

We now need to add the two fields to the `users` database table as defined in the specification. Create a migration script using the following command:

```
$ ruby script/generate migration AddFlickrUserFields
```

```
      exists  db/migrate
      create  db/migrate/023add_flickr_user_fields.rb
```

Now edit this file, `db/migrate/023add_flickr_user_fields.rb`, as shown in Listing 11-12.

Listing 11-12. *Migration Script to Add the Flickr User Details*

```
class AddFlickrUserFields < ActiveRecord::Migration
  def self.up
    add_column :users, :flickr_username, :string
    add_column :users, :flickr_id, :string
  end

  def self.down
    remove_column :users, :flickr_username
    remove_column :users, :flickr_id
  end
end
```

Execute the migration script to add the fields to the database:

```
$ rake db:migrate
```

```
== AddFlickrUserFields: migrating ==============================================
-- add_column(:users, :flickr_username, :string)
   -> 0.0445s
-- add_column(:users, :flickr_id, :string)
   -> 0.0251s
== AddFlickrUserFields: migrated (0.0701s) =====================================
```

We can now add support for these to the User model and views.

Adding the Flickr Username to the Edit User View

To allow the users to enter their Flickr usernames to their profiles, we simply need to add an extra field to the user edit view. Open this file, app/views/users/edit.rhtml, and add the extra text entry field as shown in Listing 11-13.

Listing 11-13. *Adding the Flickr Username to the User Edit View*

```
<h2>Edit your account</h2>

<p><%= link_to 'Show my profile', user_path(@user) %></p>

<%= error_messages_for :user %>

<% form_for :user,
            :url => user_url(@user),
            :html => { :method => :put } do |f| -%>
  <p>Email:<br /><%= f.text_field :email, :size => 60 %></p>
  <p>Flickr Username:<br />
    <%= f.text_field :flickr_username, :size => 60 %>
  </p>
  <p>Password:<br /><%= f.password_field :password, :size => 60 %></p>
  <p>Password Confirmation:<br />
    <%= f.password_field :password_confirmation, :size => 60 %></p>
  <p>Profile:<br /><%= f.text_area :profile, :rows => 6, :cols => 60 %></p>
  <%= submit_tag 'Save' %>
<% end -%>
```

This field will now be submitted when the form is saved.

Retrieving the User's Flickr nsid

As we discussed before, to specify a user in the Flickr API methods, we need to use the user's nsid, a unique ID for each Flickr user.

In order to obtain this field, we will use the Flickr API call `flickr.people.findByUsername`. If you take a look at the documentation for this method at `http://www.flickr.com/services/api/flickr.people.findByUsername.html`, you will see that we need to supply the arguments `api_key` and `username`, and the call will return an XML response including the nsid that we require.

To make an API call to Flickr, we have a choice among three ways of making a request: REST, XML-RPC, and SOAP. As we have seen when adding an API to the RailsCoders application, REST is by far the simplest way of calling a remote method, as you just submit your query as a URL. The specification on how to make a REST API call to Flickr is at `http://www.flickr.com/services/api/request.rest.html`—submit your query in the following format:

```
http://api.flickr.com/services/rest/?method=flickr.test.echo&name=value
```

So, to perform the query to retrieve the user details for the Flickr member with the username railscoders, the REST query would be as follows:

```
http://api.flickr.com/services/rest/?method=flickr.people.findByUsername& ➡
username=railscoders&api_key=abcd
```

Obviously, insert your own Flickr API key in place of abcd. This would receive the following response:

```
<rsp stat="ok">
  <user id="7611484@N08" nsid="7611484@N08">
    <username>railscoders</username>
  </user>
</rsp>
```

Ruby comes with a built-in XML parser called REXML, so we can easily extract the nsid from this XML to obtain the nsid for the user.

Since we only want to retrieve this when the User model is saved and the flickr_username attribute is not empty, we will also update our before_save callback.

We can add the code to perform this request to our User model now. Open the User model file, app/models/user.rb, and edit as shown in Listing 11-14, updating the callback and adding the get_flickr_id method.

We need to add a check for the flickr_username attribute within the callback, since we already have migrations that create users before this attribute is added. If we attempt a migration from an empty database, this callback would cause the previous migrations to fail, as we would be attempting to access an attribute that did not exists. Adding the has_attribute? check ensures that the callback will not try to access the flickr_username and flickr_id unless the attributes have been added to the user table.

Listing 11-14. *Updates to the User Model File*

```
class User < ActiveRecord::Base
  ...
  def before_save
    self.hashed_password = User.encrypt(password) if !password.blank?
    if self.has_attribute?('flickr_username') && !self.flickr_username.blank?
      self.flickr_id = self.get_flickr_id
    end
end

  ...
  def get_flickr_id
    # build the flickr request
    flickr_request = "http://api.flickr.com/services/rest/?"
    flickr_request += "method=flickr.people.findByUsername"
    flickr_request += "&username=#{self.flickr_username}"
    flickr_request += "&api_key=#{FLICKR_API_KEY}"

    # perform the API call
    response = ""
    open(flickr_request) do |s|
      response = s.read
    end

    # parse the result
    xml_response = REXML::Document.new(response)
    if xml_response.root.attributes["stat"] == 'ok'
      xml_response.root.elements["user"].attributes["nsid"]
    else
      nil
    end
  end

end
```

If you take a look at the get_flickr_id method, you will see that performing an API call via REST is incredibly simple. First of all, we build the REST request URL, and we open it using the open command. We can then read the output of this into the response string. This performs an HTTP GET to the URL that we specified.

Since the response is in an XML string, we use REXML to create a new XML object from the raw text sent back from Flickr; REXML allows us to dig into the XML to retrieve specific data. In this case, we just check the stat attribute of the <rsp> tag. If this is equal to ok, the query was successful, and we extract the nsid and return it to the calling method. If the query failed, we return nil.

If you now take a look at the before_save callback, you will see that in addition to the existing password hashing, we now check the flickr_username attribute. If this is not blank, the callback sets the flickr_id attribute using the get_flickr_id method that we just created.

We can try using this now to check that it works correctly. Open your browser, and log in as a regular user. Click the profile link in the sidebar menu to edit your user profile, enter your Flickr username into the relevant form field, and click Save.

Your user details will be saved and a call made to Flickr to retrieve the nsid of your Flickr account. Check your database to make sure that the flick_id field of your account has been updated.

Now that we can obtain each user's Flickr nsid, we can retrieve that user's latest photos from Flickr.

Displaying a User's Latest Flickr Photos

To obtain a list of a user's latest photographs on Flickr, we simply request an RSS feed of that user's photographs. You can request feeds for one or many users, or you can search for photos with certain tags. Details of the feeds available are at http://www.flickr.com/services/feeds.

Since we want to get details of only particular photos, we need to look at the public photo feeds, which are detailed at http://www.flickr.com/services/feeds/docs/photos_public. This also shows the list of formats in which the feeds are available. Ruby comes with an RSS parser already built in, so it is easiest for us to use an RSS feed. If we use the RSS 2.0 feed with enclosures, the feed will include a URL for each photo along with the photo description and title.

Using this information, we can request the photo feed for the Flickr user railscoders using the following URL:

```
http://api.flickr.com/services/feeds/photos_public.gne?id=7611484@N08& ➥
format=rss_200_enc
```

This will respond with an RSS feed similar to the following:

```
<?xml version="1.0" encoding="utf-8"?>
<rss version="2.0"
  xmlns:media="http://search.yahoo.com/mrss/"
  xmlns:dc="http://purl.org/dc/elements/1.1/"
  >
  <channel>
    <title>railscoders' Photos</title>
    <link>http://www.flickr.com/photos/railscoders/</link>
    <description>A feed of railscoders' Photos</description>
    <pubDate>Wed, 28 Mar 2007 07:47:15 -0800</pubDate>
    <lastBuildDate>Wed, 28 Mar 2007 07:47:15 -0800</lastBuildDate>
    <generator>http://www.flickr.com/</generator>
    <image>
      <url>http://farm1.static.flickr.com/151/buddyicons/7611484@N08.jpg?
        1175093565</url>
      <title>railscoders' Photos</title>
      <link>http://www.flickr.com/photos/railscoders/</link>
    </image>
```

```
  <item>
    <title>CIMG1068</title>
    <link>http://www.flickr.com/photos/railscoders/437601124/</link>
    <description>&lt;p&gt;&lt;a href=&quot;http://www.flickr.com/people/
railscoders/&quot;&gt;railscoders&lt;/a&gt; posted a photo:&lt;/p&gt;
&lt;p&gt;&lt;a href=&quot;http://www.flickr.com/photos/railscoders/437601124/&quot;
title=&quot;CIMG1068&quot;&gt;&lt;img
src=&quot;http://farm1.static.flickr.com/148/437601124_005d91dc1c_m.jpg&quot;
width=&quot;240&quot; height=&quot;180&quot; alt=&quot;CIMG1068&quot;
style=&quot;border: 1px solid #ddd;&quot; /&gt;&lt;/a&gt;&lt;/p&gt;
&lt;p&gt;This brought me here&lt;/p&gt;</description>
      <pubDate>Wed, 28 Mar 2007 07:33:04 -0800</pubDate>
      <dc:date.Taken>2006-12-30T16:39:00-08:00</dc:date.Taken>
      <author>nobody@flickr.com (railscoders)</author>
      <guid isPermaLink="false">tag:flickr.com,2004:/photo/437601124</guid>

      <enclosure url="http://farm1.static.flickr.com/148/437601124_b10bdf4af7_o.jpg"
          type="image/jpeg" />
      <media:content
url="http://farm1.static.flickr.com/148/437601124_b10bdf4af7_o.jpg"
          type="image/jpeg"
          height="2112"
          width="2816"/>
      <media:title>CIMG1068</media:title>
      <media:text type="html">&lt;p&gt;&lt;a
href=&quot;http://www.flickr.com/people/railscoders/&quot;&gt;railscoders&lt;/a&gt;
posted a photo:&lt;/p&gt;
&lt;p&gt;&lt;a href=&quot;http://www.flickr.com/photos/railscoders/437601124/&quot;
title=&quot;CIMG1068&quot;&gt;&lt;img
src=&quot;http://farm1.static.flickr.com/148/437601124_005d91dc1c_m.jpg&quot;
width=&quot;240&quot; height=&quot;180&quot; alt=&quot;CIMG1068&quot;
style=&quot;border: 1px solid #ddd;&quot; /&gt;&lt;/a&gt;&lt;/p&gt;
&lt;p&gt;This brought me here&lt;/p&gt;</media:text>
      <media:thumbnail
url="http://farm1.static.flickr.com/148/437601124_005d91dc1c_s.jpg" height="75"
        width="75" />
      <media:credit role="photographer">railscoders</media:credit>
      <media:category scheme="urn:flickr:tags">japan plane airplane</media:category>
    </item>
  </channel>
</rss>
```

As you can see, there is a lot of information contained here about the photos, but the information we are interested in is the image enclosure:

```
<enclosure url="http://farm1.static.flickr.com/148/437601124_b10bdf4af7_o.jpg"
type="image/jpeg" />
```

This is a direct line to the original version of the uploaded image. However, we want to display thumbnails on our profile page, not huge, many-megapixel images. Thankfully, it is very easy to obtain different versions of this image. If you look at the end of this image URL, you will notice that it ends in _o.jpg. The o means that this is the original image. If we replace o with t (for "thumbnail"), we can access a thumbnail version of this image.

■Tip You can also use l for "large," m for "medium," and s for "square" to access different sizes of the same image.

Looking again at the RSS feed sent back by Flickr, we can see that each item has a link to the photo page on Flickr. We will use this as a link for each photo shown.

Now that we know how to retrieve an RSS feed, we can add the code to do this to our User model. Open the file app/models/user.rb, and edit it as shown in Listing 11-15, adding the flickr_feed method to the end of the file before the final end statement. We also need to add the line require 'rss/2.0' to the top of the file as shown, to make sure that we can access the Ruby RSS parsing library.

Listing 11-15. *The Modifications to the User Model File*

```
require 'digest/sha2'
require 'rss/2.0'

class User < ActiveRecord::Base
  ...
  def flickr_feed
    flickr_request = "http://api.flickr.com/services/feeds/photos_public.gne?"
    flickr_request += "id=#{self.flickr_id}"
    flickr_request += "&format=rss_200_enc"

    rss_content = ""
    open(flickr_request) do |s|
      rss_content = s.read
    end
    return RSS::Parser.parse(rss_content, false)
  end

end
```

This method simply constructs the RSS feed URL as a string then uses the open command to do an HTTP GET of this URL. The resulting string of the RSS feed is then parsed using the Ruby RSS Parser and the returned to the calling method.

We can now use this flickr_feed method to show the latest photos on the profile page. Open the users controller file, app/controllers/users_controller.rb, and edit the existing show method as shown in Listing 11-16.

Listing 11-16. *Update to the Users Controller Show Method*

```
def show
  @user = User.find(params[:id])
  @entries = @user.entries.find(:all, :limit => 3, :order => 'created_at DESC')
  @photos = @user.photos.find(:all, :limit => 3, :order => 'created_at DESC')
  @flickr_feed = @user.flickr_feed if @user.flickr_id
end
```

If the user has a flickr_id set, the controller retrieves the feed of the photos for this user from Flickr, and this feed is made available to the view.

Now, open the corresponding view file, app/views/users/show.rhtml. Add the code in Listing 11-17 to the end of this file.

Listing 11-17. *Addition to the User Show View to Display the Flickr Photos*

```
...
<% if @flickr_feed %>
<h3>Flickr Photos</h3>
<p>
  <ul id="photos">
  <% @flickr_feed.items.values_at(0..3).each do |item| %>
    <% if !item.nil? %>
    <li>
      <%= link_to image_tag(item.enclosure.url.gsub('_o.jpg', '_t.jpg')),
               item.link %>
    </li>
    <% end %>
  <% end %>
  </ul>
  <%= link_to "See more", @flickr_feed.channel.link %>
<p>
<% end %>
```

This first checks to see if the instance variable @flickr_feed is set. If the feed is available, the first four items in the feed are displayed. For each item shown, we select the direct link to the photo with item.enclosure.url and use the string gsub method to replace _o.jpg with _t.jpg, enabling us to display the thumbnail versions of the images. We also add a link to the user's Flickr home page using the channel.link attribute of the feed.

Try using this now. Log in to the application, make sure that your Flickr username is set correctly in your profile, and view your user profile page. At the bottom of the page, a section is added displaying the latest four photos that you have uploaded to Flickr, along with a link to your page on Flickr, as shown in Figure 11-4.

Try clicking one of the Flickr thumbnails to go directly to the respective photo on Flickr, and use the "See more" link to go to your Flickr page.

Figure 11-4. *The user profile page showing the latest Flickr photos*

Further Development Using Mashups

The possibilities opened up by integrating our application with other sites are endless. Hundreds of web applications now offer extensive APIs, and we can easily integrate with them and extend our application in many different ways.

You may wish to build on the simple mashup that we created here to extend the mapping feature. It would be easy to search for other photos that have been marked as being in the surrounding area and add them as markers on to the map, allowing users to see other photos taken in the area.

Since Flickr allows such extensive integration with its site, you may wish to make more use of it, allowing users to send their photos directly from the RailsCoders photo gallery to their Flickr account.

Take a look at some of the other APIs listed on `http://www.programmableweb.com` to get some ideas of the types of data available and to see some great examples of mashups.

Summary

In this chapter, we integrated our site with Google Maps and Flickr. Doing this allowed us to embed maps in our photo gallery and include the latest photos from users on their profiles.

To embed Google Maps to our site, we used the YM4R/GM plug-in, which provides a simple Ruby interface to the Google Maps JavaScript API. We wrote a simple JavaScript function to allow users to set the real-world location of their photos by dragging and clicking on a map.

We used the Flickr API via REST to retrieve a user's Flickr ID by specifying the Flickr username. We next used that username to obtain an RSS feed of the user's photos, which was parsed and used to display the latest four photos on the RailsCoders user profile page.

In the next chapter, we will go back to our blogging system and extend it to allow users to create their own unique layout and styles to personalize their blog.

CHAPTER 12

■ ■ ■

Adding User-Created Themes to the Blogging Engine

In Chapter 6, we added blogs to RailsCoders that allows users of the site to create their own blogs. Currently, all blogs on RailsCoders look similar to other pages on the site; there is no way for a user to personalize the look of a blog. This would be a desirable feature, because most bloggers wish to personalize their blogs, either by using or adapting an existing template or creating their own design from scratch.

It is possible to allow users to create their own ERb templates, which could be stored in the database or just as files that are rendered when someone views the blogs. However, since we know that ERb allows any Ruby code to be embedded within it, including code that accesses the server's file system, this would be a very bad idea. Malicious users could easily hack the site and cause a lot of problems.

To solve this problem, we will use a templating plug-in for Rails called Liquid, which allows us to have user-editable templates that only have access to objects that you have specified and disallows embedded Ruby code within the templates.

The Blog Template Requirements

To add user-definable templates to the existing blogging system, we will need to modify the existing entries controller and create a new controller to allow users to edit their templates. We will call this controller `usertemplates_controller`.

We also need to add a model that will store the templates created by users. We will call this model Usertemplate.

■Caution We are using a model called "Usertemplate" rather than "Template," because "Template" is a reserved word in Rails. If you try to create a model or controller called "Template," you will simply end up with a lot of slightly confusing errors.

We require a database table called `usertemplates` to store the actual templates created by each user.

Each user can have a number of templates, so each `usertemplate` object belongs to a user, requiring a user `id` field. A `name` field is needed to define what type of template it actually is. This is so we can allow different templates for different blog pages, such as the standard blog entry list and the entry show page, showing one particular entry along with all comments for that entry. A template `body` field is required to hold the actual template itself. We will limit the body field to 10,000 characters.

The database fields necessary for this `usertemplates` table are shown in Table 12-1.

Table 12-1. *The usertemplates Database Schema*

Field Name	Field Type	Description
id	integer	The primary key
name	string	The name of the template
body	text	The actual body of the template

For the user's blog pages, the templates that we will allow the user to define are `blog_index`, the main blog page listing the latest blog posts of a particular user, and `blog_entry`, a page for viewing a single blog entry that shows the blog entry along with any comments that have been left about this entry.

When a user creates a new account on RailsCoders, they will not have defined any templates, so when rendering the blog views, we will check if the user has defined any templates. If no templates exist for the user or if the body field is empty, we will render the default RailsCoders entries templates.

The usertemplates controller will allow our users to edit the body of their templates. It will follow the same structure as our other controllers, but we will not allow the user to create a new template—only to edit the `blog_index` and `blog_entry` templates. Also, they will not be allowed to delete a template. When the user visits the `index` method of the usertemplates controller, we will check to make sure that the templates `blog_index` and `blog_entry` exist in the database for the particular user. If not, we will create the objects with empty body fields, allowing them to edit them.

Therefore, we must implement the methods `index`, `edit`, and `update` for the usertemplates controller.

Liquid Templates

As I mentioned, we will be using a Rails plug-in called Liquid to render the templates. Liquid was developed by Tobias Lütke, and you can find the Liquid Templates home page at `http://home.leetsoft.com/liquid`.

Liquid allows users to create their own templates but prevents them from running insecure code on your server. It also allows you to store templates in a database. Since all of our users' data is stored within a database, this makes it very easy for us to extend our database and store their personalized templates in a database too.

Liquid is in active development, so it is a good idea to keep an eye on and contribute to the Google Group at `http://groups.google.com/group/liquid-templates` and the wiki accessible from the Liquid home page.

The Liquid API

Using Liquid is very simple. The simplest method of rendering a template is to instantiate a Liquid Template object and call the `parse` method with your template as a parameter. You can then render this object as HTML by calling the `render` method and passing in the necessary variables.

For example, you could parse a very simple template like this:

```
@template = Liquid::Template.parse("Hello {{user}}, it is now {{time}}.")
```

You could then render this using the given variables as follows:

```
@template.render( 'name' => 'Freddy', 'time' => Time.now.to_s )
```

The template we parsed only has access to the variables passed to it by the `render` method. However, if we pass a user object to the `render` method rather than just a string, the template would have access to all of the methods of the user object, including potentially dangerous methods. This then creates a similar problem when allowing the user to write ERb templates. To solve this, Liquid allows us to create drops. Liquid drops act as a wrapper around a regular Ruby object, allowing you to provide a user with just the attributes of an object that you define. They also allow you to add extra functionality to templates by creating extra accessible methods in a drop. We will create a number of drops, allowing our users to access safe versions of the User, Entry, and Comment models.

Liquid also allows us to create filters. Liquid filters are simply Ruby methods that allow you to provide text filters to the template author. They take one parameter, perform some action, and return a string to be entered into the rendered template. Liquid provides a number of built-in filters, such as `upcase`, `downcase`, `strip_html`, and a date reformatter. After you have installed the Liquid plug-in, look at its source at `vendor/plugins/liquid/lib/liquid/standardfilters.rb` to see the provided filters. It is very simple to add new filters to meet the specific requirements of your application.

Liquid Markup

Liquid templates use two types of markup, similar to the ERb templates we have created for the rest of the application. In Liquid, output is surrounded by {{ and }}, while tags, which control the logic in the template, are surrounded by {% and %}.

For example, to output a user's name, we might use markup like the following:

```
Hello {{ user.username }}
```

As we mentioned previously, we can add filters to outputs, modifying the output to match our requirements. We can also chain filters together using | (the pipe character). Some examples of filters to modify the given output follow:

```
Hello {{ user.username | upcase }}
The time is now {{ now | date "%Y %h" }}
Visit {{ 'my blog ' | link_to 'http://alanbradburne.com', 'Alan's Blog' }}
```

Here's what they do:

- The first example takes the username of the user object and passes it through a filter called upcase, which simply makes the username uppercase.

- The next example formats the current time into a format specified by the date filter.

- The third example creates a link using the link_to filter. This takes a URL and an alt attribute, adding the relevant link to the string that is passed into the filter.

We need to have some way of adding logic to the template to control what is output to the browser. We do this using Liquid's tags. There are a number of built-in tags, including comment, if/else, for, and ifchanged. These act in similar ways to the statements you are used to in Ruby. For example, to iterate through elements of an array using the for loop, you would do the following:

```
{% for entry in entries %}
  {{ entry.title }}<br />
{% endfor %}
```

Within a for loop, there are a number of helper variables available, such as forloop.first, forloop.last, and forloop.length. These can be very useful when designing templates, because they allow you to add special styling to items in tables or lists, depending on their position.

Conditional statements are performed like this:

```
{% if user %}
  {{ user.username }}
{% else %}
  No user selected
{% endif %}
```

For a full list of markup with examples, go to the Liquid project wiki at http://home.leetsoft.com/liquid/wiki/DesignerHowTo.

As you can see, Liquid gives the user the tools to create complex templates while preventing direct access to the internals of the Rails application.

Installing Liquid

Liquid is installed as a Rails plug-in. Simply open a terminal window, and from the application's directory, install with the following command:

```
$ ruby script/plugin install svn://home.leetsoft.com/liquid/trunk/liquid/
```

```
A    /Users/alan/Rails/railscoders/vendor/plugins/liquid
A    /Users/alan/Rails/railscoders/vendor/plugins/liquid/test
A    /Users/alan/Rails/railscoders/vendor/plugins/liquid/test/include_tag_test.rb
A    /Users/alan/Rails/railscoders/vendor/plugins/liquid/test/test_helper.rb
```

```
A    /Users/alan/Rails/railscoders/vendor/plugins/liquid/test/helper.rb
...
A    /Users/alan/Rails/railscoders/vendor/plugins/liquid/example/server/templates/
products.liquid
A    /Users/alan /Rails/railscoders/vendor/plugins/liquid/example/server/templates/
index.liquid
A    /Users/alan/Rails/railscoders/vendor/plugins/liquid/README
Exported revision 144.
```

We can now access the Liquid methods from any controller.

Building the Blog Templates Feature

Now that we know what the feature must do and have Liquid installed, we can begin building the templating feature.

Creating the Liquid Drops

We are going to place the Liquid drop files that we write in the directory app/drops/. Create this directory now.

In order for Rails to know to look in this directory, we need to add it to the Rails configuration. We will also add the directory that we will use to store the Liquid filters that we will write in the next section. Open the config/environment.rb file, and find the config.load_paths statement at line 23. The line will be commented out with an example directory as a parameter. Uncomment the line, and replace the example path with the drops directory and the filters directory (we will create these directories in a moment), as follows:

```
...
Rails::Initializer.run do |config|
  ...
  # Add additional load paths for your own custom dirs
  config.load_paths += %W( #{RAILS_ROOT}/app/drops ➥
#{RAILS_ROOT}/app/filters )
  ...
```

We now need to create the drops themselves. First of all, create the user drop file, app/drops/user_drop.rb. Enter the code shown in Listing 12-1.

Listing 12-1. *The User Drop File*

```
class UserDrop < Liquid::Drop
  def initialize(user)
    @user = user
  end
```

```
  def username
    @user[:username]
  end

  def email
    @user[:email]
  end

  def profile
    @user[:profile]
  end

  def blog_title
    @user[:blog_title]
  end
end
```

This class lists the only data that is available to a Liquid template when it is passed a user object. Other attributes, such as hashed_password, are not accessible, only the username, email, profile, and blog_title. If you wish to give your users access to other attributes of the User model, you would just add them as extra methods here.

The initialize method is executed when the UserDrop object is instantiated and the other methods simply return the relevant data.

In order for this Liquid drop to be accessible to the template, we also have to add a method called to_liquid to the User model. This method simply instantiates the UserDrop object and passes it to the Liquid render method.

Open the User model file, app/models/user.rb, and add the to_liquid method at the end of the file as follows:

```
require 'digest/sha2'
require 'rss/2.0'

class User < ActiveRecord::Base
  ...
  def to_liquid
    UserDrop.new(self)
  end
end
```

We now need to create the drops for the Entry and Comment models. Create the entry drop file, app/drops/entry_drop.rb, and add the code in Listing 12-2.

Listing 12-2. *The Entry Drop File*

```
class EntryDrop < Liquid::Drop
  def initialize(entry)
    @entry = entry
  end
```

```
  def title
    @entry[:title]
  end

  def body
    @entry[:body]
  end

  def comments_count
    @entry[:comments_count]
  end

  def permalink
    "/users/#{@entry.user.id}/entries/#{@entry.id}"
  end

  def comment_post_url
    "/users/#{@entry.user.id}/entries/#{@entry.id}/comments"
  end
end
```

Note that we have added a drop called permalink. This allows the user writing the template to easily access the URL of the entry by simply referring to an entry attribute called permalink. The drop called comment_post_path returns the path that a new comment should be posted to. This will be used on the entry view page to allow users to create new comments.

Now add the to_liquid method to the Entry model. Open the file app/models/entry.rb, and add the method as follows:

```
class Entry < ActiveRecord::Base
  ...
  def to_liquid
    EntryDrop.new(self)
  end
end
```

Finally, create the comment drop file, app/drops/comment_drop.rb, and add the code in Listing 12-3.

Listing 12-3. *The Comment Drop File*

```
class CommentDrop < Liquid::Drop
  def initialize(comment)
    @comment = comment
  end

  def author
    @comment.user.username
  end
```

```
  def body
    @comment[:body]
  end

  def created_at
    @comment[:created_at]
  end
end
```

In this drop file, the `author` method provides the user with the attribute `author`. This is not a direct attribute of the Comment model, but we can access it and return it to the template as if it were.

Now, open the app/models/comment.rb file, and add the following `to_liquid` method:

```
class Comment < ActiveRecord::Base
  belongs_to :entry, :counter_cache => true
  belongs_to :user
  validates_length_of :body, :maximum => 1000

  def to_liquid
    CommentDrop.new(self)
  end
end
```

Creating the Liquid Filters

Since our users can write blog entries using the Textile markup system, we need to add a Liquid filter allowing the templates to have access to a `textilize` method. To do this, we need to create a Liquid filter.

We will also create a filter called `link_to_entry`, which will allow the user to easily link to an individual entry by just specifying the entry object and the filter.

Create the directory for the Liquid filters that we specified in the config/environment.rb file, app/filters/. Next, create a filter file called app/filters/text_filters.rb, and enter the code in Listing 12-4.

Listing 12-4. *The Liquid Text Filters File*

```
module TextFilters
  include ActionView::Helpers::TagHelper

  def textilize(input)
    RedCloth.new(input).to_html
  end

  def link_to_entry(entry)
    content_tag :a, entry['title'], :href => entry['permalink']
  end
end
```

The `textilize` filter simply converts the input text, which is marked up with Textile, into HTML using RedCloth, the Ruby package for processing Textile markup.

The `link_to_entry` filter takes an `entry` object as input and builds an `<a>` tag with a link to the entry's permalink and the entry title as the link text. In order to use the Rails helper method `content_tag`, we have to include the ActionView code at the beginning of the file.

We can now create the `usertemplate` model, controller, and views.

The Usertemplate Model

Generate the skeleton code for the Usertemplate model using the Rails generate script:

```
$ ruby script/generate model Usertemplate
```

```
    exists  app/models/
    exists  test/unit/
    exists  test/fixtures/
    create  app/models/usertemplate.rb
    create  test/unit/usertemplate_test.rb
    create  test/fixtures/usertemplates.yml
    exists  db/migrate
    create  db/migrate/024_create_usertemplates.rb
```

Edit the generated migration file, and add the fields as defined in the specification. Also, add an index on the user_id and name fields, since that is how we will be retrieving the templates from the database. Open the migration file db/migrate/024_create_usertemplates.rb, and edit it as shown in Listing 12-5.

Listing 12-5. *The Usertemplates Migration File*

```
class CreateUsertemplates < ActiveRecord::Migration
  def self.up
    create_table :usertemplates do |t|
      t.column :user_id, :integer
      t.column :name, :string
      t.column :body, :text
    end
    add_index :usertemplates, [:user_id, :name]
  end

  def self.down
    drop_table :usertemplates
  end
end
```

Now, execute this migration using the following command:

```
$ rake db:migrate
```

```
== CreateUsertemplates: migrating ===========================================
-- create_table(:usertemplates)
   -> 0.0281s
-- add_index(:usertemplates, [:user_id, :name])
   -> 0.0322s
== CreateUsertemplates: migrated (0.0607s) ==================================
```

We next need to edit the Usertemplate model file and add the relationship with the User model and a validation. Open the file app/models/usertemplates.rb, and edit it as shown in Listing 12-6.

Listing 12-6. *The Usertemplate Model File*

```
class Usertemplate < ActiveRecord::Base
  belongs_to :user

  validates_length_of :body, :maximum => 10000
end
```

We also need to add the reciprocal relationship to the User model. Open the app/models/user.rb file, and add the has_many relationship as follows:

```
require 'digest/sha2'
require 'rss/2.0'

class User < ActiveRecord::Base
  ...
  has_many :friendships
  has_many :friends, :through => :friendships, :class_name => 'User'
  has_many :usertemplates

  def before_save
  ...
```

The Usertemplates Controller

We will now create the controller that allows a user to edit the user templates for an account. We will use the generate script to create the usertemplates controller:

```
$ ruby script/generate controller Usertemplates
```

```
     exists   app/controllers/
     exists   app/helpers/
     create   app/views/usertemplates
     exists   test/functional/
     create   app/controllers/usertemplates_controller.rb
     create   test/functional/usertemplates_controller_test.rb
     create   app/helpers/usertemplates_helper.rb
```

Since this will act as a REST resource, we need to add the resource definition line to the routes file. Open `config/routes.rb`, and add the `map.resources` line as follows:

```
ActionController::Routing::Routes.draw do |map|
  ...
  map.resources :photos
  map.resources :tags
  map.resources :usertemplates

  map.resources :users, :member => { :enable => :put } do |users|
    ...
```

We should add a link to the controller in the sidebar menu too. Open the file `app/views/layouts/_menu.rhtml`, and add the link to the usertemplates controller in the section only shown to logged-in users, as follows:

```
...
<% if is_logged_in? %>
  <li>Logged in as: <i><%= logged_in_user.username -%></i></li>
  <li><%= link_to 'My Profile', edit_user_path(logged_in_user) -%></li>
  <li><%= link_to 'My Friends', friends_path(:user_id => logged_in_user) -%></li>
  <li><%= link_to 'My Photos', user_photos_path(:user_id => logged_in_user) -%></li>
  <li>
    <%= link_to 'Upload Photo', user_new_photo_path(:user_id => logged_in_user) -%>
  </li>
  <li>
    <%= link_to 'New Blog Post', new_entry_path(:user_id => logged_in_user) -%>
  </li>
  <li><%= link_to 'Blog Templates', usertemplates_path -%></li>
  <li>
    <%= link_to 'Logout', {:controller => 'account', :action => 'logout'},
          :method => :post %>
  </li>
<% else %>
```

Now, open the generated controller file, `app/controllers/usertemplates_controller.rb`, and enter the code in Listing 12-7.

Listing 12-7. *The Usertemplates Controller File*

```
class UsertemplatesController < ApplicationController
  before_filter :login_required

  def index
    @usertemplates = @logged_in_user.usertemplates.find(:all)

    if @usertemplates.empty?
      @logged_in_user.usertemplates << Usertemplate.new(:name => 'blog_index',
                                                         :body => '')
```

```
      @logged_in_user.usertemplates << Usertemplate.new(:name => 'blog_entry',
                                                         :body => '')
      @usertemplates = @logged_in_user.usertemplates.find(:all)
    end
  end

  def edit
    @usertemplate = @logged_in_user.usertemplates.find(params[:id])
  rescue ActiveRecord::RecordNotFound
    redirect_to :action => 'index'
  end

  def update
    @usertemplate = @logged_in_user.usertemplates.find(params[:id])

    if @usertemplate.update_attributes(params[:usertemplate])
      flash[:notice] = 'Template was successfully updated.'
      redirect_to usertemplates_path
    end
  rescue ActiveRecord::RecordNotFound
    redirect_to :action => 'index'
  end
end
```

The code in this file does a number of things:

- `before_filter` ensures that the methods in this file are accessible only by logged-in users and that the object `@logged_in_user` is available.

- When the `index` action is executed, the program checks to see if the two user templates `blog_index` and `blog_entry` exist for the logged-in user. If they do not, they are created.

- The `edit` action simply retrieves the `usertemplate` object with the specified id, as long as it belongs to the logged-in user.

- `update` saves the updated user template.

Next, we need to create the view for this controller.

The Usertemplate Views

First, we'll create the `index` view. Create the file `app/views/usertemplates/index.rhtml`, and enter the view code in Listing 12-8.

Listing 12-8. *The Usertemplate Index View*

```
<h1>Your Blog Templates</h1>

<table>
  <tr>
    <th>Template Name</th>
    <th>Description</th>
  </tr>
  <tr>
    <td><%= link_to 'blog_index', edit_usertemplate_path(
              @usertemplates.find {|ut| ut.name == 'blog_index'} ) -%></td>
    <td>The main template for your blog</td>
  </tr>
  <tr>
    <td><%= link_to 'blog_entry', edit_usertemplate_path(
              @usertemplates.find {|ut| ut.name == 'blog_entry'} ) -%></td>
    <td>The template for viewing one entry</td>
  </tr>
</table>
```

This presents the user with the list of editable templates. We have used the Ruby find method within the link_to statement to display the id corresponding to the particular template.

Clicking the template name takes the user to the edit page for that template. Create this view file now, app/views/usertemplates/edit.rhtml, and enter the code in Listing 12-9.

Listing 12-9. *The Usertemplate Edit View*

```
<h2>Editing <%= @usertemplate.name %></h2>

<%= error_messages_for :usertemplate %>

<% form_for(:usertemplate,
              :url => usertemplate_path(@usertemplate),
              :html => { :method => :put }) do |f| %>
  <p><%= f.text_area :body, :rows => 25, :cols => 80 %>
  <p>
    <%= submit_tag "Save" %> or <%= link_to 'cancel', usertemplates_path %>
  </p>
<% end %>
```

Now that our users can edit their user templates, we need to modify the entries controller to render the users' blogs with these templates if they exist.

Rendering Liquid Templates

Open app/controllers/entries_controller.rb, and take a look at the existing index and show methods.

Currently, we just render the index and show view files as normal. We now want to be able to render a Liquid user template if the user has specified one. If a user does not have any user templates defined, we should still render the regular .rhtml view.

Modify the index and show methods as shown in Listing 12-10.

Listing 12-10. *The Updated Entries Controller File*

```
def index
  @user = User.find(params[:user_id], :include => :usertemplates)
  @entry_pages = Paginator.new(self, @user.entries_count, 10, params[:page])
  @entries = @user.entries.find(:all, :order => 'created_at DESC',
                                :limit => @entry_pages.items_per_page,
                                :offset => @entry_pages.current.offset)

  @usertemplate = @user.usertemplates.find_by_name('blog_index')
  if @usertemplate and @usertemplate.body.any?
    @page = Liquid::Template.parse(@usertemplate.body)
    render :text => @page.render({'user' => @user, 'entries' => @entries},
      [TextFilters])
  end
end

def show
  @user = User.find(params[:user_id], :include => :usertemplates)
  @entry = Entry.find_by_id_and_user_id(params[:id],
                                        params[:user_id],
                                        :include => [:comments => :user])

  @usertemplate = @user.usertemplates.find_by_name('blog_entry')
  if @usertemplate and @usertemplate.body.any?
    @page = Liquid::Template.parse(@usertemplate.body)
    render :text => @page.render({'user' => @user,
      'entry' => @entry, 'comments' => @entry.comments},
      [TextFilters])
  end
end
```

We now have a condition in each of the methods that parses and renders a user's blog_index template if one is available. If there is no matching usertemplate, Rails automatically renders the normal view file.

When rendering a Liquid user template, we pass the Liquid drops for the user, entry, and comment objects along with the TextFilters module that we created earlier.

We can now finally try creating a new template for our blog.

Manual Testing

You will have to restart the Rails application server to pick up changes to the environment.rb file. Do this and log in to the RailsCoders application as a regular user.

First of all, try viewing your blog by going to your profile and clicking on the "See all of your blog" link to view your blog. Since you have not created a new template yet, it will be rendered using the normal Rails view files.

In the sidebar menu, there is now a Blog Templates link. Click this to view the user templates available for you to edit, as shown in Figure 12-1. Since this is the first time that you have attempted to edit your user templates, the controller will have to create the empty templates and save them before showing this page.

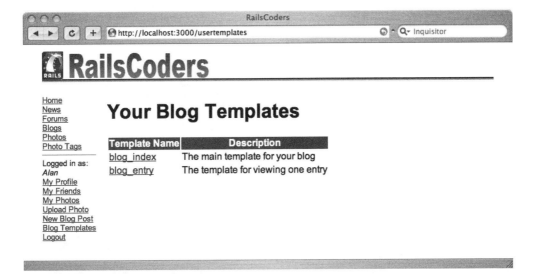

Figure 12-1. *The usertemplates index view*

Click the blog_index template link to edit the Liquid template for the blog index page.

We now need to create a blog template from scratch using the Liquid drop objects and the Liquid filters that we have been passed.

■**Tip** It would be a good idea to include details of the Liquid drop objects and Liquid filters available as a help page for your users.

A very simple blog_index template is shown in Listing 12-11. Enter this into the text box on the edit template page and save the template.

Listing 12-11. *A Sample blog_index User Template*

```
<html>
<head>
  <title>{{ user.blog_title }}</title>
  <style>
<!--
body { background: #111; color: #eee; font-family:arial,sans-serif; }
a { color: #c66; }
-->
  </style>
</head>

<body>
  <h1>{{ user.blog_title }}</h1>

  {% for entry in entries %}
    <h2>{{ entry | link_to_entry }}</h2>
    {{ entry.body | textilize }}
  {% endfor %}
</body>
</html>
```

We can now take a look at your main blog page to see the new template in action. Go to your blog via your profile page or the Blogs sidebar link. The page shown will now be in a style that's totally different from the rest of the site, as shown in Figure 12-2.

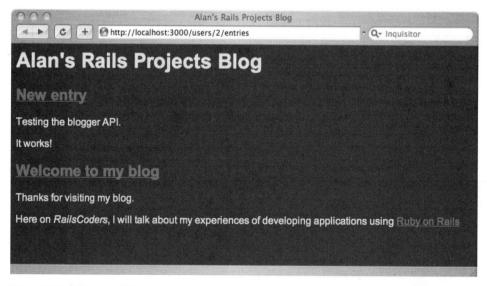

Figure 12-2. *The main blog view with the new user template*

If you click an entry title, the entry view page will still be in the regular style of the RailsCoders site, since we haven't defined a user template for blog_entry yet. Go back to your Blog Templates page, and click the blog_entry link. Listing 12-12 shows a simple page that lists all of the comments for an entry along with a new comment form.

Listing 12-12. *A Sample blog_entry User Template*

```
<html>
<head>
  <title>{{ user.blog_title }} - {{ entry.title }}</title>
  <style>
<!--
body { background: #111; color: #eee; font-family:arial,sans-serif; }
a { color: #c66; }
-->
  </style>
</head>

<body>
<h1>{{ user.blog_title }}</h1>
<h2>{{ entry.title }}</h2>
{{ entry.body | textilize }}

{% for comment in comments %}
<p>
  {{ comment.author }} said:<br />
  {{ comment.body }}
</p>
{% endfor %}
<form action="{{ entry.comment_post_path }}" method="post">
  <p>
    <textarea cols="40" id="comment_body" name="comment[body]" rows="4"></textarea>
    <br />
    <input name="commit" type="submit" value="Save Comment" />
  </p>
</form>
</body>
</html>
```

This page simply shows the selected entry and lists all of the comments for the entry. The page also includes a basic form to allow users to add new comments. We use the comment_post_path filter to return the post path for the form.

Save this template, and go back to view your blog. Click an entry title to view a specific entry. The page will now be in the same style as the main blog page, as shown in Figure 12-3.

Make sure that the comment form path is working correctly by entering a new comment and clicking Save Comment.

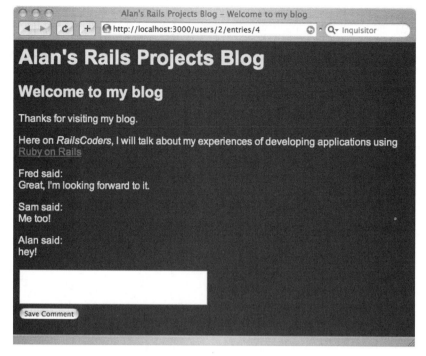

Figure 12-3. *The blog entry view with the new user template*

Now that you can see that the templating feature is working correctly, you may wish to design some better templates or create more filters to provide more features to the template authors.

Testing the Usertemplates Controller

We should automate the tests for the usertemplates controller using the functional test system. First of all, create usertemplates fixtures, adding three user templates, two belonging to the user id 1, as specified in the user fixtures, the other belonging to user id 2.

The test/fixtures/usertemplates.yml file follows:

```
valid_blog_index_for_joe:
  id: 1
  user_id: 1
  name: blog_index
  body: a template
valid_blog_entry_for_joe:
  id: 2
  user_id: 1
  name: blog_entry
  body: a template
valid_blog_index_for_admin:
  id: 3
```

```
user_id: 2
name: blog_index
body: my template
```

Now edit the functional test file for the usertemplates controller, test/functional/
usertemplates_controller_test.rb. The full test file is shown in Listing 12-13. You will see that
the login_as helper simulates a user logging into the application. The index, edit, and update
methods are the only ones that need to be tested.

We have also included two extra tests that log in as user id 1, but try to edit and update
user templates that belong to user id 2. The expected result is to not allow editing of another
user's templates, so user 1 is redirected to the index page.

Listing 12-13. *The User Templates Functional Test File*

```
require File.dirname(__FILE__) + '/../test_helper'
require 'usertemplates_controller'

# Re-raise errors caught by the controller.
class UsertemplateController; def rescue_action(e) raise e end; end

class UsertemplateControllerTest < Test::Unit::TestCase
  fixtures :usertemplates, :users

  def setup
    @controller = UsertemplatesController.new
    @request    = ActionController::TestRequest.new
    @response   = ActionController::TestResponse.new
  end

  def test_should_get_index
    login_as(:valid_user)
    get :index
    assert_response :success
    assert assigns(:usertemplates)
  end

  def test_should_get_edit
    login_as(:valid_user)
    get :edit, :id => 1
    assert_response :success
  end

  def test_should_update_usertemplate
    login_as(:valid_user)
    put :update, :id => 1, :usertemplate => { :body => 'a different template'}
    assert_redirected_to usertemplates_path
  end
```

```
  def test_should_fail_get_edit_for_other_user
    login_as(:valid_user)
    get :edit, :id => 3
    assert_response :redirect
    assert_redirected_to :action => 'index'
  end

  def test_should_fail_update_for_other_user
    login_as(:valid_user)
    put :update, :id => 3, :usertemplate => { :body => 'a different template'}
    assert_response :redirect
    assert_redirected_to :action => 'index'
  end
end
```

Before you run these functional tests, you need to bring the test database up to date by opening a terminal window and entering the following command:

```
$ rake db:test:prepare
```

Now, run the tests with the following command:

```
$ ruby test/functional/usertemplates_controller_test.rb
```

```
Loaded suite test/functional/usertemplates_controller_test
Started
.....
Finished in 0.889032 seconds.

5 tests, 9 assertions, 0 failures, 0 errors
```

Further Development of the User Templates

This feature could be developed further in many ways:

- Since developing a whole template from scratch is pretty difficult, you may wish to provide your users with a number of sample templates that they can copy into the blog_index and blog_entry templates and edit to their liking.

- You will likely wish to add more filters and possibly extend the drops further, providing more tools to help your users build templates.

- At the moment, the CSS for the user templates is simply embedded within the user template body itself, but you may wish to create another template called `blog_css`, separating the CSS from the template bodies. This would allow the `blog_index` and `blog_entry` templates to access a common CSS file.

- You may wish to make even more use of Liquid. Since it provides a very solid templating framework that protects your application's code, it would be possible to template your whole application in this way. This would allow other people to completely restyle the application without breaking the functionality of the site.

Summary

In this chapter, we added support for user-defined themes for the blogging feature of RailsCoders. This utilized the Liquid templating plug-in to give our users the freedom to completely redesign their blogs from scratch, while protecting our application from malicious code.

We created a new model called Usertemplate to store the user-designed templates. To support these templates, we created a number of drops, versions of objects that only have access to the methods or attributes of a model that we define. We can also extend drops to provide useful attributes for the creation of templates. We also created some custom Liquid filters, allowing the user template to access Textile markup and provide links to individual entries.

In the next chapter, we will look at how you can create a version of your site that is optimized for small-screen devices, such as mobile phones and PDAs.

■■■

## CHAPTER 13

Adding a Mobile Interface

We now have a fully functioning social networking community site. But currently it is only available to users while they are sitting at their desktop or laptop computers. And, in many countries in the world, more people access the Web from a mobile phone than from PCs. In this chapter, we will develop an alternate interface to our application, allowing the site to be used on mobile phones or other small-screen devices, such as PDAs or smartphones. This will allow our users to keep in touch with their contacts on the site at any time, even when they are away from their computers.

The Mobile Web

Some smartphones have the capability to display full XHTML web pages, but the majority of phones cannot load regular web pages. In order to allow browsing on devices with limited screen size, memory, and input methods, special versions of XHTML have been developed: XHTML Basic and XHTML Mobile Profile (XHTML MP).

XHTML Basic, as you might guess by the name, is a subset of XHTML designed for devices that cannot support the full set of XHTML features. XHTML MP is a superset of XHTML Basic that supports some extra tags from standard XHTML but is not supported by as many mobile browsers. Since we want as many users as possible to be able to use our site, we should ensure that our site validates as XHTML Basic.

Almost every mobile phone that can be purchased today is capable of displaying pages delivered in XHTML Basic. Older phones will not be able to, as they may use an older mobile markup system, Wireless Markup Language (WML). However, we can almost guarantee that any tech-savvy user of our site who wishes to use a mobile version of our application will have a reasonably modern phone, so we can focus on the modern standard.

Since XHTML Basic and XHTML MP are subsets of XHTML, we can simply use a regular XHTML-compatible browser to view and test our mobile site. Of course, nothing beats testing on a real device to check that everything is working exactly right, but since there are far too many models of mobile phones in the world to physically test on, we will just rely on our trusty web browser.

XHTML Basic allows us to use CSS to add styling to our site, so we are not stuck with text-only pages. However, CSS support is not consistent across phones—some support more CSS attributes than others.

While the markup language and technical constraints are important, there are equally important issues in the design of applications to be used on resource-limited devices. Web pages that are displayed and used on a mobile phone using a small screen and simple keypad have very different requirements than a page on a desktop or laptop computer.

Some of the issues to consider follow:

- A mobile user is likely to have a slow Net connection, so it is a good idea to keep the number of images on a mobile site to a minimum and make sure that any images that are used are very small—a couple of kilobytes at most—and that they are the correct dimensions for a small screen. Loading a 640×480-pixel image into a phone isn't very practical.

- Since a mobile device has a limited screen size, the amount of text rendered on a page is quite small. Displaying a page with a huge amount of text isn't a good idea.

- The user's interaction with the site will be quite different. It is more likely that a mobile user will use the site primarily to view pages and rarely enter text, so the interface should be optimized towards this.

- Navigation on your mobile site should be made as simple and quick as possible. Having a navigation list on every screen and using the HTML accesskey attribute to allow a user to quickly and easily access a page is good practice.

All of these issues should be carefully considered while designing a mobile-focused web application. In order to help developers understand the constraints and produce useable mobile web applications, the World Wide Web Consortium (W3C) has set up a special group, the W3C Mobile Web Initiative (MWI). Their web page can be found at http://www.w3.org/Mobile.

The W3C Mobile Web Best Practices Working Group is part of the W3C MWI; their task is to investigate and recommend best practices for mobile application developers. They can be found at http://www.w3.org/2005/MWI/BPWG and have released a very useful document called "Mobile Web Best Practices: Basic Guidelines." This document recommends best practices for designing mobile web pages and can be found at http://www.w3.org/TR/mobile-bp. I highly recommend referring to this document and taking note of its recommendations if you are developing any kind of mobile web application.

The RailsCoders Mobile Site Requirements

Keeping in mind the recommended best practices for mobile web development, we can start to think about what information we want to show on our mobile RailsCoders site and how we can best optimize the user interface.

The mobile version of RailsCoders should contain exactly the same information and work with the same data model as the full Web version. Only the interface to the data should change.

The mobile site will be accessible using the URL http://railscoders.net/mobile/. It is also a good idea to provide a redirection from the URL http://m.railscoders.net, making it easier to enter into a mobile keypad. This redirection would be set up by the web server rules, rather than in Rails.

Since it is unlikely that the site will need to be administered using a mobile device, we will not develop an administration interface accessible from the mobile site.

The Layout

The main layout for the mobile site should be consistent throughout the site, in the same way as the full version. We should use the same color scheme and logo to maintain our site's identity, although we should create a smaller, mobile-optimized logo to make sure that the site loads quickly.

Each page should have a navigation section, linking to each part of the site. To make switching sections quick for users, accesskey shortcuts should be assigned to each option and be consistent on each page. To enable quick access to the main content of the page, the navigation section should be placed at the bottom of the page. Figure 13-1 shows the RailsCoders mobile page layout.

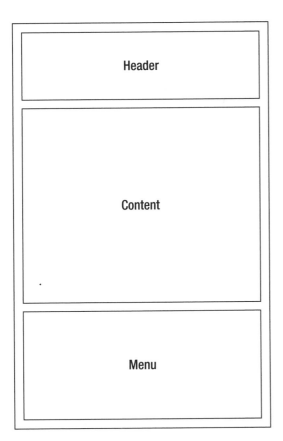

Figure 13-1. *The layout of the mobile RailsCoders site*

We will use a Rails layout file in the same way as the full XHTML version. This will allow us to use exactly the same markup for the template and then insert the required content for each page.

User Profiles

Since the user's profile page is a central point for a user, we should provide the user's profile in a similar way to on the Web, showing the username and profile text. We should also show the titles of the user's latest blogs along with tiny versions of the latest photos uploaded.

Accounts

Since we want to allow our users to log in on the mobile site, we need to provide a mobile version of the login page.

Pages

The pages are essential in providing information about the site, so we need to provide views to allow them to be shown.

News Articles

The news articles should be available to viewers of the mobile site. Since the news articles may be quite large, the index view should display only the title and category of the news article. Also, to make the page smaller and easier to navigate, we will only show five articles at a time. Clicking the title of an article will display the entire article.

Forums

The RailsCoders forums are a central part of the site, so they must be available on the mobile version. However, to make them easily navigable, we will need to simplify the way the pages are laid out. Currently, the pages are rendered using tables, but on the mobile site, we will just use a list.

- For the forum list, we will just show the name of the forum and link to the topic list. We will not show the count of the number of topics.

- The topics list will list only the topics, not the number of posts or the creator of the topic. We will add a link to the page for creating new topics.

- The list of posts within a topic will show the author's name before the topic. We will provide a link to allow users to reply to a topic.

We will support creation of new topics and posts from the mobile device. While it is unlikely that a user will enter a large amount of text on a phone keypad, it could be useful for requesting information while away from the main computer.

Blogs

The user's individual blogs should be accessible from the mobile site. However, since the screen size is much smaller, we will show only the titles of the entries in the index view. To view the entire entry, the user must click the title. The pagination links will allow a reader to read more articles, which will be displayed along the following lines:

- The blog feature allows users to write their own templates to display their blog pages as they wish. Since they haven't created a mobile-specific site, we cannot guarantee that it will display properly on a mobile browser. To solve this, we will ignore any user-generated blog templates and display blog entries on a standard template.

- Since a blog entry may be very long, the standard blog view should show a truncated version of each entry, containing only the first 500 characters. If it is truncated, there should be a link to the full version of the blog post.

- Each entry should also show the number of comments for the post. This will link to the full entry view, displaying all of the comments.

- The blogs controller will show the title and creator's username of the five most recently added entries on the site.

We will not provide support to allow a user to create a new blog entry or for others to add comments via the mobile web site, since it is unlikely that users will want to enter a large amount of text from their phone keypads.

Photo Gallery

When we developed the gallery feature, we anticipated the mobile version by creating a smaller thumbnail called `tiny`. We will use this for the gallery view, allowing us to show a number of photos at a time on the screen. Each photo will have a corresponding link to a page showing the `thumb` version of the photo.

Developing Mobile RailsCoders

The mobile version of RailsCoders should use as much of the existing code as possible. Because Ruby is object oriented, this is a very simple process. To create the mobile version, we will simply create new Rails controllers that inherit from the existing controllers. These new mobile controllers can then override any controller methods that need to change.

Structure of the Mobile Application

If we place these new controllers in a directory within the existing `controllers` directory, Rails will automatically expect their corresponding views to also be within a subdirectory of the existing `views` directory. This means that we can create a whole new set of view files that work either with exactly the same controller code, if we do not override the action code, or with our modified controller code, if we override any methods. Therefore, we only have to write code for actions where the controller behavior is different from the existing code.

Controllers in any subdirectories of the `controllers` directory will automatically be accessible by prefixing the controller name with the name of the subdirectory. For instance, a controller called `controllers/mobile/pages_controller.rb` will be accessible at `http://localhost:3000/mobile/pages`. These controllers must specify their subdirectory in the namespaces of their classes, so the pages controller within the `mobile` directory is defined using `class Mobile::PagesController`.

All of these mobile controllers will be defined as resources to Rails, meaning that they will follow the same convention in using the standard Rails resource URLs and action method names.

Creating the Mobile Layout and Style Sheet

The mobile layout file is similar in structure to the existing `application.rhtml` layout file, but we need to update it with the correct DOCTYPE and CSS file. We can also change the markup if we need to.

Create the file `app/views/layouts/mobile.rhtml`, and add the markup in Listing 13-1.

Listing 13-1. *The Mobile Layout File*

```
<!DOCTYPE html PUBLIC "-//W3C//DTD XHTML Basic 1.0//EN"
  "http://www.w3.org/TR/xhtml-basic/xhtml-basic10.dtd">
<html>
  <head>
    <title>RailsCoders</title>
    <%= stylesheet_link_tag 'mobile' %>
    <%= yield :head %>
  </head>
  <body>
    <div id="container">
      <div id="header">
        <h1>RailsCoders</h1>
      </div>
      <div id="content">
        <% if flash[:notice] -%>
          <div id="notice"><%= flash[:notice] %></div>
        <% end -%>
        <% if flash[:error] -%>
          <div id="error"><%= flash[:error] %></div>
        <% end -%>
        <%= yield %>
      </div>
      <div id="menu">
        <%= render :partial => 'shared/mobilemenu' %>
      </div>
    </div>
  </body>
</html>
```

To go along with this, we need to add the navigation partial view referenced by this, the `mobilemenu` file. Create the file `app/views/shared/_mobilemenu.rhtml`, and add the code in Listing 13-2.

Listing 13-2. *The mobilemenu Partial View*

```
<ul>
  <li>0 <%= link_to 'Home', mobile_index_url, :accesskey => '0' %></li>
  <li>1 <%= link_to 'News', mobile_articles_path, :accesskey => '1' %></li>
  <li>2 <%= link_to 'Forums', mobile_forums_path, :accesskey => '2' %></li>
  <li>3 <%= link_to 'Blogs', mobile_blogs_path, :accesskey => '3' %></li>
  <li>4 <%= link_to 'Photos', mobile_photos_path, :accesskey => '4' %></li>

  <% if is_logged_in? %>
    <li><%= link_to 'Logout', mobile_logout_path %></li>
  <% else %>
    <li><%= link_to 'Login', mobile_login_path %></li>
  <% end %>

</ul>
```

You will notice that the links point to resource shortcuts starting with `mobile_`. These are links to a different version of the resource. We will set up these new resource mappings in the next section.

Also, each of the main areas of the site now has an `accesskey` set. This links one of the numeric keys on the mobile handset to a particular area, allowing the user to quickly navigate the site. For instance, to return the home page from any page on the site, all they have to do is hold down the 0 key.

We should also create a mobile CSS file. Create the file `public/stylesheets/mobile.css`, and add the CSS shown in Listing 13-3. Not all mobile browsers support all CSS attributes, so we need to keep our mobile CSS simple.

Listing 13-3. *The Mobile CSS File*

```
a { color: #b00; }
a:hover { background-color: #b00; color: #eee; }

#menu ul {
  background-color: #fcc;
  border-top: 1px solid #666;
  list-style: none;
  padding: 0px;
}
```

The Resource Mappings

In the mobile navigation menu, we created links to mobile versions of the resources, such as `mobile_articles_path`, `mobile_forums_path`. We need to create the mappings for these resources in the routes file.

Open the `config/routes.rb` file, and create a new section for the mobile routes below the regular route definitions but before the closing end statement. The resource mappings for our mobile resources are shown in Listing 13-4.

Listing 13-4. *Mobile Resource Mappings in the routes.rb File*

```
# Mobile Routes

map.resources :pages,
              :controller => 'mobile/pages',
              :path_prefix => '/mobile',
              :name_prefix => 'mobile_'

map.resources :articles,
              :controller => 'mobile/articles',
              :path_prefix => '/mobile',
              :name_prefix => 'mobile_'

map.resources :blogs,
              :controller => 'mobile/blogs',
              :path_prefix => '/mobile',
              :name_prefix => 'mobile_'

map.resources :photos,
              :controller => 'mobile/photos',
              :path_prefix => '/mobile',
              :name_prefix => 'mobile_'

map.resources :categories,
              :controller => 'mobile/categories',
              :path_prefix => '/mobile',
              :name_prefix => 'mobile_' do |categories|
  categories.resources :articles,
                :controller => 'mobile/articles',
                :name_prefix => 'mobile_category_'
end

map.resources :users,
              :controller => 'mobile/users',
              :path_prefix => '/mobile',
              :name_prefix => 'mobile_' do |users|
  users.resources :photos,
                :controller => 'mobile/user_photos',
                :name_prefix => 'mobile_user_'
  users.resources :entries,
                :controller => 'mobile/entries',
                :name_prefix => 'mobile_'
end
```

```
map.resources :forums,
              :controller => 'mobile/forums',
              :path_prefix => '/mobile',
              :name_prefix => 'mobile_' do |forums|
  forums.resources :topics,
                   :controller => 'mobile/topics',
                   :name_prefix => 'mobile_' do |topics|
    topics.resources :posts,
                     :controller => 'mobile/posts',
                     :name_prefix => 'mobile_'
  end
end

map.mobile_index '/mobile', :controller => 'mobile/pages',
                            :action => 'show',
                            :id => "1"

map.mobile_show_user  '/mobile/user/:username', :controller => 'mobile/users',
                                                :action => 'show_by_username'
map.mobile_all_blogs  '/mobile/blogs', :controller => 'mobile/blogs',
                                       :action => 'index'
map.mobile_all_photos '/mobile/photos', :controller => 'mobile/photos',
                                        :action => 'index'
map.mobile_login  '/mobile/login', :controller => 'mobile/account',
                                   :action => 'login'
map.mobile_logout '/mobile/logout', :controller => 'mobile/account',
                                    :action => 'logout'
```

These resource mappings are similar to the regular mappings, but they specify a different controller, URL path, and name prefix to use when referring to the resource by a shortcut such as mobile_pages_path.

These resources are distinct from the regular resources, since they point to a different controller and use a different name.

As before, we have nested resources for the articles when accessed with a category and for the forum topics and posts. These work in exactly the same way as the regular mappings, except using the new controllers. Notice, however, that the mobile nested mappings do not specify the path_prefix attribute. This should only be done for the top-level resource. Since you will only specify the nested resource together with the higher level resource, the higher level requires the path_prefix of /mobile, not the nested resource.

We have also added a mobile_index mapping, allowing us to set a default page for the URL http://railscoders.net/mobile/.

The mobile_all_blogs and mobile_all_photos mappings link to the index actions within the relevant controllers, in the same way as their regular controllers do.

The Mobile Controllers and Views

We can now create the mobile versions of the controllers.

Inside your app/controllers/ directory, create a new directory called mobile. Within this directory, we will create a new controller for the mobile version of each resource. Next, inside the directory app/views/, create another new directory, also called mobile. Within this directory, we will create the mobile views for the corresponding controllers.

The Pages Resource

Create a new file called app/controllers/mobile/pages_controller.rb. Within this, we need to create a controller that inherits from the existing pages controller. We then need to override the default layout, specifying out new mobile layout file.

For the action methods, the only nonadministrative action accessible for the pages controller is the show action. Since we want this to work in exactly the same way as the regular version, we do not have to override the show method.

The complete mobile pages_controller.rb file is shown in Listing 13-5.

Listing 13-5. *The Mobile Pages Controller File*

```
class Mobile::PagesController < PagesController
  layout 'mobile'
end
```

To go along with this, we need to create the corresponding mobile views for this controller. Since we only need to support the show action, we only need to create this one view.

First, create a new subdirectory of the app/views/mobile/ directory called pages. Next, create the file app/views/mobile/pages/show.rhtml. This file must simply display the title and the body of the page. The full page view file is shown in Listing 13-6.

Listing 13-6. *The Mobile Pages Show Action*

```
<h2><%= @page.title %></h2>
<p><%= @page.body %></p>
```

You can now take a look at this mobile view using your regular browser. Go to http://localhost:3000/mobile/pages/1. The welcome page will be shown using the new mobile layout and templates.

The Articles Resource

The specification for the mobile articles controller calls for a slight change from the regular controller. The index action for the normal articles controller paginates the list of articles to show ten articles at once. Because of the small screen size of a mobile device, we want to change this to show only five articles at one time.

Because this controller can be called either directly or nested within a category, we need to check for the presence of a category_id parameter in the request. If the parameter is present, we need to return only articles within that category. If it is not present, we retrieve articles irrespective of the category. Also, only articles that have their published attribute set to true should be shown.

The only other nonadministrative action is the show action. The current controller action method can be used unchanged, since all the method does is retrieve the article and display it.

Create the new controller file, app/controllers/mobile/articles_controller.rb. Add the code shown in Listing 13-7.

Listing 13-7. *The Mobile Articles Controller*

```
class Mobile::ArticlesController < ArticlesController
  layout 'mobile'

  def index
    if params[:category_id]
      @articles_pages, @articles = paginate :articles,
        :include => :user,
        :per_page => 5,
        :order => 'published_at DESC',
        :conditions => "category_id = #{params[:category_id].to_i} AND
                        published = true"
    else
      @articles = Article.find_all_by_published(true)
      @articles_pages, @articles = paginate :articles,
        :include => :user,
        :per_page => 5,
        :order => 'published_at DESC',
        :conditions => "published = true"
    end
  end
end
```

This controller again overrides the layout, specifying the mobile layout. The inherited index method is overridden with similar code to the parent articles controller but with a limit of five articles per page instead of ten.

We now need to create the views for the index and show methods. But first, create the directory for the mobile articles views, app/views/mobile/articles/.

Create the index view app/views/mobile/articles/index.rhtml, and enter the view code in Listing 13-8.

Listing 13-8. *The Mobile Articles Index View*

```
<h2>News Articles</h2>

<% if @articles_pages.page_count > 1 %>
  <p class="pagination">Pages: <strong>
    <%= pagination_links @articles_pages, :params => params %>
  </strong></p>
<% end %>
```

```
<% @articles.each do |article| %>
  <div class="article">
    <h3><%= article.title %></h3>
    <% if article.category %>
      <p class="category">
        Category: '<%= link_to article.category.name,
                          mobile_category_articles_path(article.category) %>'
      </p>
    <% end %>

    <p>
      <%= article.created_at.to_s(:short) %> by <%= article.user.username %><br />
      <%= link_to 'Read the full article', mobile_article_url(article) %>
    </p>
  </div>
<% end %>

<% if @articles_pages.page_count > 1 %>
  <p class="pagination">Pages: <strong>
    <%= pagination_links @articles_pages, :params => params %>
  </strong></p>
<% end %>
```

This includes the pagination links at the top and bottom of the page to make it easy for a user to navigate the pages.

As defined in the feature specification, the index view does not show the full article or synopsis, only the title, the category, the author, and a link to the full article.

Now create the show action view, app/views/mobile/articles/show.rhtml. This page shows the title and the full body of the article. Add the code in Listing 13-9.

Listing 13-9. *The Mobile Articles Show View*

```
<h2><%= @article.title %></h2>
<p>
  <%= @article.created_at.to_s(:short) %><br />
  <%= textilize(@article.body) %><br />
</p>
<p><%= link_to 'Back to article list', mobile_articles_url %></p>
```

The Forums, Topics, and Posts Resources

The mobile forum feature consists of the forums, topics, and posts controllers. The mobile views need to be simplified compared to the Web versions, but should display most of the same information.

As with the previous mobile controllers, we need to focus only on the nonadministrative actions, as administration of the forums is not necessary for the mobile views.

First of all, we should create the forums controller. Create the file app/controllers/mobile/forums_controller.rb, and add the code in Listing 13-10.

Listing 13-10. *The Mobile Forums Controller*

```
class Mobile::ForumsController < ForumsController
  layout 'mobile'

  def show
    redirect_to mobile_topics_path(:forum_id => params[:forum_id])
  end
end
```

We do not have to override the index action, as the current version is fine. The show action simply redirects to the topics controller. Since we need to redirect to a different shortcut, we need to override the current method.

Since the index action is the only one that displays anything, we only have to write this one view for the forums controller. Create the app/views/mobile/forums/ directory and the file app/views/mobile/forums/index.rhtml. Add the simplified forums index view shown in Listing 13-11.

Listing 13-11. *The Mobile Forum Index View*

```
<h2>Forums</h2>

<% @forums.each do |forum| -%>
  <div class="forumname">
    <%= link_to forum.name, mobile_topics_path(:forum_id => forum) -%>
  </div>
  <div class="forumdescription">
    <%= forum.description -%>
  </div>
<% end -%>
```

In the topics controller, since we want to allow mobile users to create new messages in the forum, the actions that we need to look at are the index, show, new, and create actions. The current index action just returns a paginated list of topics with ten topics per page, so that is fine. However, we should override the show method in the same way as we did for the forums controller, redirecting to the mobile version of the posts resource.

The new action does not require changing, as it simply shows the form for entering a new topic. But the create action needs to be overridden to redirect to the mobile version of the posts controller.

Create the controller file app/controllers/mobile/topics_controller.rb, and add the code shown in Listing 13-12.

Listing 13-12. *The Mobile Topics Controller*

```
class Mobile::TopicsController < TopicsController
  layout 'mobile'

  def show
    redirect_to mobile_posts_path(:forum_id => params[:forum_id],
                                  :topic_id => params[:id])
  end

  def create
    @topic = Topic.new(:name => params[:topic][:name],
                       :forum_id => params[:forum_id],
                       :user_id => logged_in_user.id)
    @topic.save!
    @post = Post.new(:body => params[:post][:body],
                     :topic_id => @topic.id,
                     :user_id => logged_in_user.id)
    @post.save!

    redirect_to mobile_posts_path(:topic_id => @topic, :forum_id => @topic.forum)
  end

end
```

To store the topics' mobile views, create the directory app/views/mobile/topics/.

The index view for the topics controller should just display the name of the topic with a link back to the topics list and the list of topics, along with the pagination links. Also, if the user is logged in, there should also be a link to the new action, allowing the user to create a new topic. Create the file app/views/mobile/topics/index.rhtml, and enter the code shown in Listing 13-13.

Listing 13-13. *The Mobile Topics Index View*

```
<h2>Forum : <%= @forum.name -%></h2>

<h3>Topics</h3>

<p>
<% if is_logged_in? -%>
  <%= link_to 'Post New Topic', mobile_new_topic_path(:forum_id => @forum) -%>
<% else -%>
  <%= link_to 'Login to post a new topic', mobile_login_url -%>
<% end -%>
</p>
```

```
<% if @topics_pages.page_count > 1 %>
  <p class="pagination">Pages: <strong>
    <%= pagination_links @topics_pages, :params => params %>
  </strong></p>
<% end %>

<ul>
<% @topics.each do |topic| -%>
  <li><%= link_to topic.name,
                  mobile_posts_path(:forum_id => @forum, :topic_id => topic) -%>
  (<%= pluralize(topic.posts_count, 'post') -%>)</li>
<% end -%>
</ul>

<% if @topics_pages.page_count > 1 %>
  <p class="pagination">Pages: <strong>
    <%= pagination_links @topics_pages, :params => params %>
  </strong></p>
<% end %>
```

We also need to create the view for the new action. This should just be a simple form that submits to the mobile topics controller. Create the file app/views/mobile/topics/new.rhtml, and enter the code from Listing 13-14.

Listing 13-14. *The Mobile Topics New View*

```
<h2>New Topic</h2>

<%= error_messages_for :topic -%>
<%= error_messages_for :post -%>

<% form_for :topic, :url => mobile_topics_path do |f| -%>
  <p>Subject:<%= f.text_field :name -%></p>
  <p>Message:<%= text_area :post, :body -%></p>
  <%= submit_tag 'Save' %>  or
  <%= link_to 'cancel', mobile_topics_path(:forum_id => params[:forum_id]) %>
<% end -%>
```

The mobile posts controller is similar to the topics controller, in that it requires the index, new, and create actions to be available. The index and show actions do not need to be changed from their regular version, but the create controller should be overridden to redirect to the mobile posts index action after creating the new post.

Create the file app/controllers/posts_controller.rb, and add the code shown in Listing 13-15.

Listing 13-15. *The Mobile Post Controller*

```
class Mobile::PostsController < PostsController
  layout 'mobile'

  def create
    @topic = Topic.find(params[:topic_id])
    @post = Post.new(:body => params[:post][:body],
                     :topic_id => @topic.id,
                     :user_id => logged_in_user.id)

    if @post.save
      flash[:notice] = 'Post was successfully created.'
      redirect_to mobile_posts_path(:forum_id => @topic.forum_id,
                                    :topic_id => @topic)
    else
      render :action => "new"
    end
  end
end
```

Create the directory for the mobile posts views, app/views/mobile/posts/. The create action does not require a view file, as it just redirects after creating the post. The index view should present a list of posts within a topic, together with the pagination links if necessary, and a link to create a new post within this topic if the user is logged in.

Create the file app/views/mobile/posts/index.rhtml, and add the code in Listing 13-16.

Listing 13-16. *The Mobile Posts Index View*

```
<h2><%= @topic.name -%></h2>

<h3>
  <%= link_to 'Forums', mobile_forums_path -%> >
  <%= link_to @topic.forum.name, mobile_topics_path(:forum_id => @topic.forum) -%> >
  <%= @topic.name -%>
</h3>

<p>
<% if is_logged_in? -%>
  <%= link_to 'Post Reply', mobile_new_post_path(:forum_id => @topic.forum,
                                                 :topic_id => @topic) -%>
<% else -%>
  <%= link_to 'Login to post a new topic', mobile_login_url -%>
<% end -%>
</p>
```

```
<% if @posts_pages.page_count > 1 %>
  <p class="pagination">Pages: <strong>
    <%= pagination_links @posts_pages, :params => params %>
  </strong></p>
<% end %>

<% @posts.each do |post| -%>
  <p>
    <%= link_to  post.user.username, mobile_user_path(post.user) -%> said:<br />
    <%= textilize(post.body) -%>
  </p>
<% end -%>

<% if @posts_pages.page_count > 1 %>
  <p class="pagination">Pages: <strong>
    <%= pagination_links @posts_pages, :params => params %>
  </strong></p>
<% end %>
```

The new post view is a simple form to accept a new forum post and send it to the mobile post controller. Create the file app/views/mobile/posts/new.rhtml, and enter the code from Listing 13-17.

Listing 13-17. *The Mobile Posts New View*

```
<h2>New Post</h2>

<%= error_messages_for :post -%>

<h3>Topic: <%= @topic.name %></h3>
<% form_for :post, :url => mobile_posts_path(:topic_id => @topic,
                                            :forum_id => @topic.forum) do |f| -%>
  <p>Message:<br /><%= f.text_area :body -%></p>
  <%= submit_tag 'Save' -%> or
  <%= link_to 'Cancel',
            mobile_topics_path(:id => @topic, :forum_id => @topic.forum) -%>
<% end -%>
```

The Users Resource

We will not support creating a new user via the mobile site, but we do want to provide access to the profile of each user, meaning that we need to provide support for the show action. Since we are not supporting an administration interface on the mobile version of RailsCoders, we do not need to create a view for the index action, showing all of the users.

The current controller's show action simply retrieves a User model and renders the show view. Since this is exactly what we need for the mobile view, we do not need to override the method.

Create the mobile users controller file, app/controllers/mobile/users_controller.rb, and enter the code from Listing 13-18.

Listing 13-18. *The Mobile Users Controller*

```
class Mobile::UsersController < UsersController
  layout 'mobile'
end
```

The show view needs to display the selected user's profile, along with that user's latest activity on the site, such as the latest blog entries and photographs, as with the full, Web profile page.

Create the directory for the mobile user views, app/views/mobile/users, and create the show view file, app/views/mobile/users/show.rhtml. Add the view code shown in Listing 13-19 to this file.

Listing 13-19. *The Mobile User Show View*

```
<h2><%= @user.username %></h2>
<p><%=h @user.profile %></p>

<h3>Blog Entries</h3>
<ul id="entries">
<% @entries.each do |entry| %>
  <li><%= link_to entry.title, mobile_entry_path(:user_id => @user, :id => entry) %>
<% end %>
</ul>
<p>
  <%= link_to "See all of #{@user.username}'s blog",
              mobile_entries_path(:user_id => @user) %>
</p>

<h3>Photos</h3>
<ul id="photos">
<% @photos.each do |photo| -%>
  <li>
    <%= link_to image_tag(photo.public_filename('tiny')),
                mobile_photo_path(:user_id => photo.user, :id => photo) %>
  </li>
<% end %>
</ul>
<p>
  <%= link_to "See all of #{@user.username}'s photos",
              mobile_photos_path(:user_id => @user) %>
</p>
```

The Entries Resource

For the users' blogs, we need to produce an interface to the entries resource. Since the entries show action displays any comments for the blog entry and we do not need to accept new comments from the mobile interface, we do not need to provide a separate interface to the comments resource.

Since we also will not support creating new blog entries on the mobile site, we need to consider only the index and show actions for the mobile entries controller. The current entries controller's index action returns ten items per page. As discussed in the specifications, we will just show the titles of the five most recent blog entries on the index page. Since the existing entries controller index action renders pages using a Liquid usertemplate if the user has defined one, we need to override it so that the entries views are always rendered using the default style.

The show action also needs to be overridden to show the individual entries without any styling. Create the mobile entries controller, app/controllers/mobile/entries_controller.rb, and add the code shown in Listing 13-20.

Listing 13-20. *The Mobile Entries Controller File*

```ruby
class Mobile::EntriesController < EntriesController
  layout 'mobile'
  def index
    @user = User.find(params[:user_id], :include => :usertemplates)
    @entry_pages = Paginator.new(self, @user.entries_count, 5, params[:page])
    @entries = @user.entries.find(:all, :order => 'created_at DESC',
                        :limit => @entry_pages.items_per_page,
                        :offset => @entry_pages.current.offset)
  end


  def show
    @user = User.find(params[:user_id], :include => :usertemplates)
    @entry = Entry.find_by_id_and_user_id(params[:id],
                        params[:user_id],
                        :include => [:comments => :user])
  end
end
```

Now create the directory for the mobile entries views, app/views/mobile/entries/. As discussed, the index view will just show the titles of the entries, linking to the show action. Create the index view file, app/views/mobile/entries/index.rhtml, and enter the code in Listing 13-21.

Listing 13-21. *The Mobile Entries Index View*

```rhtml
<h2><%= @user.username %>'s blog</h2>

<% if @entry_pages.page_count > 1 %>
  <p>
    <% if @entry_pages.current.previous %>
      <%= link_to '&laquo; Previous', :page => @entry_pages.current.previous %>
    <% end %>
```

```
    <% if @entry_pages.current.next %>
      <%= link_to 'Next &raquo;', :page => @entry_pages.current.next %>
    <% end %>
  </p>
<% end %>

<ul>
<% @entries.each do |entry| -%>
  <li>
    <%= link_to entry.title, mobile_entry_path(:user_id => @user, :id => entry) -%>
    (<%= entry.created_at.to_s(:short) %>)
  </li>
<% end -%>
</ul>

<% if @entry_pages.page_count > 1 %>
  <p>
    <% if @entry_pages.current.previous %>
      <%= link_to '&laquo; Previous', :page => @entry_pages.current.previous %>
    <% end %>
    <% if @entry_pages.current.next %>
      <%= link_to 'Next &raquo;', :page => @entry_pages.current.next %>
    <% end %>
  </p>
<% end %>
```

The show view is very simple; it just displays the title and body of the entry. Create the view file app/views/mobile/entries/show.rhtml, and add the code in Listing 13-22.

Listing 13-22. *The Mobile Entries Show View*

```
<h2>
  <%= link_to "#{@user.username}'s blog",
              mobile_entries_path(:user_id => @user.id) %>
</h2>
<h3><%=h @entry.title %></h3>
<p><%= textilize(@entry.body) %></p>
```

The Blogs Resource

To view the most recently created posts by any users, rather than by one specific user, we'll use the blogs controller.

Since we only need to show a list of the titles of the posts and the usernames of the authors, we only need to create an index view. The existing blogs controller already retrieves the correct variables, so all we need to do is add a mobile blogs controller that inherits from the existing blogs controller and then create a corresponding mobile index view.

Create a mobile blogs controller, app/controllers/mobile/blogs_controller.rb, and enter the code in Listing 13-23.

Listing 13-23. *The Mobile Blogs Controller*

```
class Mobile::BlogsController < BlogsController
  layout 'mobile'
end
```

Now create a directory for the mobile blogs view, `app/views/mobile/blogs/`. Within this directory, create the index view, `app/views/mobile/blogs/index.rhtml`, and enter the view code in Listing 13-24.

Listing 13-24. *The Mobile Blogs Index View File*

```
<h2>Recently updated blogs</h2>

<% @entries.each do |entry| %>
  <p>
    <%= link_to entry.user.username,
              mobile_entries_url(:user_id => entry.user) %><br />
    '<%=h entry.title %>' was posted <%= time_ago_in_words(entry.created_at) %> ago
  </p>
<% end %>

<% if @entry_pages.page_count > 1 %>
  <p class="pagination">Pages:
    <%= pagination_links @entry_pages, :params => params %>
  </p>
<% end %>
```

The Photos Resource

To view the latest photos on the site that have been uploaded by all users, we need to create a mobile `photos` resource. The `photos` resource only implements one action, `index`.

We do not need to override the existing actions, since the existing code retrieves the data we require—nine photos from a specific user. Although the Web view displays the nine photos in a 3×3 grid, we will just display them in a list for the mobile view.

Create the mobile `photos` controller file, `app/controllers/mobile/photos.rb`, and enter the code in Listing 13-25.

Listing 13-25. *The Mobile Photos Controller File*

```
class Mobile::PhotosController < PhotosController
  layout 'mobile'
end
```

For the `index` view, we simply want to show a list of the images together with links to view a larger version. As discussed in the specifications, we will use the thumbnails called `tiny` for this `index` view.

Create the necessary directory and view the file for the `index` view, `app/views/mobile/photos/index.rhtml`, and enter the code in Listing 13-26.

Listing 13-26. *The Mobile Photos Index View File*

```
<h2>All Photos</h2>

<% if @photo_pages.page_count > 1 %>
  <p class="pagination">
    <% if @photo_pages.current.previous %>
      <%= link_to '&laquo; Previous', :page => @photo_pages.current.previous %>
    <% end %>
    <% if @photo_pages.current.next %>
      <%= link_to 'Next &raquo;', :page => @photo_pages.current.next %>
    <% end %>
  </p>
<% end %>

<ul id="photos">
  <% @photos.each do |photo| -%>
    <li id="photo-<%= photo.id %>">
      <%= link_to image_tag(photo.public_filename('tiny')),
                  mobile_user_photo_path(:user_id => photo.user, :id => photo) %>
    </li>
  <% end %>
</ul>
```

The user_photos Resource

To view photos by a specific user, we use the user_photos resource. This needs to support the index and show actions. Since we will not support uploading or editing of photos from the mobile site, we do not need the new, create, edit, update, or destroy actions.

We do not need to override any existing methods; the regular index and show actions perform exactly as we require.

Create the file app/controllers/mobile/user_photos_controller.rb, and enter the code in Listing 13-27.

Listing 13-27. *The Mobile Photos Controller File*

```
class Mobile::UserPhotosController < UserPhotosController
  layout 'mobile'
end
```

Now create the directory for the mobile photo views, app/views/mobile/user_photos/. Create the index view file, app/views/mobile/user_photos/index.rhtml, and add the view code in Listing 13-28. As with the index view from the mobile photos resource, we will show the thumbnail using the tiny size.

Listing 13-28. *The Mobile user_photos Index View*

```
<h2><%= @user.username %>'s Photos</h2>

<% if @photo_pages.page_count > 1 %>
  <p class="pagination">
    <% if @photo_pages.current.previous %>
      <%= link_to '&laquo; Previous', :page => @photo_pages.current.previous %>
    <% end %>
    <% if @photo_pages.current.next %>
      <%= link_to 'Next &raquo;', :page => @photo_pages.current.next %>
    <% end %>
  </p>
<% end %>

<ul id="photos">
  <% @photos.each do |photo| -%>
    <li id="photo-<%= photo.id %>">
      <%= link_to image_tag(photo.public_filename('tiny')),
                mobile_user_photo_path(:user_id => photo.user, :id => photo) %>
    </li>
  <% end %>
</ul>
```

The show view is very simple, showing just the photo, the body, and the title. In this view, the thumbnail size called thumb will be used to show a large version of the photo. Create the file app/views/mobile/user_photos/show.rhtml, and add the code in Listing 13-29.

Listing 13-29. *The Mobile user_photos Show View*

```
<h3>
  <%= link_to "#{@photo.user.username}'s Photos",
            mobile_user_photos_path(:user_id => @photo.user) %>
</h3>
<h2><%=h @photo.title %></h2>

<%= image_tag @photo.public_filename('thumb'), :id => 'photo' %>

<p><%=h @photo.body %></p>
```

The Account Login Page

Finally, we need to create the mobile account controller and login page. The mobile account controller performs the same actions as the regular controller, but we need to override both the authenticate and logout methods, as we need to change the redirections to point to the mobile URLs.

Also, we need to change the logout method to accept a regular HTTP GET, instead of a POST, request. For the regular controller, we require the logout request to be a POST request, which makes sure that web accelerator applications, such as Google Web Accelerator, do not log out a user while trying to preload a page and accidentally cause the session to be destroyed.

However, to make a text link perform a request as an HTTP POST, Rails uses JavaScript. Many phones support a form of JavaScript, but we cannot guarantee that it is supported. Since applications such as the Google Web Accelerator will not be running on a mobile phone, we can safely allow a GET request to the logout URL to log out a user.

Create the mobile account controller, app/controllers/mobile/account_controller.rb, and enter the code in Listing 13-30.

Listing 13-30. *The Mobile Account Controller File*

```
class Mobile::AccountController < AccountController
  layout 'mobile'

  def authenticate
    self.logged_in_user = User.authenticate(params[:user][:username],
                                             params[:user][:password])
    if is_logged_in?
      flash[:notice] = "You have successfully logged in."
      redirect_to mobile_index_url
    else
      flash[:error] = "I'm sorry, either your email or password was incorrect."
      redirect_to :action => 'login'
    end
  end

  def logout
    reset_session
    flash[:notice] = "You have been logged out."
    redirect_to mobile_index_url
  end
end
```

We have to create only one mobile view file, the login form. This is simply a form accepting the username and password of a user who submits the form to the mobile account controller.

Create the mobile account views directory, app/views/mobile/account/, and the login form view, app/views/mobile/account/login.rhtml. Now enter the code in Listing 13-31.

Listing 13-31. *The Mobile Account Login View*

```
<h2>Login</h2>

<% form_for :user, :url => {:action => 'authenticate'} do |f| -%>
  <p>Username:<%= f.text_field :username %></p>
  <p>Password:<%= f.password_field :password %></p>
  <%= submit_tag 'Login' %>
<% end %>
```

Manual Testing

We can now try using the mobile site. Since we cannot easily access the local web server running on your machine from a mobile device, we will use a standard desktop web browser that supports XHTML Basic to test the site. Firefox or Opera are good choices for this.

Make sure that your Rails application is running, and go to the mobile home page, `http://localhost:3000/mobile/`. You will see the page shown in Figure 13-2.

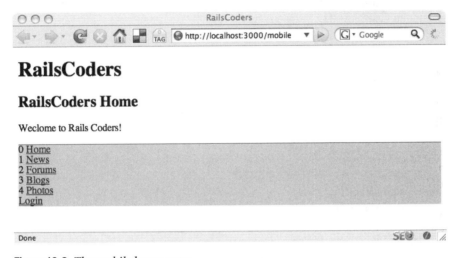

Figure 13-2. *The mobile home page*

Note If you wish, you could create a unique page for this mobile home page and set it as the default `mobile_index` page in the `routes.rb` file.

Now try using the mobile interface to look around your site, checking that the views work as expected.

Try logging in and using the forum interface to create a new topic and to reply to an existing post; make sure that the items are created and that the redirections correctly go back to the mobile view.

Testing the Mobile Site

Since our mobile site uses much of the same code as our regular site, we should take this into account while deciding what we need to test:

- We have not altered or added to the models in any way, so we do not have to add any specific unit tests for the mobile site.

- The existing controllers have not been changed, so we do not need to change our existing functional and integration tests.

- The main focus of the code for our mobile site has been in sending different views and redirecting to different pages where necessary. For this, we should consider doing integration testing.

To investigate how we can use integration tests to check the behavior of our mobile application, we will test the login function. So, if an attempt to log in fails, the user is redirected to the login page, but if the login is successful, the user is directed to a page shown by the mobile pages resource.

Create a new integration test file, test/integration/mobile_login_stories_test.rb, and enter the test code in Listing 13-32.

Listing 13-32. *The Mobile Login Integration Tests*

```ruby
require "#{File.dirname(__FILE__)}/../test_helper"

class LoginStoriesTest < ActionController::IntegrationTest
  fixtures :users, :pages

  def test_valid_mobile_login
    get 'mobile/login'
    assert_response :success
    assert_template 'mobile/account/login'

    post 'mobile/account/authenticate',
        :user => {:username => 'joe', :password => '12345'}
    assert_response :redirect
    follow_redirect!
    assert_response :success
    assert_template 'mobile/pages/show'
  end

  def test_invalid_mobile_login
    get 'mobile/login'
    assert_response :success
    assert_template 'mobile/account/login'

    post 'mobile/account/authenticate',
        :user => {:username => 'joe', :password => 'wrong'}
    assert_response :redirect
    follow_redirect!
    assert_response :success
    assert_template 'mobile/account/login'
  end
end
```

As you can see, these tests check that the correct mobile template is being used to show the login page and the show action of the pages controller.

Try running these tests now:

```
$ ruby test/integration/mobile_login_stories_test.rb
```

```
Loaded suite test/integration/mobile_login_stories_test
Started
..
Finished in 1.288459 seconds.

2 tests, 10 assertions, 0 failures, 0 errors
```

We could follow this with a number of stories for each of the controllers in which we have overridden a method to make sure that the correct responses are given to each action.

Further Development of the Mobile Site

There are many ways in which you may wish to develop this mobile interface further. At the moment, it provides a basic interface to viewing the site, along with an option to add posts to the discussion forum.

You may wish to allow users to create blog posts or add comments to a blog entry while on the move. Since we have already added an interface to add posts to the forum, you can see that it is easy to add input forms to the blog feature.

You may also want to add an administration interface to allow yourself access to certain administrative functions through a mobile device. This may be useful for forum moderators, allowing them to perform their role through a PDA or mobile device.

Summary

In this chapter, we created a new interface to the RailsCoders site, allowing it to be used on a small-screen device, such as a mobile phone. To do this, we reused existing model and controller code, overriding controller methods when necessary.

We created a new set of views for the mobile site by simplifying the views and making the site easy to navigate on a small screen with a limited keypad.

In the final chapter, we will examine how you can release your web application to the world. We will look at how to deploy your application onto a server and how you can start to monitor and optimize your application.

■ ■ ■

## CHAPTER 14

Deploying, Optimizing, and Scaling the Application

In this chapter, we will look at how you can take your application live by deploying it on a production server and how you can monitor, optimize, and scale your application as it starts to grow. As you might expect, there are a number of tools available for Rails that help automate the deployment procedure. The most important tool that we will be using for deployment tasks is Capistrano.

Optimizing your application for dealing with heavy loads and a large number of users is highly dependent on your specific application and requirements. Optimizing Rails applications is a constant area of research within the Rails community, and methods for getting the most out of your system and strategies for scaling are continually evolving. In this chapter, I will describe some of the best practices and options available at the moment and how to get involved and stay on top of new optimization techniques.

Since Rails uses a share-nothing architecture, where each request is unique and does not rely on any state to be maintained on a specific server, scaling Rails can simply be a matter of providing more servers to process the requests.

Deploying RailsCoders

Deploying your application, that is making it live can be a daunting task, and running your application in production mode may uncover some problems with your application. Therefore, I recommend that, during development, you regularly deploy your code to a server. This way, you can check both your deployment process and your application code.

Development Mode vs. Production Mode

Until now, we have been using our application in development mode. This means that Rails does not try to cache or optimize the running of your application, so any changes you make to the code are always visible in your running application. This is a great help while we are developing, but it is not necessary when your application is deployed in a production environment.

When you run your application in production mode, Rails attempts to process the requests as fast as possible by caching model information from the database schemas and by not reloading classes after every request, which speeds up request processing. Production mode also uses a different database configuration from your test and development modes, so you do not have to worry about corrupting your live database during development and testing.

Session Storage

During development, we have been using the default method of storing session IDs, that is, the file system, also known as PStore. If you look within the `tmp/sessions/` directory of your application, you will see a number of files corresponding to the sessions created when you logged in to the application.

In production, it is not a good idea to use the file system for session storage. While it works well for very small systems and development, it requires a lot of housekeeping to keep the number of session files low, since performance degrades as the number of session files increases. This method cannot scale well above a single server, since the session files would need to be accessible to all servers. Also, using files can sometimes cause file-locking issues with Mongrel. To solve this, there are many different methods you may use to store your sessions data. We will look at some of these now.

ActiveRecordStore

The simplest method is known as `ActiveRecordStore`; it's built into Rails and uses the database to store all the session data. There are even some predefined `rake` tasks to create a migration that adds the necessary database table and to perform maintenance tasks.

You will still need to delete old sessions from the database, but this can easily be done with a `cron` job and the provided `rake` tasks.

■**Tip** `cron` is a tool found on Unix systems that allows you to run commands on a given schedule. You can find an introduction to `cron` at `http://www.linuxhelp.net/guides/cron`.

SqlSessionStore

As an alternative to the built-in database session store, Stefan Kaes, the author of the Rails Express blog, has created a plug-in called `SqlSessionStore`. This works in a similar way to the `ActiveRecordStore` but uses optimized SQL queries and is, therefore, faster.

The Rails Express blog at `http://railsexpress.de` has more information about `SqlSessionStore` as well as other great advice about getting the best performance from your Rails application.

Memcached

A very fast and scalable, but more complicated to configure, solution is `memcached`. `memcached` is a general purpose memory-based caching system that simply stores a very large hash table in memory. It can be distributed across a number of servers and can, therefore, provide a large and very fast cache for sessions. It was originally developed by Danga Interactive to provide caching for LiveJournal.

You can find out more information about configuring Rails to use memcached at http://nubyonrails.com/articles/2006/08/17/memcached-basics-for-rails.

Setting Up ActiveRecordStore

Since ActiveRecordStore is simple to configure and built into Rails, we will use this as our session store.

In order to change the RailsCoders application to use ActiveRecordStore rather than the default PStore, enter the following rake command:

```
$ rake db:sessions:create
```

```
     exists  db/migrate
     create  db/migrate/026_add_sessions.rb
```

You now need to perform the migration:

```
$ rake db:migrate
```

```
== AddSessions: migrating ========================================================
-- create_table(:sessions)
   -> 0.1202s
-- add_index(:sessions, :session_id)
   -> 0.2011s
-- add_index(:sessions, :updated_at)
   -> 0.1880s
== AddSessions: migrated (0.5105s) ===============================================
```

Next, you need to tell Rails to use the database as the session store. This is done in your environment.rb file. Open this file, config/environment.rb, and uncomment the following line:

```
config.action_controller.session_store = :active_record_store
```

Once you have restarted your application server, your application will use ActiveRecordStore as the session store.

Choosing a Host

Choosing a hosting provider comes down to a number of options. The first choice you will have to make is whether to go for shared hosting, where you will share a server with other people, or some kind of private server. This may be either a virtual private server (VPS) or a dedicated machine.

VPS VS. DEDICATED SERVER

A VPS appears to you as a dedicated server, in that you have a unique IP address, you have root user access to the box, and it is up to you to configure and maintain the box. However, a number of VPS instances can be run on the same physical machine.

This means that you are sharing resources such as the CPU, hard drives, and network bandwidth with other users on the same machine. With a dedicated server, you have a complete machine dedicated to you. In practice, because of the burstable nature of web sites, you will not notice performance problems unless your site becomes very popular. When it does, you can easily move to a dedicated server.

Using a VPS is a very good way to get started hosting your application. You will gain experience configuring and maintaining a server, and when your site becomes busy enough to justify a move to a dedicated machine (or to more than one), the procedure is exactly the same as a VPS.

Shared Hosting

If you choose to use a shared host, make sure that it supports Rails, as many do not. If Rails is supported, it is highly likely that the host will provide information about how to configure and deploy your application on its servers. Since shared hosts have different configurations, it is very difficult to give instructions here, and you should follow your provider's instructions to ensure that your application works in that hosting environment.

VPS or Dedicated Server Hosting

When deploying your application on a VPS or dedicated server, you have many options for the configuration of your production environment. While the choice of operating system is totally up to you, you will find that using a Unix-based server will make deployment, monitoring, and maintenance of your application much easier. At the moment, trying to find help with a Rails production environment using Windows is going to be very difficult. Therefore, I highly recommend using a Unix-based OS such as Linux or FreeBSD.

Since we have used Ubuntu as our Linux development platform, I will describe deployment tasks using Ubuntu. However, the deployment process will be similar on other Unix-based operating systems.

Choosing a Web Server

Throughout the development of our application, we have been using Mongrel to serve all pages and resources to the browser. When you run a Rails production site, you will want to manage the serving of pages slightly differently. While you could just have Mongrel receive and process all requests, there are many ways to improve on this.

First of all, you will want to run more than one Mongrel process at a time. When Mongrel processes a request, for part of the time that it's processing, it is blocked from accepting any new requests, since Rails is not thread-safe. Therefore, having more than one Mongrel process available to handle incoming requests means that requests are not being queued up, waiting for the process to become available. The optimum number of Mongrel processes to run depends on many factors, including the amount of memory in your server, how your application is written, and how much caching is used. For a great guide on how to choose the optimum number of Mongrel processes to run, read the article by Zed Shaw, the creator of Mongrel, at `http://mongrel.rubyforge.org/docs/how_many_mongrels.html`.

Also, although Mongrel is great at serving up dynamically created Rails pages, it is not the fastest tool for serving static content such as images—a standard web server can do this much faster. Therefore, we will use a web server to capture incoming requests. Depending on the request, it will either be forwarded to an instance of Mongrel or, if it is a request for a static file, served directly by the web server.

The web server should also act as a load balancer, allowing us to distribute requests across a number of Mongrel instances. These instances may be on the same machine, or they could even be on multiple machines.

There are a large number of web servers and load balancers to choose from. Some of the most popular follow:

- Apache (`http://httpd.apache.org`) is currently the most famous and widely used web server on the Internet. It is an open source project and is very powerful and flexible, but it is also resource hungry. Therefore, it may not be the best choice for a shared environment or memory-constrained VPS.

- lighttpd (`http://lighttpd.net`) is another open source web server, and it has a very light memory footprint. It is very fast and efficient and a great choice for serving Rails applications. At the time of this writing, there are problems with the `mod_proxy` implementation, making it currently unsuitable for use in conjunction with Mongrel. However, the software is under constant development, and I highly recommend that you read the project's blog for the latest updates.

- LiteSpeed (`http://litespeedtech.com`) is a closed source web server that has very good support for Rails. There is a free version available, but for high-traffic websites, you will need to purchase a license.

- Nginx (`http://nginx.net`), pronounced engine-x, is a very fast, very lightweight open source web server that provides load balancing and incredibly fast static file serving.

The best method of configuring a production Rails environment with a web server and load balancer is constantly under debate. Also, the choice of web server may be outside of your control if you are in a corporate environment. Then too, you may simply have a personal preference. To find out more about the various configuration methods, it is a good idea to get involved in the Rails deployment group at Google Groups: `http://groups.google.com/group/rubyonrails-deployment/`.

I will demonstrate deploying the application using Apache, since it is the most common web server in use at the moment.

Automating Deployment with Capistrano and Deprec

To help us automate our application deployment tasks, we are going to use a couple of utilities, Capistrano and Deprec.

Capistrano (formerly known as SwitchTower) was developed by Jamis Buck, one of the Rails core development team. It is a tool that allows you to write deployment recipes, which are instructions on how and where your application should be deployed. In the most simple scenario, a deployment recipe will be just the location of your source code together with the addresses of your production server and database server. However, if you have a more complex configuration, you can write recipes that perform multiple tasks on multiple servers, such as performing backups, creating links, and restarting application servers. This is similar in concept to the tools Ant and `make`.

■**Note** The full manual for Capistrano can be found online at `http://manuals.rubyonrails.com/read/book/17`.

Deprec, short for Deployment Recipes, was written by Mike Bailey and is a collection of Capistrano recipes that allow you to set up a production server with the minimum amount of effort. The Deprec home page can be found at `http://deprec.rubyforge.org`.

The version of Deprec that we will be using (1.3.1) will automatically install and configure an Ubuntu 6.06 server with Rails, Apache, Subversion, and MySQL. At the time of this writing, Deprec only works on Linux or Mac OS X. There are documented workarounds for Windows available at `http://brainassembly.blogspot.com/2007/02/deploying-rails-from-windows.html`, but future releases of Deprec are likely to work with Windows.

■**Note** Deprec is currently being very actively developed, so I highly recommend that you check the Deprec home page to find out the latest developments and changes to the software.

Preparing Your Server

In order to use Deprec, your server will need to be running Ubuntu 6.06.1 Desktop or Server Edition. You do not need to install Rails on the machine manually; Deprec will do this for you.

■**Note** You may wish to practice deploying your application with a local machine running Ubuntu Desktop Edition, or you may wish to rent a remote VPS.

Capistrano and Deprec communicate with your servers using Secure Shell (SSH), but Ubuntu does not come with an SSH server installed by default, so you will need to install the SSH server software yourself.

Do this by opening a terminal window on the Ubuntu server and entering the following command:

```
$ sudo apt-get install openssh-server
```

On both Ubuntu Desktop and Server, you should create a user on the machine that you will use to deploy the application. You may find it useful to create a user specifically for deployment. For instance, to create a user called `deploy` on the server, use the following command:

```
$ sudo useradd --create-home --groups admin deploy
```

Set a password for this user using the following command:

```
$ sudo passwd deploy
```

To make your life easier, creating a personal SSH key will allow you to log in and deploy to your server without constantly entering your password. If you already have an SSH key, skip this step. If not, from your home directory on your development machine, enter the following command:

```
$ ssh-keygen -t rsa
```

This will create two files, id_rsa and id_rsa.pub, in a directory called .ssh within your home directory.

Installing Capistrano and Deprec

You now need to install Capistrano to your local development machine. Capistrano is distributed as a Ruby gem, so you simply install it with the following command:

```
$ gem install capistrano --include-dependencies
```

```
Successfully installed capistrano-1.4.1
```

Deprec is also distributed as a Ruby gem. Install it with the following command:

```
$ gem install deprec --include-dependencies
```

```
Successfully installed deprec-1.3.1
```

Configuring Your Application for Capistrano and Deprec

Before you create a deployment recipe, you need to set up Capistrano to use the Deprec recipes. This is done by creating a file called .caprc in your application's root directory that simply consists of the command require 'deprec/recipes'.

You can easily do this by entering the following command while in the railscoders directory:

```
$ echo "require 'deprec/recipes'" >> ./.caprc
```

To check that Capistrano is now using the Deprec recipes, list the predefined Capistrano tasks by entering the following command:

```
$ cap show_tasks
```

A long list of the available recipes is shown. If the install_rails_stack recipe is listed as follows, Deprec is installed correctly:

```
...
install_rails_stack              setup_rails_host takes a stock standard ubuntu
                                 'dapper' 6.06.1 server and installs everything
                                 needed to be a rails machine
...
```

You now need to create a deployment recipe for your application, specifying where the application will be deployed and the name of the application. Do this by entering the following command from the root directory of your application:

```
$ deprec --apply-to .
```

```
    exists  config
    create  config/deploy.rb
```

This creates a new configuration file called config/deploy.rb, which is shown in Listing 14-1.

Listing 14-1. *The Deployment Configuration File, deploy.rb*

```
require 'deprec/recipes'

# ============================================================================
# ROLES
# ============================================================================
# You can define any number of roles, each of which contains any number of
# machines. Roles might include such things as :web, or :app, or :db, defining
# what the purpose of each machine is. You can also specify options that can
# be used to single out a specific subset of boxes in a particular role, like
# :primary => true.

set :domain, "www.mynewsite.com"
role :web, domain
role :app, domain
role :db,  domain, :primary => true


# ============================================================================
# REQUIRED VARIABLES
# ============================================================================
# You must always specify the application and repository for every recipe. The
# repository must be the URL of the repository you want this recipe to
# correspond to. The deploy_to path must be the path on each machine that will
# form the root of the application path.

set :application, "application"
set :deploy_to, "/var/www/apps/#{application}"
```

```
# XXX we may not need this - it doesn't work on windows
# XXX set :user, ENV['USER']
set :repository, "svn+ssh://#{user}@#{domain}#{deploy_to}/repos/trunk"
set :rails_env, "production"

# Automatically symlink these directories from current/public to shared/public.
# set :app_symlinks, %w{photo, document, asset}


# ==============================================================================
# APACHE OPTIONS
# ==============================================================================
set :apache_server_name, domain
# set :apache_server_aliases, %w{alias1 alias2}
# set :apache_default_vhost, true # force use of apache_default_vhost_config
# set :apache_default_vhost_conf, "/etc/httpd/conf/default.conf"
# set :apache_conf, "/etc/httpd/conf/apps/#{application}.conf"
# set :apache_ctl, "/etc/init.d/httpd"
# set :apache_proxy_port, 8000
# set :apache_proxy_servers, 2
# set :apache_proxy_address, "127.0.0.1"
# set :apache_ssl_enabled, false
# set :apache_ssl_ip, "127.0.0.1"
# set :apache_ssl_forward_all, false
# set :apache_ssl_chainfile, false



# ==============================================================================
# MONGREL OPTIONS
# ==============================================================================
# set :mongrel_servers, apache_proxy_servers
# set :mongrel_port, apache_proxy_port
set :mongrel_address, apache_proxy_address
# set :mongrel_environment, "production"
# set :mongrel_config, "/etc/mongrel_cluster/#{application}.conf"
# set :mongrel_user, user
# set :mongrel_group, group


# ==============================================================================
# MYSQL OPTIONS
# ==============================================================================


# ==============================================================================
# SSH OPTIONS
# ==============================================================================
# ssh_options[:keys] = %w(/path/to/my/key /path/to/another/key)
# ssh_options[:port] = 25
```

Open the `deploy.rb` file, because you need to modify this file to suit your own configuration.

The first change is to set the location of your production server. This is done by changing the `set :domain` statement at line 12. If you have a remote server with a registered host name, you should enter this. I will be demonstrating with a server on my local network, so I will just enter the IP address of this server as follows:

```
...
# :primary => true.

set :domain, "192.168.1.6"
role :web, domain
role :app, domain
...
```

You now need to set the location of your source code repository, as Capistrano will currently only deploy by checking out code from a source control repository. If you are already using an SCM, you should enter the location of this repository in the `set :repository` statement at line 30. Capistrano assumes that you are using Subversion. If you are using different source control software, you can add a configuration line: `set :scm`. The currently supported modules are `:subversion`, `:cvs`, and `:darcs`.

However, if you are not currently using SCM, you can add an extra statement defining the production server to be the SCM machine. To do this, add the following statement at line 16:

```
...
role :app, domain
role :db,  domain, :primary => true
role :scm, domain
...
```

You now need to set the name of the application at the `set :application` statement at line 25. Set this to the same name as the application directory that you used when you originally created your Rails application. Since my application is called `railscoders`, the line looks like this:

```
...
set :application, "railscoders"
set :deploy_to, "/var/www/apps/#{application}"
...
```

Next, edit line 29 to set the name of the user on the server that will be used to deploy the application. We set up a user called `deploy` earlier, so we will use this. Change the line as follows:

```
...
# XXX we may not need this - it doesn't work on windows
# XXX set :user, ENV['USER']
set :user, "deploy"
set :repository, "svn+ssh://#{user}@#{domain}#{deploy_to}/repos/trunk"
...
```

Now edit the SSH options at line 73, giving the path to your SSH keys on your local development machine. Deprec will copy the public key to the remote server, but you need to specify the filename of the private key, for example:

```
...
# ssh_options[:keys] = %w(/path/to/my/key /path/to/another/key)
ssh_options[:keys] = %w(/Users/alan/.ssh/id_rsa)
# ssh_options[:port] = 25
```

Depending on the setup of your server, you may also need to change the port used to connect to the machine using SSH. This will normally be the default of port 25.

Next, you can copy your SSH key to the production server by entering the following command on your development machine:

```
$ cap setup_ssh_keys
```

```
  * executing task setup_ssh_keys
  * executing "sudo  test -d ~/.ssh || mkdir ~/.ssh"
    servers: ["192.168.1.6"]
Password:
    [192.168.1.6] executing command
    command finished
  * executing "sudo  chmod 0700 ~/.ssh"
    servers: ["192.168.1.6"]
    [192.168.1.6] executing command
    command finished
    servers: ["192.168.1.6"]
  * uploading /home/alan/.ssh/authorized_keys
 ** uploading data to 192.168.1.6:/home/alan/.ssh/authorized_keys
  * done uploading data to 192.168.1.6:/home/alan/.ssh/authorized_keys
    upload finished
```

You can now use SSH to connect to your server from your development machine without entering your password every time.

You should also make sure that the production settings in your database configuration file, config/database.yml, are as you require. Deprec will create and set up a production database using the values in this file, so you should change the database username and password. As an example, my settings are shown in Listing 14-2.

Listing 14-2. *The Production Settings in the Database Configuration File*

```
...
production:
  adapter: mysql
  database: railscoders_production
  username: railscoders
  password: cOmp73xpa55wd
  host: localhost
```

It is good practice not to use the MySQL root user and to make sure you set a password for the user that you use. In this case, I have used a MySQL user called railscoders with a password of cOmp73xpa55wd. This user should only have permissions to access the railscoders_production database. We will create this user in the "Preparing the Server for your Application" section, after MySQL has been installed.

Installing the Rails Software Stack

The installation of all the software required to run Rails on your server is automated by a Deprec recipe, install_rails_stack. Simply enter the following command on your development machine:

```
$ cap install_rails_stack
```

```
* executing task install_rails_stack
  * executing task setup_user_perms
  * executing "sudo  grep 'deploy:' /etc/group || sudo /usr/sbin/groupadd deploy"
    servers: ["192.168.1.6"]
  ...
 ** [out :: 192.168.1.6] /etc/rc3.d/S20httpd -> ../init.d/httpd
 ** [out :: 192.168.1.6] /etc/rc4.d/S20httpd -> ../init.d/httpd
 ** [out :: 192.168.1.6] /etc/rc5.d/S20httpd -> ../init.d/httpd
    command finished
```

This will take a little while, as it has to retrieve all of the software from the Internet and compile and install it.

There are also Deprec recipes to install other software that may be required by your application. In our case, RailsCoders makes use of ImageMagick and RMagick. You can install these on the production server by entering the following command on your development machine:

```
$ cap install_rmagick
```

```
  * executing task install_rmagick
  * executing task install_image_magic
  ...
```

The RailsCoders application also uses some extra gems, ar_mailer and RedCloth. We need to manually install these on the server. Log in to your remote server using SSH, for example:

```
$ ssh deploy@192.168.1.7
```

Now install the necessary gems using the following command:

```
$ sudo gem install ar_mailer redcloth
```

```
Successfully installed ar_mailer-1.1.0
Installing ri documentation for ar_mailer-1.1.0...
Installing RDoc documentation for ar_mailer-1.1.0...
Successfully installed RedCloth-3.0.4
```

Preparing the Server for Your Application

Next, you need to create the application-specific directories on the server. To do this, from the project's root directory on your development machine, enter the following command:

```
$ cap deprec_setup
```

During this setup process, you will be asked to enter the MySQL database password. MySQL is installed with a blank password for the root user, and this is the password that is required, so just press the Enter key to enter the blank password.

The Deprec script will automatically create the production database user that is specified in the database.yml file.

You should also take this opportunity to change the MySQL root user password. To do this, enter the following command, substituting your own choice of password:

```
$ mysqladmin -u root password Sup3rS3cr3t
```

Setting Up a Subversion Server

If you are already using an SCM and you have entered the details of your repository into the deploy.rb file, you should skip this step.

However, if you are not already using an SCM, this step will create a new Subversion repository in the production server, add your code to the repository, and check out the code to your development machine.

Capistrano only deploys code from an SCM repository, so even if you do not want to use an SCM (although I highly recommend that you do), you must create a repository for your code.

Run the Deprec task to set up the SCM for you:

```
$ cap setup_scm
```

After adding your code to the newly created repository, Deprec will check out a working copy of the code into a directory with the suffix _machine. You should now archive the copy of the application that you have been using and use this version, which is under source control. In my case, the directory is railscoders_machine.

Change to this directory with the following command:

```
$ cd ../railscoders_machine
```

Deploying Your Application

We are now ready to actually deploy the application to the server. In the newly created source-controlled directory, enter the following command:

```
$ cap deploy_with_migrations
```

```
  * executing task deploy_with_migrations
  * executing task update_code
  * querying latest revision...
  ...
 ** [out :: 192.168.1.6] mongrel::stop reported an error. Use mongrel_rails
mongrel::stop -h to get help.
 ** [out :: 192.168.1.6] mongrel_rails stop -P log/mongrel.8001.pid -c
/var/www/apps/railscoders/current
 ** [out :: 192.168.1.6] Starting 2 Mongrel servers...
    command finished
```

Finally, you need to restart the Apache web server with the following command:

```
$ cap restart_apache
```

```
  * executing task restart_apache
  * executing "sudo  /etc/init.d/httpd restart"
    servers: ["192.168.1.7"]
Enter password for /Users/alan/.ssh/id_rsa:
    [192.168.1.7] executing command
 ** [out :: 192.168.1.7] httpd not running, trying to start
    command finished
```

That's it—your site is now deployed and running on your production server. To test this, simply go to the site with your browser. You will be presented with the default RailsCoders home page.

Optimizing and Scaling RailsCoders

Previously, we haven't really worried about optimizing our application, except for adding some database indexes. However, now that our application is in the wild, we should start to consider ways to improve the response speed for our users.

Watching the Log Files

Look first in your application's log files to start understanding any performance problems. If you take a look at the log file for your application on your local development server, log/development.log, you will see the actual SQL queries made for each page request. For example, the show action of the articles controller produces an output like this:

```
Processing ArticlesController#show (for 127.0.0.1 at 2007-03-27 22:21:40) [GET]
  Session ID: e30c6bb8ae9352a334b352d650b0df43
  Parameters: {"action"=>"show", "id"=>"10", "controller"=>"articles"}
  Article Columns (0.003368)   SHOW FIELDS FROM articles
  Article Load (0.000457)   SELECT * FROM articles WHERE (articles.`published` = 1
AND articles.`id` = '10') LIMIT 1
Rendering actionshowlayoutfalsecontent_typetext/html within layouts/application
Rendering articles/show
  Category Columns (0.035837)   SHOW FIELDS FROM categories
  Category Load (0.002032)   SELECT * FROM categories WHERE (categories.`id` = 1)
Rendered layouts/_menu (0.12141)
Completed in 0.19310 (5 reqs/sec) | Rendering: 0.14069 (72%) | DB: 0.04169 (21%) |
200 OK [http://localhost/articles/10]
```

You can see here that the actual time spent processing the database query is shown, along with the total time spent processing the request.

If you look at the production.log file on the production server, you will notice that the full SQL query is not shown, but the time taken rendering the page is still shown. If you are finding that a particular page is taking a long time to respond, the log files are the first place you should look to help you understand if its slow response is being caused by the SQL query.

The MySQL EXPLAIN command will detail how the SQL query is processed and may help you see how to improve the query or where to add extra indexes.

Caching

The easiest way to improve the speed of your application is to use caching. Rails supports a number of different levels of caching; the level of caching you can use depends on the amount of user-specific data on a page.

By default, caching is disabled for the development environment and enabled for the production environment. If you wish to temporarily enable caching for development mode, edit your config/environments/development.rb file by changing the setting for config.action_controller.perform_caching to true as follows:

```
config.action_controller.perform_caching            = true
```

Page Caching

The fastest and simplest method of caching in Rails is page caching. However, you can only make use of page caching if the entire page is identical for all users and if the page is available for all users, that is, it's not a page accessible by only logged-in users.

Currently RailsCoders does not have any pages that are exactly the same for all users. Since we always render the sidebar, and it changes depending on whether the user is logged in or not, we cannot use page caching unless we change the behavior of our application.

We might want to change the pages controller to use a different layout that does not include the sidebar menu. Then, it would be possible to cache the index and show methods of the pages controller. You would do this by adding caches_page statement within the PagesController class as follows:

```
caches_page :index, :show
```

When page caching is used and specified for a specific method in a controller, the first time that page is requested, the rendered page is saved as a static HTML file within the public directory of your application. The actual file is stored in a subdirectory of public corresponding to the controller name. For instance, the page /pages/1-welcome-page would be stored in public/pages/1-welcome-page.html.

When another user attempts to access this page, the static page is returned by the web server rather than the request being processed by Rails, resulting in a very fast response.

However, you need to bear in mind what happens if the contents of this page actually change. Since every request for that cached page will be returned by the web server rather than Rails and, therefore, the contents are never updated, we need a mechanism for indicating when the cached page expires. You can either do this on a specific event or at a specific time interval, using cron.

To make a page expire on an event, you create classes called cache sweepers. These work in a similar way to callbacks, allowing you to make pages expire on the events after_create, after_update, and after_destroy.

For a very complete tutorial on using page caching, go to http://www.railsenvy.com/2007/2/28/rails-caching-tutorial. Page caches can provide very fast responses, since they bypass running Rails entirely. However, they are also very limited, allowing you to only cache pages that will be completely identical for every user.

Action Caching

Action caching is similar to page caching, except that the requests are processed by Rails rather than just by the web server. This means that a before_filter in your controller class will be run before the cached page is returned. Because of this, you can have items that are only available to a logged-in user.

Action caching renders the page on the first request and saves this rendered page. By default, the page is saved in the tmp/cache/ directory of your application. Since this caches the entire output of an action, action caching is also limited to pages that are the same for all users. In the case of our application, the sidebar also limits the use of action caching, since the same page may be rendered differently for different users.

■**Note** In the same way as page caching, you create cache sweepers to empty the cache on specific actions.

Action caching is slower than page caching, since the server has to process the request by Rails, but since all Rails has to do is output a prerendered file, it does not have to perform any database queries or perform any other processing.

Fragment Caching

Fragment caching involves caching just a section of a page rather than the entire page. This makes it very useful for sites, like RailsCoders, where every page is dynamic. With fragment caching, you can cache snippets of a page, such as a list of objects on a page or any other section that either requires a complex SQL query or takes a reasonable amount of time to process and render by Rails.

You add fragment caches within an ERb file by putting the cacheable data within a Ruby block called `cache`. The first time the page is rendered, the output of this block is saved to a file within the `tmp/cache/` directory of your project.

The next time the page is rendered, this cached fragment will be automatically loaded and inserted into the page output. However, the controller method will still be executed, meaning that any SQL queries will be executed even though the output is cached. To prevent this, you can add conditional statements in your action methods to check if a fragment already exists for this action before performing the query.

■**Note** You can also make fragment caches expire by defining cache sweepers.

For a complete explanation and tutorial of action and fragment caching, see `http://www.railsenvy.com/2007/3/20/ruby-on-rails-caching-tutorial-part-2`.

Fragment caching is very powerful, as it allows you to target slow or complex sections within certain pages.

Benchmarking

To assess the speed of your site and the impact of any optimizing that you do, you should consider performing benchmarking test of your application. Valid benchmarking tests are important in helping you get the most from your server and your application, but they can be somewhat complex to set up.

For a thorough explanation on how to perform benchmarking tests using the `httperf` tool, there is an excellent screencast by Geoffrey Grosenbach available at `http://peepcode.com/products/benchmarking-with-httperf`.

By benchmarking your application, you can also find the optimum number of Mongrel processes that you should run on your server. If you try to run too many, your server will run out of memory and start to use swap, so you need to make sure you run as many as possible without running out of memory.

Summary

In this chapter, we talked about the different options available for hosting your Rails application, along with the merits of different web servers.

I showed you how to change your application to use the database for the session store and talked about the other session storage options. We then installed Capistrano and Deprec and used them to install all of the necessary tools onto the production server, along with automatically setting up the database, SSH keys, and source control software. We then deployed the RailsCoders application onto the server, along with performing the database migrations.

The RailsCoders application is now live, so we talked about ways we can study the performance of the application and optimize the performance of the site by adding caching. Best practices for optimizing Rails applications are constantly evolving. As the popularity of your site grows, you may need to adapt your application to scale properly. To stay on top of the latest developments regarding Rails performance, you should read the Rails Express blog and the Rails blogs and groups discussed in Chapter 1.

Index

■Symbols & Numerics

% prompt, 223
37signals, Basecamp tool, 4

■A

accessing Ruby RSS parsing library, 324
account controller
  for adding users and groups, 49
  creating, 57–58
  functional test for, 70–72
  mobile interface, 373
account login view, mobile interface, 374
accounts, mobile site, 354
action caching, 394
Action Web Service (AWS), 181, 186
ActionMailer module
  configuring, 217–218
  e-mail template and, 219
  multi-part e-mails and, 222
ActionPack package, 6
actions
  See also index action; show action
  adding, articles controller, 96–97
  comments controller create, 226
  create, 37–38, 239
  delete forum, 130
  destroy, 240
  edit, 39–40, 204, 239
  naming, 220
  new, 37–38, 203–204, 238
  newsletter feature, 239–240
  restricting to moderators, 142–143
  sendmails, 39–40, 240
  update, 204
ActiveRecord migrations, 30

ActiveRecord package, 6, 279
ActiveRecordStore method, 380–381
acts_as_attachment plug-in, 192
acts_as_taggable gem, 279
acts_as_taggable plug-in, 279
acts_as_taggable_on_steroids plug-in
  installing, 282–283
  using in photo gallery, 279–282
Add a new friend page, 264
adding users and groups
  administration views
    creating, 63
    user edit, 66–67
    user index, 64–65
  controllers
    account, 49, 57–58
    creating, 55
    roles, 50
    users, 50, 55–57
  extending user management system, 81
  overview of, 47
  Role model
    creating, 72–74
    join table and, 48–49
  roles
    adding, 72, 90–91
    administering, 76–79
    functional testing, 79–80
    of user, checking, 74–76, 126
  session-handling library, 53–54
  sessions and cookies, 50
  testing
    functional, 68–72, 81
    unit, 67–68

user account views
   creating, 58
   login, 61
   new user, 58–61
   user show, 62–63
   User model
      creating, 51–53
      database fields required for, 48
      defining, 47
addressee of e-mail, looking at, 226
Admin user, 74
administering roles, 76–79
administration views, creating
   overview of, 63
   user edit, 66–67
   user index, 64–65
Ajax (Asynchronous JavaScript and XML), 278
Ajax callbacks, 292
Allen, Dean, 83
Amazon Web Service Simple Storage
      Service, 192
Apache web server, 383
APIs
   See also Blogger API; Flickr API,
      integrating; Google Maps API,
      integrating
   for blogging engine, 155, 188–189
   further development using mashups, 326
   HTTP authentification for, 103–105
   Liquid, 331
   MetaWeblog, 156, 181
   Movable Type, 156
   public, free, 301, 327
   XML, 101–102
app/models/page.rb file, editing to add
      validations, 32
application manager (Instant Rails), 10
application.js file, 313
application.rb file, 54
applicationwide helper file listing, 236
ar_mailer plug-in
   description of, 219
   installing, 230–232

Article model
   creating, 87
   database fields for, 84
article views
   articles admin, 100
   edit article, 100
   new article, 99
   overview of, 98–99
   show article, 99
article, new, creating, 101
articles admin view, 100
articles controller
   actions, adding, 96–97
   creating, 92–93
   description of, 86
   functional tests for, 112–113
   mobile interface, 360–361
   pagination, 93
   returning XML data, 94
   RSS and Atom feeds, 94–96
articles index view, mobile interface, 361–362
articles show view, mobile interface, 362
Assign Role link, 79
Asynchronous JavaScript and XML (Ajax), 278
Atom feeds and articles controller, 94–96
attachment_fu plug-in
   database fields for, 193
   description of, 192
   installing, 196
   methods, 194
automating deployment with Capistrano
      and Deprec
   configuring application, 385–389
   deploying application, 391–392
   installing Capistrano and Deprec, 385
   overview of, 383
   preparing server, 384–385
   preparing server for application, 391
   Rails software stack, installing, 390
   setting up subversion server, 391
AWS (Action Web Service), 181, 186

B

Bailey, Mike, 384

bandwidth and file size, 191

Bartelme, Wolfgang, 269

Basecamp tool (37signals), 4

benchmarking, 395

blog entry view with new user template, 345

blog entry, displaying, 168

blog name helper method, 161

blog settings migration, 159

blog title, adding to edit user profile page, 162

blog, description of, 153

Blogger API
    description of, 156
    method calls, defining, 182–183
    method code, writing, 184–186
    methods, 180–181

blogging engine
    See also blogging system
    building
        blog name helper method, 161
        blog title, adding to edit user profile page, 162
        blogging scaffolding code, generating, 156–157
        models' relationships and variations, 160
        resource mapping, 161
    controllers and views
        blogs controller, 178
        blogs index view, 179
        comments controller, 173–175
        edit entry view, 170–171
        entries controller, 164–165
        entries index view, 169–170
        entries show view, 166–168
        new entry view, 165
        overview of, 163
        removing generated layouts, 163
    further development of, 189
    migrations for, 158–159

new comment notifier, building
    automating mailer tests, 228–230
    calling mailer from comments controller, 226–227
    mailer model, creating, 220–223
    manually testing, 223–226
    testing mailer from within application, 227

notifying owners of new comments in blog, 219

overview of, 153

requirements for
    APIs, 155
    blogs controller, 155
    Comment model, 154
    comments controller, 155
    entries controller, 155
    Entry model, 153
    User model, 154

testing
    automated, of API, 188–189
    comments controller, 176–177
    desktop blogging client, using, 186–187
    entries controller, 171–173
    Web services, 186

user profiles, adding latest blog entries to, 177–178

XML-RPC interface, creating
    Action Web Service and, 181
    Blogger API method calls, defining, 182–183
    Blogger API method code, writing, 184–186
    overview of, 180–181
    Web service code, generating, 181

blogging system
    See also blogging engine
    adding user-definable templates to
        further development of, 348
        installing Liquid, 332
        Liquid API and, 331
        Liquid markup and, 331–332
        Liquid plug-in and, 330

manually testing, 343–346

requirements for, 329–330

testing usertemplates controller, 346–348

building templating feature

creating Liquid drop files, 333–336

creating Liquid filters, 336–337

rendering Liquid templates, 342

Usertemplate model, 337–338

usertemplate views, 340–341

usertemplates controller, 338–340

blogs controller

creating, 178

description of, 155

mobile interface, 370

blogs index view

blogging engine, 179

mobile interface, 371

blogs, mobile site, 354

body field, 26

body of text-only part of e-mail, displaying, 226

Buck, Jamis, 383

built-in testing, 6

■C

caching

action caching, 394

counter cache, 117, 124, 153

fragment caching, 395

page caching, 393–394

calling mailer from comments controller, 226–227

Capistrano

configuring application for, 385–389

deploying application, 391–392

installing, 385

overview of, 383

preparing server, 384–385

preparing server for application, 391

setting up subversion server, 391

categories controller, 86, 105–107

Category model

creating, 88

database fields for, 85

category views

admin, 109

edit, 108

index, 108

new, 108

category_id, nullifying on deletion, 89

Çelik, Tantek, 249

checking roles of user, 74–76, 126

commands

generate, 92

generate controller, 33–34

rails, 14

rake, 68

script/generate migration, 29

Comment model, 154

comments controller

calling mailer from, 226–227

creating, 173–175

description of, 155

functional tests, 229–230

testing, 176–177

comments table migration, 158–159

config/routes.rb file, 22

configuring

ActionMailer, 217–218

application for Capistrano and Deprec, 385–389

Rails to use database, 18–19

content management system

See also controllers, creating; Page model

default page, setting up, 41

extending, 44

layout, creating, 23–26

sidebar menu, adding link from, 41

controller layer, 5

controllers

See also specific controllers

for adding users and groups, 49–50

for blogging engine, 155

creating
    account, 57–58
    deleting pages, 40
    displaying pages, 36
    editing pages, 39–40
    links and permalinks, creating, 36–37
    listing available pages, 34–36
    new pages, adding, 37–38
    overview of, 33–34, 55
    users, 55–57
for discussion forum, 119
for friends list
    building, 258–259
    testing, 272–273
for mobile application, 355
for News module, 86
for photo gallery, 195
for tagging system in photo gallery
    creating, 285
    tags, writing, 286
    user tags, writing, 288
for viewing tags, 278
mobile interface
    account, 373
    articles, 360–361
    blogs, 370
    entries, 368
    forums, 362
    pages, 360
    photos, 371
    post, 365
    topics, 363
    user show view, 368
    user_photos, 372
    users, 367
usertemplates
    creating, 338–340
    description of, 330
    testing, 346–348
convention over configuration design
        principle, 4
cookies, for adding users and groups, 50

counter cache
    for blogging service, 153
    for discussion forum, 117
    posts, adding to users model, 124
create action, 37–38, 239
Create New Newsletter screen, 242
cron tool (Unix), 380
CSS
    for forum tables, adding, 127
    for photo gallery, 208
cURL utility, 101

■**D**

database
    configuring Rails to use, 18–19
    creating, 18
    Page model
        creating, 28–33
        description of, 26–27
    pages controller file, 27
    testing, 19–20
    for testing, creating, 42
    using as storage system, 193
database fields
    Article model, 84
    Category model, 85
    Comment model, 154
    db_files table, 193
    Entry model, 153
    forum model, 118
    friendships schema, 250
    for models using attachment_fu
        plug-in, 193
    newsletter, 219
    Photo model, 195, 302
    post model, 119
    Role model, 48
    Role_Users join table, 49
    Tag model, 280
    Tagging model, 280
    topic model, 118
    User model, 48, 154
    Usertemplate model, 330

database migrations. *See* migrations

database software and community web
    sites, 7

date format, defining, 62

db_files table, 193

dedicated server hosting, 381–382

default mappings, 22

default page, setting up, 41

defining
    Blogger API method calls, 182–183
    date format, 62
    post model, 119
    relationships among models, 88
    Role model, 48
    topic model, 118
    User model, 47–48
    validations, 89

delete forum action, 130

deleting
    See also removing
    pages, 40
    posts, 141
    topics, 136

deploying application
    automating with Capistrano and Deprec
        configuring application, 385–389
        deploying application, 391–392
        installing Capistrano and Deprec, 385
        overview of, 383
        preparing server, 384–385
        preparing server for application, 391
        Rails software stack, installing, 390
        setting up subversion server, 391
    deployment mode vs. production
        mode, 379
    host provider, choosing, 381–382
    session storage, 380–381
    web server, choosing, 382–383

deployment mode, running application
    in, 379

Deprec
    configuring application for, 385–389
    deploying application, 391–392
    installing, 385
    overview of, 383
    preparing server, 384–385
    preparing server for application, 391
    Rails software stack, installing, 390
    setting up subversion server, 391

desktop blogging client, testing using,
    186–187

destroy method, 40

developer community, 17

development mode
    ActionMailer and, 218
    e-mail delivery and, 224

disabling users, 65

discussion forum
    building
        checking user role for moderator
            rights, 126
        forum, topic, and post models, 120–121
        layout template and style sheet,
            modifying, 126–127
        migration scripts, 123–125
        model relationships, 121–122
        model validations, 122–123
        nested resource route mappings,
            adding, 126
    description of, 117
    forum controller and views
        delete forum action, 130
        forum index action, 127
        forum index page, 128
        forum new and edit pages, 129–130
        manually testing, 131
        new forum, creating, 129
        show action, 129
    further development of, 150–151
    link to sidebar menu, adding, 141

posts controller and views
  deleting post, 141
  editing post, 139–141
  new post, creating, 138–139
  posts index page, 136–137
requirements for
  controllers, 119
  moderator role, 119
  overview of, 117
  post model, defining, 119
  topic model, defining, 118
restricting actions to moderators, 142–143
testing
  fixtures, creating, 143–144
  functional, 144–150
  overview of, 143
  topics and posts, 141
topic controller and views
  deleting topics, 136
  editing topics, 135
  new topic view, 133–135
  topic index action, 131–132
  topic index page, 132–133
  topic show action, 136
displaying
  body of text-only part of e-mail, 226
  latest Flickr photos, 322–325
  location data as map, 308–311
  pages, 36
domain-specific language (DSL), 6
don't repeat yourself (DRY) design
    principle, 4

■**E**
Ecto, testing using, 186–187
edit action, 39–40, 239
edit article view, 100
edit category view, 108
edit entry view, 170–171
edit photo view, 204
edit user profile page, adding blog title to, 162
edit user view, adding Flickr username to, 319
edit.rhtml file, 66–67

editing
  blog title, 162
  pages, 39–40
  posts, 139–141
  topics, 135
editing photo screen, 297
editor role
  adding, 90–91
  for News module, 85
e-mail, sending
  See also newsletter feature
  ActionMailer module, 217–218
  further development of system for, 244
  new comment notifier, building
    automating mailer tests, 228–230
    calling mailer from comments
      controller, 226–227
    mailer model, creating, 220–223
    manually testing, 223–226
    testing mailer from within
      application, 227
  requirements for
    newsletters, 219–220
    notification of new comments in
      blog, 219
    overview of, 218
empty migration, running, 19
enabling users, 65
entity relationship diagrams for Article and
    Category models, 85
entries controller
  creating, 164–165
  description of, 155
  mobile interface, 368
  testing, 171–173
entries helper file, 161
entries index view
  blogging engine, 169–170, 175
  mobile interface, 369–370
entries show view
  blogging engine, 166–168, 175
  mobile interface, 370
entries table migration, 158

Entry model, 153
entry view
    blog, 345
    edit, 170–171
    new, 165
    show, 166–167
ERb templating system, 24
error messages for method, 37
extending
    blogging engine, 189
    content management system, 44
    discussion forum, 150–151
    e-mail system, 244
    friends list, 274
    mashups, 326
    mobile interface, 377
    news blog system, 115
    photo gallery, 215
    tags, 298
    templates, 348
    user management system, 81

■F
Fakes, Tom, 287
FCKeditor, 44
feature requirements, specifying for site, 21
file size, 191
file system
    session storage and, 380
    using for storage of uploaded files, 194
file_column plug-in, 192
flash, success notices stored in, 38
flash messages, 58
Flickr API, integrating
    building feature
        key, obtaining, 318
        latest photos, displaying, 322–325
        overview of, 317
        user database fields, creating, 318–319
        user nsid, retrieving, 320–322
        username, adding to edit user view, 319
    further development using mashups, 326

overview of, 316
    requirements for, 317
form for method, 37
forum controller and views
    delete forum action, 130
    description of, 119, 127
    forum index action, 127
    forum index page, 128
    forum new and edit pages, 129–130
    manually testing, 131
    new forum, creating, 129
    show action, 129
forum index action, 127
forum index page, 128
forum index view, 363
forum model
    building, 120–121
    validations, 122–123
forum model file, 121
forum new and edit pages, 129–130
forums, mobile site, 354
forums controller, mobile interface, 362
forums functional tests, 145–146
fragment caching, 395
framework, 4
Fried, Jason, 4
friends index page, 264
friends list
    controller
        building, 258–259
        testing, 272–273
    database migrations, creating, 251–253
    description of, 247
    friends resource
        building, 254–257
        description of, 249–251
    further development of, 274
    requirements for, 249
    showing users' latest activities, 251
    sidebar menu links, adding, 267–268
    styling, 269–271
    testing, 274

user's latest activity, updating, 257–258

views

edit, 266–267

index, 260–262

new, 262–266

XFN and, 247–249

functional testing

account controller, 70–72

back-end, of blogging API, 188–189

comments controller, 176–177

discussion forum

forums functional tests, 145–146

overview of, 144

posts controller functional tests, 148–150

topics functional tests, 146–148

entries controller, 171–173

friends controller, 272–273

mailer model, 229–230

news blog system, 112–114

overview of, 68

photo gallery, 212–215

roles, 79–81

user controller, 68–70

G

Garrett, Jesse James, 278

gems

acts_as_taggable, 279

installing Ruby on Rails as, 7

RedCloth, 84, 86–87

generate command, 92

generate controller command, 33–34

generated layouts, removing, 163

geocoder, 312

geographical fields, adding

to photo edit and new pages, 306–307

to photo schema, 305–306

Google Maps API, integrating

building feature

displaying location data as map, 308–311

geographical fields, adding, 305–307

key, obtaining, 303

selecting location of photo using map, 312–315

YM4R/GM plug-in, installing, 303–304

overview of, 301–302

requirements for, 302

Grosenbach, Geoffrey, 28

H

Hansson, David Heinemeier, 4, 279

Harman, Steve, 270

has and belongs to many (HABTM) relationship, 73, 249

has_many_polymorphs ActiveRecord plug-in, 279

hash, 48

header, e-mail, viewing, 226

helper methods

blog name, 161

paginate, 93

textilize, 84

uploading files, 212

xfn_rel_tag, 261–262

Hibbs, Curt, 9

Hodel, Eric, 219

host provider, choosing, 381–382

HTTP authentication for API

adding, 103–104

testing, 104–105

I

id field, 26

image file size, 191

ImageMagick, 195–196

index action

articles, 98

forums, 127

newsletters, 236–237

photos, 205

posts, 141

topics, 131–132

user photos, 204

index method, 34–36

index view
    articles, 361–362
    blogs, 179, 371
    categories, 108
    entries, 169–170, 175, 369–370
    forums, 128, 363
    friends, 260
    newsletters, 237
    pages, 35, 40
    photos, 205, 371
    posts, 137, 366–367
    tags, 287–288
    topics, 132, 364–365
    updated, 35
    user photos, 204–205, 372
    user tags, 289
    users, 64–65
    usertemplate, 340, 343
in-memory testing, 28
installing
    acts_as_taggable_on_steroids plug-in,
        282–283
    ar_mailer, 230–232
    attachment_fu plug-in, 196
    Capistrano and Deprec, 385
    ImageMagick and RMagick, 196
    on Linux, 12–13
    Liquid plug-in, 332
    on Mac OS X, 11–12
    overview of, 8
    Rails software stack, 390
    RedCloth gem, 86–87
    on Windows, 9–10
    YM4R/GM plug-in, 303–304
Instant Rails, 9–10
integrating Flickr API
    building feature
        key, obtaining, 318
        latest photos, displaying, 322–325
        overview of, 317
        user database fields, creating, 318–319

        user nsid, retrieving, 320–322
        username, adding to edit user view, 319
    overview of, 316
    requirements for, 317
integrating Google Maps API
    building feature
        displaying location data as map,
            308–311
        geographical fields, adding, 305–307
        key, obtaining, 303
        selecting location of photo using map,
            312–315
        YM4R/GM plug-in, installing, 303–304
    overview of, 301–302
    requirements for, 302
integrating OpenID into user accounts
        system, 81
integration testing
    description of, 79
    example of, 80
    mobile site, 376
    news blog system, 114–115

■J
join models, 249
join tables, 49, 72–74

■K
Kaes, Stefan, 380
key, obtaining
    Flickr API, 318
    Google Maps API, 303

■L
layout
    creating, 23–26
    generated, removing, 163
    mobile interface, 356
    mobile site, 353
layout template for discussion forum,
        modifying, 126–127
libraries
    Object/Relationship Mapping, 6
    Ruby RSS parsing, accessing, 324

session-handling, 53–54

tagging, 278–282

TMail, 225

lighttpd web server, 383

link to method, 35

links

 creating, 36–36

 from sidebar menu

  for discussion forum, 141

  for friends list, 267–268

  to gallery and new photo pages, 207

  for News module, 109

  to newsletters, 241

  overview of, 41

 to tag browser

  adding links on user profile page, 296

  adding tag links to photo show view, 295

  adding tags to sidebar menu, 295

 User and Role models, 49

Linux

 installing ImageMagick and RMagick on, 196

 installing on, 12–13

Liquid plug-in

 adding user-definable templates to blogging system, 330

 API, 331

 description of, 329

 drop files, creating, 333–336

 filters, creating, 336–337

 installing, 332

 markup, 331–332

 templates, rendering, 342

listing available pages, 34–36

listings

 account controller file, 57–58

 account controller functional test, 71

 add_tag method, 290

 add_tag RJS file, 293

 adding blog title to edit user profile page, 162

 adding tag index link to sidebar menu, 295

admin view of categories, 109

application layout file, 24

application.js file, 313

application.rb file, modifications to, 54

applicationwide helper file, 236

articles admin view, 100

articles integration test, 114

atom.rxml file, 95

backend controller file, 184

back-end functional tests, 188–189

Blogger API definition file, 183

Blogger Web service file, 184–186

blogs controller file, 178

blogs index view file, 179

categories controller file, 106–107

categories index view, 108

category create view, 108

category edit view, 108

comment drop file, 335

comment notification e-mail template, 221

comments controller create action, 226

comments controller file, 173

comments functional tests, 176–177

CSS style sheet

 to display XFN icons, 270–271

 for tag cloud, 288

deployment configuration file, deploy.rb, 386–388

edit article view, 100

edit page view, 39

edit post view, 140

edit_tag partial view, 291

edit_tag partial view updated, 294

entries controller file, 164–165

entries controller file updated, 342

entries controller functional tests file, 171–173

entries helper file, 161

entries index view, 169–170

entry drop file, 334

entry edit view file, 170–171

entry model, modifications to, 257

entry show view to add delete link, 175

Flickr username, adding to user edit view, 319

forum edit view, 130

forum index view, 128

forum model file, 121

forum new view, 130

friends controller file, 258–259

friends controller functional test file, 272–273

friends index view file, 260

friends resource mapping in routes.rb file, 254

friendship edit view, 266–267

friendship model file, 255

friendship model file updated, 255–257

friendship partial view, 260

friendship_with_edit partial view, 261

functional tests
   account controller, 71
   articles controller, 112–113
   back-end, 188–189
   comments, 176–177
   entries controller, 171–173
   friends controller, 272–273
   photos controller, 212–215
   topics controller, 146–148
   user templates, 347
   users controller, 69

gmaps_api_key.rb configuration file, 304

HTML new comment notification e-mail template, 222

index view updated, 35

Liquid text filters file, 336

login stories integration test file, 79

login system module, 53

login view, 61

mappings for entries, comments and blogs resources, 161

menu partial file updated, 267

menu view file updated, 41

migrations
   to add editor role, 90
   to add fields to user table, 159
   to add geographical coordinates to Photo model, 305
   to add last activity to users table, 253
   to add moderator role, 124
   to add posts counter cache to users model, 124
   to add tagging support, 283
   ar_mailer, 231
   to create comments table, 158–159
   to create entries table, 158
   Flickr user details, adding, 318
   friendships table, 252–253
   for newsletter, 233
   for Page model, 30
   for photos table, 198
   role_users table, 73
   user table, 51
   Usertemplates, 337

mobile account controller file, 374

mobile account login view, 374

mobile articles controller, 361

mobile articles index view, 361

mobile articles show view, 362

mobile blogs controller, 370

mobile blogs index view, 371

mobile CSS file, 357

mobile entries controller file, 369

mobile entries index view, 369

mobile entries show view, 370

mobile forum index view, 363

mobile forums controller, 362

mobile layout file, 356

mobile login integration test, 376

mobile pages controller file, 360

mobile pages show action, 360

mobile photos controller, 371–372

mobile photos index view, 371

mobile photos show view, 373

mobile posts index view, 366

mobile posts new view, 367

mobile resource mappings in routes.rb
file, 357–359

mobile topics controller, 363

mobile topics index view, 364

mobile topics new view, 365

mobile user show view, 368

mobile user_photos index view, 372

mobile users controller, 367

mobilemenu partial view, 356

new article view, 99

new blog entry view file, 165

new blog post link, creating, 167–168

new friendship view file, 262–266

new newsletter view, 239

new page view, 37

new post view, 139

new topic view, 134

new user view, 58–59

newsletter edit view, 239

newsletter index view, 237

newsletter mailer method, 241

newsletter show view, 238

newsletters controller, 234

notifier mailer model, 220

page index view updated, 40

page show view, 36

page test fixtures file, 43

Photo model, 199

    modifications to, 258

    modifications to, for tagging, 284

    unit tests, 210–212

photos controller, 200

plain text newsletter template, 241

post model, modifications to, 257

post model file, 122

posts controller functional tests, 149–150

posts index view, 137

production settings in database
configuration file, 389

remove_tag action method, 294

remove_tag RJS template, 295

roles controller file, 76

roles index file, 77

roles table migration file, 72

roles_users table migration file, 73

route mappings file, updates to, 285

routes file updated, 55

routes.rb file, 357–359

rss.rxml file, specifying RSS feed of
articles, 94

sample blog_entry user template, 345

sample blog_index user template, 343

show article view, 99

show blog entry view file, 166–167

sidebar menu for user index view, 65

sidebar menu partial file, 26

    updated for administering roles, 78

    updated for new user view, 59–60

stylesheet for RailsCoders site, 25–26

tag cloud helper, 287

tag controller file, 286

tags index view, 287

topic index view, 132

topic model file, 121

topics controller functional tests, 146–148

unit tests

    for comment notification, 228

    for Photo model, 210–212

user drop file, 333

user edit view, 66–67

user index view, 64

User model file, 52

    modifications to, 254

    modifications to for RSS feed, 324

    modifications to for tagging, 284

    updates to for Flickr integration, 320

user partial view, 64

user photos controller, 201–203

user show view, 62

    displaying Flickr photos, 325

    updated, 296

user table migration file, 51

user tags controller file, 288

user tags index view, 289
user tags show view, 289
user templates functional test file, 347
user unit test file, 67
user view file updated, 268
user_photos
    edit page, modifications to, 306, 313
    new page, modifications to, 307
    show file updated, 309
    update to new view, 314
user_photos edit file updated, 291
user_photos_controller
    edit method, modifications to, 312
    show action updated, 309
    update to new method of, 314
user_tags show view updated, 296
users controller file, 55–57
users controller functional test, 69
users controller show method
        updated, 324
usertemplate edit view, 341
usertemplate index view, 340
Usertemplate model file, 338
usertemplates controller file, 339
Usertemplates migration file, 337
view file
    for edit photo action, 204
    for new photo action, 203–204
    for photo show action, 206
    for photos index action, 205
    for user photos index action, 204
view for articles index action, 98
xfn_rel_tag helper method, 261–262
LiteSpeed web server, 383
location data, displaying as map, 308–311
location of photo, selecting using map,
        312–315
Locomotive, 11–12
log files, watching, 16, 224, 392–393
logging out of site, 60
login screen with error message, 61
login stories integration test file, 79

login system module, 53
login view, creating, 61
Lütke, Tobias, 330

■M
Mac OS X, installing on, 11–12
MacroMates, TextMate, 7
mailer model
    automating testing of, 228–230
    calling from comments controller,
        226–227
    creating, 220–223
    description of, 217
    manually testing, 223–226
    testing from within application, 227
main blog view with new user template, 344
manually testing
    forum controller, 131
    mobile interface, 375–377
    new comment notifier, 223–226
    news blog system, 110
    photo gallery, 208–209
    user-definable templates, 343–346
mapping
    See also mapping feature; resource
        mapping
    newsletter resource, 233
    photos resource, 200
    resource, 32
    REST resources for News module, 91–92
mapping feature
    building
        displaying location data as map,
            308–311
        geographical fields, adding, 305–307
        Google Maps API key, obtaining, 303
        selecting location of photo using map,
            312–315
        YM4R/GM plug-in, installing, 303–304
    requirements for, 302
mapping service. See Google Maps API,
        integrating

mappings
    default, 22
    nested resource route, adding to
        discussion forum, 126
    REST, 22
Markdown markup system, 84
mashups
    See also Flickr API, integrating; Google
        Maps API, integrating
    description of, 301
    further development using, 326
Matsumoto, Yukihiro, 3
memcached, 380
Messina, Chris, 269
metaprogramming, 6
MetaWeblog API, 156, 181
methods
    See also helper methods
    ActiveRecordStore, 380–381
    add_tag, 290
    attachment_fu plug-in, 194
    Blogger API, 180–181
    default action, 27
    destroy, 40
    edit, 312
    error messages for, 37
    form for, 37
    index, 34–36
    link to, 35
    logout, 72
    MetaWeblog API, 156
    new, 314
    remove_tag, 294
    test logout, 72
    text area, 38
    text field, 38
    validates length of, 33
    validates presence of, 32
Meyer, Eric, 249
microformats, 247. *See also* XFN (XHTML
    Friends Network)

migrations (migration scripts)
    ActiveRecord, 30
    to add editor role, 90
    to add last activity to users table, 253
    to add tagging support, 283
    ar_mailer, 231
    for blogging engine, 158–159
    discussion forum, 123–125
    empty, running, 19
    Flickr API integration, 318
    friendships table, 252–253
    for mapping feature, 305
    for newsletter, 233
    for Page model, 30
    performing, 19–20
    for photo gallery, 198–199
    roles table, 72
    roles_users table, 73
    users table, 51, 159, 253
    uses of, 28
    Usertemplates, 337
mobile home page, 375
mobile interface
    controllers and views
        account login page, 373–374
        articles index view, 361–362
        articles resource, 360–361
        articles show view, 362
        blogs resource, 370–371
        entries index view, 369–370
        entries resource, 368
        entries show view, 370
        forum index view, 363
        forums resource, 362
        pages resource, 360
        photos resource, 371–373
        post resource, 365
        posts index view, 366–367
        posts new view, 367
        topics index view, 364–365
        topics new view, 365

topics resource, 363
user show view, 368
user_photos resource, 372
users resource, 367
further development of, 377
layout file and style sheet for, 356–357
manually testing, 375–377
need for, 351
requirements for
accounts, 354
blogs, 354
forums, 354
layout of, 353
news articles, 354
overview of, 352
pages, 354
photo gallery, 355
user profiles, 354
resource mappings, 357–359
structure of, 355
XHTML and, 351–352
Mobile Web Best Practices, 352
model layer, 5
model relationships, discussion forum,
121–122
model validations, discussion forum, 122–123
models
See also specific models
defining relationships among, 88
relationships and validations for blogging
engine, 160
model-view-controller (MVC) architecture,
5–6, 21
moderator rights, checking user role for, 126
moderator role
description of, 119
migration to add, 124
restricting actions to, 142–143
Molina, Marcel, Jr., 192
Mongrel, 382–383
monitoring log files, 16, 224, 392–393

Movable Type API, 156
Mullenweg, Matthew, 249
MVC (model-view-controller) architecture,
5–6, 21
MySQL
adding to Locomotive path, 12
database password, 391

■N

naming actions, 220
navigation of mobile site, 352
nested resource route mappings, adding to
discussion forum, 126
new action, 37–38
new article view, 99
new category view, 108
new entry view, 165
new forum, creating, 129
new photo view, 203–204
new post, creating, 138–139
new topic view, 133–135
new user view, creating, 58–61
news articles, mobile site, 354
News module
Article model, creating, 87
article views
articles admin, 100
edit article, 100
new article, 99
overview of, 98–99
show article, 99
articles controller
actions, adding, 96–97
creating, 92–93
pagination, 93
returning XML data, 94
RSS and Atom feeds, 94–96
categories controller, creating, 105–107
Category model, creating, 88
category views
admin, 109
creating, 105
edit, 108

index, 108

new, 108

controllers and views, creating, 91

defining

relationships among models, 88

validations, 89

editor role, adding, 90–91

further development of, 115

HTTP authentication for API, adding, 103–104

link to sidebar menu, adding, 109

mapping REST resources, 91–92

new article, creating, 101

nullifying category_id on deletion, 89

overview of, 83

requirements for

Article model, 84

articles controller, 86

categories controller, 86

Category model, 85

editor role, 85

Textile markup system, 83–84

testing

API authentication, 104–105

functional, 112–114

integration, 114–115

manually, 110

overview of, 110–112

XML API, 101–102

updating published_at field, 89

newsletter feature

See also sending e-mail

building

ar_mailer, installing, 230–232

create action, 239

destroy action, 240

edit action, 239

link to newsletters, adding to sidebar, 241

newsletter index action and view, 236–237

newsletter mailer, creating, 241

newsletter model, 234

newsletter new action and view, 238

newsletter resource, mapping, 233

newsletter show action and view, 237–238

newsletters controller, 234–236

overview of, 230

sendmails action, 240

skeleton resource, creating, 232–233

update action, 240

requirements for, 219–220

testing newsletter mailer, 242–244

newsletter mailer

creating, 241

testing, 242–244

newsletter model, creating, 234

newsletter resource, mapping, 233

newsletters controller, creating, 234–236

Nginx web server, 383

notifier, building

automating mailer tests, 228–230

calling mailer from comments controller, 226–227

mailer model, creating, 220–223

manually testing, 223–226

overview of, 219–220

testing mailer from within application, 227

nullifying category_id on deletion, 89

■O

Object/Relationship Mapping (ORM) library, 6

Olson, Rick, 47, 192

one-way hashing algorithm, 48

OpenID, integrating into user accounts system, 81

optimizing application, 392–395

OS X, installing ImageMagick and RMagick on, 196

■P

page caching, 393–394
Page model
    accessing with pages controller file, 27
    creating
        adding validations, 32–33
        mapping resource, 32
        migrations and, 28–29
    description of, 26–27
    testing, 42–44
pages
    adding new, 37–38
    mobile site, 354
pages controller, mobile interface, 360
pages controller file, 27
pages index view, 35
paginate helper method, 93
partial file, 26
passwords, storing, 47
percent (%) prompt, 223
performing, migration, 19–20
permalinks, creating, 36–37
photo edit page, adding geographical fields
        to, 306–307
photo gallery
    See also Photo model; tags
    attachment_fu plug-in and, 192–194
    controllers
        photos, 200
        user photos, 201–203
    further development of, 215
    generating scaffolding code, 197
    latest photos, adding to user profile,
        207–208
    links to gallery and new photo pages,
        adding, 207
    mobile site, 355
    overview of, 191
    photos resource, mapping, 200
    requirements for, 194–195
    styling, adding, 208
    testing

    functional, 212–215
    manually, 208–209
    photo fixtures, creating, 210
    unit, 210–212
    User model, adding reciprocal
        relationship to, 200
    views
        edit photo, 204
        new photo, 203–204
        photos index, 205
        user photos index, 204–205
        user photos show, 206
    working with uploaded files, 191–192
    writing migration, 198–199
Photo model
    creating, 199
    defining, 195
    storing location data and, 302
    unit tests for, 210–212
    updating for tagging, 284–285
photo new page, adding geographical fields
        to, 307
photo schema, adding geographical fields to,
        305–306
photo show page, with embedded Google
        map, 310
photo show view, 206, 295
photo upload page with embedded Google
        map, 315
photos
    adding tags to
        allowing users to add tags, 290–293
        allowing users to remove tags, 293–295
    latest, displaying, 322–325
    mapping feature for, 302
photos controller
    creating, 200
    functional tests for, 212–215
    mobile interface, 371
photos index view, 205, 371
photos resource, mapping, 200
photos show view, mobile interface, 373
photos tag cloud, 297

phpBB open source forum implementation, 117

plug-ins. *See specific plug-ins*

polymorphic associations, 279

post controller, mobile interface, 365

post model

building, 120–121

defining, 119

validations, 123

post model file, 122

posts, testing, 141

posts controller and views

deleting post, 141

description of, 119

editing post, 139–141

functional tests, 148–150

new post, creating, 138–139

posts index page, 136–137

posts counter cache, adding to users model, 124

posts index action, 141

posts index page, 136–137

posts index view, mobile interface, 366–367

posts new view, mobile interface, 367

preparing server

for application, 391

for deploying application, 384–385

production mode, running application in, 379

PStore, 380

published_at field, updating, 89

PunBB open source forum implementation, 117

R

Raaum, Ryan, 11

radio_button helper, 257

RadRails text editor, 7

rails command, 14

Rails console, 223

Rails deployment group, 383

Rails Express blog, 380

Rails software stack, installing, 390

RailsCoders Web site

creating skeleton of, 14–16

description of, 1

layout for, creating, 23–24

requirements for, 2, 21

sidebar menu partial file, 26

software required to build, 7

style sheet for, 25–26

rake command, 68

rake tool, 31

RedCloth gem, 84, 86–87

registering for Flickr, 317

relationship, specifying for friends list, 248

relationships among models

for blogging engine, 160

defining, 88

Remote JavaScript (RJS) files, 292

Remote JavaScript (RJS) template files, 293

removing

See also deleting

generated layouts, blogging engine, 163

tags from photo objects, 293–295

rendering Liquid templates, 342

Representational State Transfer (REST) routes, 22, 301

resource mapping

for blogging engine, 161

mobile interface, 357–359

overview of, 31

for tagging system in photo gallery, 285

REST (Representational State Transfer) routes, 22, 301

REST resources, mapping for News module, 91–92

restful authentication plug-in, 47

restricting actions to moderators, 142–143

retrieving Flickr user nsid, 320–322

returning XML data, 94

REXML parser, 320

RHTML file, 94

RJS (Remote JavaScript) files, 292

RJS (Remote JavaScript) template files, 293

RMagick, 195–196

Role model, 48, 72–74

roles

adding, 72, 90–91

administering, 76–79

editor, 85, 90–91

functional test for, 79–81

moderator, 119, 124, 142–143

of user, checking, 74–76, 126

roles controller, for adding users and
groups, 50

roles controller file, 76

roles index file, 77

roles table migration file, 72

roles_users table migration file, 73

Roos, Chris, 28

routes.rb file

adding mapping to end of, 57

mobile resource mappings in, 357–359

update to, 55

RSS feeds and articles controller, 94–96

RSS parsing library, accessing, 324

Ruby

history of, 3

uses of, 4

Ruby console window (Instant Rails), 10

Ruby on Rails

built-in testing, 6

description of, 2–4

metaprogramming, 6

model-view-controller architecture, 5–6

RubyCocoa framework, 4

RubyGems packaging system, 7

RXML file, 94

■S

scaffold resource generator, 120, 143, 232

scaffolding code for blogging system,
generating, 156–157

scaling application, 392–395

script/generate migration command, 29

script/generate tool, 87

Secure Shell (SSH), 384

security issues with uploaded files, 191

selecting location of photo using map,
312–315

sending e-mail

See also newsletter feature

ActionMailer module, configuring,
217–218

further development of system for, 244

new comment notifier, building

automating mailer tests, 228–230

calling mailer from comments
controller, 226–227

mailer model, creating, 220–223

manually testing, 223–226

testing mailer from within
application, 227

requirements for

newsletters, 219–220

notification of new comments in
blog, 219

overview of, 218

server, preparing

for application, 391

for deploying application, 384–385

session storage, 380–381

session-handling library, 53–54

sessions, for adding users and groups, 50

SHA-256 hashing algorithm, 48

shared hosting, 382

share-nothing architecture, 379

Shattered Ruby (game), 4

Shaw, Zed, 383

show action

controller, 36

discussion forum, 129

mobile page, 360

newsletter, 237–238

photo, 206

topic, 136

show view

article, 99, 362

entry, 166–168, 175, 370

newsletter, 238

page, 36

photo, 206, 295, 373

tag, 288

user, 62–63, 296, 325, 368

user tag, 289, 296

showing users' latest activities, 251

sidebar menu, adding tags to, 295

sidebar menu links

for discussion forum, 141

for friends list, 267–268

for News module, 109

to newsletters, 241

overview of, 41

for photo gallery, 207

sidebar menu partial file, 26

Simple Storage Service (Amazon Web Service), 192

skeleton of Rails application, creating, 14–16

skeleton resource, creating, 232–233

SMTP, configuring ActionMailer to use, 218

software requirements for building RailsCoders Web site, 7

source control management, 14

specifying feature requirements for site, 21

speed of Net connection for mobile user, 352

SQLite, 28

SqlSessionStore plug-in, 380

SSH (Secure Shell), 384

starting Rails console, 223

status window (Instant Rails), 9

storage system, using database as, 193

storing passwords, 47

structure of mobile application, 355

style sheet

for discussion forum, modifying, 126–127

for mobile interface, 357

for photo gallery, 208

for RailsCoders site, 25–26

styling friends list, 269–271

Subversion client software, 303

subversion server, setting up, 391

■T

tag clouds, 277

tag index view, 287–288

Tag model, database fields, 280

tag show view, 288

Tagging model, database fields, 280

tags

acts_as_taggable_on_steroids plug-in, 279–283

adding to photo

allowing user to add tags, 290–293

allowing user to remove tags, 293–295

adding to photo gallery

controllers, creating, 285

controllers, writing, 286–288

database tables, creating, 283–284

overview of, 282

Photo and User models, updating for, 284–285

resource mapping, adding, 285

tag index view, 287–288

tag show view, 288

user tags index view, 289

user tags show view, 289

further development of, 298

libraries available, 278–279

linking to tag browser, 295–296

manually testing, 296–297

requirements for, 277–278

tags controller, 286

templates

comment notification e-mail, 221

HTML new comment notification e-mail, 222

plain text newsletter, 241

user-definable, adding to blogging system

creating Liquid drop files, 333–336

creating Liquid filters, 336–337

further development of, 348

installing Liquid, 332

Liquid API and, 331

Liquid markup and, 331–332

Liquid plug-in and, 330
manually testing, 343–346
rendering Liquid templates, 342
requirements for, 329–330
testing usertemplates controller,
  346–348
Usertemplate model, 337–338
usertemplate views, 340–341
usertemplates controller, 338–340
templating plug-in. *See* Liquid plug-in
test logout method, 72
test mode and ActionMailer, 218
test-driven development, 7
testing
  API authentication for News module,
    104–105
  automated, of blogging API, 188–189
  built-in, 6
  comments controller, 176–177
  database, 19–20
  desktop blogging client, using, 186–187
  discussion forum, 143–150
  Ecto, using for, 186–187
  entries controller, 171–173
  forum controller manually, 131
  friends controller, 272–273
  friends list, 274
  functional
    account controller, 70–72
    back-end, 188–189
    comments, 176–177
    entries controller, 171–173
    friends controller, 272–273
    news blog system, 112–114
    overview of, 68
    photo gallery, 212–215
    roles, 79–81
    topics controller, 146–148
    user controller, 68–70
    user templates, 347
  in-memory, 28

integration
  description of, 79
  example of, 80
  mobile site, 376
  news blog system, 114–115
mailer, 227–230
manually
  forum controller, 131
  mobile site, 375–377
  new comment notifier, 223–226
  news blog system, 110
  photo gallery, 208–209
  user-definable templates, 343–346
new comment notifier, 223–226
news blog system, 110–115
newsletter mailer, 242–244
overview of, 67
photo gallery, 208–215
tags, 296–297
topics and posts, 141
unit
  comment notification, 228
  mailer model, 228–229
  Page model, 42–44
  photo gallery, 210–212
  user, 67–68
user-definable templates, 343–346
usertemplates controller, 346–348
Web services for blogging engine, 186
XML API for News module, 101–102
text area method, 38
text editor, RadRails, 7
text field, 26
text field method, 38
Textile markup system, 83–84
textilize helper method, 84
TextMate (MacroMates), 7
thumbnails for photos in gallery, 205
TinyMCE, 44
title field, 26
TMail library, 225

tools
See also specific plug-ins
Basecamp, 4
cron, 380
rake, 31
script/generate, 87
YM4R, 302
topic controller and views
deleting topics, 136
description of, 119
editing topics, 135
functional tests, 146–148
new topic view, 133–135
topic index action, 131–132
topic index page, 132–133
topic show action, 136
topic index action, 131–132
topic index page, 132–133
topic model
building, 120–121
defining, 118
validations, 122
topic model file, 121–122
topic show action, 136
topics, testing, 141
topics controller, mobile interface, 363
topics count field, 117
topics index view, mobile interface, 364–365
topics new view, mobile interface, 365
traditional routes, 22

■U
Ubunto 6, 12–13
Ubuntu 6.06.1 Desktop or Server Edition, 384
unit testing
comment notification, 228
mailer model, 228–229
Page model, 42–44
photo gallery, 210–212
user, 67–68
update action, 39–40

updating
published_at field, 89
User model, 284–285, 320
user's latest activity, 257–258
upgrading Rails, 8
uploaded files, working with, 191–192
uploading files
helper methods for, 212
new photo with location data, 307
web form for, 194
user account views, creating
login view, 61
new user view, 58–61
user show view, 62–63
user database fields, creating, Flickr API
integration, 318–319
user edit view, 66–67
user index view, 64–65
user management system, extending, 81
User model
adding reciprocal relationship to, 200
for blogging engine, 154
creating, 51–53
database fields required for, 48
defining, 47
linking with Role model, 49
modifications to for RSS feed, 324
updating for Flickr integration, 320
updating for tagging, 284–285
user nsid, retrieving, 320–322
user partial view, 64
user photos controller, creating, 201–203
user photos index view, 204–205
user profile page
See also friends list
adding friends to, 247
adding latest blog entries to, 177–178
adding latest photos to, 207–208
adding links to tag browser on, 296
mobile site, 354
showing latest Flickr photos, 325

user role, checking, 74–76, 126

user show page, 63

user show view

  displaying Flickr photos, 325

  mobile interface, 368

  user account views, creating, 62–63

user signup form, 60

user table migration, 159

user tags controller, 288

user tags index view, 289

user tags show view, 289

user-definable templates, adding to
    blogging system

  creating Liquid drop files, 333–336

  creating Liquid filters, 336–337

  further development of, 348

  installing Liquid, 332

  Liquid API and, 331

  Liquid markup and, 331–332

  Liquid plug-in and, 330

  manually testing, 343–346

  rendering Liquid templates, 342

  requirements for, 329–330

  testing usertemplates controller, 346–348

  Usertemplate model, 337–338

  usertemplate views, 340–341

  usertemplates controller, 338–340

user_photos

  edit page, modifications to, 306, 313

  new page, modifications to, 307

  show file, updates to, 309

  update to new view, 314

user_photos controller, mobile interface, 372

user_photos index view, mobile
    interface, 372

user_photos_controller

  edit method, modifications to, 312

  show action, updates to, 309

  update to new method of, 314

user.rb model file, 52–53

users

  allowing to add tags to photos, 290–293

  allowing to remove tags from photos,
    293–295

  checking roles of, 74–76

  enabling and disabling, 65

users controller

  for adding users and groups, 50

  creating, 55–57

  functional test for, 68–70

  mobile interface, 367

Usertemplate model, 329, 337–338

usertemplate views, 340–341

usertemplates controller

  creating, 338–340

  description of, 330

  testing, 346–348

usertemplates index view, 343

■V

validates length of method, 33

validates presence of method, 32

validates_captcha plug-in, 151

validations

  adding, 32–33

  for blogging engine, 160

  defining, 89

Vellut, Guilhem, 302

view layer, 5

viewing e-mail header, 226

views

  See also entry view; index view; show view

  friends edit, 266–267

  friends index, 260–262

  friends new, 262–266

  mobile interface

    account login, 374

    articles index, 361–362

    articles show, 362

    blogs index, 371

    entries index, 369–370

entries show view, 370

forum index, 363

overview of, 360

photos index, 371

photos show, 373

posts index, 366–367

posts new, 367

topics index, 364–365

topics new, 365

user_photos index, 372

newsletter feature

index, 236–237

new, 238

show, 237–238

tag index, 287–288

tag show, 288

user tags index, 289

user tags show, 289

usertemplate index, 340–341

Viney, Jonathan, 279

virtual private server (VPS), 381–382

W

watching log files, 16, 224, 392–393

Weaver, Evan, 279

web server, choosing, 382–383

web service code, generating, 181

web services for blogging engine, testing, 186

web sites

See also RailsCoders web site

API list, 301, 327

cURL utility, 101

developer community, 17

Flickr API documentation, 316

Google Maps API, 302

Liquid plug-in, 330

Markdown, 84

Mongrel, 383

Ruby, 3

Subversion client software, 303

Textile, 84

web servers, 383

World Wide Web Consortium Mobile Web Initiative, 352

YM4R tools, 302

Web 2.0 and REST architectures, 301

welcome page, 16

Windows

installing ImageMagick and RMagick on, 196

installing on, 9–10

World Wide Web Consortium Mobile Web Initiative, 352

writing Blogger API method code, 184–186

WxRuby framework, 4

X

XFN (XHTML Friends Network)

attribute icons, 269–271

description of, 247–249

xfn_rel_tag helper method, 261–262

XHTML Basic, 351–352

XHTML Mobile Profile (MP), 351–352

XML API for News module, testing, 101–102

XML data, returning, 94

XML-RPC blogging interface, creating

Action Web Service and, 181

Blogger API, 182–186

overview of, 180–181

web service code, generating, 181

Y

YAML, 18

YM4R/GM plug-in, 302–304

FIND IT FAST

with the Apress *SuperIndex*™

Quickly Find Out What the Experts Know

Leading by innovation, Apress now offers you its *SuperIndex*™, a turbocharged companion to the fine index in this book. The Apress *SuperIndex*™ is a keyword and phrase-enabled search tool that lets you search through the entire Apress library. Powered by dtSearch™, it delivers results instantly.

Instead of paging through a book or a PDF, you can electronically access the topic of your choice from a vast array of Apress titles. The Apress *SuperIndex*™ is the perfect tool to find critical snippets of code or an obscure reference. The Apress *SuperIndex*™ enables all users to harness essential information and data from the best minds in technology.

No registration is required, and the Apress *SuperIndex*™ is free to use.

❶ Thorough and comprehensive searches of over 300 titles

❷ No registration required

❸ Instantaneous results

❹ A single destination to find what you need

❺ Engineered for speed and accuracy

❻ Will spare your time, application, and anxiety level

Search now: *http://superindex.apress.com*

You Need the Companion eBook

Your purchase of this book entitles you to buy the companion PDF-version eBook for only $10. Take the weightless companion with you anywhere.

We believe this Apress title will prove so indispensable that you'll want to carry it with you everywhere, which is why we are offering the companion eBook (in PDF format) for $10 to customers who purchase this book now. Convenient and fully searchable, the PDF version of any content-rich, page-heavy Apress book makes a valuable addition to your programming library. You can easily find and copy code—or perform examples by quickly toggling between instructions and the application. Even simultaneously tackling a donut, diet soda, and complex code becomes simplified with hands-free eBooks!

Once you purchase your book, getting the $10 companion eBook is simple:

❶ Visit **www.apress.com/promo/tendollars/**.

❷ Complete a basic registration form to receive a randomly generated question about this title.

❸ Answer the question correctly in 60 seconds, and you will receive a promotional code to redeem for the $10.00 eBook.

THE EXPERT'S VOICE™

2855 TELEGRAPH AVENUE | SUITE 600 | BERKELEY, CA 94705

Offer valid through 12/07.